What People Are Saying About
The Truth About Mental Illness . . .

"Clear, practical, scholarly and strong. In this important book, Charles Whitfield documents the basis of trauma psychology. Highly recommended for clinicians and anyone looking to recover from 'mental illness'."

—Raymond Dreitlein, Ph.D.
private practice, Berkeley Heights, NJ
faculty, Rutgers University Institute on Alcohol and Drug Studies

"Serious students, consumers, and clinicians of all theoretical orientations have a must-read here. In *The Truth About Mental Illness,* Charles L. Whitfield, M.D., documents the strong relationship between childhood trauma and common mental illnesses, supporting his arguments with clear summaries of vast research data. He balances these with thoroughly enlightening case studies. Whitfield provides credible evidence on how modern psychiatric practice errs in its biological and genetic theory of mental illness and offers specific treatment solutions that challenge current psychiatric drug treatments. He offers hope to millions of patients. An important contribution to the mental health field."

—Judith S. Miller, Ph.D.
professor of psychology, Columbia University
author, *Direct Connection: Transformation of Consciousness*

THE TRUTH
about
MENTAL ILLNESS
CHOICES FOR HEALING

Charles L. Whitfield, M.D.

Bestselling author of *Healing the Child Within*

Health Communications, Inc.
Deerfield Beach, Florida

www.hcibooks.com

Library of Congress Cataloging-in-Publication Data

Whitfield, Charles L.
    The truth about mental illness : choices for healing / Charles L. Whitfield.
        p.   cm.
    ISBN 0-7573-0107-X
    1. Mental illness—Treatment—Evaluation. I. Title.

RC437.5.W48 2004
616.89'1—dc22   2004042415

Publisher: Health Communications, Inc.
                3201 S.W. 15th Street
                Deerfield Beach, FL 33442-8190

Cover and inside book design by Lawna Patterson Oldfield
Inside formatting by Anthony Clausi and Dawn Von Strolley Grove
Cover photo ©PictureQuest

Contents

Tables

Figures

Sidebar Summaries

Acknowledgments

I give special appreciation and acknowledgment to my wife Barbara Whitfield for her patience and input. Also thanks to the several people who read sections of this book and gave their feedback. These include Steve Gold, Ph.D.; Steven Wonderlich, Ph.D.; Vincent Felitti, M.D.; Rob Anda, M.D., MS; Jeffrey Johnson, Ph.D.; Diane Rullo, Ph.D.; John Read, Ph.D.; Judith Miller, Ph.D.; Colin Ross, M.D.; John Kab; Robynne Moran; Shanta Dube, MPH; Josh Kendall; Bruce Greyson, M.D.; Michael De Bellis, M.D.; William Wirshing, M.D.; Loren Mosher, M.D.; Barbara Sanders, Ph.D., Paul Lysaker, Ph.D.; Ray Dreitlein, Ph.D.; Paul Fink, M.D.; Pat Webbink, Ph.D.; Richard Chefetz, M.D.; Sammy Ray; Brenda Mazzocchi; Emma Stupp, Mike Shagina and Bob Scaer, M.D.

Also special thanks to the staff at Health Communications, including Peter Vegso, Allison Janse, Christine Belleris, Bret Witter, Kathy Grant and Paola Fernandez.

I thank all of my patients who over the decades have inspired and informed me with their truth and their courage.

I'm grateful for all the recent research studies by hundreds of dedicated clinical and basic scientists who continue to validate the truth about the link between trauma and illness.

Dedication

I dedicate this book to all people with "mental illness" throughout the ages who have been misunderstood and mistreated.

I also dedicate this book to the tireless researchers who have authored these many articles summarized herein, and to the countless clinicians who know enough to take a careful trauma history and, if present, address it appropriately.

Introduction

In the first book in this two-part series—*The Truth About Depression*—I showed that 1) there are numerous misconceptions being circulated throughout society about depression, and that 2) there is also a strong and *scientifically documented link* between depression and childhood and later trauma. In this second volume, *The Truth About Mental Illness,* I continue with the same theme by discussing in detail the further misconceptions that have been claimed about other kinds of mental illness, as well as their continued strong link with repeated childhood and later trauma.

Throughout history we have looked for the cause of mental illness, and we still don't know it. The two major theories have long been and remain: nature (genes, biology) versus nurture (environment, family).

Our mistake has been to focus on only one or the other. In fact, based on our current knowledge, it appears that both nature and nurture are active factors in most people with mental disorders. These afflictions include:

- Depression and suicidality
- Anxiety disorders
- Alcohol & other drug problems
- Schizophrenia & other psychoses
- Attention deficit disorder (ADD) & violence
- Eating disorders
- Dissociative disorders

In this book I take a new look at these most common kinds of mental illness. While many helping professionals and consumers have realized the connection between childhood trauma and the onset of mental disorders, most have not. Some may be partially aware but don't know how strong the trauma-mental disorder link is.

This book will:

1) Show the strong and perhaps even causal relationship between repeated childhood trauma and common mental illnesses,

2) Show some of the risks, side effects, marginal efficacy, and high cost of psychoactive drugs commonly used today, and

3) Provide an alternative treatment and recovery program for people who have mental disorders and a history of childhood and other traumas.

Mental illness is common. It may affect up to 40 percent of the United States population during their lifetime. Since about 1960 psychiatry has gradually been building a biological base for the mental illness that it treats. While some have criticized it, its evolving *Diagnostic and Statistical Manual* (DSM) has helped clarify a number of ways that psychiatrists and other clinicians have come to view some of the more painful aspects of the human condition. During this time, countless articles and books were published to support their growing idea that most mental illness is due to a genetically transmitted brain problem. With the help of the drug industry, this theory spread throughout medicine and the helping professions, and eventually into the public belief system.

But as I will show throughout this book, this idea remains only a theory. Depending on the particular mental illness in question, the evidence for its reality varies from only fair to weak, as I discuss in chapter 4 of the previous volume.* So while there is various evidence that some mental illnesses are caused by a genetically transmitted brain problem, there is a large and growing body of data that suggests that repeated childhood and later trauma are at least as, if not more powerful, in causing several common mental illnesses.

It may be timely now to promote the role of the helping professions in the treatment of traumatized children and adults, as well as the personal power of trauma survivors to help themselves heal. This is because the documented evidence in the clinical scientific literature has increased since 1980 to show a strong link between trauma and mental disorders. In these two books I describe this evidence for each of the most common mental illnesses. The most studied and commonly reported disorder linked with a history of childhood trauma is *depression,* which I cover in the first volume. There I also presented principles of trauma, its effects, and its treatment and recovery. In this book I continue by reviewing the next most reported trauma-linked disorders. These are: *addictions,* including alcohol and other drug problems, eating disorders and nicotine dependence, *post-traumatic stress disorder, anxiety disorders, dissociative disorders, personality disorders, psychosis,* and *behavior problems,* including *violence.*

The data found in the more than 300 scientific reports that I summarize and cite raise potentially important questions and concerns for all child, adolescent and adult victims of trauma and the clinicians who assist them.** How can we improve our awareness

---

* In this book I will refer to *The Truth About Depression* as the previous (or prior) volume or book.

**In my research over the years I have likely missed some important articles, chapters and books that support the numerous findings that I cite here in this book. I hope that the authors of studies I may have missed will tell me of their work so that I can add it to this collection of important but overlooked data proving my observations. (They can contact me through my Web site, *www.cbwhit.com.*)

of and our approach to people who have experienced childhood and later trauma? Given this new knowledge, how can mental health services best be improved? And how can survivors of trauma recognize its effects on themselves and then find effective recovery aids, including knowledgeable and experienced health professionals? While assistance from clinicians may provide an important way for trauma survivors to help identify the causal factors for their pain and help them discover how best to handle it, it is ultimately up to the affected individual to become aware of the link between their pain and their past trauma.

We can step out of the box of our conservative and sometimes limited beliefs about the nature and cause of mental illness. I ask the reader to consider opening your mind to the possibility that repeated trauma from childhood could be contributing to or even causing some mental illness. And perhaps with this new information you will understand an important alternative to healing it. Armed with this understanding, people with depression and other so-called mental illnesses can now consider more possibilities and choices as they heal. At the same time, some of their family may now be able to support these alternative forms of healing. This book offers state of the art information that I hope will allow affected people and their families, their clinicians, and other important people in their lives to expand their understanding of the mystery of mental illness.

I ask that the reader bear with me when the reading may be dry. By translating this wealth of otherwise dense and complex information into a more reader friendly and useful format, this may be the first time that anyone has gathered and explained the truth about mental illness and our choices to heal it.

Charles L. Whitfield, M.D.
Atlanta, Georgia, January 2004

Statement of Intent

This book is not intended to replace the counsel of a licensed therapist in sorting out and healing from any mental or emotional problem or disorder. Each person's case is unique and deserves individual attention. The references in the back of this book may assist the reader with the further exploration and explanation of this important information. This information is not the final word on the subject and may represent only the tip of the iceberg of the many dimensions of trauma.

For the reader: To make this large amount of detailed research data most useful, please refer to the list of Tables and Figures in the front of the book on page vii, as well as their locations, and as I refer to each of them in the text.

Most psychiatric drugs commonly cause an often psychologically and physically painful withdrawal syndrome. If you are taking them, do not stop without consulting a physician with expertise in their actions.

1   THE TRUTH ABOUT MENTAL ILLNESS

The truth about mental illness is that it is not as advertised. It is not what some special interest groups tell us. It is not what drug companies and some mental health groups may claim. It is not simply a group of genetically transmitted disorders of brain chemistry. It does not reliably respond to psychoactive drugs. And these drugs are not their only available recovery aid.*

These special interest groups may have misled us.

Their special interest is in large part about money, power and influence in the diagnosis and treatment of common mental health problems. Much of what they tell us about mental illness is actually in their own best interest. It is not always in the interest of the people who experience the pain.

At the top of the list of these groups is the drug industry. While drug companies have produced some effective pharmaceutical

---

*I began to describe these facts in *The Truth About Depression,* where I focused on the most common mental illness—depression. Because these principles for depression are also true for the most other common mental illnesses, in the first three pages of this introductory chapter I describe the state of the dysfunctional mental health system today using similar wording as in chapter 1 of that first volume. The rest of this chapter is new.

agents, such as antibiotics, insulin, and others, they fall short when it comes to mental illness. But to help market and sell their drugs, they have often resorted to making up a limited and *still unproven* theory about the cause of mental illness. This theory is that most mental illnesses are caused by genetic and other biological defects that are somehow inherent in our makeup. In other words, they claim that we are born with faulty genes and brains—which their chemical will fix. A problem is that after a century of looking for a cause, and since 1960 looking for a "magic bullet" drug, we still do not know what causes mental illness, and our drug treatments for them do not work very well.

Influenced and often financially supported by the drug industry, and probably for other reasons, health insurance companies, including those who call themselves "managed care," some academics, professional organizations, some mental health advocacy groups and government agencies have bought this unproven theory. These groups, which some have called a major part of the "mental health industry," have used this limited theory as a basic principle in the diagnosis and treatment of people hurting with what they call "mental illness." On the surface they espouse the more accurate and balanced bio-psycho-social theory of mental illness. But they focus primarily on the biological aspects of these disorders and commonly ignore or even neglect the physical, psychological and social traumas in the person's past and current history.

Though it is in their name, managed "care" companies don't really appear to care. They are a pure business. They are *managed money*. Some have called them "managed greed." Their goal appears to be to make as much money as they can without getting into legal trouble. For starters, just look at the salaries of their CEOs. Forget helping sick people in need. Most do everything they can to delay or disapprove coverage, and not pay clinicians appropriately for their services. Some, such as the nonprofit HMO Kaiser-Permanente, are exceptions to the rule.

In my thirty-eight years as a physician, and the last twenty-six years of that time as a psychotherapist, I have seen and assisted countless patients with a wide variety of mental and physical illnesses. Whether their problem was depression, an anxiety disorder, an addiction, or some other illness, in most of them I have not seen convincing evidence that the cause of their disorders was solely a genetic or another biological defect. (There is also no published proof for the biogenetic theory of mental illness.[97, 542, 768]) In fact, I regularly saw evidence for another equally, if not more important factor: a history of repeated childhood trauma. Among all of these people, I have rarely seen one who had a major psychological or psychiatric illness who grew up in a healthy family.

Over the past century numerous observers have looked at trauma, and how it affects us. But since 1980 there has been an outpouring of more than 300 clinical scientific studies that have shown a strong link between repeated childhood trauma and the development of subsequent mental illness—often decades later. In most of these investigations the authors have controlled for other potential associations with mental symptoms and disorders (called "modulating" or "confounding" variables in the research trade), and they have found them to play a less important role than did the trauma itself. These findings have major implications for the prevention and treatment of mental illness, which I address throughout this and the prior book.

AN EXEMPLARY STUDY

As an example, one of those studies was conducted on a large sample of people living in upstate New York. The resulting information that it gave us is not just psychologically helpful—it is remarkable. Psychologists and researchers Jeffrey Johnson, Patricia Cohen and their colleagues looked at 593 families and their children.[532] Their aim was to compare and sort out the effects of *parental mental illness* versus *faulty parenting* on the children's subsequent development of mental illness. The faulty or maladaptive parent behaviors included *psychological* and *physical abuse,* and *neglect,* all of which are forms of childhood trauma. They evaluated each family member four different times over the long course of eighteen years. At the start of the study the children were on average six years old, and so were about twenty-four years old by its end. At each of these four evaluations, they conducted detailed psychosocial and psychiatric interviews with every participant.

Their results showed that parents with mental disorders had enacted more faulty parenting behaviors than did the parents who had no mental illness. In turn, faulty parenting was associated with a highly significant risk for their children's having a subsequent mental illness as teens or young adults. Indeed, most of the children who received poor parenting, and thus experienced varying degrees of repeated childhood trauma, developed these mental illnesses *whether or not* their parents had a mental illness. However, the children of parents with no mental illness, but who still had faulty parenting, had the *same amount of subsequent mental illness,* as shown in Figure 1.1. Parents with a mental disorder had twice as many faulty parenting behaviors than the comparison parents without a mental disorder. This finding could explain a possibly *erroneous interpretation* from other and less comprehensive research studies that a particular *mental illness* is *genetically transmitted*. Thus, as shown in Figure 1.1, the children of mentally ill parents were not at increased risk for having mental disorders *unless there was a history of faulty or maladaptive parental behavior* (i.e., child abuse or neglect).

Figure 1.1 The Graded Relationship Between Childhood Trauma and Subsequent Mental Disorders (Among Offspring of 593 Parents with and Without Mental Disorders, in 18-Year Follow-Up)[532]

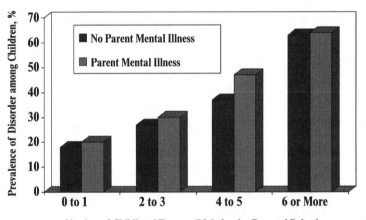

The mental disorders that were looked for and found most commonly in both the parents and the children were among the most common disorders, and included: depression, anxiety disorder, substance abuse/chemical dependence, personality disorder and disruptive behavior disorders.* Looking at the lower left corner of Figure 1.1, we can see that the prevalence (i.e., percentage with a mental disorder) of these mental illnesses for the children who had 0 to 1 kinds of childhood trauma was about 20 percent; this was essentially the control or comparison group. But in this study, as the number of faulty parenting behaviors/traumas goes up, so does the prevalence of subsequent mental illness among their children. When there were six or more kinds of trauma present, the prevalence of mental illness increased by a factor of *over three times* that of the control group.

These serious and life-threatening psychiatric disorders were clearly more common (by the above factor of at least three times) than they are known to exist in the general population. These numbers (in epidemiology called "odds ratios" or "risk factors") each represent multiples of 100 percent, so that a risk factor of 2 means that their chance for having that particular illness was 200 percent greater, or twice as often as people with no repeated childhood trauma (CT). As an example, smoking cigarettes is well known to double a person's risk of having a heart attack. Epidemiologists consider such a *doubling* of a risk factor ratio to represent a *strong* or *substantial* degree of risk, and an odds ratio of 3 to be *extremely high*. This study of people's lives over 18 years revealed five kinds of mental illness to occur over three times more often for children who had six or more kinds of faulty parenting than for those who had no identified childhood trauma. When compared to most risk factors that both researchers and the public are used to seeing, these figures are impressive.

---

* The further breakdown of these mental disorders included: alcohol or other drug abuse, attention deficit hyperactivity disorder (ADHD), oppositional defiant disorder, conduct disorder, generalized anxiety disorder, panic disorder, social phobia, obsessive-compulsive disorder, major depression, personality disorders, including antisocial personality disorder, and post-traumatic stress disorder.

Don't let these terms and numbers fool you. In the field of epidemiology (the study of illness across populations), these odds ratios, or increases over the control group, do not represent just a slight increase. They are high numbers. Their results are telling us about how dangerous it is not to recognize, treat and prevent repeated childhood trauma. This message is true for people with illness that occurs decades after their experience of the repeated trauma, as I show throughout this book.

The take-home message of this important study is that childhood trauma is significantly associated with subsequent mental illness *irrespective of the presence of mental illness in the parents.*[532] While parental mental illness was associated with the later development of mental illness among their children, *none* of these associations *remained statistically significant after controlling for maladaptive parental behavior.* Thus, as others have shown (e.g., Anda et al. 2001), it is the faulty parenting, i.e., the *childhood trauma* and *neglect* that accompanies the parent's mental illness, that is *most significantly related* to the children's *mental illness,* and not the parents' mental illness itself.

This study gives us another important message: the *more traumas* to the children, the *more likely* that there will be later *mental illness* among them.[532] It tells us this by showing a dramatic *graded increase* of the relationship between the trauma and its effects (Figure 1.1). In the fields of epidemiology and public health, this pattern of such an increasing relationship, also called a "stair-step" or "dose-response effect," is considered to be a significant and important finding. These results show that *the more unrecognized, unaddressed,* and *untreated* is childhood trauma, the *more* will there be subsequent *mental illness.*

While these results are impressive, if other researchers were unable to replicate this study's results, its findings would be invalidated. But the opposite has happened, as I will show throughout this book. Nearly every study that has examined a potential relationship between repeated childhood and later trauma and mental illness has found it to occur to a statistically significant degree. These investigations have also found a similar trauma-disorder link for depression, which I described in the prior volume.

The truth about mental illness is that the published clinical and basic scientific evidence is strong in showing the link between having a history of repeated childhood trauma and the development of subsequent mental illness. The truth is that psychoactive drugs, legal or illegal, prescribed or not, are not as effective as we would like them to be in ameliorating the symptoms of mental illnesses.

The truth is that the very diagnosis of "mental illness" may be inaccurate and at times even totally invalid for many people so labeled. And the most important truth is that people with mental illness have several more choices that they can use to heal their pain than to use drugs alone.

In the next chapter I will address some truths about the disorder that many researchers say commonly lies at the core of the link between childhood trauma and mental illness: post-traumatic stress disorder. In the subsequent chapters I will address other common mental disorders. In chapter 19 I review the real link between trauma and *physical* illness. In chapter 20 I discuss how most psychiatric drugs don't work well. In chapter 21 I review some principles of healing from the pain of trauma-related mental illness, which I continue discussing in the Epilogue.

2 POST-TRAUMATIC STRESS DISORDER

"When I felt burdened by fear or depression, I had to remind myself that I wasn't crazy. I just had PTSD."

John, forty-one years old, one year in recovery

I have found post-traumatic stress disorder (PTSD) to be the most accurate, inclusive and potentially useful of all of the *DSM* diagnostic categories. Its *accuracy* begins with the fact that many of the common mental disorders are strongly associated with, and in some cases possibly caused by, repeated childhood and other trauma. At the least they are often aggravated by it, as shown throughout this and the prior book. It's *inclusiveness* rests in the fact that its diverse symptoms can be manifested by several other common disorders, including *depression, substance abuse/chemical dependence, anxiety* and *panic disorder, somatization disorder,* and *dissociative* and at times *psychotic disorders*. PTSD also often occurs as a co-morbid condition with any one or more of these. And its *usefulness* lies in its ability to reframe and at times clarify a common cause of human suffering as being caused simply by unmetabolized trauma. Knowing about it thereby frees sufferers from the fear, guilt, and shame that they are somehow responsible—bad, sick, crazy or stupid—by showing that they are instead, just wounded.

Trauma occurs when any act, event or experience harms or damages the physical, sexual, mental, emotional or spiritual integrity of our true self. Simple upsetting or disrupting of it is not usually enough to cause actual harm, unless it is repeated over time and is of human origin. And if we are vulnerable, i.e., if our true self is already wounded or hurt from prior trauma, then we may be more likely to develop additional or more severe symptoms and signs of post-traumatic stress when we are exposed to additional trauma. The American Psychiatric Association has described a spectrum of psychosocial *stressors* which range from mild to severe (Table 2.1). These are but a *few examples* of traumas, but are useful ones to consider, since several psychiatrist and psychologist authors ranked them according to their estimated levels of severity.[15]

LIMITATIONS OF DIAGNOSTIC CRITERIA

We can define a traumatic experience in many different ways. What is a trauma to one person may not be traumatic to another. Before recovery, a person might define a trauma differently than that person might do after being in recovery for a while. And during recovery our understanding of a trauma often changes.

In 1980, the original *DSM-III* committee defined a trauma as a "recognizable stressor that would evoke symptoms of significant distress in almost everyone." Seven years later (in a revision, *DSM-III-R*), they narrowed it down to any event that was "outside the range of usual human experience and that would be markedly distressing to almost anyone".[15] Their major purpose for doing so may have been to distinguish unusual stress, with which most people are unprepared to deal, from everyday stress.[240] Unfortunately, in their most recent definition in *DSM-IV* they have focused mostly on the person's physical integrity wherein they react with intense fear, a definition which I and others[920,921] view as being clinically limiting and inappropriate (see item A in Table 2.2).*

Table 2.1. Severity Rating of Psychosocial Stressors (from *DSM-III*)

Severity	Adult Examples	Child/Adolescent Examples
1. **None**	No apparent psychological stressor	No apparent psychological stressor
2. **Minimal**	Minor violation of the law; small bank loan	Vacation with family
3. **Mild**	Argument with neighbor; change in work hours	Change in schoolteacher; new school year
4. **Moderate**	New career; death of close friend; pregnancy	Chronic parental fighting; change to new school; illness of close relative; sibling birth
5. **Severe**	Serious illness in self or family; major financial loss; marital separation; birth of child	Death of peer; divorce of parents; arrest; hospitalization; persistent and harsh parental discipline
6. **Extreme**	Death of close relative; divorce	Death of parent or sibling; repeated physical or sexual abuse
7. **Catastrophic**	Devastating natural disaster; concentration camp experience	Multiple family deaths

*For example, in the *DSM-III-R* definition (the second one cited above), how easily can we agree on the word *usual*? And how can we determine what "markedly distressing to almost anyone" means? Davidson and others have written about the importance of the subjective perception and appraisal in response to a traumatic event. Two people may respond differently to the same event. With this more accurate understanding, we can begin to examine the "specific details that need to be understood about each traumatic experience, including the *characteristics* of the *event* itself and the *perceptions, feelings,* and *meanings* for the victim".[240] I and many clinicians who assist trauma survivors prefer to focus more on items B, C, D, E, and especially F from the diagnostic criteria for PTSD (Table 2.2). Item F says that "the disturbance causes clinically significant distress or impairment in social, occupational, or *other important areas of functioning*" [my emphasis].

Table 2.2. PTSD Diagnostic Criteria from *DSM-IV* (309.81)[16]

A. The person has been exposed to a traumatic event [or events] in which both of the following have been present: 1. the person has experienced, witnessed, or been confronted with an event or events that involve actual or threatened death or serious injury, or a threat to the physical integrity of oneself or others. 2. the person's response involved intense fear, helplessness, or horror.

B. The traumatic event is persistently **re-experienced** in at least *one* of the following ways:
   1. recurrent and intrusive distressing recollections of the event, including images, thoughts, or perceptions.
   2. recurrent distressing dreams of the event.
   3. acting or feeling as if the traumatic event were recurring (includes a sense of reliving the experience, illusions, hallucinations, and dissociative flashback episodes, including those that occur upon awakening or when intoxicated)
   4. intense psychological distress at exposure to internal or external cues that symbolize or resemble an aspect of the traumatic event
   5. physiologic reactivity upon exposure to internal or external cues that symbolize or resemble an aspect of the traumatic event

C. Persistent **avoidance** of stimuli associated with the trauma and numbing of general responsiveness (not present before the trauma), as indicated by at least *three* of the following:
   1. efforts to avoid thoughts, feelings, or conversations associated with the trauma
   2. efforts to avoid activities, places, or people that arouse recollections of the trauma
   3. inability to recall an important aspect of the trauma
   4. markedly diminished interest or participation in significant activities
   5. feeling of detachment or estrangement from others
   6. restricted range of affect (e.g., unable to have loving feelings)
   7. sense of a foreshortened future (e.g., does not expect to have a career, marriage, children, or a normal life span)

D. Persistent symptoms of increased **arousal** (not present before the trauma), as indicated by at least two of the following:
   1. difficulty falling or staying asleep
   2. irritability or outbursts of anger
   3. difficulty concentrating
   4. hypervigilance
   5. exaggerated startle response

E. Duration of the disturbance (symptoms in B, C, and D) is more than one month

F. The disturbance causes clinically significant distress or impairment in social, occupational, or other important areas of functioning.

Specify if: Acute: if duration of symptoms is less than three months; Chronic: if duration of symptoms is three months or more. *Specify if:* With Delayed Onset: onset of symptoms at least six months after the stressor

Figure 2.1. Major Components of PTSD

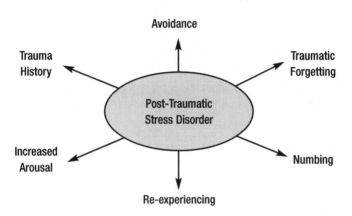

RECOGNITION

The three main clusters of symptoms in PTSD include a *re-experiencing* of the trauma in various ways, a persistent *avoidance* of stimuli that are associated with the trauma, and persistent symptoms of increased *arousal*. In addition to the trauma history, there is also usually a numbing of the person's awareness of their inner life, especially their feelings, and frequently some degree of traumatic forgetting (Figure 2.2).

Difficulty remembering aspects of traumatic experiences is so common in PTSD that it is used in at least ten of its approximately twenty diagnostic criteria in the *DSM-IV*. Indeed, rather than being the exception after experiencing a trauma, as some skeptics claim, memory difficulties tend more often to be the rule, which many clinicians and researchers have described.[137, 138, 486, 1095, 1092, 1093] Thus, an important part of healing from PTSD lies in the process of

..ses of PTSD from an Historical Perspective

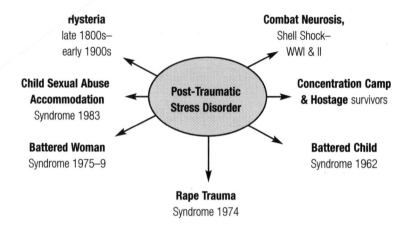

remembering what happened in our traumatic experience. This remembering is not simply cognitive, but is also experiential. As we heal, we re-experience the trauma with increasing awareness in a constructive, non-dissociated consciousness, which evolves during the recovery process.

GUISES OF PTSD

Like alcoholism and other chemical dependence, PTSD is also a *great masquerader.* It can mimic and present as any one or more of the most common psychiatric illnesses described in the *DSM* and this book. PTSD may occur in multiple and varied guises and associations, from anxiety to depression to dissociative and personality disorders to psychosis. Thus, health professionals and others should maintain a high index of suspicion for the possible presence of PTSD among most of the people they evaluate and assist.

PTSD has presented itself in many guises throughout history. In the late 1800s and early 1900s, during the time of Janet, Freud and their colleagues, it was called *hysteria* and was seen most often in traumatized young women. During World Wars I and II it was seen most often in young men, and was called *shell shock* or *combat neurosis*. And when people are taken hostage or kept and abused in concentration camps, what usually results is also PTSD (Figure 2.2).

Even though children have been physically and otherwise abused for millennia, we did not begin to recognize it until about 1962, when the *battered child* syndrome was described, another guise of the disorder. Twelve to fifteen years later, two more variations of PTSD were described: the *rape trauma* syndrome in 1974 and the *battered woman* syndrome in 1975 to 1979. One of the more recently recognized guises is the *child sexual abuse accommodation* syndrome, described by psychiatrist Roland Summit in 1983.[1001] PTSD is also commonly seen among adult children of dysfunctional families and occurs often in people with other mental and physical disorders.

While these guises may have various things in common, including their association with PTSD, people who are afflicted with any of them tend to be laden with fear, shame and guilt. *Fear* because of the terror of the unhealed original trauma. *Shame* because our political, social and helping professional systems are generally so unfamiliar about what to do to help survivors of childhood trauma, and may be fearful of facing their own wounds that they tend to project their own unhealed shame onto the victims of these many kinds of abuse. Rather than assist and help, not doing so often hinders and

Stress is neither "good" nor "bad." However, depending on how we choose to use it, stress may be positive or negative in our life. It can thus be growth-inducing, or it can cause illness and suffering, or both. Transient stress is usually short-lived, especially if it is dissipated with muscle action or with another fairly quick and ameliorating response, and thus itself is not damaging. Such a response has been called *eustress* (Seyle 1974, Pelletier 1977, Cox 1979, Nuernberger 1981, Girdano & Everly 1979).

However chronic stress, also called *distress* (Seyle 1974), occurs when the person has an incomplete and thus unhealthy response to a demand, and tension remains and accumulates. Distress is a prolongation and a continuation of acute stress and may accumulate and linger indefinitely. When stress is prolonged in this manner, it can fatigue the body, often targeting certain organs. These target organs vary among individuals. Chronic stress and distress can continue for months or years without the person knowing or feeling it. Physiologically, the stress response consists of a nonspecific arousal caused by stimulation of the adrenergic or sympathetic nervous system. Here the hypothalamus releases corticotropin releasing hormone (CRH), which stimulates the pituitary gland to release ACTH, which then causes the adrenal gland to release cortisol, aldosterone, and norepinephrine and epinephrine (adrenalin) into the bloodstream. The blood glucose rises, as do serum triglycerides and free fatty acids. Often erroneously called "stress," the stimulus that causes the arousal is more accurately called a "stressor."

retraumatizes. And *guilt* because we as survivors feel that we somehow *caused* the abuse, even though we did not.

Central to all of the above is that when we are traumatized and then naturally and appropriately try to express our resulting pain, in these dysfunctional systems we are repeatedly *invalidated* for doing so. Being invalidated not only blocks and often destroys our natural mechanisms for healing, but it frequently inflicts a double trauma on the victim. Most all of the invalidations (whether individual or collective) against our genuine attempts to heal are thus just another kind of trauma—known as *re-traumatization,* also called revictimization (discussed on page 207).

The *intensity* of the trauma, *characteristics* or *kind* of trauma, and our *subjective response* to it, including our *opportunity* and *ability* to *process* and *heal* the traumatic experience, are all important in influencing the personal and clinical consequences that result from the trauma. To have been mistreated by our parents or another person who is supposed to be protective of our welfare and well-being is traumatic enough. But to heap on top of that trauma their blocking of our ability to grieve the traumatic experience and heal ourselves is equally as traumatic. Other than their original traumas, survivors tend also to experience more stressful life events and revictimization than others.[296] Some of these latter people may have *complex* PTSD.

COMPLEX PTSD

Complex PTSD (sometimes called Disorder of Extreme Stress Not Otherwise Specified, or DESNOS) is another, yet extreme, guise of PTSD that is commonly seen among trauma survivors who were exposed to repeated trauma, especially during childhood. In addition to the above usual symptoms of PTSD, these people may also experience increased *dissociation,* marked *relationship difficulties, revictimization, somatization,* extreme *disrupted feelings* and *emotions,* and a *lost sense of self* and *meaning* in their life.* As

---

*As clinical and research trauma psychiatrist Judith Herman described it, the person with complex PTSD usually has a history of subjection to totalitarian control over a prolonged period (months to years). Examples include hostages, prisoners of war, concentration-camp survivors and survivors of some religious cults. Examples also include those subjected to totalitarian systems in family life, such as survivors of domestic battering, childhood physical or sexual abuse, and organized sexual exploitation. The specific findings may be: 1) Alterations in affect (feelings) regulation, including: persistent dysphoria (emotional pain), chronic suicidal preoccupation, self-injury, explosive or

described in chapters 6, 8 and 9 of the prior book, developmental research is finding that many brain and hormonal abnormalities occur from early repeated trauma, and appear to cause difficulties with memory, learning, and regulating impulses and emotions. All of these trauma effects may contribute to severe behavioral difficulties (such as impulsivity, aggression, sexual acting out, eating disorders, alcohol/drug abuse and self-destructive actions), emotional regulation difficulties (such as intense rage, depression or panic) and mental difficulties (such as extremely scattered thoughts, dissociation and amnesia). As adults, people with complex PTSD are often diagnosed with depressive, personality or dissociative disorders. Their recovery and improvement often takes much longer, may progress at a much slower rate, often interspersed with frequent crises, and requires a sensitive and structured treatment program delivered by a trauma specialist.

---

extremely inhibited anger (these may alternate), compulsive or extremely inhibited sexuality (may alternate); 2) Alterations in consciousness, including: amnesia or hyperamnesia for traumatic events, transient dissociative episodes, depersonalization/derealization, reliving experiences, either in the form of intrusive post-traumatic stress disorder symptoms or in the form of ruminative preoccupation; 3) Alterations in self-perception, including: sense of helplessness or paralysis of initiative, shame, guilt, and self-blame, sense of defilement or stigma, sense of complete difference from others (may include sense of specialness, utter aloneness, belief no other person can understand, or nonhuman identity); 4) Alterations in perception of perpetrator, including: preoccupation with relationship with perpetrator (includes preoccupation with revenge), unrealistic attribution of total power to perpetrator (caution: victim's assessment of power realities may be more realistic than clinician's), idealization or paradoxical gratitude, sense of special or supernatural relationship, acceptance of belief system or rationalizations of perpetrator; 5) Alterations in relations with others, including: isolation and withdrawal, disruption in intimate relationships, repeated search for rescuer (may alternate with isolation and withdrawal), persistent distrust, repeated failures of self-protection; 6) Alterations in systems of meaning: loss of sustaining faith, sense of hopelessness and despair. Complex Post-Traumatic Stress Disorder Recommended *DSM* diagnostic criteria, from *Trauma and Recovery* by Judith Herman, 1992 Basic Books.

History 2.1.

Marta was a forty-three-year-old woman who came to me for assistance with a life in chaos. She had recurring depression, anxiety and repeated failed relationships and job difficulties. She had severe premenstrual syndrome, recurrent asthma, smoked two packs of cigarettes a day and had been raped twice in the past ten years. She had been diagnosed with depression, borderline personality disorder, bipolar disorder and had been hospitalized several times for these. She had been treated with numerous antidepressant drugs and benzodiazepine sedatives with little or no improvement. Five years ago, during her last relationship with a man, she felt safe enough to remember increasingly more details of being brutally physically and psychologically abused by her father and neglected by her mother as a child. She had partial memories of having been sexually abused by her father and another unidentified man. None of her recent clinicians had addressed her trauma history, nor had any of them before that inquired about possible trauma.

I saw her weekly in individual psychotherapy for six months, during which time she had such marked swings in her emotions and ability to function that she was unable to join our trauma-focused therapy group. She had to be hospitalized twice for brief psychotic episodes, at which time the attending psychiatrist made a provisional diagnosis of bipolar disorder, although over the next few years she did not have another psychotic or manic episode. Because of her continuing severe premenstrual syndrome pain, her gynecologist performed a hysterectomy and removed her ovaries, after which her mood swings improved enough for her to join our therapy group. Over the next three years, her chaotic and painful life began to improve, and at this point she has been able to keep a job and an ongoing relationship with a man for over a year, which, she says, is a record for her. She realizes that she has more issues to address.

Although the details may vary, Marta's story is typical for many people with complex PTSD. Before she could begin the long and difficult trauma effects healing work in a Stage Two recovery program, she first needed to stabilize in a Stage One program, during which she did a number of things to help herself stabilize (these stages are further described in chapter 14 of the prior book and summarized in Table 2.3 below). These included stopping smoking cigarettes (one of the most difficult but helpful choices), improving her diet and nutrition, beginning an exercise program, seeing me in weekly individual psychotherapy sessions, and having appropriate attention given to her gynecological problem. It is unfortunate that most people with this very disruptive disorder of complex PTSD do not get the opportunity to heal their pain in a trauma-focused recovery program. Instead, many suffer through their personal and work lives, use the health care system much more than average, including frequent hospitalizations, while the health care and health insurance systems tend to ignore the role of trauma as a major causal factor in mental and some physical illness.

Table 2.3. Recovery and Duration According to Stages

Recovery Stage	Condition	Focus of Recovery	Approximate Duration
3	**Human/spiritual**	Spirituality	Ongoing
2	**Past trauma effects**	Trauma-specific recovery program	3–5+ years
1	**Stage 0 disorder**	Basic illness, full recovery program	Months to 3 years
0	**Active illness**	Usually none	Indefinite

3 POST-TRAUMATIC STRESS DISORDER — CONTINUED

THE EVIDENCE

With the above introduction to PTSD in chapter 2, I am not suggesting that we find it under every rock that we turn over. I am simply describing what I have seen over my long career as a physician. It is well-understood that PTSD is caused by unprocessed trauma. But what does the scientific literature say about the link between childhood trauma and this common mental and physical illness called PTSD? I believe that it clearly documents, supports and expands the link. A problem is that there are not as many data-based studies that show this link as there are for depression and for alcohol and other drug problems. Part of the reason is that *most* of the over 300 studies on the mental and physical health effects of childhood trauma simply *did not look* for PTSD. This lack may be surprising to many, since PTSD has been described as a core effect of repeated childhood trauma (described further below).[873] Some have even shown evidence that PTSD due to child sexual abuse is similar to PTSD due to combat trauma.[297]

Clinical Studies

When compared to the other mental disorders such as depression, anxiety disorder, personality disorders, addictions and psychotic disorders, to make a diagnosis of PTSD, a history of past significant trauma is not only expected—it is required. It is a given. The trauma, unprocessed and unmetabolized, causes the disorder. Because of this obvious link, fewer researchers have looked for PTSD among their traumatized subjects. I found 54 reports that looked for PTSD among their clinical samples of survivors of childhood trauma, as shown in Table A3.1 on page 270 of the Appendix. These studies were published from 1985 through 2003, and they evaluated a total of 28,894 subjects in clinical settings, including their controls. Their results also showed not only a strong association, with odds ratios of up to *46 times* the controls (an astronomical number in epidemiology), but also a high co-morbidity among the traumatized samples, consisting of substance abuse, chemical dependence, depression, suicidality, anxiety, dissociative disorders, and aggressive, violent and antisocial behaviors.

Community Studies

I also found twenty-one reports on non-clinical, community samples of trauma survivors whose authors looked for PTSD (Table A3.2). These were reported from 1990 through 2002, evaluating a total of 39,344 subjects and their controls. With one exception, where 54 child sexual abuse survivors showed no significant increase in *current* PTSD symptoms[431] but did show an increase in *lifetime* PTSD symptoms, all of the other twenty studies showed a statistically significant increase in PTSD of up to *ten times* that found among the control subjects. Their results also showed a high co-morbidity, including a significant increase in depression, suicidality, anxiety, substance abuse/chemical dependence (SA/CD), and, in one report, ADHD, conduct and hyper-activity problems, and a decrease in self-esteem.[833]

Prospective Studies

I found ten reports of prospective studies, where people were initially evaluated, and then reevaluated over time. Reported from 1996 and 2003 by over twenty-five authors who studied 7,221 subjects, these, too, found a significant increase in PTSD or PTSD symptoms—up to *sixteen times* that for the control subjects—among the survivors of childhood trauma, as shown in Table A3.3. They also found a significant increase in depression, suicidality, anxiety, alcohol and other drug problems, aggression, violence and antisocial behavior.

Index Case Studies

I found three index case studies (these were included in Table A 4.1). For example, Coons and colleagues evaluated twenty-six people with PTSD. Of the women (most of the group), 72 percent had a history of significant childhood trauma, and all of the men had experienced combat trauma. The two other studies looked at 58 women and another 132 adults with PTSD, and found that all of them had a history of childhood trauma.[202, 1120]

Meta-Analysis and Literature Reviews

In 1996 Neumann and colleagues conducted a meta-analysis* on thirty-eight studies published from 1974 through 1992 on the effects of child sexual abuse on women. They found an increase in

---

*See page 89 for definition of meta-analysis.

PTSD and symptoms of traumatic stress, as well as other disorders and symptoms, as shown in Table 3.5. In 1993, Rowan and Foy reviewed the literature on child sexual abuse and found that PTSD describes the *core features* of the detrimental effects of child sexual abuse. In addition to PTSD, their common findings included: depression, substance abuse, increased fears and phobias, sexual and relationship problems, obsessive-compulsive disorder, somatization, self-destructive behaviors, insomnia and nightmares, trauma reenactments and revictimization, aggressive behaviors, and feeling isolated, guilty, angry and distrustful.

Also published in 1993, Kendall-Tackett and colleagues reviewed forty-five studies that were published from 1984 through 1991 on the effects of child sexual abuse. In four of these studies, where PTSD was looked for, they found an average of 53 percent (range 20 to 77 percent) of CSA survivors to have PTSD, which is about *forty times* the percentage found among children in the general population. They noted that the evidence for PTSD as a *central effect* of child sexual abuse lies in its high frequency, especially among preschool and school-age victims, as opposed to older-aged survivors of child abuse. Even so, they pointed out that PTSD is not specific to child sexual abuse, since it affects many children who were abused or traumatized in other ways. They also noted that many children in studies that did not look for PTSD may have actually had the disorder, since they did manifest post-traumatic stress symptoms such as fears, nightmares, somatic complaints, autonomic nervous system arousal and guilt feelings.

Finally, in 2002, research psychologist Elizabeth Paolucci and her colleagues published a meta-analysis of the effects of child sexual abuse reported among thirty-seven studies, most of which are listed in this book. They found a medium to strong link between CSA and subsequent PTSD. In addition these combined and re-analyzed data from thirty-seven independent studies show a significant relationship between CSA and later co-morbidity, including depression, suicidality, sexual promiscuity, victim-perpetrator cycle and sometimes, poor academic performance.[770]

SUMMARY

These eighty-five original databased reports from numerous independent researchers on diverse population samples of survivors of childhood trauma from different countries confirm what I and many other trauma-knowledgeable clinicians have observed in our practices: PTSD is *common* among childhood and adult trauma survivors. These results came from data on 75,459 people, which by any measure is a large sample for scientific endeavors. Analysis of the data shows increased risks (odds ratios) for having PTSD of up to forty-six times that of the control samples, which varies from highly significant to astronomical numbers. I summarize all of these studies in Table 3.5.

Screening for PTSD among people with other *high risk* disorders for an association with childhood trauma, such as *depression, anxiety disorder, alcohol* and *drug problems, eating disorders, nicotine addiction, personality disorders, dissociative disorders, behavior problems* and *psychosis,* is important in documenting further co-morbidity that may need attention and as a way to assist them in their process of healing.[1139] Knowing that they are *not mentally ill,* but instead, that they have PTSD, can be helpful as a way to begin to heal their fear, guilt and shame. As they recover, they learn that they are not bad, sick, crazy or stupid. They learn that they are just wounded, and that their painful symptoms are the *effects* of the *trauma.* All of this new and correct information may help them to be more interested in healing by working a recovery program.

Like the diagnostic criteria for other disorders, those for PTSD can also be a double-edged sword: While they are usually useful, they can be limiting at times. Not all people who have been significantly traumatized will fulfill all of the required diagnostic criteria for PTSD. Therefore, as databased studies have shown, the *absence* of diagnostic criteria for PTSD as suggested in the *DSM-IV* does *not rule out or invalidate* having a history of childhood or other trauma.[591, 776, 920, 921] Similarly, there are some people with PTSD who may not be able to remember or accurately describe having experienced a significant trauma. This lack of memory is commonly due to dissociative amnesia, a firm and well-documented diagnostic criterion for PTSD. Indeed, while about a third of CSA survivors always cognitively remembered having been sexually abused, and another third only partially remember it, the final third have *no memory for the abuse*.[137, 1089, 1093]

Some traumatized children and adolescents will thus not show PTSD outwardly. Instead, they often show other, more surface problems, such as depression, anxiety and/or acting-out behavior problems, including ADHD. [591, 776, 1016] The onset of full PTSD is often *subtle* and *delayed* in time from the traumatic event itself.*

---

*In chapters 8 and 9 of *The Truth About Depression* I described how repeated childhood trauma stresses and often damages the brain and nervous system. Research psychiatrist Martin Teicher and his colleagues (2002) said, "Severe early stress and maltreatment produces a cascade of events that have the potential to alter brain development. The first stage of the cascade involves the stress-induced programming of the glucocorticoid, noradrenergic, and vasopressin-oxytocin stress response systems to augment stress responses. These neurohumors then produce [negative] effects on neurogenesis, synaptic overproduction and pruning, and myelination during specific sensitive periods. Major consequences include reduced size of the mid-portions of the corpus callosum; attenuated development of the left neocortex, hippocampus, and amygdala along with the abnormal frontotemporal electrical activity; and reduced functional activity of the cerebellar vermis. These alterations, in turn, provide the neurobiological framework through which early abuse increases the risk of developing post-traumatic stress disorder (PTSD), depression, symptoms of attention-deficit/hyperactivity, borderline personality disorder, dissociative identity disorder, and substance abuse."

Often the traumatized person appears to hold back the pain of the trauma until later, commonly when they feel safe enough to begin to express some of it.[776]

Table 3.5. PTSD and Childhood Trauma: Clinical, Community, Prospective, Index Case Studies & Reviews

Year/Authors	Study	PTSD	Other Trauma Effects/ Full table page
Clinical **54 Studies** 1985–2003	28,894 people	↑ to 46x controls	Overly strict use of *DSM–IV* category A for PTSD may cause false negatives. ↑ Co-morbidity Table on page 270
Community **21 Studies** 1987–2002	39,344 people CT v. controls	↑ to 7.7x controls	↑ legal, job problems Table on page 278
Prospective **10 Studies** 1996–2003	7,221 people CT v. controls	↑ to 16x controls	↑ Co-morbidity Multiple dimensions. Table on page 280
Meta-analysis/ Lit. Reviews 1993–2002	6 literature reviews & meta-analyses	↑ association with CT	↑ Co-morbidity Table on page 283
Summary **85 Studies by Independent International Authors** 1985–2003	**75,459 CT People and Controls**	↑ **to 46x Clinical** ↑ **to 7.7x Community** ↑ **to 16x Prospective** ↑ **to 100% CT in Index Cases**	↑ **Co-morbidity** **All document CT link** **Key:** CT = childhood trauma, Sx = Symptoms or signs, ↑ = increased

RECOVERY AIDS

The principles for healing from PTSD are similar to most of the principles for healing from most of the other disorders and problems described throughout this and the prior book. This is because these various disorders all so commonly stem from repeated trauma. Thus, the stage-oriented approach I described in chapter 14 of the first book, reproduced here as Table 2.3 on page 20, also applies here—as it does throughout these disorders that so commonly result from repeated childhood trauma. Also, the various choices for healing depression described in its chapter 11 of that book are also useful in healing from trauma. I am not suggesting that anyone use a "shotgun" or a "one size fits all" approach here. As Wilson and colleagues (2001) and others[341, 926] describe, this is a specific recovery strategy that has multiple dimensions. Even so trauma is trauma, and while its effects vary, they can still be constructively addressed by a relatively generic approach to healing from its effects, while at the same time addressing the person's individual problems and needs.[398] Thus, the treatment for PTSD, by using a stage-oriented approach, is similar to the treatment for most trauma-related disorders.[486]

In Figure 3.1 I show a flowchart or decision tree that may be helpful in approaching PTSD. Here, I see two main goals. The first is to recognize and *diagnose* PTSD, which does not always take a trauma-savvy clinician to do. And the second is *addressing* any other concomitant or *co-morbid disorder(s)* that may be present. If one is present, it should be diagnosed and treated appropriately, usually from a Stage One perspective. If PTSD is also present (which is common when looked for), it is useful to tell the person that they have it, and then begin to explain what it is, as well as to review

Figure 3.1. PTSD Symptoms:
Flowchart for Decision Making in Recovery

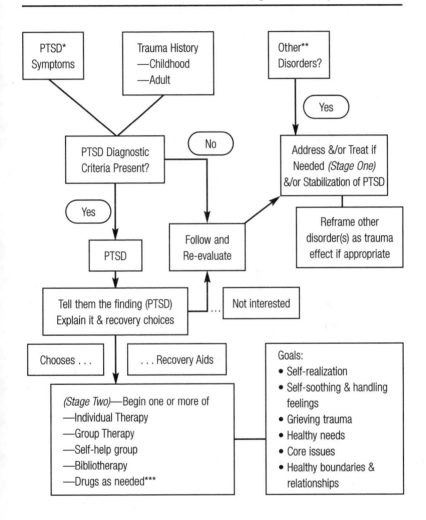

* PTSD symptoms: See Tables 2.2, and text. May first need stabilization in a Stage One Recovery Program.
**PTSD may occur in multiple and varied guises, associations, and co-morbidities, from anxiety to depression, to dissociative and personality disorders, to psychosis.
***Caution: Avoid using benzodiazepines longer than a week (these are highly addicting). Drug treatment alone is not usually sufficient for treating or healing PTSD or any other trauma-related disorder or problem.

their various recovery choices. I list these recovery choices at the bottom of Figure 3.1, along with the goals of recovery.

Trauma and its effects can be addressed and treated at any time in the course of its natural history. Immediately after experiencing a trauma, victims usually need to make effective interventions—or, in the case of children, to have a number of interventions made for them—by setting healthy boundaries.[1094] They need to be validated that the trauma happened and that it hurt, and that they will be protected from further abuse. For people who have been traumatized acutely or recently, principles of debriefing and other methods are described in the clinical literature (e.g., reference 1107). Other treatment and recovery methods are evolving.

The effectiveness of drug treatments for PTSD varies. For example, acutely, just after a trauma, beta-blocker drugs may help. Bremner describes that in the acute aftermath of rape, emergency department physicians who administer a beta-blocker such as propranolol demonstrated that doing so blocks many of the hurtful and dysfunctional aftereffects of the rape trauma.[115] Used long-term, these drugs may help relieve hyperarousal symptoms, as may buspirone and some SSRI antidepressant drugs. Anticonvulsant drugs (carbamazepine, valproic acid and phenytoin) may help subtly reduce symptoms, and although more studies are needed there is some evidence that they may help promote neuronal regeneration in the hippocampus.[115] Benzodiazepine sedatives (highly addicting)[56, 115] and lithium are not helpful long-term.[115]

When a person with PTSD comes to a clinician for help with a problem, they are often in one of the disorder's two common polar-opposite mental and emotional states: 1) *shut down and numb* (i.e., from parasympathetic nervous system arousal) or 2) *hyperaroused, hypervigilant* and often with *increased anxiety* (from sympathetic nervous system arousal). Depending on which of these two seemingly opposite conditions they present with, the clinician may diagnose and treat them for *that specific one,* only to have them shift to the other state minutes, hours or days later. In this situation, in the absence of a clear diagnosis of PTSD, the person may be being only partially diagnosed and treated. Of course, a major goal of recovery from PTSD is to attain a natural state of inner peace, which tends to evolve slowly over the long course of the healing process.

Using drugs alone to treat PTSD symptoms and signs is not usually effective. In 1998, researchers Michelle Van Etten and Steven Taylor conducted a meta-analysis on 61 treatment outcome trials that were included among 39 studies on PTSD. The various treatment methods evaluated included drugs, psychological therapies and placebo or other controlled treatments. As shown in Table 3.6, psychological treatments were most effective. These included psychotherapy, behavioral therapy, EMDR (eye movement desensitization and reprocessing), hypnosis and relaxation therapy. Based on the significant percentage of dropouts (one in three) for drug-treatment studies—likely due to their high toxicity and side effects combined with their limited overall effectiveness—using drugs alone to treat PTSD produced only fair results in lessening its painful symptoms. By contrast, psychotherapy and other psychological recovery aids had a low dropout rate and gave significantly better results. In this meta-analysis the causal traumas for most of these people with PTSD were military combat (51 percent), rape or assault (19 percent), or a mix of traumas (30 percent), but the authors did not mention a history of childhood trauma. Clinical and research neurologist Robert Scaer underscores the common observation, that if looked for, people with more severe PTSD often have been *previously traumatized* before their initially identified traumas. These earlier traumas commonly occurred in childhood,[920, 921] so that the person already had an overt or covert PTSD before their revictimization as an adolescent or adult (I discuss revictimization further in chapter 19 on page 207).

Table 3.7. Meta-Analysis Summary for PTSD Treatment*

Treatment Type	# Trials	Dropout Rate	Effectiveness (effect size)**	Overall Success
Psychological	27	**Low** (14%)	**Good** to **very good** (1.2 to 1.5**)	**Good**
Drug	19	**Significantly high** (32%)	**Fair** to **good** (0.69 to 1.0)	**Fair**
Controls: • Placebo • Wait list • Supportive Psychotherapy***	15	**Low** (16%)	**Some** to **fair** (0.43 to .77**)	**Smaller** (except for **supportive psychotherapy, which was fair**)

*Compiled from Van Etten & Taylor 1998.
**Coded in "effect size" numbers (the larger, the better).[291]
***Of the control methods, only supportive psychotherapy was significantly *helpful*
(I believe this method should have been included in the psychological treatment group).

Closely related to PTSD and trauma in general are the anxiety disorders, which I prefer to call disorders of fear, and which I address in the next chapter.

4 DISORDERS OF ANXIETY AND FEAR

F_{ear} is a feeling of painful apprehension, an uncomfortable sense that we are about to lose something. It is an uneasiness that we commonly feel in our body, usually in an area somewhere from our abdomen to our chest, as "butterflies," or a "knot" in our stomach, a pounding heart, or simply a subtle but bothersome feeling of tension or worry. If we hold it long-term, our body can manifest it as aches and pains, insomnia and other symptoms. My personal and clinical experience is that *anxiety* is another word for fear. But using the term "anxiety" alone to name its pain separates us from the awareness and motivation that using the simple word *fear* instead can give us. While it can be useful at times, anxiety is a kind of twentieth-century code word that we have coined which in reality often ends up separating and removing us from what we may be actually experiencing in our important inner life. Fear is basic and closer to its trigger. Anxiety is neither.

I know fear. It is an old, sometimes friend. If a car is about to hit me, fear can motivate my attention enough so that I will take the responsibility to get out of its way fast. If I haven't done my income taxes by early April, feeling fear of losing money can help me get them finished and in the mail by April 15, after which I can relax. Using the term "fear" instead of "anxiety" to describe this kind of pain can help me to become aware of what is happening in my inner life so that I can now take responsibility for correcting a potential or real problem, or stop worrying about an imaginary one. But when I call that same feeling anxiety, doing so can lessen my awareness, motivation and ability to do something about whatever I may be concerned.

I may also think that because it is so vague or distant, that anxiety is not mine, and I am therefore not responsible for having it, and I may seek help for it from a physician or a therapist. The downside of doing that may be that the physician may compound my problem by giving me a benzodiazapine or another kind of sedative drug, which may separate me even further from my inner life, including my feelings. Or by focusing on it as only anxiety, the therapist may miss the actual causes of my fear. The upside may be that the physician or therapist may carefully prescribe and assist me in a course of action that allows me to eventually lessen my pain and heal. In such a situation, knowing what to do and when to do it is in part what this chapter and this book are about.

While I usually prefer to call this painful feeling fear, because anxiety is so entrenched in the clinical literature and our everyday vocabulary, for consistency and documentation I will call it anxiety in those cases.

Anxiety is a common painful feeling in both our daily life and as a symptom or part of many mental disorders. These disorders include depression, the addictions, PTSD, dissociative disorders, personality disorders, psychosis, as well as the primary anxiety disorders described below. For example, about 80 percent of people with depression report experiencing a bothersome anxiety, and most people with the other disorders commonly experience anxiety. Also, many people with physical problems or disabilities may experience varying degrees of fear or anxiety. This is why—before making a diagnosis of an anxiety disorder—we have to rule out other disorders that are commonly associated with fear, as I outline at the end of the next chapter.

ANXIETY DISORDERS

Anxiety disorders are said to be the most common psychiatric illnesses in the United States. Every year, an estimated 19 million Americans experience an anxiety disorder, which cost the U.S. economy almost $42 billion yearly, with about half of the costs going for non-psychiatric medical care. People with PTSD and panic disorder had the highest rates of medical and psychiatric service use. Greenberg and colleagues found that people with an anxiety disorder are up to five times more likely to go to a physician, and six times more likely to be hospitalized than those without such a disorder.[428]

The *DSM-IV* lists ten "anxiety disorders," half of which are the most common, including: 1. *generalized anxiety disorder* (GAD), commonly called simply "anxiety disorder," 2. *panic disorder,* 3. *social phobia* (or *social anxiety disorder*) and other *specific phobias,* 4. *obsessive-compulsive disorder* (OCD), and 5. *PTSD.* For each of the first four of these I provide in the accompanying sidebars a summary of the *DSM-IV* diagnostic criteria, followed by the code number (used only for recordkeeping and insurance purposes). The final three sidebars are at the end of this chapter. (I covered PTSD in the previous two chapters.)

History 4.1

James was forty-four years old, married with three children, and came to me for help with a drinking problem. He had a history of hypertension and a year before a psychiatrist diagnosed generalized anxiety disorder and prescribed a benzodiazepine drug, which James soon discontinued because he felt too sedated and dysphoric. My evaluation showed him to have early stage alcoholism. When he stopped drinking, his blood pressure normalized and his anxiety lessened appreciably. He reluctantly attended a few AA meetings, and denied that he had alcoholism, focusing instead on his belief that he had "GAD," which I was unable to diagnose. He was psychologically abused by both parents as a boy and still had a strained relationship with his father, his mother having died five years before. He chose not to work on his childhood trauma issues.

His story illustrates that: 1. a firm diagnosis of GAD cannot be made when the person is using a drug that often causes anxiety (e.g., alcohol in his case); 2. active alcoholism can simulate or cause many psychological and physical disorders (e.g., GAD and hypertension in his case), which usually improve or clear with cessation of drinking alcohol; and 3. he had a clear history of childhood psychological abuse repeatedly by both parents and had difficulty connecting his anxiety or alcoholism with it.

Most of the people with symptoms of anxiety disorder that I have seen had another illness or disorder that caused their anxiety, as have some people with a phobia or OCD. At any age, fear and anxiety are common acute and long-term *effects* of *trauma.* In most of my patients, I usually screen for PTSD and other disorders, including alcohol and other drug problems, since these are so common and treatable. If I have to use an anti-anxiety drug, I generally prescribe buspirone, and almost never prescribe a benzodiazepine for chronic fear or anxiety. Benzopdiazepine drugs do have a place in acute-care medicine and psychiatry, such as for sedation in frightening medical procedures and conditions, e.g., a heart attack, or when used for *no more than* a week in cases of acute, severe emotional upset.

I have seen countless adult survivors of childhood trauma who came to me for assistance with lessening their panic attacks or another anxiety disorder. They nearly all say that their prior clinicians had not taken a trauma history from them, and that they personally had never connected it with their symptoms.

Generalized Anxiety Disorder
(nonspecific fear, anxiety neurosis) (300.02)

- Excessive [and unrealistic] anxiety and worry about several events or activities for more than half the days during at least 6 months
- Difficulty controlling these feelings
- Associated 3 or more of the following symptoms, some of which are present for over half the days in the past 6 months:* feels restless,edgy, keyed up; tires easily; trouble concentrating; irritability; increased muscle tension and aches; trouble sleeping (initial insomnia or restless, unrefreshing sleep)**
- The symptoms cause clinically important distress or impair work, social or personal functioning.

Exclusions: 1. Aspects of *another Axis I disorder* do not provide the focus of the anxiety*** 2. The disorder is not directly caused by a *general medical condition* or by *substance* (i.e.,drug) use, including medications and drugs of abuse. 3. It does not occur only during a *mood disorder, psychotic disorder, post-traumatic stress disorder* or *pervasive developmental disorder.*

---

*Children need fulfill only 1 of these 6 symptoms.
**A child or adult with these symptoms or signs may be inappropriately labeled with ADHD or ADD.
***Aspects of another Axis I disorder include worry about: weight gain (anorexia nervosa); contamination (obsessive-compulsive disorder); having a panic attack (panic disorder); separation from home or relatives (separation anxiety disorder); public embarrassment (social phobia); or having physical symptoms (somatoform disorders).

THE POLITICS OF ANXIETY & FEAR

Anxiety and depression are our most common emotional problems, and they often coexist. People in the mental-health system have tried to understand these and other mental problems so they can better help people who suffer from them. But in doing so, many of them may have erred. Influenced by the drug industry and other special interest groups, they have misunderstood or overlooked a major cause of these common mental illnesses: repeated childhood and later trauma. They have made the erroneous assumption that anxiety disorders, depression and other mental illnesses are primarily due to chemical problems in the brain and that they are best treated with drugs. But this theory is still unproven (discussed on page 254). To help sell their drugs further, the drug industry and their hired academics have made up new diagnostic categories of mental illnesses that their drugs will theoretically treat (for example, generalized anxiety disorder, further described on page 220).

A major problem is that most of the drugs don't work well, and they are toxic and expensive (see chapter 20 on page 215). The politics of psychiatry, psychology, and other special interest groups and the government are intertwined and complex, and they often spin off to harm the health consumer as much as they may help. I have not found one study that proves the reigning biogenetic theory of mental illness. But I have found a large number of databased reports that, taken as a whole, provide strong evidence that childhood and later trauma are associated with, and probably causal of, common mental illness. In the next chapter I summarize those studies on anxiety and anxiety disorders, as well as some effective approaches for healing.

In the following sidebars I outline the *DSM-IV*'s diagnostic criteria for the remaining three common anxiety disorders: panic disorder, phobias and obsessive-compulsive disorder.

Panic Disorder
("unprovoked" panic attacks) (300.21)

- Recurrent unexpected panic attacks. [Panic disorder is anxiety felt in separate recurrent bouts, also called panic attacks]
- For a month or more after at least 1 of these attacks has had 1 or more of: Ongoing concern that there will be more attacks; Worry as to the meaning or consequences of the attack (for health, control, sanity); Material change in behavior, such as doing something to avoid or combat the attacks.

Exclusions: 1. The panic attacks are not directly caused by a *general medical condition* or by *substance use,* including medications and drugs of abuse. 2. The panic attacks are not better explained by another anxiety or mental disorder.*

---

* Panic attacks can occur in the following anxiety disorders, which should be ruled out: social phobias; specific phobias; obsessive-compulsive disorder; post-traumatic stress disorder. Children who have panic attacks on leaving home should be evaluated for separation anxiety disorder.

Social or Specific Phobia
(300.23/300.29) Three kinds:
social, agoraphobia and specific.

- A strong, persistent fear that is excessive or unreasonable. It is set off (cued) by a specific object or situation that is present or anticipated, e.g.: Social situations*; Other situational (airplane travel, being closed in); Natural environment (thunderstorms, heights, etc.); Blood, injection, injury; Animal (spiders, snakes); Other (situations that might lead to illness, choking, vomiting)
- The phobic stimulus almost always provokes an anxiety response, which may be either a panic attack or anxiety.
- The person realizes that the fear is unreasonable or excessive**
- And avoids the stimulus or endures it with intense anxiety or distress.
- Those under age 18 must have the symptoms for 6 months or more.

Exclusions: Symptoms are not better explained by a different mental disorder, including other anxiety disorders,*** and not directly caused by a general medical condition or by substance use, including medications and drugs of abuse. Dysmorphic disorder, pervasive developmental disorder or schizoid personality disorder.

---

*Social Phobia: Marked and repeated fears of a social or performance situation that involves facing strangers or being watched by others. Fears showing anxiety symptoms or behaving in some other way that will be embarrassing or humiliating. If the social phobia is generalized, look for Axis II diagnosis of avoidant personality disorder. *Children* cannot receive this diagnosis unless they have demonstrated the capacity for age-appropriate social relationships. The anxiety must occur not just with adults, but with peers. They may express the anxiety response by crying, tantrums, freezing or withdrawing. They may not recognize that the fear is unreasonable or out of proportion.
**Children with specific phobia may express the anxiety response by clinging, crying, freezing or tantrums. They may not have insight that their fear is unreasonable or out of proportion. Children who avoid leaving home should be evaluated for separation anxiety disorder.
*** Other anxiety disorders should be ruled out before diagnosing specific phobia: social phobias (avoids public eating or other activities for fear of embarrassment); obsessive-compulsive disorder (fears dirt or contamination); PTSD (for example, avoids movies about Vietnam); agoraphobia (with or without panic disorder).

Obsessive-Compulsive Disorder (300.3)

Either or both of: ***Obsessions*** (thoughts, impulses or images)

1. Recurring, persisting, inappropriate thoughts, impulses or images intrude into awareness, causing marked anxiety or distress (not just excessive worries about ordinary problems)
2. Tries to ignore, suppress or neutralize these ideas by thoughts or compulsive behavior
3. Knows ideas are a product of their own mind

Compulsions (behaviors or rituals)

1. Feels the need to repeat physical behaviors (checking the stove to be sure it is off, handwashing) or mental behaviors (counting things, silently repeating words)
2. Behaviors occur as a response to an obsession or by strictly applied rules
3. Aim is to reduce or eliminate distress or to prevent fear over something dreaded.
4. These behaviors are either not realistically related to the events they are supposed to counteract or are clearly excessive for that purpose

- At some time recognizes that the obsessions or compulsions are unreasonable or excessive (children do not have to have insight)
- The obsessions and/or compulsions are associated with at least 1 of: Cause severe distress; Take up time (more than an hour per day); Interfere with the patient's usual routine or social, work or personal functioning

Exclusions: 1. If has another Axis I disorder, the content of obsessions or compulsions is not restricted to it. 2. other Axis I disorders that must be ruled out: *appearance* (Body Dysmorphic Disorder); *food* (Eating Disorders); being *seriously ill* (Hypochondriasis); *guilt* (Mood Disorders); *sexual* fantasies or urges (Paraphilias); *drugs* (Substance Use Disorders); *hair pulling* (Trichotillomania). 3. symptoms not directly caused by a general medical condition or by substance use, including medications and drugs of abuse.

5 DISORDERS OF ANXIETY AND FEAR
—— CONTINUED

CAUSAL FACTORS

Fear is a natural feeling that happens in our everyday life. It can become a problem when it bothers us so much that it interferes with our ability to function. In my clinical experience, although it can happen independently, it occurs most often as a part of another problem or disorder, such as depression, PTSD or an addiction, and/or simply as a response to trauma or other stressors.

Countless articles, chapters and books have been written about anxiety. The Anxiety Disorders Association of America (2001) believes that anxiety disorders may develop from a complex set of risk factors, including life events, personality, genetics and brain chemistry. It is still debated how these potential causal factors interact. Once the anxiety patterns emerge, a cycle of fear and avoidance is learned. That learned pattern is then kept in motion by "fear-enhancing" habits. Stress, especially chronic distress, commonly precedes anxiety disorders. One of the most frequent kinds of distress is that which is associated with childhood trauma. Here is what the clinical and scientific literature says about that association.

Retrospective Studies

I found seventy-three retrospective studies that reported an association between anxiety, anxiety disorders and childhood trauma. As shown in Tables A 5.1 and A 5.2 in the Appendix, thirty-five of them were from people evaluated among *clinical* samples ($n = 13,212$ people) and 38 from those in *community* samples ($n = 63,223$ people). When compared with their matched control groups, they all showed a significantly increased incidence and/or prevalence of anxiety or anxiety disorder among adults and some children who had experienced repeated childhood trauma. Five of these found an increase in phobias among childhood trauma survivors.[808, 934, 935, 982] I also found five studies that looked for obsessive-compulsive disorder[155, 982] which found that OCD was increased up to *five times* among survivors of childhood trauma when compared to controls. Except for these, most of the seventy-three reports did not differentiate specific kinds of anxiety disorders (except for ruling out PTSD). They looked for the experience of a non-ordinary or bothersome anxiety, and all of these studies found it to a statistically significant degree among CT survivors when compared to matched controls.

Prospective Studies

While the above high number (seventy-three) of retrospective studies provides firm evidence of a real trauma-anxiety relationship, prospective studies can make the link stronger. I found twelve such reports, which I summarize in Table A5.3 of the Appendix. The study sample of these totaled 7,593, people with an additional study on 593 families, including their matched controls. These were all followed for a period of from fifteen months (in one study) to twenty years. Over such prolonged follow-up periods, these peer-reviewed reports give us a remarkable look at the natural history of the many painful effects of repeated childhood trauma. When compared to their controls, those traumatized as children show an increase of up to *six times* the anxiety and anxiety disorders (i.e., up to 600 percent more than was found among the controls), plus the numerous other mental and physical disorders shown in the table. These results are consistently strong, and clearly support the seventy-three retrospective studies described above.

Index Case Studies

I found fifteen studies that evaluated 10,609 people *with anxiety disorders* and their controls for a history of childhood trauma. All fifteen studies found a statistically significant increase of a history of trauma among those with anxiety disorders up to 64 percent, which is a high number. They also showed an increased amount of co-morbidity.

SUMMARY OF DATA

Taken as a whole, these 100 reports provide strong evidence to document the link between repeated childhood trauma and anxiety that countless clinicians have observed over time among their patients and clients as summarized in Table 5.5. These include seventy-three studies on large clinical and community samples (n = 76,435 people), twelve prospective studies, and fiffteen index case studies, for a total of sixty-seven peer-reviewed, published reports on 94,637 study subjects. Even more remarkable, these studies include but one, which I add as an example,[98] of the *eighty-five reports of PTSD* as a result of childhood trauma. Anxiety/fear is a prominent symptom of PTSD, which is also classified as an anxiety disorder. One cannot have PTSD without usually experiencing a bothersome to severe anxiety. (If we were to add these 85 PTSD studies to the 99 retrospective, prospective and index case reports on anxiety, the result would total 184 reports (see chapters 2 and 3 for details on PTSD).*

In most of these studies, the authors *controlled for other* possible confounding or confusing *variables* and they *still arrived* at the results shown in these tables. The consistent finding showing this trauma-anxiety link across 100 separate reports, representing four diverse research designs (clinical and community retrospective, index case and prospective samples), using various methods of measurement, by numerous authors in nearly all independent studies on such a large number of people in several countries, increases the likelihood that this highly replicated relationship between repeated childhood trauma and anxiety is a real phenomenon, as opposed to being an artifact of methodology, sample variation, or measurement error that may have occurred in single studies.

Several literature reviews also summarize and synthesize multiple studies on the effects of childhood trauma. For example, research psychologist Kathleen Kendall-Tackett and her colleagues reviewed 45 such studies in 1993 and found that among 13 of these 45 studies that anxiety and fear was reported in 13 to 68 percent of the 1,165 *children* evaluated. Ammerman and colleagues did a literature review in 1986 on 83 articles and found a similar result, as have others.

---

*Anxiety is also well known to be present among at least 80% of depressed people. But most of the studies that evaluated the relationship between depression and trauma did not look for anxiety or anxiety disorders. However, we could make a "best guess" by estimating that of the original 276 scientific reports that I found which linked depression with childhood and other trauma, among the 174,039 people studied, that 80% of them (i.e. 220 studies on some 139,231 people had bothersome anxiety).[1090]

Table 5.5. Anxiety, Anxiety Disorders & Childhood Trauma: Clinical, Community, Prospective, Index Case Studies, & Meta-Analysis/Literature Reviews*

(See Tables A5.1-4 for details.)

Year/Author	Study	PTSD	Other Trauma Effects
Clinical **35 Studies** 1972–2003	13,212 people CT v. controls	↑ to 15x controls (5 found phobia, 4 found OCD)	↑ Co-morbidity Table on page 284
Community **38 Studies** 1987–2003	63,223 people CT v. controls	↑ to 11x controls	↑ Co-morbidity Table on page 290
Prospective **12 Studies** 1996–2003	7,593 people CT v. controls	↑ to 6x controls	↑ Co-morbidity Multiple dimensions. Table on page 296
Index Case **15 Studies** 1993–2002	10,609 anxiety disordered or affected	↑ to 64% had a CT history	↑ Co-morbidity Table on page 298
Meta-Analysis/ *Literature* *Reviews* 1986–1993	2 literature reviews	Both show ↑ association with CT	↑ Co-morbidity Text on page 46
Summary **100 Studies by** **Independent** **International** **Authors** **1972–2003**	**94,637 CT** **people and** **controls**	**↑ to 15x Clinical;** **↑ to 11x** **Community;** **↑ to 6x** **Prospective;** **↑ to 64% CT in** **Index Cases**	**↑ Co-morbidity** **All document CT link**

Key: CT = childhood trauma, Sx = symptoms or signs, ↑ = increased

All of the above data tells us that the trauma-anxiety link is real among a large number of people with a history of childhood trauma. If that connection is true, how can we best use our knowledge of it to help people with disorders of anxiety and fear?

RECOVERY AIDS

As for most problems or disorders, choosing one or more recovery aids will usually be based on first *finding the cause*—in this case, of the fear or anxiety. The fear/anxiety may be telling us of an underlying problem. Knowing the cause or causes will allow a more efficient search for how to lessen or eliminate the symptom or problem. For ordinary fear/anxiety, formal recovery aids are usually not needed. People commonly handle them on their own. For long-standing, problematic, or disordered fear, it may be useful to evaluate it by using a decision tree or flowchart, as shown in Figure 5.1. On conducting an initial evaluation, attention should be paid to ruling out more complex causes or forms of anxiety, as shown in the first footnote of the figure. Once a specific anxiety disorder is identified, the person can begin a Stage One recovery program (as outlined in Table 2.3 on page 20), which focuses on lessening the anxiety and/or associated disordered behavior, while attending to any co-morbidity as appropriate. If there is a history of significant childhood trauma, then serious consideration should be given to using a Stage Two trauma-focused recovery program on a long-term basis. Individual and/or group psychotherapy is usually an efficient way to begin this whole process.

The fear in anxiety disorder (recently named *generalized* anxiety disorder, and previously called anxiety neurosis) has been somewhat disguised as being "free-floating" anxiety. This vague term means

Figure 5.1. Anxiety Disorder— Flowchart for Decision Making

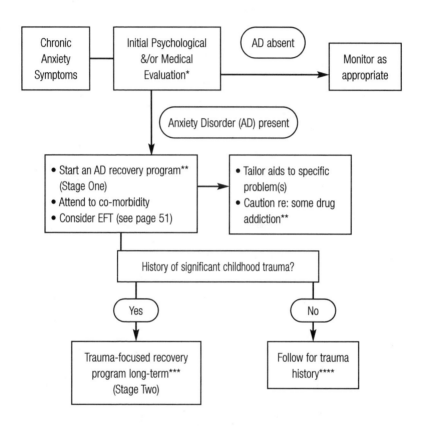

* Rule out more complex forms or causes of anxiety, e.g., PTSD, addiction, dissociative disorder, inordinate relationship conflicts, serious physical problems and effects of childhood trauma.

** Avoid using benzodiazepine sedative drugs to treat anxiety, insomnia or depression. Buspirone is an acceptable, non-addicting anti-anxiety drug.

*** Long-term group therapy, individual therapy, self-help group attendance, etc., as described in prior volume.

**** Because many trauma survivors authentically forget the trauma (dissociative amnesia), or they may not be able to accurately name what happened to them as having been traumatic, keep an open mind that a substantial number of these people may eventually remember a serious trauma history.

Table 5.6. Some Physical and External Causes
of Fear and Anxiety *(expanded from references below)*

1. Threats of violence or loss; age regression
2. Hormonal—hyperthyroidism, hypoadrenalcorticalism, hypoglycemia
3. Brain—temporal lobe epilepsy
4. Drug effects—caffeine, theophylline, aminophylline, salbutamol, antidepressant drugs, antipsychotics, cocaine, amphetamines, psychedelic drugs and other stimulants
5. Drug withdrawal—alcohol, other sedatives (especially benzodiazepines), antidepressant drugs (effects may occur early and during longer-term use as well), anti-psychotic drugs, mood stabilizers, opiates.

Causes of Anxiety or Fear Among Children and Adolescents

0–6 months	Loss of support, loud noises
7–12 months	Strangers, heights; sudden, unexpected and looming objects
1 year	Separation from parents; toilet training, injury, strangers
2 years	A multitude of sources, including loud noises (vacuum cleaners, sirens/alarms, trucks and thunder), animals (e.g., large dogs), dark rooms, separation from parents, large objects or machines, change in person's environment, strange peers
3 years	Masks, darkness, animals, separation from parents
4 years	Separation from parents, animals, darkness, noises (including at night)
5 years	Animals, "bad" people, darkness, separation from parent, bodily harm
6 years	Supernatural beings (e.g., ghosts, witches, "Darth Vader"), bodily injuries, thunder and lightning, darkness, sleeping or staying alone, separation from parents
7–8 years	Supernatural beings, darkness, media events (e.g., news reports on the threat of nuclear war or child kidnapping), staying alone, bodily injury
9–12 years	Tests and examinations in school, school performance, bodily injury, physical appearance, thunder and lightning, death, darkness
Teens	Social performance, sexuality

From *Treating Children's Fears and Phobia: A Behavioral Approach,* by R. Morris and T. Kratochwill, Pergamon Press 1983
U.S. Dept. of Health and Human Services: A Report of the Surgeon General - executive summary. Rockville, MD, 1999
Green B: Problem-based psychiatry. Churchill Livingston, NY 1996

that the painful fear feeling has no clear link with any causal or aggravating person or event. To those who use this term I ask, "How exactly did you evaluate the fear/anxiety? Did you check for exogenous (external) causes? Did you look for and rule out a history of past trauma and the possible presence of PTSD?" Table 5.6 shows a list of such common and uncommon physical and external causes of anxiety in adults and children.

If an anti-anxiety drug is indicated or required, in my experience buspirone (BuSpar) is usually the safest one to use. Although it usually takes two to four weeks to act on lessening or taking the edge off of fear/anxiety, it is generally non-addicting and does not have the numbing and strongly addicting characteristics of benzodiazepines sedatives. It also usually helps to prevent an escalation of fear into panic. The initial dose of buspirone is 5 milligrams three times daily, as tolerated, with a gradual increase in the dose every few days, as prescribed.

Recent Advances

Based on recent discoveries involving the body's subtle energies, such as has been shown for centuries by using acupuncture and acupressure treatment, a new method of addressing bothersome emotional pain issues called *emotional freedom techniques* (EFT) has been clinically effective in thousands of cases. There is some published data to show its effectiveness. Numerous licensed clinicians worldwide are using it successfully to help treat people's fear/anxiety, anger, shame and inordinate grief, as well as PTSD. It can also help lessen some physical symptoms, including headaches, body pains and breathing problems. Expanded from early acupressure methods from pioneers such as Roger Callahan Ph.D., (who in the 1980s developed the similar *thought field therapy*), the technique's developer Gary Craig has observed that, properly applied, over 80 percent of people who use it achieve either noticeable improvement or complete cessation of their problem. Indeed, he believes that EFT is useful to reduce the symptoms of most emotional and physical diseases. This simple method for helping us heal may be an important missing piece to the healing puzzle for a number of reasons, including that it often works where nothing else will, it is usually rapid, long-lasting and gentle, no drugs or equipment are involved, its basics can be learned by anyone, and it can be self administered and is relatively gentle. I have seen it used since 1991 on several of my patients with success. To find a clinician who is skilled in using it and more information about it, Craig's Web site is *www.emofree.com.* He offers an excellent manual that explains the basics of EFT as a free download.

In his book *The Body Bears the Burden,*[920] neurologist Robert Scaer said, "TFT [Thought Field Therapy], an unusual technique devised by Callahan, is based on a theory that 'perturbations' in the 'thought field'—i.e., any negative emotion, phobia, or anxiety—cause disruption in the body's energy system. This state of energy imbalance is measurable through a diagnostic process of strength testing based on the technique of applied kinesiology, which in turn is related to the concepts of meridian energy flow on which acupuncture is based. The treatment involves instructing the patient to tap [with the tip of their finger] strategic acupuncture meridian points determined by the diagnostic procedure, while simultaneously imaging or remembering a traumatic event, memory, phobia, or emotion. Frequently the process is blocked by 'psychological reversals,' a presumed reversal of meridian polarity. These reversals are then corrected by tapping on the outside of the hand while saying three times, 'I fully accept myself even though I have this problem.' The patient then goes through a nine-step procedure involving a ritualized combination of eye movements, counting, and humming a few bars of a song while performing hand tapping. During this process, the patient's self-assessed SUDS (e.g. anxiety) rating is documented sequentially, with the goal being reduction of the scale to a 1 [out of 10]."

Dr. Scaer continues, "The arcane nature of TFT, its radical departure from any standard concept of psychotherapy, and the supposed 'quick fix' that it provides have predictably exposed it to the condemnation and ridicule of many research psychologists. These very features, however, have probably contributed to its remarkably widespread use by community-based psychotherapists frustrated by treatment failures with standard therapy for PTSD, and also to the success of Callahan's training seminars."[920]

History 5.1

Sally was a forty-four-year-old woman who as a child was repeatedly raped by her father. Her mother ignored these assaults and both parents ridiculed her constantly. She has worked in individual and group therapy for three years. While crying in an individual session, she complained that her fear of being raped, fear of losing her job and her home has increased to the point where she is now afraid to go out. I suggested EFT as an adjunct to her other therapy, and she commented that she would try anything because she was desperate. Her EFT-trained therapist later told me, "I explained to her that we needed to isolate each specific fear and work on them one at a time. She picked her lingering fear of being raped first and rated it as a nine on a scale of one to ten. I first tapped rapidly on the fleshy part of the outside of her hand just below her little finger while she repeated three times: 'Even though I have this fear of being raped, I love and accept myself.' (This is done in case there is a psychological reversal.) Then she repeated 'fear of being raped' each time I tapped (between five and seven times at each meridian point). Sometimes, I reminded her to increase intensity of her fear as much as she could. She then followed me in the rapid eye movement, humming and counting (to engage the left hemisphere of the brain) and we repeated the tapping series. This procedure took three minutes. I then asked her to rate her fear of being raped again on a scale of one to ten. She emphatically answered that it was gone. (On recheck six weeks later it was still gone.)

"She then asked me to proceed with her other fears. We didn't need to do the tapping on the hand for reversal. I showed her how to tap by tapping on myself while she repeated the next phrase: 'fear of losing my job,' and then 'fear of losing my home.' We needed to do only the tapping, not the other parts, and those fears decreased to the point where she reported no longer having them."

I believe that this treatment aid can be an adjunct to lessening disabling fear and anxiety while the person does their deeper healing work in individual and/or group therapy. It is best used under the guidance of a therapist who has specific training in this method.

Another common effect of trauma is the defense against emotional pain called dissociation, which at times develops into a dissociative disorder. I address these in the next two chapters.

6 DISSOCIATION AND DISSOCIATIVE DISORDERS

Here, I look at two frequent issues: dissociation and dissociative disorders. To better understand dissociative disorders, I will first summarize the psychological defense against emotional pain called dissociation.

DISSOCIATION

People who have experienced abuse or trauma frequently report: "I went numb," "I just wasn't there," or "I left my body." To dissociate means to *separate*. Dissociation is a ". . . process whereby information—incoming, stored or outgoing—is actively deflected from integration with its usual or expected associations." Clinical and research psychologist David Spiegel further defined dissociation as being ". . . analogous to working in one directory of a computer without being able to access the main menu, indicating the presence of other directories and without path commands enabling the directory to find information needed from another directory. The presence of the material in one directory makes the computer act as

though the other material does not exist".[968] Psychologist Frank
Leavitt defines dissociation as an altered mental state wherein our
connections to our experience are partially or fully decreased.[624]

We can dissociate across a spectrum of *healthy trance states* to
defending against *emotional* pain to having PTSD and/or a *dissociative disorder,* as shown in Figure 6.1.

Figure 6.1. Spectrum of Dissociation

Healthy Dissociation		"Grey Zone"		**Unhealthy** Dissociation	
Healthy Trance States	Defending Against the Pain of Being Abused as a Child	Defending Against the Pain of Being Abused as an Adult	PTSD	Dissociative Disorder (DD)	Dissociative Identity Disorder (MPD)

Dissociation is a *protective* and *useful* survival defense for growing up in an unhealthy family and world. When we are being mistreated or abused, dissociating allows us to separate from our
awareness of our inner life, especially our painful feelings and
thoughts. Here it serves a useful purpose. But after we grow up and
leave that family, to dissociate frequently from all pain may no
longer be necessary or particularly useful, especially if we are now
around safe people. But what was an adaptive and useful skill in
defending against the pain of childhood abuse may continue into
adulthood as a maladaptive habit.

Dissociation may be *maladaptive* in two ways. First, as just
mentioned, the adult-pain dissociator who has left the abusive
environment of home and neighborhood may now live in a safe

environment, yet they may continue to dissociate unnecessarily, thus hampering their interactions and relationships. Or second, they may remain in their abusive environment or move into another one, and while their ability to dissociate may still be useful, it may block their ability to access their inner life accurately and appropriately (see Figure 6.2). In either of these situations, the person may age-regress frequently, which can also rob them of their ability to feel in charge of their life and to enjoy it. Age regression is a dissociative state, and many of the principles for its healing apply for many of the other varieties of dissociation. (see refs 1089, 1094 and 1095.)

As adults, if we habitually dissociate because of our childhood trauma, we may feel as though we have lost the "point of contact"

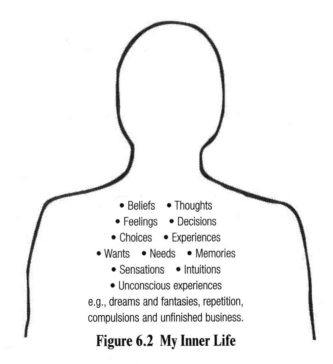

- Beliefs   • Thoughts
- Feelings   • Decisions
- Choices   • Experiences
- Wants   • Needs   • Memories
- Sensations   • Intuitions
- Unconscious experiences
e.g., dreams and fantasies, repetition, compulsions and unfinished business.

Figure 6.2 My Inner Life

with our inner and outer reality. We often feel "out of touch," with the present moment, "artificial," or as though we are "play acting." As we heal we take control of the mechanism of dissociating and become more in touch with our authentic inner life in the present moment.

Areas of Dissociation

We may dissociate our awareness and experience in any of several of our life areas—the physical, mental, emotional and spiritual. The following include some examples.

Physical: Out-of-body experience, psychogenic or hysterical anesthesia or paralysis, some drug intoxication, physical self-harm, violence to another, overeating, purging or starving.

Mental: Separating or distancing from one or more inner-life components, such as our beliefs, thoughts and memories; fantasizing, intellectualizing; "splitting off."

Emotional: Separating from our *feelings,* whether painful or joyful, "numbing out," smiling or laughing at pain, "poker face" or a mask, age-regressing.

Spiritual: All of the above, as exemplified by age-regression, plus feeling separated from others and the God of our understanding.

We may dissociate in any one or more of these areas in a healthy or an unhealthy way. We may also dissociate as an individual, or collectively as a group. Individuals may dissociate frequently, e.g., when they mean, "*I* get angry," instead, they say "*You* get angry" or "*One* gets angry." An example of collective dissociation is calling something by another name, such as when we call homelessness "displaced person status," or when we call fear "anxiety," and sadness or grief "depression." Others and I describe dissociation in more detail elsewhere.[960, 1089]

DISSOCIATIVE DISORDERS

Healthy trance states like daydreaming, writing a song or poem, listening to a symphony, or even a jogger's high, are common. Also common is the psychological defense of dissociation in reaction to the stress and traumas of everyday life. Actual disorders of dissociation are relatively common (as in dissociative amnesia) to rare (dissociative fugue), as shown in the first column of Table 6.1. Here I also describe their salient characteristics. For example, *dissociative amnesia* is relatively common among survivors of trauma—hence its alternative name of *traumatic* amnesia. As of 1999 there was documentation in sixty-eight databased studies that showed that about a third of CSA survivors *completely* forget long-term that they were sexually abused, while another third always remember it, with the middle third having *partial* amnesia for the trauma.[137, 138, 1089] Dissociative identity disorder (DID) and the other dissociative disorders (DDs) frequently involve some degree of dissociative amnesia. I address memory further in history 6.3 and at the end of this chapter.

History 6.1.

Amy was a forty-four-year-old single, recovering alcoholic woman with dissociative identity disorder. She was referred to me by a colleague for work on healing the effects of her severe childhood trauma. When I first saw her she knew that she had DID, with about six "alter" personalities, but she knew little about them. As I worked with her over time in individual and group therapy, I noted that she had great difficulty identifying

Table 6.1. Characteristics of Dissociative Disorders

Dissociative Disorder/Code		Characteristics Summary
Dissociative Identity Disorder *Uncommon*	300.14	Person has at least two distinct identities or personality states, which repeatedly take control of their behavior.** Each personality has its own relatively lasting pattern of sensing, thinking about and relating to self and world.**
Dissociative Amnesia *Relatively Common Effect of Trauma*	300.12	Inability to recall important personal information, usually concerning trauma, and it is more extensive than could be explained by ordinary forgetfulness. (see also page 73)
Dissociative Fugue *Rare*	300.13	Person suddenly and unexpectedly travels and cannot recall personal history. May be confused about identity or assume a new identity; partial or complete.*** All not solely as a part of DID.*
Depersonalization Disorder *Rare*	300.6	A lasting or recurring feeling of being detached from person's own body; feels like an outside self-observer, as if in a dream. Throughout the experience, knows this is not really the case (reality testing is intact).* Absence of other major psychological or dissociative disorder.
Dissociative Disorder Not Otherwise Specified *Uncommon*	300.15	Serious and disabling dissociative symptoms that do not fit any of the above disorders.*

* Not directly caused by a general medical condition or by substance use, including medications and drugs of abuse.
** In children, the symptoms cannot be attributed to fantasy play, including imaginary playmates.
*** Cause clinically important distress or impair work, social or personal functioning.

and expressing her feelings. She had only fragmentary memories about the severe abuse and neglect that she suffered as a child. However, when her alter personalities surfaced they were better able to name and express her feelings and describe her traumatic memories. When she became stressed or sleep-deprived, she frequently "switched," as an alter personality would assume her identity, and this experience aggravated her stress level such that she drank, missed work, and finally lost her job.

Early in the course of her recovery, she relapsed into alcoholic drinking several more times, necessitating four hospitalizations. She eventually strengthened her alcoholism recovery program and began to stabilize, and then found a job where she could support herself. In individual and group therapy, over time she began to slowly get to know her alters and, more importantly, to feel, own and express her feelings more authentically. She spent the next four years in the active stage of grief work, feeling and expressing the ungrieved pain of her severe childhood trauma and neglect. She ultimately switched less often and is now approaching a state of "integration," wherein she is able to live as and from her true self (called the "core" personality by DID clinical researchers and authors).

Amy's story illustrates the difficulty that people with DID experience as they try to heal. Before she could enter into a Stage Two full-recovery program, she had to stabilize her almost chaotic life, which was aggravated by her flooding memories of the trauma and frequent alcoholic relapses wherein she tried to lessen her pain. As with most people with DID, she had several other (co-morbid) disorders, including alcoholism, depression and PTSD. My experience is that people with dissociative disorders represent an extreme end of the effects of trauma and that they usually require more time and patience to recover. Amy has now been active in her trauma-focused recovery work for over six years.

History 6.2.

Tony was a forty-six-year-old divorced dentist who had the disorder called *dissociative fugue* since he was a young man. He came for assistance with trying to heal from a life of frustration and pain. He had to stop practicing dentistry because of disability from his dissociative fugue and severe PTSD. He was sexually and psychologically abused by his mother after having been abandoned by his father when he was two years old. He had great difficulty expressing his feelings in both individual and group therapy. After three years of recovery work, he went to work for a dental clinic that provided services for a low-income neighborhood. Gradually his fugue states, in which he unpredictably dissociated and traveled, only to awaken and not remember what he had done, decreased. He is now in his fifth year of work on his recovery and is moderately improved from his debilitating symptoms.

Both Amy and Tony's histories show how long and painful the process of recovery is for many people with dissociative disorders. Recovery is commonly aggravated by the presence of multiple co-morbidities, such as depression, addictions and PTSD. Most of the people with DID and many with the other dissociative disorders have seen several health professionals, many of whom have paid little attention to their childhood trauma issues. They have commonly lost jobs and become disabled and so financially strapped that they have difficulty paying for their treatment. These disorders are toward the far end of the spectrum of severity regarding the effects of trauma, approaching those with debilitating schizophrenia, which I discuss in chapters 17 and 18.

When we dissociate in a *healthy* way, we may focus our awareness on only one or two areas of our experience. Or we may shift, and scan many areas. Dissociation is thus a great facility and skill through which we may explore and experience parts of our life. *Unhealthy* dissociation can be differentiated from the healthy kind by 1) a significant alteration in a person's sense of *identity,* as seen in DID and fugue states—as well as in the common numbed dissociation of our true self when we let our false self run our life—and by 2) a partial or complete loss of *memory* for a traumatic event[968, 969] and by 3) the other maladaptive kind of dissociation described earlier in this chapter.

In all my years of practice, I have never seen a person with a dissociative disorder who grew up in a healthy family. These dissociative disorders, along with PTSD and anxiety disorders, appear to be mostly disorders of *fear.* Each of these people grew up in a dysfunctional family that usually repeatedly shamed and threatened them, leaving the child in a continuous state of post-traumatic fear that manifested as either *hyperstimulation, hyperactivity,* or a feeling of *numbness,* or an alternating of these.

With no healthy models to teach us otherwise and no safe people or places to share and process our inner and outer life, and because they are often so painful or confusing, we may split off any of these components of our experience and bury them deep within the unconscious part of our psyche. This is similar to what I have referred to as "The Child or True Self going into hiding" (as shown on page 69 of *The Truth About Depression*). This dissociation, separation or splitting off one or more of these components may come about in any pattern or sequence. A common pattern is when a person *cognitively remembers* aspects of a traumatic experience but dissociates from their associated feelings, sensations or images for a long duration of time, as the following history illustrates.

History 6.3.

At age thirty, Susan came for counseling because she had recently felt a repulsion for her five-year-old son and had begun to reject him physically and emotionally. After several counseling sessions she began to remember that her mother had treated her the same way when she was five, although more severely. It was at this age when she had realized that her mother was very disturbed. While she had always cognitively remembered that she had been sexually abused by a baby-sitter at age six and by her grandfather at age nine, she had *forgotten her painful emotions* that were *attached to the experience* of being molested. While talking about it with her therapist, her painful feelings gradually returned. She then remembered telling her mother immediately after being molested by her grandfather (her mother's father), and her mother's dissociating and completely ignoring her. At that time, Susan realized that he molested her mother as a child also. When she was thirty she told her aunt, who believed her and validated her experience. After expressing her story and her pain, she was able to grieve the trauma that she had not been able to before. Her feeling of repulsion for her son then gradually disappeared.

Susan's experience is an example of a frequent pattern of dissociation after trauma that is not allowed to be processed initially. It shows how, even in those who have always cognitively remembered trauma, that, having dissociated from the hurt, they may still have ungrieved pain to experience and work through. During her process of remembering and grieving, she said, "It was as though my memories were under a stairway in the dark recesses of my mind. A part of me always knew they were there, but I never wanted to shine the light on them." While she was able to resolve her presenting complaint in four months of weekly psychotherapy, three years later she continues to work on her residual associated pain and core issues, and her functioning as an individual, wife and mother show clear improvement. (I summarize the process of trauma memory recovery at the end of the next chapter.)

7 DISSOCIATION AND DISSOCIATIVE DISORDERS
— CONTINUED

In this chapter I will first focus on trauma-related causal factors for *dissociation* itself, after which I will turn to these causal factors for the dissociative *disorders*.

CAUSAL FACTORS OF DISSOCIATION

Retrospective and Prospective Studies

Researchers have studied dissociation by looking at it as being a component of normal and natural responses to trauma. I found thirty such studies conducted on 2,961 people in diverse, mostly clinical situations and settings, published from 1985 to 2002, as shown in Table A7.1 on page 300 of the Appendix. Nearly all compared the characteristics of people who had been traumatized as children with control groups of people who reported no trauma history. Dissociation was a significant finding, often major, among all of the trauma survivors. Most also reported multiple co-morbidities, which is common among trauma survivors.

As is true for most of the studies that I have summarized throughout this book, the specific symptom or disorder looked for—here, the presence of dissociation, or below, a dissociative disorder—was usually but *one part* of the total effects found among the survivors of childhood trauma. Like low self-esteem, the survival defense mechanism of dissociation is a common, if not almost universal finding among survivors of repeated trauma. While nineteen of these twenty clinical studies were conducted using a retrospective design, one used a prospective one,[811] which supports the validity of the retrospective studies.

Community Studies

I found sixteen community studies, all of which reported similar results as the clinical and prospective ones (see Table A7.2 on page 304 of the Appendix). For example, one of the studies reported a significant trauma-dissociation link, and also found no significant perceptual *distortions* among its sample of 259 college students,[886] which supports the fact that dissociation is *not* a *psychotic process*. Another study concluded that child sexual abuse itself was a significant associated factor among all of the several detrimental effects found, including dissociation.[843] And another suggested that the increased dissociation may also be due to the ill effects of growing up in a toxic family environment.[746] This dissociation is commonly a normal reaction to trauma. Twelve of these studies found the presence of multiple co-morbidities. Two found an increasing graded relationship between repeated childhood trauma and the degree of dissociation.[907, 908]

CAUSAL FACTORS IN DISSOCIATIVE DISORDERS

All forty-six of these above-described studies looked for and found a significant amount of dissociation among trauma survivors, and, of these, the thirty clinical ones found an increase in dissociation and/or *disorders* of dissociation among trauma survivors. In eleven separate reports, published from 1984 to 1997, six research teams examined 1,167 people with dissociative identity disorder (DID, also called multiple personality disorder, or MPD) and found that in general from 75 to 97 percent had substantial to severe childhood trauma histories. Another one studied six people with atypical dissociative disorders and eleven with dissociative amnesia, and twenty with DID, and found that from 82 to 100 percent had childhood trauma histories. Five of these studies showed a high degree of multiple co-morbidity, while most of the remaining five studies did not look for it. *None failed to find a significant link* between CT and dissociative disorders. Three reported psychotic and/or neurologic symptoms, as shown in the table. One showed a significant improvement among fifty-four people with DID using a trauma-focused recovery program over a two year follow-up period.[303] The improvement included a significant decrease in their depression, anxiety, alcohol and/or drug problems, dissociation, somatization, hospitalizations, and number of psychiatric drugs needed. A summary of these eleven published reports is shown in Table A7.3.

In summary, I found sixty databased, peer-reviewed published reports conducted by diverse researchers in different countries using different study methods on different sample populations (clinical, community, prospective and index cases) that came to a consistent and replicated conclusion: that repeated childhood trauma was significantly associated with subsequent dissociation and dissociative disorders (Table 7.4).

Table 7.4. Dissociation, Dissociative Disorders & Childhood Trauma: *Clinical, Community, Prospective, Index Case Studies,* & *Literature* Reviews* *(see Tables A7.1-3, p. 300 for details)*

	Study	Dissociation/ Disorder	Other Trauma Effects/ Full Table Page
Clinical **30 Studies** 1985–2002	2,961 people CT v. controls	↑ to 2x controls	↑ Co-morbidity Table on page 300
Community **16 Studies** 1988–2002	5,502 people CT v. controls	↑ to 5.4x controls	↑ Co-morbidity Table on page 304
Prospective **3 Studies** 1998–2002	1,103 children CT v. controls	↑ (included in Tables A7.1, 2 & 3)	↑ Co-morbidity
Index Case **11 Studies** 1984–1997	1,167 Dissociative Disordered	↑ to 100% had a CT history	↑ Co-morbidity Table on page 306
Literature Reviews 2001	2 example literature reviews	↑ association with CT	↑ Co-morbidity
Summary **60 Studies by Independent International Authors** 1985–2003	**9,630 CT people and their controls**	↑ **to 2x Clinical;** ↑ **to 5.4x Community;** ↑ **in 3 Prospectives;** ↑ **to 100% CT in Index Cases**	↑ **Co-morbidity** **All document CT link**

Key: CT = childhood trauma, Sx = symptoms or signs, ↑ = increased

TRAUMA MEMORIES ARE CORRECT IN ESSENCE

Since ordinary memory is often inaccurate, some critics have rightly expressed concern about the possibility that retrospective reports of childhood trauma could also be inaccurate. To address this concern, several independent researchers looked at this question from different perspectives and by using different research methods over a seventeen-year span from 1985 to 2002. I found nine examples of such investigations. Six were databased studies on 6,546 people and three were extensive reviews of the current research literature available from 1998 through 2002. As summarized in Table 7.5 on the next 2 pages, these examples show that not only is trauma memory different than ordinary memory, but it is also generally accurate in its essence, i.e., in this case that the childhood trauma occurred. These reports from diverse authors and study samples show that 1) trauma memory is generally accurate and 2) trauma memory data from retrospective studies is usually reliable. These findings have also been substantiated by over 300 published studies on trauma effects, including over thirty prospective studies, that have replicated the same results. This is in contrast to the disinformation promoted by "false memory" advocates, who in well over a decade of their claims have not produced any published convincing empirical evidence of the existence of a "false memory syndrome." This observation, backed by a strong research base, may make us wonder: Who has the false memory?

Table 7.5. Self-Reporting and Remembering Accuracy of

Year/Author	Study Characteristics	Findings among trauma survivors
1985 Robins et al.	52 alcoholics or depressives 39 controls	Memories of child environment experience mostly valid
1988 Berger et al.	Study 1: 4,695 college students, Study 2: 34 social service managed teens	12% were physically injured by parent, yet only 2.9% said they were abused
1993 Brewin et al.	Extensive review of retrospective report accuracy	Central features of trauma memories are likely to be reasonably accurate
1997 Bifulco et al.	87 twin sister pairs evaluated	High cross-corroboration of trauma memories
1998 Brown et al.	Extensive review & analysis of literature on dissociative amnesia & critical literature	All 68 reports that studied CSA memory found DA** in about 1/3 of subjects
2000 Fergusson et al. Prospective	1,265 children followed 21 years from birth	Significant false *negative* reports about trauma
2001 Richter & Eisermann	220 psych inpatients	Memories of parenting were generally consistent & credible
Whitfield et al.	Special volume on misinformation by CSA memory critics (including organized accused & convicted child molesters)	Extensive reviews showed no databased evidence for a "false memory syndrome"
2002 Wilsnack et al.	154 CSA women, structured interview, 37 with dis. amnesia	Only 3 of 37 remembered with help of a clinician
1985–2002 9 Reports	**6 Studies (on 6,546 people) 3 Reviews (of numerous reports)**	**Trauma memory is generally accurate (when positive)**

*For ethical and humanistic reasons, prospective studies cannot be conducted in CSA and other childhood traumas. Even so, when researchers find already-existing abused populations to evaluate and follow, they can

Childhood Trauma: 9 Example Studies or Reviews

Other Findings	Comments
A significant number had true memories	Psychiatric disorders did not appear to bias reports
Under-reporting of trauma is common	Most abused failed to label themselves as having been abused
Confirming reports are given more weight than negative ones	Linking trauma memories to current pain is helpful
Childhood trauma memories are mostly valid	
Most of the 63 cited *critical* reports did not examine memory for CSA	Dissociative amnesia is a real and common phenomenon among CSA survivors
Single negative reports are unreliable	Numerous effects of trauma found
Depressed patients	High stability of memories
Memory critics often use a contrived denial system on trauma memory	Examples given and discussed of an extensive disinformation campaign by accused child molesters
Clinician-assisted recall is rare	Childhood sexual abuse memories are mostly valid
Some critics' bias may be substantial.	**Retrospective trauma memory data are usually reliable.**

do so ethically, as these reports have shown, and all of them found dissociative (traumatic) amnesia to occur in a substantial percentage of CSA survivors (Brown et al. 1998). **DA = dissociative amnesia

RECOVERY PRINCIPLES

Addressing dissociation involves becoming more aware of it when it happens to us. A starting point is to learn about a common form of dissociation called *age-regression,* and what it is and how to handle it. I describe age-regression in some detail in my books *A Gift to Myself* (page 181) and *Memory and Abuse* (page 155). Healthy and unhealthy dissociation happens throughout the long process of recovery from any of the various effects of trauma, some of which I have described in this and the prior volume, and in more detail in my above two books. For example, clinical and research psychiatrist Frank Putnam sees the spectrum of dissociation as also involving *clusters* of these trauma effects, which he calls primary (1°), secondary (2°), and tertiary (3°) listed in Table 7.6. When it occurs, attending to each of these effects by healthy expression of our inner-life with safe people will usually increase the chance for an earlier recovery.

Other authors have described principles for healing from DID and other dissociative disorders.[193, 593] As is true for most of the other disorders that are aggravated or caused by trauma, using a

Table 7.6. Effects of Childhood Trauma: Dissociative Symptom Clusters

(expanded from Putnam 1997)

1°	Dissociative process symptoms, disordered memory & amnesia [Acute stress disorder; age regression*]
2°	Anxiety, depression, somatization, ↓ self-esteem (shame), [PTSD*]
3°	Chemical dependence & other substance abuse, self-destructive behaviors (including suicide attempts), promiscuity & other sexualized behaviors, etc.

* My additions. From Putnam FW (1997). *Dissociation in Children & Adolescents: A developmental perspective,* Guilford Press, NY.

stage-oriented approach is most helpful, as I have described in Table 2.3 on page 20. Stage One recovery for DID is to recognize and name it, and then stabilize from its disruptive effects. In Stage Two we do the trauma work directly by the long process of *uncovering, remembering* and *naming* our traumas and then grieving about their hurtful effects. Each time that we work through a memory or a painful issue, we tend to get stronger. Most of the recovery aids in Table 12.1 on page 148 of the prior volume may be useful to accomplish this task. Of these, individual and group therapy may be especially helpful.

Processing Dissociated Memories

People in recovery from dissociative and other "mental disorders" tend to have a broad range of past and ongoing pain, such as intrusive post-traumatic stress symptoms, dissociative symptoms, and painful psycho-physiological reactivity.[137, 486] Reliable recovered memories are typically accompanied by significant emotional distress and the occurrence of psychological and emotional symptoms concurrent with recovery of the memory.[137, 225, 1089, 1092]

Recent research has addressed the natural history of recovered memories, which my colleagues Dan Brown, Alan Scheflin and I have described in some detail.[137] Memory of the trauma usually persists *both* as an overt, verbal or explicit narrative memory *and* a hidden, covert, implicit behavioral and somatic memory. While these clinical findings often evolve in the order shown in Figure 7.1 below, they may also evolve in a different sequence. Working through these phases over time in the process of recovering the narrative memory strengthens recovery by *decreasing dissociation* and leading to a sense of *mastery over* the traumatic experience.[137]

Figure 7.1. The Natural History of the Evolution of Memory Recovery in Childhood Sexual Abuse*

(from Brown, Scheflin & Whitfield 1999)

Clinical Findings**	Example References
1. Transference re-enactments (in &/or out of therapy)***	Burgess et al. 1995; Terr 1994; Laplanche & Pontalis, 1973
↓	
2. Somatic & psychological symptoms	Cameron 1996; van der Kolk & Fisler 1995; Pomerantz 1999
↓	
3. Flashbacks, abreactions & age regressions	above plus: Roe & Schwartz 1996; Kristiansen et al., 1995; Whitfield 1995,1997,1998
↓	
4. Dreams & nightmares	Whitfield 1995,1997, 1998; Kristiansen et al. 1995
↓	
5. Fragmented narrative memory (triggered by reminder events)	Cameron 1996; Kristiansen et al. 1995; van der Kolk & Fisler 1995
↓	
6. Obsessive thoughts of trauma	Terr 1994
↓	
7. Organized narrative memory	van der Kolk & Fisler 1995 (none showed initial return of memory as narrative memory, which tended to occur last)

* Working through these stages as they occurred decreased dissociation and led to a sense of mastery over the trauma.

** Clinical findings are from Davies & Frawley 1994, Whitfield 1995, 1997, 1998, and other cited references, and all may be manifestations of PTSD. Triggering events commonly initiate these kinds of memory (Whitfield, 1995b). These clinical findings tend to progress from being vague to clearer over the extended time of recovery.

*** These clinical findings may occur in different sequences, e.g., #2 may be the initial experience, then skip to #5, and then continue as #6 and #7.

Symptoms Often Get "Worse"
Before They Get Better

Clinical and research psychologists Diana Elliott and John Briere evaluated 113 adults who had been sexually abused as children and compared them with 385 controls (those with no history of CSA). They found that those with the most recent recovered memories of the traumas were the most symptomatic, when compared with those who had a longer abuse memory and those who had always remembered the abuse, and especially when compared to the controls,[306] as shown in Figure 7.2. Other clinicians and I have observed these findings in countless survivors who we have assisted as they healed.[137, 138, 486, 920, 1086] This is important information, since the trauma survivor and the person's family and friends often believe that the survivor is mentally ill and/or making up the trauma memory. They often need to be reassured that neither is true. Rather, their *symptoms* and *concerns* are *part of the natural history of recovery from trauma.*[137, 138, 1086]

In recovery, as we heal in the company of safe people, we can begin to *recognize* when we are dissociating (age regressing). If we are in group or individual therapy, the others can mirror what they see and hear. Other therapy group members can also describe what is coming up for them from their inner lives as we tell our stories and describe how we are feeling. We can also experiment with *deliberately* trying to *dissociate.* Bringing what was formerly unconscious into our conscious awareness can be empowering. As we dissociate—that is, alter our state of consciousness by separating or distancing from our full awareness—we can practice increasing or decreasing the clarity of our experience. We can thereby gain more awareness and control over what once may have felt was out

Figure 7.2. Symptom Scores Among CSA Survivors (broken lines) **Compared to Control Sample** (bottom, solid line)

(from Elliott & Briere 1995, by permission)

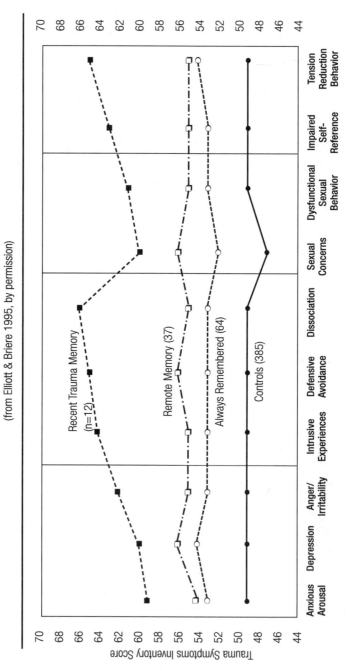

of control for us. Identifying which people or situations may *trigger* the experiences of dissociation is also useful. Then we can begin to set healthy boundaries and limits around them so that they will not continue to hurt us.

When we dissociate, we involuntarily alter our state of consciousness. The person who can move spontaneously from one state of consciousness to another can have several advantages. One is that in recovery they may eventually be able to access their unconscious feelings and other inner life material more easily. And they can go in and out of therapeutic trance more easily. While fear is often still a block for some, they may be able to make more constructive use of experiential techniques in their recovery.

Psychiatrist and past president of the *International Society for the Study of Dissociation* Richard Chefetz said, "An additional way to think of dissociation is as an automatic adaptation to emotion in the extremes of living. Dissociation is a way to 'manage' the effects of overwhelming and intolerable emotional pain. For example, dissociation that detaches these painful feelings from the knowledge of a person's life history results in a feeling of 'numbness.' Inability to feel feelings may also be secondary to profound, chronic, painful states of neglect. Feelings arise out of what cognitive neuroscientists call 'affect,' primitive non-verbalizable bodily states. Our everyday language is filled with these body-referenced feeling states: light-hearted, weighed down heavy with depression, worried sick, flushed with shame, frozen with fear, etc. Dissociation of feeling states of mind is facilitated by losing a sense of what is happening in our bodies. When this reaches a profound level out-of-body experience, feeling unreal, depersonalization, occurs. Derealization, the world looking fake, phony, or as if seeing the world through a fog or veil, also destroys the context of feeling feelings by depriving sight of its vividness, a dream-like derealized state may be the result. In this case too, with everything foggy, we don't know how we feel. Dissociation, as an experience, can be seen primarily as a regulator of emotion, feeling states. In the next chapter, as Dr. Whitfield talks about the addictions, consider that addictions regulate emotional states too. There is a high price, and the solution works temporarily. It leaves people trapped in a repeating cycle of psychic pain and the induced numbness of alcohol, binge-purge cycles, etc."

As Dr. Chefetz indicates, some trauma survivors use alcohol and other drugs to dissociate from their pain, which I address in the next chapters.

8 ALCOHOL AND OTHER DRUG PROBLEMS

*"I drank to lessen my painful feelings. I thought they would
kill me. I knew no other way to stay alive and sane. It took me
a while to see that alcohol was doing the opposite—it was
aggravating my pain and insanity. I had to grieve to let it go."*

Mary (thirty-one-year-old therapy group member)

DEFINITION AND DIAGNOSIS

In my thirty-five year career assisting people with alcohol and
other drug problems, the most useful definition I found for alcoholism and chemical dependence is *recurring trouble* associated with
drinking or using other psychoactive drugs—whether they are legal
or not. The *trouble* may occur in one or more of the person's major
life areas, including: *relationships, education, legal, financial,
medical* or *job-related.* Alcoholism and other chemical dependence
(CD) is a protean disease, and may be the most common "great
masquerader" today. It can mimic many mental and physical illnesses. Thus, a thorough alcohol and drug history should be taken
for most people who present with mental or physical symptoms.

At the first suspicion of an alcohol or drug problem, one or more screening tests can be used, as shown in Figure 8.1. I ask most of my patients to take the *Michigan Alcoholism Screening Test* (MAST), the MAST *Addendum* and the CAGE questionnaire.[61] If they score positively on any one or especially a combination of these screening tests, I usually tell them the diagnosis (alcoholism, chemical dependence or the like), that it is a disease, that it is not their fault for having it, and that there is a way out. The way out is by stopping using alcohol and psychoactive drugs one day at a time, and changing from within. Effective ways to change from within may include employing any of a number of recovery aids, especially self-help groups such as Alcoholics Anonymous and Narcotics Anonymous, an addiction-recovery focused therapy group, individual psychotherapy, bibliotherapy and others.

Ralph (forty-six-year-old psychotherapy group member, full history described below): *I didn't know I had been abused. My resulting shame is what made me sick and drove my alcoholism. I put all my other feelings behind a wall just to avoid feeling shame. When I felt "depressed," I now know I was actually feeling sadness, hurt, fear and panic. I couldn't identify what caused them, which I later learned was my abuse as a child. My shame and self-hate is from the abuse, not from me. I know it will come to visit me again, but now I know what to call it. Shame is an emotional hallucination, a lie. The abuse pain was the problem. I kept running from that pain by using alcohol and drugs—or whatever else I could find.*

Figure 8.1. Alcohol or Drug Problem
Flowchart for Decision Making

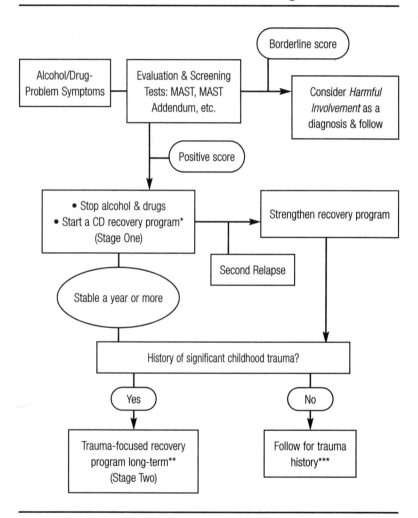

* Avoid using benzodiazepine sedative drugs to treat anxiety, insomnia or depression. Buspirone is an acceptable, non-addicting antianxiety drug.

** Long-term group therapy, individual therapy, self-help group attendance, etc.

*** Because many trauma survivors authentically forget the trauma (dissociative amnesia), or they may not be able to accurately name what happened to them as having been traumatic, keep an open mind that a substantial number of these people may eventually remember a serious trauma history.

Relapse

I call this initial phase of recovery *Stage One,* as I showed previously in the Table on page 20. It may take many months or years of working such a program to bring about a stable recovery. If the person *relapses,* they may consider *strengthening* their recovery program by 1. *adding* one or more aids, 2. attending to these and prior aids *regularly,* and 3. working them more faithfully. If they relapse again, it may be time to look more carefully at their childhood trauma history.

ADDRESSING CHILDHOOD TRAUMA

In my experience in assisting countless people with CD in their recoveries I have not met one who grew up in a healthy family. Rather, they have usually grown up in troubled, dysfunctional, abusive and/or neglectful families. In that environment they became traumatized and wounded, as I describe in chapter 6 and 7 of the prior volume.

Eventually, the person may be able to identify the troubled nature of their upbringing. Some may even elect to begin working a trauma-focused recovery program. I call this part of their recovery *Stage Two* (shown on page 20), which usually takes several years to complete. Its most effective components include first, attendance at a trauma-focused weekly therapy group, and a concomitant self-help group such as ACoA, Al-Anon and/or CoDA. Individual psychotherapy will also be helpful as needed or desired, along with selected bibliotherapy.

Like other illness, the truths about addiction are many and sometimes complex. I have assisted people in their recoveries from alcohol and other drug problems since 1965. For about the first ten years of that time, my approach was to treat them for the toxic physical effects of these drugs and suggest that they stop drinking and using drugs. While doing so was appropriate, that was all I knew to do at that time. In my training, no one had taught me any further truth about these addictions. By 1973, I had learned that it would help to explain to my patients exactly *how to* stop drinking and begin recovery. Still later, I learned how common it was for addicted people to have experienced trauma growing up. Finally, over the last fifteen years I read the numerous research reports that have documented the link between addictions and childhood trauma. Their findings are remarkable, as I describe below.

> **Ralph:** *I was repeatedly abused as a child. I had been raped and neglected for days at a time. Under the hurt is my anger I need to express. If I believed that I was "sick or bad," then they (my parents and abusive brother) were "good." If they were good, then I could survive. The memory fades, but the feeling doesn't, so I have remained wary of my feelings. I would give anything not to remember. My family and I tried to pretend the abuse away, and my mother especially denied the extent of my brother's illness. I ended up treating my real self like my abusive parents and brother did. I want to control him and make him obey my orders.*

EXAMINING THE EVIDENCE

Retrospective Studies

The evidence for the link between alcohol and other drug problems and having a history of repeated childhood trauma is strong.

To date I am aware of a total of 153 databased research studies that document this firm association. Of these 153 published reports (summarized in the next chapter on page 91), 90 are based on retrospective studies conducted on *clinical* and *community* samples, wherein identified general and high-risk populations were carefully surveyed and evaluated (summarized in the Appendix as Table A8.1 on page 308). Most of these large samples of people with a history of childhood trauma were compared with a matched control group that did not report such a history. The few with no control groups used data from prior reports on the general population.

Any one of these studies alone would not establish a definite link between the two variables of addiction and childhood trauma (Table A8.1). What makes these results so strong is the combination of six factors:

1. The fact that there were 90 *independent* groups of observers studying many *different populations* (usually from a hospital, clinic, or a community)—that were from *different* geographical *locations*.
2. The *large number* of people evaluated, which total 237,886 subjects.
3. The fact that *control groups* were used for comparison of results in most of these studies.
4. The fact that these *researchers* were *widely published* and *well respected* among their peers.
5. The fact that essentially all were published in *peer-reviewed* journals or reports.
6. That with only one exception,[950] they *arrived at the same results*. This is strong, if not overwhelming evidence.

These results supported the nearly ninety independent research teams to conclude that there was a *definite* link, association and relationship between the presence of an addiction and having a history of childhood trauma. The most common potential source of error among these studies was that they were based on retrospective reports of the individuals sampled. While the validity of *retrospective study results* can be called into question, many independent researchers have examined the validity of trauma memory in retrospective studies in different settings using different methods and have found that their results are mostly reliable, as shown in Table 7.5 on page 70.

So if there was a trauma-addiction link, what *kind* of link? Was it *coincidental?* Was it perhaps a *common* association or relationship? Was it *usual?* Could it be *causal?* To explore these possibilities we need more information. We also need other kinds of study designs. This is because no matter how carefully planned and executed they may be, most individual research studies have one or more weak points—from a small number of people studied, to an inadequate or even absent control group, to a failure to ask one or more key questions. These and other deficiencies are often addressed and overcome when subsequent researchers learn from the mistakes of their peers' earlier work, by using improved study designs, and by replication by other researchers.

Prospective Studies

Replication supports causality. The more replication of an association by different and independent observers, the stronger the likelihood for an association's being causal. When prospective and index case studies are so replicated, in addition to the clinical and community sample studies, the link becomes even stronger.

One of the most reliable and respected research designs is the *prospective* study.[139, 748] Here, traumatized people and their non-traumatized controls are evaluated and followed over time. But prospective research is more difficult to do. It is more expensive, usually requires more researchers on a study team, and takes a lot of patience and persistence. In the case of including childhood trauma as a key variable, there is also the obvious ethical admonition that it is unacceptable to abuse or neglect anyone and then study them. So, as we might expect, there are substantially fewer prospective reports that address the possible addiction-trauma link. Currently, I am aware of 21 of these, which evaluated 15,873 people, as shown in Table A8.2 on page 316 in the Appendix. All of them show a strong association between addiction and trauma.

Clinical and research psychologist Dan Brown has carefully evaluated three of these prospective studies and says that their results are so strong that he believes that they indicate that childhood trauma appears to be *causal* of the substance abuse and chemical dependence in these large populations (Table 8.2). He says that as well, childhood trauma appears to be *causal* of several other disorders or problems, including, for childhood **sexual** abuse: *PTSD, anxiety disorders, dissociative disorders, somatization disorders, sexual problems, difficulty handling feelings, low self-esteem,* and the eventual finding of *multiple co-morbidity*.[139] For **physical** abuse, *substance abuse* and *chemical dependence* are *possibly* causally related to that childhood trauma. (I refer to this table in other chapters). Others have shown that when combined, both of these kinds of trauma tend to cause these problems even more often.

Table 8.3. Effects of Childhood Trauma as Shown by
Selected Prospective Studies* (compiled from Brown 2002)

Effects Replicated and Appear Causal

Sexual Abuse	Physical Abuse	Both
Substance abuse	Aggression & violence	Depression
Chemical dependence	Antisocial behavior	Suicidality
PTSD		
Anxiety Disorders		
Dissociative Disorders		
Somatization Disorders		
Sexual problems *(hypersexual behaviors, promiscuity, older sexual partners)*		
Disordered affect regulation		
Self-sense defects		

Multiple co-morbidity later

Effects Significant, Replicated in Retrospective Studies and Possibly Causal

Sexual Abuse	Physical Abuse	Both
Self-harming	Substance abuse	Social withdrawal
ADHD (Putnam 1998,	Chemical abuse	Social problems
Silverman et al. 1996)		Severe obesity**

*From Burgess et al. 1996, Silverman et al. 1996, Widom et al. 1996-99, Putnam 1998, Kendler et al. 2000, Brown 2000 **From replicated retrospective studies only (see chapters 10 and 11).

Index Cases

There are two other study designs that show a trauma-addiction link. The first involves "index cases," or identifying people with substance abuse or chemical dependence and then evaluating them for having a history of childhood trauma and other possible associations. Conducted over a twenty-six-year time span by independent authors on 42 different populations (and comprising a total of 7,836 people), most found similar results. For example, the investigators in three of these independent studies[84, 102, 1110] found similar if not almost identical results: about half of the people in the study sample reported having a history of childhood *sexual* abuse (Table A8.3). This result is remarkable for two reasons. The finding of half, or 50 percent of people with SA/CD with a history of child sexual abuse in these three reports is from 1.5 to 2 times larger than the current estimations of one in three or four girls in the general population as having been sexually abused as children. And since about one-third of CSA survivors traumatically *forget* their abuse and another one-third *partially* forget it (the remaining third *always* remembered it[137, 138, 1086, 1089, 1092]), a substantial percentage of those who reported having no such memories may have completely forgotten their abuse. The other studies reported a trauma history of up to 90 percent having experienced *severe* childhood trauma, which makes the evidence here even stronger.

I continue this discussion in the next chapter.

9 ALCOHOL AND OTHER DRUG PROBLEMS
— CONTINUED

Ralph: *I was afraid, especially of my abusing eighteen-year-old brother coming in to my bed since I was five. I guess that's not normal. After that I lose the memory. My parents expected me to behave as though the abuse wasn't happening, that he wasn't molesting me. Why me? Because I'm bad. I caused it. I hid under the couch or locked the door when I was in the bathroom.*

Meta-Analysis: The final study design is called *meta-analysis*. More than a literature review, here the data from several previously reported studies are *reanalyzed together* using special statistical methods. The analyst can expand the results of several similar yet independent studies into a more unified statistical result, which can provide a potentially more accurate approximation of the originally found relationship.

In 1996, Neumann and colleagues conducted a meta-analysis on thirty-eight studies on the effects of child sexual abuse on women that were published from 1974 through 1992. They found similar results, as shown in Table A9.1 in the Appendix. In 1998, Simpson and Miller also conducted a meta-analysis and found a twofold increase of alcohol and other drug problems among the survivors of childhood trauma. I also list the results of nine literature reviews in Table A 9.1 in the Appendix, which show similar results.

Summary of Studies

Taken as a whole, these reports provide strong, if not overwhelming, evidence to document the link between trauma and effect (i.e., alcohol and other drug abuse and dependence [SA/CD]) that countless clinicians have observed over time with their patients and clients. These include 90 studies on large clinical and community samples, 42 studies on people with SA/CD (index cases), and 21 prospective studies, for a total of 153 peer-reviewed, published reports on 261,595 study subjects. In addition I found two meta-analyses of over eighty studies and nine literature reviews that supported these 153 reports, as summarized in Table 9.2.

In most of these studies, the authors controlled for other variables, and still arrived at the results shown in these tables. The consistent finding showing this link across these 153 separate reports, representing five diverse research designs (including meta-analysis), using different methods of measurement, by more than 300 authors in nearly all independent studies on such a large number of people from several countries greatly increases the likelihood that this demonstrated relationship between childhood trauma and substance abuse/chemical dependence is a real phenomenon, as opposed to being artifacts of methodology (e.g., retrospective, prospective or index case analysis), sample variation, or measurement error that may have occurred in single studies.

This is impressive evidence. If clinicians and scientists in medicine, psychiatry, psychology, sociology or anthropology had found

Table 9.2. Substance Abuse/Chemical Dependence and Childhood Trauma: 90 Clinical & Community Studies, 21 Prospective Studies, 42 Index Studies and 11 Meta-Analyses/Reviews

Year/ Authors	Study	SA/Chemical Dependence	Other Effects	Comments/ Other
Clinical/ Community 90 studies 1942–2003	237,886 CT v. Controls	2–38x	4–12x depression ↑ –15x anxiety	Multiple Co-morbidity Common Table on page 308
Prospective 21 studies 1978–2003	15,873 CT v. Controls	1.2–10x, incl. other drugs & nicotine	1.1–4x depression ↑ anxiety, PTSD, ADHD, Conduct dis, ED, APD	Multiple Co-morbidity Common ↓ self-esteem Table on page 316
Index Case 42 studies 1975–2003	7,836 people with CD & their controls	30%–90% CT	Multiple Co-morbidities	All support trauma link Table on page 320
Analyses & Reviews 1986–2003	2 Meta-analyses 9 Literature reviews	↑ Link	↑ co-morbidity ↓ self-esteem	All support trauma link Table on page 324
Summary 153 Studies 1942–2002	261,595 CT people and controls	2–38x Clin/Com; 1.2–10x Prospec; 30–84% CT in Index Cases	↑ Co-Morbidity 1.1–12x depression; ↑ –15x anxiety; etc.	Multiple Co-morbidity common All support trauma link

* ↑ = Increased, CT = childhood trauma; SA/CD = Substance abuse/chemical dependence; CSA = child sexual abuse; x = times; ED = eating disorder, APD = antisocial personality disorder.

this much and this degree of a "dose-response" (i.e., trauma effect) relationship on any two factors (called "variables" in the research trade) that they were investigating, many of them would be talking cause and effect. Whether or not there may also be a genetic component in operation here, the data documents the conversion of traumatic emotional and mental experiences into serious disease later in life. In epidemiology—having been reproduced by an estimated 140 or more independent teams of investigators on many thousands of people (here 261,595)—these results are almost unique in their magnitude.

The data show that childhood trauma is common, destructive, and has an effect that lasts for a lifetime. This trauma may be the most important determinant of the health and well-being of our nation and our world.[327] As an example, the havoc that untreated alcohol and other drug problems alone brings to us all in the U.S. exceeds $200 billion annually in work, family and public losses, clinical services and crime. Extrapolating to other countries, this loss is likely over $1 trillion worldwide. The continued trauma to the spouses and children of harmfully involved and addicted parents and other close people can perpetuate the vicious cycle. Is there a way out?

Trauma—the Sleeping Giant

The treatment implications of these results shown throughout this and the prior book are far-reaching and their prevention implications are daunting. As is true for the other common mental illnesses and some physical ones, a problem has been that this information has been buried in clinical and scientific journals and books, thinly sandwiched in between an overwhelming array of biological, psychological and sociological articles that tend to ignore the sleeping giant of trauma. Most clinicians are not trained to work with it. Physicians would rather deal with traditional organic disease. Many psychiatrists would rather refer to brain neurotransmitters and prescribe psychoactive drugs. Some psychologists, social workers and counselors pay little attention to childhood trauma. And few researchers include it in their investigations.

Over time, I have assisted numerous addicted patients who stabilized (Stage One recovery), and then patiently and painfully worked through issues related to the effects of their childhood trauma (Stage Two). When they did so, their quality of life improved on a number of levels long-term—including not drinking or using drugs. Through their long recovery process, they and I have witnessed this strong link between trauma and its effect yet again from a therapeutic and healing perspective. An example follows.

History 9.1

Ralph was a forty-six-year-old recovering alcoholic and chemical-dependent man who was referred for a recent relapse, with suicidal ideation. He had been actively chemical dependent from age eighteen to twenty-eight, then abstinent and in recovery in AA (an important part of Stage One recovery) for fifteen years. When he moved from a distant state, he found it difficult to connect with people in AA here. Within three months he relapsed on alcohol, and a year later, after he was again six months' sober, his spouse died suddenly in front of him. His resulting painful feelings led him to a psychiatrist who prescribed a benzodiazepine (clonazepam/Klonopin) and an antidepressant drug (bupropion/Wellbutrin). A few months later his dog died, and shortly afterwards his chronically ill mother, whom he had taken care of in his home for over a year, died. He had started individual therapy with another therapist and began to realize that he had never grieved these losses, although he continued to take the above drugs and had taken some opiates addictively as well. He also drank six cups of coffee and smoked two to three packs of cigarettes daily.

He was referred to me for further evaluation. My initial impression of his condition was: 1) active addiction to benzodiazepines, caffeine and nicotine, and 2) suicidal ideation. I suggested that he stop the benzodiazepines (gradually, over time), and stop the caffeine and nicotine; take melatonin for sleep; start buspirone (BuSpar) for his excess fear/anxiety; attend AA meetings regularly and continue to see his therapist; continue the suicide contract with his individual therapist; and continue to take Wellbutrin. I also eventually suggested that he consider joining our trauma-focused therapy group, which he did. Since that initial visit he has not been suicidal again.

During subsequent sessions with me, he described having a history of serious childhood trauma in the form of severe physical (by older brother), sexual (mother and brother), and mental/emotional abuse and neglect by both parents and brother. He fulfilled the *DSM-IV* diagnostic criteria for PTSD, and after several individual sessions joined our weekly therapy group which focuses on Stage Two recovery issues.

In group therapy, he worked on appropriate issues over the next three years, while remaining sober. Although he did not stop smoking, he showed much progress in his healing. He has talked recently several times about the pain he had experienced. For example, he said, "My pain is not the problem. The cause of it is. To survive, I blinded myself to my and others' feelings and behavior. To become aware of others' feelings about me is scary because it may confirm how bad I am and how I feel about myself. I'm mostly afraid, but underneath that is shame. Underneath that is anger. Smoking cigarettes has kept it all down for me." Currently, after working hard in individual and group therapy over time, he is beginning to feel more positive, hopeful and grateful for his progress.

His life has taken on a quality that he never knew could happen for him. He believes that his addictions were a way to cover up the pain he carried from his abusive childhood. He continues to take Wellbutrin and smoke cigarettes.

Ralph's history shows several important recovery principles in action. First, the principle of *parsimony,* which says that observers should assume no more causes than are necessary to explain what they see. This idea is also called *Occam's razor:* that if two or more theories explain the same observations, the simplest theory is most likely to be true. In Ralph's case, he was alcohol- and chemical-dependent, depressed, had PTSD and anxiety, low self-esteem and was continuing to relapse on alcohol and other drugs. Some biologic psychiatrists believe that there is a defective gene and/or neurochemical process for every psychiatric illness, although after nearly a century of intensive searching, none has been found (as I discuss in the Epilogue and the prior volume). While a genetic propensity is a possible causal factor for some cases of chemical dependence and depression, it cannot also easily explain the PTSD, anxiety and low self-esteem here—nor the multiple co-morbidity found in countless other trauma survivors. (And even if it did, we can't change our genes.) One possible causal factor that can explain most, if not all of his misery, is severe, repeated childhood trauma. This likelihood was bolstered by his gradual yet remarkable improvement of all these disorders associated with his working a trauma-focused recovery program over time.

A second principle is that he followed a phase or *stage*-oriented sequence of recovery, first using AA and its Twelve-Step work (Stage One) and then, when appropriate, addressing his childhood trauma issues directly (Stage Two). Finally, during this time he allowed himself to *accurately name* his trauma (child abuse, neglect, sexual abuse, physical abuse, emotional abuse and the like) and then, alone and in the company of safe people over time, to *grieve* the traumatic pain that he had not been able to grieve.

My group therapy co-leader and I agree that over the three-plus years we have assisted Ralph in his healing process that we have been moved by his hard work and dedication that he has given to his recovery. At first he was sad and grieving, with a lot of shame. As he shared his shame, over time it started to lift. He began to see things differently and eventually was able to stop taking the blame for the severe abuse and neglect that was still prominent in his memory. His grieving began to reveal a new awareness within him. Soon he was not only helping others in the group, but he said that his view of life was becoming clearer and lighter.

Ralph's story also illustrates a focus of this book: finding more choices than conventional approaches to help us heal. After working a Stage One recovery program, he discovered that his bothersome relapses led him to consider beginning a Stage Two recovery program, which has now stabilized and solidified his previously rocky recovery.

*   *   *

Clinicians have long known that trauma commonly drives the process of relapse in substance abuse and chemical dependence. After stabilization (Stage One), as the relapsing person and their clinician address the trauma material both in and outside of therapy, they will be more likely to address and prevent the relapse process itself. By doing so, they will prevent the painful and costly psychological and medical problems—from disabling depression to costly accidents to life-threatening cirrhosis of the liver—that active drinking and drug using inevitably bring about.

The magnitude of the link between trauma and the disorder and the relapse provides strong support and justification for the affected individuals, their clinicians, health insurance companies and policy makers to address the detrimental driving force of trauma head on. With this information, there should be few, if any, reasons why not to focus on trauma work as an effective method of treatment and prevention of this and other disorders.

I describe the components of a full trauma-focused recovery program in chapter 12 on page 147 of *The Truth About Depression*, and in 4 other books.[1089, 1094, 1095, 1096] Others do also.[130, 193, 223, 243, 398, 486, 683, 1107] For chemical dependence, while any one or a combination of these methods may be helpful, one of the most effective is long-term group therapy whose goal is to address the trauma and its effects. Healing from these effects uses a combination of work that addresses the person's mental (cognitive), emotional (affective), physical (somatic) and spiritual (felt connection and meaning) life. All of these include a firm experiential base, which appropriate group therapy provides—often in a stronger and more effective way than, for example, treating the person with antidepressants or other drugs alone.

10   EATING DISORDERS

Eating disorders are the second-most common kind of addiction, behind first-place nicotine and slightly more frequent than third-place alcohol and drug addiction. Of the four major kinds of eating disorders, two are most common: *compulsive overeating* and *binge-eating disorder,* as shown in Table 10.1. The other two are uncommon: *bulimia nervosa* and *anorexia nervosa,* and all four have a high rate of psychological and medical consequences and co-morbidity. Eating disorders share many of the characteristics of alcoholism and other chemical dependence and thus have been described as being addictions in their own right.[395] Some of these characteristics include: *craving, obsession* or strong *compulsion* around food, *loss of control,* direct *detrimental effects* to the mind and body, *use* of a substance *to relieve painful feelings, denial* that there is a problem, *secretiveness* about using, a *progressive* nature (i.e., often tends to get worse), *family* involvement, a feeling of *guilt* or *shame* about excessive use, *continued use despite adverse consequences,* and an often *fatal* outcome. Given our recently accumulated knowledge, described below, we can now add yet another characteristic that chemical dependence and eating disorders share: a *strong relationship to* having a history of *childhood trauma.*

COMPULSIVE OVEREATING

Compulsive overeating is the most common of the eating disorders, found in about 9 percent of the population. The person is overweight, and while other causes or associations should be considered, such as hypothyroidism, they are seldom found to be the cause. It has a high co-morbidity, including depression, diabetes, arthritis and heart disease. The following are two examples of some of the effects, complexities and associations of compulsive overeating.

History 10.1

Dave was a sixty-three-year-old overeater who grew up with an anorexic, rageful and drug-addicted mother and a neglectful and normal-weight father. He had no memory of his mother's raging and beating him, although his fifty-eight-year-old sister did. He was 70 pounds overweight and had periods of extreme anger for most of his adult life until he began taking antidepressants and the antianxiety drug buspirone. He had adult-onset diabetes and high blood pressure. His wife and two of his three daughters were also seriously overweight, and they had tried Weight Watchers with brief success. After having had an angioplasty at age sixty-one, he was recently treated for having sleep apnea and at age sixty-three had triple coronary artery bypass surgery. His drug of choice has always been food.

His sister Jill, in recovery from a less severe form of compulsive overeating and PTSD for twenty years, had shared her memories of their traumatic childhood (physical and psychological abuse and neglect),

Table 10.1. Eating Disorders:
Incidence, Co-Morbidity and Other Characteristics*

Type	Incidence USA (%)**	Co-morbidity/ complications	Comments
Compulsive Overeating	9	Depression, diabetes, arthritis, heart disease, sleep apnea	Overweight. Rule out hypothyroidism (uncommon in comparison)
Binge-Eating Disorder	2–5 (2/3 ♀)	Depression, anxiety disorder, impulsivity, medical problems (see above)	Overweight. Half have a close relative with SA/CD***
Bulimia Nervosa	1 mostly ♀	Depression, SA/CD (half), BPD (1/4–1/2), impulsivity, promiscuity	Normal weight; 37% have a close relative with SA/CD
Anorexia Nervosa	0.5 mostly ♀	Depression, suicide, 12x age-matched death rate	Underweight, often to the extreme

*Compiled from Felitti 1993; Gold et al. 1997; Spearing 2001.
**For bulimia and anorexia, lifetime occurrence (prevalence) may be up to 4–5 times the incidence.
***SA/CD = substance abuse/chemical dependence; ♀ = females; BPD = borderline personality disorder.

which he cannot remember, but says he believes her (more on Jill in Case History 10.6 below). His uncle and aunt observed the abuse and neglect and validated her memories. His recent surgery has begun to give him a new understanding of why he uses food to hold down his painful feelings that used to surface as anger, and at times rage.

Dave's story shows how the unrecognized and unprocessed pain of childhood trauma can underlie major mental and physical health threats. An unwary health professional or researcher may never learn his true family history, seeing only him, his wife and two overweight daughters, and assuming that their common obesity "ran in the family"—and therefore was simply genetic. However, multigenerational photographs of his family extending over three generations show no other evidence of obesity, and his one daughter who moved out of the house when she was eighteen is not obese.

Recognizing the potential link between eating disorders and childhood trauma can be difficult and painful. This is because it may be easier for both health-care professionals, researchers and patients in the short run to blame genetics—as an intellectual form of denial. Routinely exploring and addressing the potential links between childhood trauma and obesity is difficult, painful, and protected by social inhibition and taboo.

History 10.2

Overweight since she was six, Cindy was a twenty-four-year-old single mother of a five-year-old girl. She was five feet, four inches tall and weighed 411 pounds. She described herself as a "compulsive overeater as a child, ate secretly and had an unhappy childhood." She was abused physically, sexually and psychologically since she was at least three or four years old and her parents threw her out of the house in her junior year of high school, which she never finished. She found a job, moved in with a boyfriend, and, already overweight, gradually became severely obese. She had a child, and soon her violent alcoholic boyfriend rejected her. Supported by public assistance, she tried to continue her job, but was unable, because of her extreme obesity. She found a surgeon who believed that her obesity was inherited and performed stomach bypass surgery on her. He knew of her childhood trauma, but discounted it. She then moved in with her mother who supported her. Her mother said, "Maybe she didn't get all the attention she wanted, so she used food." After the surgery, she lost weight, felt better and became more attractive, but then began drinking heavily and neglected her child.

Her mother again abandoned her. None of her subsequent professional care attended to her childhood trauma issues or helped her to look at them. She eventually allowed her alcoholic husband back for a short time, and then made him leave when he again began to abuse her. She reports much shame for doing this and for her past. She said, "I used my being overweight to protect me from men—who weren't interested in me when I was fat. I felt lonely, empty and afraid, and I overate to push away those painful feelings. I didn't know I was in a vicious cycle of overeating, pain and more over-eating. Diets didn't work for me. I had to find out what caused my pain." Cindy represents the far end on the spectrum of compulsive overeating.

BINGE-EATING DISORDER

Binge-eating disorder is the second most common, affecting up to 5 percent of the population. The person is also overweight, and half of those afflicted have a close relative with substance abuse or chemical dependence. Co-morbidity commonly includes depression, anxiety disorder and impulsivity. Proposed diagnostic criteria include the following characteristics:

- Recurrent episodes of binge eating, i.e., eating an excessive amount of food within a short period of time and a sense of loss of control over eating during the episode.
- The binge-eating episodes are associated with at least three of the following: eating much *more rapidly* than normal; eating

until feeling *uncomfortably full;* eating *large amounts* of food *when not* feeling physically *hungry;* eating *alone because* of being *embarrassed* by how much one is eating; feeling *disgusted with oneself, depressed* or very *guilty* after overeating.
- Marked distress about the binge-eating behavior.
- The binge eating occurs, on average, at least two days a week for six months.
- The binge eating is not associated with the regular use of inappropriate compensatory behaviors (e.g., purging, fasting, excessive exercise) *and* is not a part of bulimia or anorexia nervosa.[395]

While these criteria are useful, their downside can occur if a binge overeater (or their health professional) uses them to "compare themselves out," saying "I don't have that criterion, so I'm eating okay." As with bulimia, shame associated with this illness can lead to binging again, creating a cycle of binge eating. As with other eating disorders and addictions, the benefits of binge eating—temporary relief of the emotional pain—are seldom discussed.

History 10.3

Pam was a forty-year-old woman who came for assistance with healing from several painful effects of her childhood trauma. She had been sexually abused since at least age five by her father and physically and emotionally abused by both parents. She had binge-eating disorder, PTSD, depression, and had abused alcohol, cocaine and tobacco in the past. She had problems with binge overeating since age nine and currently was unable to keep much food in her house for fear that she would overeat, especially late at night when she felt intense fear and had difficulty sleeping. Six years ago she had tried attending about twenty Overeaters Anonymous meetings, but found these and AA meetings to be "boring," since she was used to intense drama related to her childhood abuse which carried over into her tumultuous romantic relationships as an adult.

In trying to sort out what was causing each of her problems, we could propose and consider any one of a number of possible etiological factors. However, all of her symptoms and problems could as well, if not more likely, be caused by a single etiology: her severe childhood trauma. She had consulted several psychiatrists, two social workers and a psychologist in the past with little or no attention to her childhood trauma issues. As it turned out, after four years of trauma-focused group and individual therapy and regular attendance at Overeaters Anonymous with a sponsor, and working its program of recovery, she was able to lessen her symptoms. For the past year, she has been in her first stable relationship with a man.

BULIMIA NERVOSA

Bulimia nervosa is characterized by episodes of *binge eating* with compensatory *behaviors to avoid gaining* weight. Diagnostic criteria include:

- Recurrent episodes of *binge eating,* characterized by eating an excessive amount of food within a discrete period of time *and* by a sense of loss of control over eating during the episode.
- Recurrent inappropriate compensatory behavior in order to prevent weight gain, such as self-induced *vomiting* or misuse of *laxatives, diuretics, enemas* or other ways (purging), fasting or excessive exercise.

- The binge eating and inappropriate compensatory behaviors both occur, on average, at least twice a week for three months.
- Self-evaluation is unduly influenced by body shape and weight. [16, 395]

The binging and purging is usually done alone and in secret, and once they purge, the person is usually relieved, although there is soon significant associated guilt and shame. Nutrition is chronically compromised in both bulimia and anorexia nervosa, which produces difficulty focusing, irritability, apathy, irrational thinking and insomnia. Body weight is usually normal and the onset of bulimia nervosa begins most often between twelve and thirty-five years old, with a mean age of eighteen. A third were previously anorexic. Even with treatment, a third will relapse by two years. [395]

History 10.4

Susan was a forty-four-year-old woman who since age nineteen had bulimia nervosa and became alcoholic over the next few years. In her early thirties, she saw a psychiatrist who prescribed several antidepressant drugs with no success. For the past seven years, she has used Overeaters Anonymous and Alcoholics Anonymous to help stabilize her addictions and work on her recovery. Three years ago, she began to become aware that she was physically and emotionally abused as a child, and she started individual therapy, where she learned that she also had PTSD, and began to work on her trauma-related issues. While she had earned a Ph.D. degree with honors and had a successful job and career, she had divorced twice and felt empty, with low self-esteem. She eventually joined a therapy group to work deeper on the painful effects of her childhood trauma. After three years in group and individual therapy, she said, "I wet my bed until I was eight years old. I had always felt sad and scared. I didn't even know what PTSD was. I had never connected my alcohol and eating problems with my painful childhood. Since doing that, my sadness and fear have decreased. I know I still have more work to do here."

Susan's story is optimistic. Although she had a painful childhood that extended into her adult life, at about mid-life she was able to begin a Stage One recovery program and after four years realized that she had experienced serious trauma as a child, which she began addressing in a Stage Two recovery program (Table 3.2 on page 20). Her recovery also demonstrates the slow and often prolonged nature of the healing process, which requires patience and persistence, which for Susan paid off.

ANOREXIA NERVOSA

Anorexia nervosa has been described since the seventeenth century and occurs worldwide. Because afflicted people seldom lose their appetite, the term "anorexia" is a misnomer. People with anorexia nervosa are usually obsessed with food. They may hoard food and may exercise daily for prolonged periods, become socially isolated and depressed. They deny their disorder, while their self-esteem becomes tied to their ability to achieve and maintain an emaciated state.[395] Diagnostic criteria include:

- Resistance to maintaining body weight at or above a minimally normal weight for age and height.
- Intense fear of gaining weight or becoming fat, even though underweight.
- Disturbance in the way in which one's body weight or shape is experienced, undue influence of body weight or shape on

self-evaluation, or denial of the seriousness of the current low body weight compared to the perceived benefits.

• Infrequent or absent menstrual periods (in females who have reached puberty).[395]

About half have the *restrictive* subtype—those who restrict their calories and use exercise to lose weight, and tend to have a decreased interest in sex. The other half have some *features of bulimia,* with binge-eating and purging, and tend to be compulsive, promiscuous, self-harming, suicidal, and misuse alcohol and other drugs. The mean age of onset is seventeen years old, and onset is said to be unusual over age forty. About 1 percent die each year from physical deterioration or suicide. About 40 percent eventually recover, and another 20 percent may become psychotic, bipolar, depressed, personality disordered, and/or abuse alcohol or drugs.

History 10.5

Dave's (from compulsive overeating History 10.1) mother, Francine, was age seventy-four at her death, and as an adult had fulfilled all of the above diagnostic criteria for anorexia nervosa. She used diuretics, enemas and laxatives inappropriately to try to further control her weight. She also had somatization disorder and was addicted to opiates and benzodiazepine sedatives for most of her adult life. While no medical workups and evaluations ever showed any evidence of organic disease, she nonetheless had twenty-six elective and several urgent surgeries by age forty-four, when both of her adult children left home. She went from doctor to doctor and pharmacy to pharmacy to maintain her drug habit. Although she had two psychiatric hospitalizations and had seen numerous physicians and nurses in her lifetime, no one addressed her drug addiction. Even with her strong history of the above high-risk disorders, no one explored a possible history of childhood trauma with her. As a child, she was emotionally abused and neglected and witnessed repeated family violence. She had a mixed narcissistic and histrionic personality disorder. She physically and emotionally abused both her children (Dave in History 10.1 and Jill in 11.1), while her husband's response was to leave them all during the abuse and return later.

Francine's story shows how the pain of childhood trauma may be associated with, if not causally related to, mental and physical health problems in adult life. Health professionals and researchers may also misinterpret such symptoms by assuming that the problems were solely physical, or because they "ran in the family" that they were genetically transmitted. Her older sister died young of cancer, and her younger sister followed a pattern of somatization disorder and prescription drug dependence, and recently was diagnosed with PTSD. Francine's numerous diagnoses and problems reflected only the surface effects of a deeper and tragic life of childhood trauma that, unrecognized and unaddressed, was then redirected onto her innocent children. No health professional or family member intervened to help her heal and to protect her children. Her health professionals spent countless amounts of time, energy and money to try to help her, and yet they missed the cause of her several problems. With our current knowledge and experience, we should now be able to prevent this kind of vicious cycle that runs in families.

11   EATING DISORDERS
—— CONTINUED

CAUSAL FACTORS AMONG EATING DISORDERS

Eating is controlled by many factors: appetite; food availability; family, peer and cultural practices; beliefs; emotions and attempts at voluntary control. *Overeating* is usually encouraged and aggravated by a distortion in the healthy balance of these factors. Dieting to a body weight leaner than needed for health is highly promoted by current fashion trends, sales campaigns for special foods, and by some occupations, such as being a model, ballet dancer, gymnast or jockey.

Eating disorders are not usually caused by a failure of willpower or behavior. They are real, treatable medical illnesses in which certain covertly adaptive patterns of eating take on a life of their own and produce overtly adaptive manifestations. The most commonly proposed theories about their cause include genetic transmission, abnormal brain chemistry and environmental stress. Certainly, brain chemistry is involved of necessity, but more likely as an intermediary mechanism rather than a cause. Reseacher Glenn Waller and his colleagues said, "Although it is now widely accepted within the research and clinical literatures that childhood sexual abuse plays some causal role in the bulimic disorders, the nature of that relationship remains to be elucidated".[1066] Some theorists minimize or ignore a history of childhood trauma as a possible causal factor.[796] In spite of that omission, there is strong evidence in the research literature for a link between eating disorders and childhood trauma. These include a large number of retrospective and prospective studies, and index cases.

Retrospective Studies

I found 58 databased, peer-reviewed studies that looked for eating disorders published from 1989 to 2003 on a total of 201,092 research subjects. All show a statistically significant association or relationship between childhood trauma and eating disorders, as shown in Table A11.1 on page 326. Eighteen of these 58 reports examined college students and other community members, and the remaining 40 studied clinical populations. All were conducted by independent research teams using varied methods and survey instruments, and yet they arrived at the same conclusion: that when compared with the control, non-traumatized subjects, there was a statistically *significant increase* in eating disorders or ED symptoms among those having a history of childhood trauma.

Thirty-seven (64 percent) of these 58 studies looked for the presence of co-morbidity and found a significant increase among the trauma survivors. This co-morbidity included depression, SA/CD, anxiety, problems with sexual functioning, early pregnancy, gastrointestinal problems, headaches, increased health care utilization (in the form of increased doctor office visits and hospitalizations), victimization as adults and self-harming behaviors. Although most of these 58 studies did not look for these specific EDs, 16 of them reported an increase in bulimia and anorexia nervosa among those with childhood trauma. Unfortunately, the focus of research that is necessary to obtain this information (i.e., that addresses the *kind* of ED and whether there was childhood or later trauma) is uncommon to rare among most of the large numbers of other published reports on eating disorders. Even so, the results of these 58 studies on a large number of poeple (n = 201,092) are impressive.

Prospective Studies

I found eleven prospective studies. As shown in Table A 11.2 on page 332 in the Appendix, these 4,734 people were followed for up to 18 years, and all showed a significant increase in eating disorders or serious ED symptoms among those with a history of repeated childhood trauma when they were compared with people with no such history. As an example, one of these (Calam et al. 1998) reported a significant increase in eating problems among 144 sexually abused children. These children were evaluated initially and one, nine, and twenty-four months later. The research team found an increase of 15 other problems over the two-year follow-up, as shown in Table 18.4 on page 183. If we were to propose that a conservative figure of 4 percent of these children in the UK, where they lived, have eating problems, then these results are remarkable in that their eating difficulties would be increased by four times the estimated normal.

Index Cases

I found 43 reports where 20,518 people who were first identified as having an ED, and their controls, were evaluated for having a history of childhood trauma (Table A11.3 on page 334 in the Appendix). From 11 to 100 percent of the people with an eating disorder had a CT history. Furthermore, these 11 to 100 percent were also found to be from 1.8 to 3.6 times more likely to have CT history than the controls. Nineteen of these studies showed a high degree of multiple co-morbidity. Only two found no link between CT and eating disorders, although one of these had methodological problems among the controls, many of whom had false-positive CT histories from a cultural artifact.[744] All of the remaining forty-one showed a significant link. For example, in the study by Rorty and colleagues on a sample of eighty bulimic women, a history of childhood trauma was significantly increased when compared with forty non-bulimic women.[852–854] They also found that the bulimic women more often reported a history of physical and emotional abuse and multiple abuses than child sexual abuse alone. In another study of 190 severely obese patients who had successfully each lost over 100 pounds, Felitti and Williams found them to have a common history of childhood trauma, although no control group was used for comparison. They found that *failure to keep weight off* was highly correlated with having a history of childhood sexual trauma. They concluded that it was *crucial* to take *a history of childhood trauma* in all *severely overweight patients*. They also found that compulsive overeating among these patients was an attempt to manage the unprocessed pain from the childhood trauma.[324]

Literature Reviews

I found seven literature reviews addressing a possible ED-trauma link. The first and most negative was by Pope and Hudson, who in 1992 selected ten reports from a larger number of them on bulimia only and concluded that there were no significant increases in having a history of childhood trauma among bulimics when compared to controls.[796] But they neglected to include several studies that found a positive bulimia-trauma link, and they appear to have misinterpreted at least two of their ten selected studies for review. These authors are controversial and are possibly biased in this and other opinions that they have published about the link between trauma and mental and physical illness.[137] Their 1994 lone databased report, with three additional co-authors, was an uncontrolled, retrospective study on mostly college students that they recruited through advertising that also found no statistically significant relationship of a history of child abuse and the severity of bulimic symptoms. In summary, Pope and Hudson have tried to negate a history of childhood trauma among people with eating disorders by focusing on child sexual abuse only, when trauma in the broadest sense, *including CSA,* is a major factor in the genesis of eating disorders.[309, 1115] Here, they may not only try to negate CSA as a possible factor, but by ignoring other forms of trauma, they negate the association of all trauma as well.

By contrast, the other six literature reviews appeared to be more objective. The second literature review was by Connors and Morse (1993), who examined ten studies, mostly on bulimia and anorexia nervosa, that were published between 1986 and 1990. They reported that *half* of these found a *significantly increased* association between EDs and childhood sexual abuse, no difference in three, and "NA" in the remaining two of their reviewed studies. They concluded that *at least one in three* ED patients had a history of child sexual abuse, which, in spite of some deficiencies in the study methods, is a substantial number and can be one part in the causal puzzle. One deficiency is that they did not look for the presence of a history of physical or emotional abuse or neglect, as being other possible factors.

Everill and Waller reviewed and analyzed nineteen studies on ED population samples and found eleven (i.e., over half) of these to have reported a *significant history of childhood trauma,* five that reported a negative association, and three about which they provided no data. But they found that the authors of the five studies that reported a "negative association" had made what Everill and Waller called "inappropriate levels of analysis" due to a real or likely failure to consider *five mediating factors*. These mediating factors that they observed between CSA and bulimic symptomatology included the presence of: *dissociation, shame* (low self-esteem), *borderline personality disorder, invalidating abuse disclosure* experiences, and cognitive/*thinking errors*. They concluded that a *child sexual abuse* history is *highly likely* to be associated with and relevant to the development and maintenance of bulimic symptoms.

In 1997, clinical and research psychologist Stephen Wonderlich and his colleagues analyzed 53 controlled studies that examined the relationship between sexual abuse and eating disorders.[1115] Of these they found that eighteen employed advanced methods from the more recent second wave of research. Eight of the first twelve (two-thirds) found a significantly positive relationship between child sexual abuse and bulimia nervosa, and five of the next six (83 percent) found a significant increase in co-morbidity among people with eating disorders. Refuting Pope and Hudson's prior negative conclusions, they found that child sexual abuse was significantly related to bulimia and also to anorexia nervosa, as well as to a significant increase in co-morbidity among people with these and other eating disorders.

Summary of Data

These 58 retrospective reports, seven prospective studies, 43 index cases and seven literature reviews provide strong evidence that childhood trauma is a significant finding and a potentially aggravating or possibly causal factor in the genesis of some eating disorders among many people (summary in Table 11.4 on the next page). These 108 studies by multiple independent researchers on 226,344 people from diverse population samples worldwide show a significant and strong link between eating disorders and having a history of repeated childhood trauma.

Researchers have found various abnormalities of brain chemistry and function among some people with EDs and may have mis-attributed these, mistaking an intermediary mechanism for a possible cause, as I discuss in chapter 7 of the prior volume. Some of these abnormalities may also be caused by the abnormal eating behavior and its effects. For example, in the 1980s, an abnormal dexamethasone suppression test was thought to be a "biochemical marker" for depression, but was later found to be associated with the decreased caloric intake of many depressed people; subsequently it has also been associated with having a history of childhood trauma.[737]

RECOVERY AIDS

Recovery from eating disorders varies according to the individual's needs and wants. The self-help fellowship of Overeaters Anonymous is a good place to start. It provides a basic and long-term structure, an active program, and a supportive fellowship that can help break the disordered eating behaviors, while lessening the isolation.

Individual psychotherapy and counseling are often helpful to provide expression of painful feelings, problems and needs, and to begin to explore potential underlying childhood trauma once the disordered eating behaviors are stabilized. Well-selected reading (bibliotherapy) can be helpful. Long-term group therapy is also

Table 11.4. Eating Disorders & Childhood Trauma: Clinical, Community, Prospective, Index Case Studies & Literature Reviews* (see Tables A11.1–3 on pages 326–38 for details)

Year/Author	Study	Eating Disorders	Other Trauma Effects
Clinical & Community **58 Studies** 1989–2003	201,092 people CT v. Controls	1.6–11x controls, incl ↑ bulimia & anorexia nervosa	↑ Co-morbidity Table on page 326
Prospective **7 Studies** 1992–2002	4,734 people Ct v. Controls	↑	↑ Co-morbidity Table on page 332
Index Case **43 Studies** 1986–2002	20,518 people with EDs & their controls	↑ to 100% had a CT history	↑ Co-morbidity Table on page 334
Literature Reviews 1992–2002	7 literature reviews	↑ association with CT 6 support CT link	↑ Co-morbidity Table on page 338
Summary **108 Studies by Independent International Authors** 1986–2003	**226,344 CT people and their controls**	↑ **to 1.6–11x Clinical/Community;** ↑ **to 82% in Prospective;** ↑ **to 100% CT in Index Cases**	↑ **Co-morbidity** **All document CT link**

Key: CT = childhood trauma, Sx = Symptoms or signs, ↑ = increased, ED = eating disorder useful. While drug treatments are recommended by some, I discourage using any benzodiazepine sedatives or appetite-suppressing stimulants. In their place, I recommend regular exercise to tolerance. Ten to twenty minutes of brisk walking will usually lift a down mood and more strenuous exercise helps curb the appetite and raise the mood even more. For the person who has serious medical complications or out-of-control eating behavior, hospital or residential treatment at a specialized eating disorder unit may be indicated. Attention to treating any co-morbid disorders or conditions should be addressed. Stomach stapling surgery for extreme obesity should be reserved for when the above methods are not successful, although Overeaters Anonymous and individual and group therapy should still be continued here. Also called "bariatric" surgery, this radical approach, even with ongoing post-operative support, is fraught with the risk of eating one's way out of the surgery, since opposing forces are commonly at work: a desire to lose weight, but a great fear of the social, psychological and sexual changes associated with major weight loss.

History 11.1

Jill (Dave's sister from History 10.1 previously) gained insight during her recovery about her compulsive overeating. She said, "I found out from my aunt and uncle that my parents never held me when they gave me a bottle. They 'propped' the bottle in my mouth with a folded towel holding up the other end. When I became a mother, every time I held my own babies to feed them, I wondered about how that affected me when I was an infant. Also, my mother was anorexic and drug-addicted. I now know that affected me, too.

"From my early childhood, I ate without tasting the food. I never knew when I felt 'full.' Like my brother Dave, I gobbled up my food in a trance. Sometimes I didn't remember whether I had eaten. My mother limited my food to try to control my weight, but I drank all the milk I wanted. I remember often drinking a big glass of milk without taking a breath. When I was eating or drinking, I wasn't in pain. The main thing on my mind was food. As I ate one meal, I was planning the next. Between meals, from age twelve, I smoked cigarettes to numb my pain.

"As an adult, in therapy, I read everything I could on overeating. My OA sponsor helped me practice staying 'awake' while I chewed and notice the flavors and textures. I learned to notice when I was full—if I waited ten minutes after a meal, I could tell. I then learned to pace myself with sweets and other junk food. Now I have a healthier relationship with food. I still look forward to the next meal, but it's not so much on my mind anymore, and I am very careful not to eat when I am distressed about something. I want to know what my distress is about instead of taking it to the table and losing it somewhere between soup and dessert."

In recovery, even before the disordered eating behaviors are well-stabilized, it may be useful to begin to explore possible underlying childhood trauma issues, as shown in Figure 11.1. If they are present, starting a Stage Two recovery program may be helpful to heal the unhealed effects and pain of the trauma, as described on pages 20 and 28. For further details on the Stage Two recovery process, the reader may consider looking at my books *Healing the Child Within, My Recovery, A Gift to Myself, Boundaries and Relationships,* and/or *Memory and Abuse.* Other useful books on eating disorder recovery may also be helpful.

Many people with eating disorders use nicotine to lose weight or to keep weight off. A problem is that nicotine, whether by tobacco smoking or using it in other ways, is a highly addictive and toxic

Figure 11.1. Eating Disorder: Flowchart for Decision Making

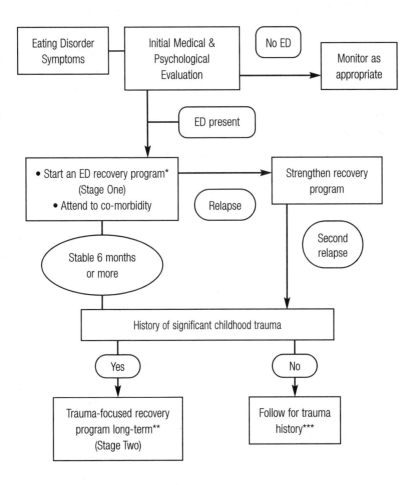

* Avoid using benzodiazepine sedative drugs to treat anxiety, insomnia or depression. Buspirone is a non-addicting and acceptable antianxiety drug.

** Long-term group therapy, individual therapy, self-help fellowship attendance, etc.

*** Because many trauma survivors authentically forget the trauma (dissociative amnesia), or may not be able to accurately name what happened to them as having been traumatic, keep an open mind that a substantial number of these people may eventually remember a serious trauma history.

drug that usually hinders recovery and healing from any life problem, including an eating disorder. Because of these and other concerns, I will address nicotine addiction in the next chapter.

12   NICOTINE ADDICTION

While there are several other kinds of addictions—such as compulsive (pathological) gambling, work addiction and sexual addictions—I have been able to find no databased documentation of their link with childhood trauma (although I suspect that there is). The only exception is for *nicotine* addiction, which is by far our largest and most destructive addiction, affecting 23 percent of adults in the United States and a higher percentage of people in many other countries.[96, 183] The most common form of nicotine addiction is cigarette smoking, which is a highly toxic nicotine delivery system. Smoking kills almost 500,000 people, over 20 percent of the total yearly deaths, in the United States. This death rate is *over five times* that for alcohol abuse and alcoholism and *over 50 times* the death rate of all illegal drug abuse and dependence *combined*. These 500,000 yearly deaths represent more than 5 million years of potential life lost. Medical costs directly related to smoking amount to over $50 billion annually.

Cigarette smoking is the leading preventable cause of premature death in the United States.[96] Cigarette smoking, or nicotine inhalation, is also a remarkably soothing self-treatment that variously can temporarily decrease *anger, appetite* and *fear* while producing a mild degree of increased intellectual acuity. Nicotine is a powerful psychoactive agent whose benefits have been concealed in recent decades by cautionary public health statements that assume risk without benefit.

Nicotine kills by its toxicity to most organ systems: cardiovascular disease (stroke, sudden death, heart attack), lung disease (asthma and chronic obstructive pulmonary disease [including chronic bronchitis and emphysema]), cancer (of the lung, mouth, throat [pharynx and larynx], esophagus, stomach, pancreas, uterus, cervix, kidney, ureter and bladder), pregnancy problems (ectopic pregnancy, spontaneous abortion, decreased fertility and impaired fetal growth and development)[954a]. Unfortunately, nonsmokers who breathe the smoke by "passive smoking" also appear to be at an increased risk for many of these same health problems. Yet the tobacco industry has long denied these problems, and most of our politicians continue to support this serious addiction by passing pro-tobacco laws and bills.

In a five-year follow-up study, research psychologist Naomi Breslan and her colleagues looked at 1,007 young adults and found that smoking increased the risk for subsequent depression, and, reciprocally, that those non-smokers who were depressed were at greater risk to smoke later, when compared to control subjects. Smoking can lead to depression, and it aggravates it. Likewise, depression leads to increased cigarette smoking. Nicotine use is a cause of co-morbidity and mortality among people with other mental disorders, especially for those with SA/CD, schizophrenia, and some personality disorders. Implicit in this observation are the psychoactive benefits of nicotine. Nicotine is a short-acting stimulant drug that—for a few minutes—*lessens emotional pain,* the most common kinds of which are 1. *nicotine withdrawal* discomfort, 2. current *stressful conflicts,* and 3. the residual and unmetabolized *pain of childhood trauma.* The latter painful feelings include especially *fear, guilt, shame* and *anger.* Underneath these are often *hurt, sadness,* and *emptiness.*

When a nicotine dependent person stops using their drug, they experience the painful feelings of nicotine withdrawal. After this brief period of detoxification, the unhealed traumatic pain gradually emerges, which, for the unaware smoker, is a common and major factor in relapse. Internist and researcher Vincent Felitti offers an interesting possibility. He observed that from the year of 1965, when 44 percent of adults smoked cigarettes and when the medical profession began to discover and appropriately expose the toxicity of smoking, that a gradual decline in the incidence of smokers occurred. This decline has for the past recent years leveled out at around 23 percent,[96,183] and Felitti has suggested that this plateau may well represent the most affected trauma survivors who are using nicotine to lessen their pain. Thus today, part of the focus on smoking cessation should be an evaluation of *all smokers'* history for *childhood* and *later trauma.*

Unfortunately few researchers have examined this link, as shown in Table 12.1. In 1994, Pelcovitz and colleagues compared twenty-seven physically abused adolescents, some of whom were also sexually abused, with twenty-seven non-abused controls. They found that the abused were cigarette smokers six times more often than the controls. They also had significantly more ADHD symptoms, delinquency, aggressive behavior, depression, conduct disorder, oppositional-defiant disorder and thought disorder. In a five-year prospective study, Swanston and colleagues (1997) compared sixty-eight sexually abused children with matched controls and found a significant increase in cigarette smoking among those with an abuse history. Felitti and colleagues (1998) found that among 9,508 adults surveyed in the ACE (Adverse Childhood Experiences) Study, the most traumatized people smoked cigarettes more than twice as often as those who reported no history of childhood trauma. They also had more addictions to other drugs, heart disease, cancer, chronic obstructive pulmonary disease, depression, suicide attempts, obesity, and other disorders and detrimental conditions.

Bell and Belicki compared 34 CSA adults with 75 controls, and found a statistically significant increase in cigarette smoking, plus other increased co-morbidity. Cohen and colleagues found similar results when they compared 99 adolescents who had been traumatized as children with 99 controls. Finally, among 1,991 twin adult pairs, Nelson and colleagues found the same results.

The totals of these six reports, plus 5 more, are remarkable. In spite of comprising only 11 studies, these evaluated 18,498 people with CT and their controls and all found a significant relationship between a trauma history and subsequent nicotine addiction. In these 11 studies (two prospective, 9 retrospective [from community and clinical samples]), 18,498 people were studied and yielded about the same results. There was a statistically significant increase in cigarette smoking (nicotine addiction) among those who had experienced childhood trauma, as well as an increase in other co-morbidity, as shown in Table 12.1.

Caffeine is another commonly used stimulant drug. Most of my patients have been regular and often heavy users, but I have not seen any study that has attempted to link caffeine use with childhood and later trauma. Heavy caffeine use aggravates insomnia, depression, anxiety, some heart arrythmias, some headaches and breast nodules.

Table 12.1. Nicotine Addiction and Childhood Trauma: 11 Studies

Year/Author	Study Characteristics	Nicotine Addiction	Other Findings
1992 Pribor & Dinwiddie	52 CSA women 23 controls	↑ (42%)	↑ co-morbidity
1994 Pelcovitz et al.	27 CPA/CSA teens, 27 controls	6x	↑ depression, aggression, delinquency, conduct disorder, oppositional-defiant disorder & thought disorder
1997 Swanston et al.	68 CSA children 84 controls followed 5 years	↑	↑ depression, suicide, anxiety, behavior problems , ↓ self-esteem; ↑ other traumas during follow-up
1998 Felitti et al.	ACE study, 9,508 patients, CT v. controls	2 + x	4.6–12.2x depression/suicide 2–10.3 self-destructiveness 4.7–10.3x SA/CD
Bell & Belicki Community	34 CSA adults 75 controls	↑	↑ SA/CD, depression, life stress
Kaplan et al.	99 CT teens 99 controls	↑	↑ depression, SA/CD, conduct disorder
1999 Agrid et al.	403 psych. patients CT v. controls	↑	
2002 Cohen et al.	99 CT teens 99 controls	↑	↑ depression, ADHD, conduct disorder
Nelson et al.	3,982 twins adult CT v. controls	↑	↑ depression, suicidality, conduct disorder, SA/CD, anxiety, revictimization
2002 Diaz et al.	3,005 girls CT v. controls	↑	↑ depression, SA/CD
2003 Breslau et al.	899 people CT v. controls	↑	↑ PTSD, SA/CD
1992–2003 11 Studies	**18,498 CTs v. controls**	**↑ to 6x**	**↑ multiple co-morbidity**

It is not the benign drug that it appears to be. But its consumption is so entrenched in the culture worldwide that most people rarely question its toxic or harmful effects. Stopping caffeine produces a two- to five-day withdrawal syndrome of difficulty focusing and afternoon headaches, but sleep and anxiety often improve and the other toxic effects usually decrease or disappear. This insidious addiction can be prevented in part by not giving it to our children.

RECOVERY AIDS

Some people can stop smoking on their own, with little difficulty. Each time a smoker lights up they usually do so to lessen the withdrawal pain, which, if they were to fully abstain, would constitute a few days of enduring the pain and difficulty concentrating. For those who can't, available helpful methods include Twelve-Step groups such as Smokers Anonymous, and the American Cancer Society and American Lung Association have effective smoking cessation programs. Individual psychotherapy may be helpful, and for those smokers with a history of childhood trauma, a Stage Two recovery program, as described on pages 20 and 28 may be helpful for the person's total healing, as well as preventing a relapse of smoking. Attention to any co-morbidity is also useful. Hypnosis can be helpful in stopping smoking. Despite optimistic advertisements, the antidepressant bupropion (Wellbutrin) and its sustained release form are only about 25 percent effective.[409]

13　PERSONALITY DISORDERS

Personality is the way we see, think and behave in our ordinary daily life. It is the way we relate to self, others and the world over time. We appear to develop most of it by age six, which underscores the importance of a healthy early environment, wherein we are at the least not abused or neglected. Ideally, to become healthy, we should also be loved and accepted. Personality traits differ from personality disorders. Personality *traits* such as passivity and aggressiveness are, according to *DSM-III-R*, "enduring patterns of perceiving, relating to, and thinking about the environment and oneself . . . exhibited in a wide range of important social and personal contexts."

These traits may become a *disorder* when our personality is narrowed down to only a few traits, which have become "inflexible and maladaptive and cause either significant impairment in social or occupational functioning or significant subjective distress." The *DSM-IV* describes a personality disorder as an enduring pattern of inner experience and behavior that deviates markedly from the expectation of the individual's culture, is pervasive and inflexible, has an onset in adolescence or early adulthood, is stable over time, and leads to distress or impairment.

The major characteristics of personality disorders (PDs) are shown in Table 13.1. The *DSM-IV* gives a more detailed description. Our concept and use of these diagnostic labels for PDs have produced a double-edged-sword result. On the one hand, they have provided a valuable understanding of the affected person's inner-life, including their pain and their often-problematic behavior. This information has helped health professionals to assist them more constructively. On the other hand, hearing others refer to them by using these diagnostic labels can naturally hurt their feelings. Their understandable emotional rejection of the painful label commonly generates conflicts with close others, who may be trying to help them. For example, their would-be helpers may walk on eggshells around them, and thus enable their continued cycle of pain and dysfunctional behavior. Of course, this pattern of denial of an emotionally laden diagnosis is not limited to PDs, since it is found among other conditions, such as addictions and psychoses, throughout psychiatry, psychology and physical medicine. It is thus with a delicate balance that both the person and their assistant may weigh, communicate and initiate action to help them identify their problems and reach their realistic goals.

CAUSAL FACTORS

We don't know what causes personality disorders. As for other mental disorders, some theorists have proposed a genetically transmitted cause. Others have observed a general stress-related model, while still others have noted an association with childhood trauma. Those most commonly linked to trauma have been borderline and antisocial PDs. For example, several studies have shown high rates of a history of childhood trauma among people with borderline personality disorder (BPD) and antisocial personality disorder (APD). Addressing BPD, psychiatrist James Chu (1999) said, "This growing body of evidence suggests that childhood abuse is often a critical factor in the development of borderline psychopathology. . . . Rather than simply focusing on traditional concepts concerning impairments of intrapsychic structure, one must also consider the developmental adaptations of young children subjected to cataclysmic events. In this context, intrapsychic structures and behaviors of borderline patients can be understood in a model that emphasizes adaptation rather than pathology."[193]

For several reasons, personality disorders have not been popular among researchers to study for a possible link with childhood trauma. Even so, I found forty-three such studies. While they are fewer compared to those for depression, addictions, anxiety disorders and the psychoses, they nonetheless represent a significant and at times impressive documentation of an actual link between some personality disorders and a history of repeated childhood trauma.

Clinical Studies

I am aware of 35 retrospective clinical studies published between 1972 and 2003 that evaluated 21,596 people who experienced childhood trauma, and their matched controls (summarized in Table A13.2 in the Appendix on page 340). These studies were conducted and reported by numerous independent authors or research teams that studied diverse populations worldwide. Fifteen found increased BPD or strong borderline symptoms and nine found APD to have a statistically significant increase among trauma survivors when compared with control subjects. Some also found an increase in paranoid (1 study), schizoid (1), avoidant (1), obsessive/compulsive (1), and

Table 13.1. Overview of Some Characteristics of Personality Disorders and Their Link with Childhood Trauma

Disorder	Overview (see DSM for specific criteria)	CT Link
Cluster A: **Paranoid** 301	Marked suspiciousness and distrust, including the belief, without reason, that others are exploiting, harming, or deceiving; belief of others' betrayal &/or hidden meanings, often angrily misinterpreting benign remarks or events; unforgiving & grudge holding; extreme jealousy.	Emotional abuse Bernstein et al. 1998
Schizoid 301.2	Very limited range of expressing and experiencing emotion; detachment from social relationships, including family; little interest in sex. Absence of psychosis or an effecting physical illness.	Emotional neglect; Kashani et al. '87 Bernstein et al. 1998
Schizotypal 301.22	Peculiarities of thinking, odd beliefs (e.g., in magical powers), and eccentricities of appearance, behavior, & interpersonal style; acute discomfort with, and reduced capacity for, close relationships.	Emotional abuse; 1 small study—no association; another large one was positive Yen et al. 2002, Bernstein 1998
Cluster B: **Antisocial** 301.7	Lack of regard for and violation of the rights of others, violating moral or legal standards, marked inability to get along with others or abide by society's rules, irresponsibility, impulsivity, and lack of remorse for transgressions; & conduct disorder since before age 15.	**Moderately strong,** by several studies Physical abuse & neglect Famularo 1999 Bernstein et al. 1998
Borderline 301.83	Lack of one's own identity, fear of abandonment, rapid mood changes, intense unstable interpersonal relationships with extremes of idealization & devaluation; marked impulsive, reckless or self-harming behavior; inappropriate, intense anger; transient, paranoid ideation, dissociative symptoms	**Strong,** by index, retrospective & prospective studies; Emotional abuse

Table 13.1. (Compiled from *DSM-IV* 1994 & Labelle 2001) *(concluded)*

Disorder	Overview (see *DSM* for specific criteria)	CT Link
Narcisstic 301.81	Superior attitude, grandiose, need to be admired; lacks empathy; preoccupied with success, power, brilliance, beauty, special-ness, entitlement, or ideal love; arrogant & exploitive, yet hypersensitive to others' opinions.	Some prospective studies Emotional abuse
Histrionic 301.5	Need to be the center of attention. Exaggerated, often inappropriate emotional displays, approaching theatricality, in every-day behavior; seductiveness. Rapidly shifting emotions. Vain, yet suggestible.	Some prospective studies Emotional abuse
Cluster C: **Avoidant** 301.82	Marked social inhibition, low self-esteem, extremely sensitive to criticism, which brings about marked fear of risking new activities.	Emotional abuse; Also any CT (Grilo & Masheb 2002, Yen et al. 2002)
Dependent 301.6	Extreme dependence on others, unable to make decisions or take responsibility or an independent stand in life areas. Fear of separation & abandonment; clinging, submissive. Marked lack of self-confidence.	Some prospective studies Emotional abuse
Obsessive Compulsive (O-CPD, not "OCD") 301.4	Preoccupation with orderliness, perfectionism, and mental and interpersonal control, at the expense of flexibility, openness, and efficiency; conscientious; miserly, hoarding, rigid.	Yen et al. 2002
PD-**NOS** 301.9	Any combination of the above that do not fit into a specific dosorder.	

histrionic/hysterical (2) PDs among trauma survivors, although some of these may have had PTSD in addition or instead,[657, 860, 1035] since PTSD was not looked for in the study or in the *DSM* at the time. A reason why the numbers of these other PDs (BPD or ASPD) are so small is that they were not looked for by many of the investigators. As others have observed,[556] and as I show throughout this and the prior book, repeated childhood trauma produces many and varied detrimental and painful effects.

Index Case Studies

I found 36 index case studies, as shown in Table A 13.3 of the Appendix on page 346. Twenty-two of these evaluated people with BPD and found a significant increase in their having a history of childhood trauma. One evaluated a large sample of chemical dependent people, who are known to have a high co-morbidity with PDs, and found a high percentage of childhood trauma among them (from 54 to 80 percent) and an increase in almost all PDs.[87] This study concluded that childhood trauma *contributes to the high prevalence of PDs* in alcohol- and drug-dependent people. It also found a significantly increased history of *emotional abuse* and *neglect* (affecting most PDs, with emotional neglect being also a factor in schizoid PD), and physical abuse and neglect (especially for those with ASPD) among those with PDs, as shown in the third column of Table 13.1 on page 132.

Prospective Studies and Literature Review

I found 5 large prospective studies on 1,897 people that evaluated and followed the traumatized children long into adulthood. Both of these found a significant increase in ASPD[660] and most other PDs[530] when the abused people were compared with matched controls (Table A 13.4 on page 350 in the Appendix). One literature review

Table 13.5. Personality Disorders and Childhood Trauma: Clinical, Prospective and Index Case Studies*

Year/Authors	Study	Personality Disorder	Other Trauma Effects /Full table page
Clinical 35 studies 1972–2003	21,596 people CT v. controls	↑ to 95% link with CT (2 said was causal)	↑ Co-morbidity Table on page 340
Prospective 5 studies 1980–1999	1,897 people CT v. controls	↑ to 6x controls	↑ Co-morbidity Table on page 350
Index 36 studies 1981–2003	2,674 people with PDs	↑ to 87% had CT history	↑ Co-morbidity Table on page 346
Summary 76 Studies by Independent International Authors 1972–2003	26,167 CT people & their controls	↑ link between CT & PDs— ↑ to 95% Clinical; ↑ to 6x Prospective; ↑ to 87% CT in Index Cases	↑ Co-morbidity All document CT link

*See Tables A13.2–4 in the Appendix for details
Key: CT = childhood trauma, ↑ = increased, PD = personality disorder

examined sixteen studies on eating disordered people and concurrently found a high association with BPD among those who had been traumatized as children.

SUMMARY OF STUDIES

Any one of these studies alone would not provide enough evidence for a significant trauma-PD link. But taken as a whole, these

76 studies by numerous independent international authors using multiple and varied study designs on 26,167 people provide a spectrum of from *strong* (for BPD and APD) to *some* (for most of the other PDs) evidence that *childhood trauma is* or *may be an important factor in the genesis of PDs.* While all personality disorders have been shown to be associated with childhood trauma, BPD is the most commonly researched that shows a clear association, enough for some researchers to suggest that the trauma is causal for it.[387, 560]

These impressive results could be low, however, since many people don't want to disclose having experienced child abuse or neglect. Psychologist Randy Noblitt (2000) said, "Imagine yourself as a patient having your first session with a mental health professional. Although a stranger to you, you are asked to disclose intimate details of your personal life. You feel nervous, embarrassed, and emotionally overexposed. You are unsure about confidentiality. You wonder whether anything that you say about yourself will later be used against you (e.g., if your mental health records are subpoenaed in a divorce or child custody hearing). The question of sexual abuse in your childhood comes up. What would you say? I cannot blame the patients for their reluctance to identify accurate histories of sexual abuse."[756] Add this to the fact that people with PDs usually have much difficulty trusting others, especially authority figures, and at least one-third of CSA survivors and a large minority of other trauma survivors have dissociative amnesia for their traumas,[137, 138] as described on page 73. These three dynamics—difficulty trusting, fear of disclosure, and dissociative amnesia—are likely operative for all the mental disorders described in this book, which would tend to contribute to underestimation of the degree of the trauma-disorder links.

14 PERSONALITY DISORDERS
── CONTINUED

The *DSM* further classifies personality disorders as "Axis II" disorders. It sees Axis I disorders, such as depression, anxiety disorders and most of the other psychiatric illnesses, as being syndromes or symptoms that are often superimposed on longstanding personality disorders.*

The *DSM's* diagnostic categories are in part arbitrary, with many of its "disorders" having a blurred relationship with one another. For example, as I noted in the prior volume, depression and PTSD are so similar as to be almost identical in many instances.[115] BPD and other PDs are also often so intermeshed categorically and clinically with other disorders, such as complex PTSD, some dissociative and psychotic disorders, and addictions, that even outside the consideration of co-morbidity one may not be able to tell the difference between them. *Trauma* may be their *most common causal* or *aggravating* link. In this regard James Chu adds, "Although an

---

*The *DSM*'s formal diagnostic and functioning code reporting system is divided into five such "axis" categories: Axis I = general psychiatric disorder, Axis II = personality disorder (if present), Axis III = concurrent medical conditions, Axis IV = stressors, and Axis V = global assessment of functioning (on a scale of 0 to 100).[15, 16]

understanding of the role of trauma in the development of borderline personality disorder may help both patients and clinicians
struggle through difficulties, it does not diminish the intensely
painful and slow process of [the personality disordered person's
struggle with] changing the sense of self, adaptations made to the
world, and the meanings attached to formative experiences".[193]

Some people with BPD and APD, as well as many with other
personality disorders, may not be able to identify a clear trauma
history. As discussed in the prior volume (pages 63 and 158), it
may not be the *individual* trauma per se that results in BPD. In fact,
nearly all of the common traumas (sexual, physical and neglect) are
accompanied by psychological abuse, also called emotional abuse,
all of which interfere with the parent-child attachment relationship.
Chu said, ". . . it is the gross disruptions of normal familial attach-
ments and the massive failure of adequate care and protection of
the child that result in distortions of normal characterologic [i.e.,
personality] development. Experiences of intrafamilial abuse and
neglect are extreme manifestations of the failure of normal parental
attachment and nurturance. Often these disruptions of attachment
and nurturance have been neither subtle nor limited to the rap-
prochement subphase [i.e., during from about age 18 to 24
months], but have existed throughout multiple phases of childhood
development".[193]

RECOVERY AND HEALING

If they are motivated to change, recovery for people with personality disorders is usually long and painful. While people with any
mental or physical disorder should be evaluated for their individual

problems and needs as part of their recovery plan, I offer some basic principles for those with PDs below.

Since addictions to alcohol, other drugs, food, gambling and the like are so common here, these problems should be screened for initially and ongoing, especially among those with Cluster B personality disorders, i.e., the "dramatic" ones: borderline, histrionic, narcissistic and antisocial PDs. Conversely, an active addiction can disrupt a non-personality-disordered person's mental functioning, behavior and life to such an extent that they may appear to have a mental disorder, including a personality disorder, when they may not actually have one. Others and I have seen numerous such people's symptoms of depression, anxiety, troubled behavior and at times even psychotic symptoms or signs improve over time just by abstaining from their drug(s) of choice and working a program of recovery. If they do not improve, they may benefit from more conventional and complementary trauma disorder recovery aids, some of which are summarized in Table 12.1 on page 148 of the prior volume.

While they may need *group therapy,* people with Cluster B PDs tend not to do well in it because of their often needing to be the center of attention and, especially among those with BPD, having a tendency to initiate or get caught up in unhealthy triangles.[1094] They are also hard to help in both group and individual therapy because of their difficulty learning to tolerate the emotional pain needed to accomplish their grief work on the effects of childhood trauma in a Stage Two recovery program (Table 14.1). Transference may be especially strong, and, e.g., those with BPD may have great difficulty with abandonment issues, as parodied in the Bill Murray movie *What About Bob?*

Health insurance programs tend to deny treatment for PDs alone. However, because co-morbidity is so common in people with them, the presence of their other disorder(s) can usually be used for billing and reimbursement purposes. Like the addictions and psychoses, many people with a PD who enter recovery are forced into it, since they usually do not believe they have a mental or behavioral problem and are seldom spontaneously motivated to change their disordered thinking and behaving.

For those who are also trauma survivors, a small percentage of people with PDs who may be so motivated may consider working a Stage Two recovery program to help them heal (see below and Figure 14.1). Here it will be to their advantage to have substantially decreased any serious acute problematic behavior and stabilized any active addictions before taking on the challenge of such hard and long work. Even with those motivated enough to begin a Stage Two recovery program, they may encounter other obstacles from within and outside. A common external obstacle is a family, friend or helping professional who invalidates their experience of childhood trauma in favor of them being "mentally ill." Internal obstacles abound. I describe one example in the following case history.

History 14.1

Olivia is a forty-eight-year-old woman who came to me in conflict with her previous therapist and therapy group. Over time, I observed her to fulfill six of the nine *DSM-IV* diagnostic criteria for borderline personality disorder (the *DSM-IV* suggests that at least five criteria be present to make this diagnosis). She had been severely sexually and emotionally abused by her father and unprotected from the abuse by her mother. She joined our therapy group and was particularly engaging and endearing with the group members and my group co-leader. She presented herself as a "model member." The other group members often looked to her as an authority on the effects of sexual abuse. She frequently summarized another group

Table 14.1. Overview of Some Characteristics of Personality Disordered People

(Compiled from Rullo 2000 & Modestin et al. 1997)

Disorder	Drug Abuse/ Chem Dep	Motivation for Recovery	Characteristics	TX approach/ Prognosis
A: Paranoid	Uncommon	Low; Isolated, "odd," most	Usually forced into treatment	1:1 therapy & disease model
Schizoid	Nicotine dependence	unhealthy of PDs, often	12 Step phobic	may help. Short sessions, support-
Schizotypal	is common	close to psychosis	Don't care for others' opinions	ive & directive. Prognosis: 1:1 fair; group doesn't help. Be concrete
B: Antisocial	Common	Low; no guilt or empathy	Dramatic, emotional, "depressed,"	Contracts, firm limits. Poor prognosis.
Borderline*	Some	Varies, 1/7–1/4	seductive, erratic . . .	±Trauma-based, limits; may disrupt
Narcisstic*	Some	in Tx for CD		group; avoid self-disclosure; watch
			Overreact, needy,	transferences. Low
Histrionic	Some	Some	drive away rel'ns, often lonely	humility
C: Avoidant*	Some; want friends,	±	Much shame; anxiety common	Empathy, support 12 Step group
Dependent	don't get them	±	Can't decide; lonely	±Trauma-based, build self-strength
Obsess. Comp. (OCPD, not "OCED")	Uncommon	±	Lack spontenaity; Perfectionistic achievers	Authoritative, non-judgmental; group, 12 Step
PD–NOS	Some	Varies	Mixture	What works

*BPD = fear abandonment, NPD = crave power, beauty & perfect mirroring; AvPD = fear rejection member's work with appropriate comments. The group worked with her on her conflicts with her previous therapist, although she declined to work on her conflicted relationship with her mother. She initiated three individual sessions with my co-leader and praised her in group sessions. Yet she eventually became angry with the co-leader and over time expressed anger and doubt about her competence, saying that she (Olivia) was severely wounded and doubted whether the co-leader was skilled enough to handle her wounds. She found another individual therapist who she believed understood her and left the therapy group abruptly, without processing her conflicts and concerns. Her last words to my co-leader (after her final group session had ended and where no one else could hear) were, "Of course, we know this is really about my mother, not you."

Olivia's story illustrates an extreme effect of childhood trauma on relationships, in this case as transference (denial, misperception and projection) with a group therapy co-leader. Olivia's trauma-personality disorder link was occasionally clear to her and at other times she not only denied it but also projected its pain onto others. In a broader context, while we all may at times have some aware-ness of the trauma-effect link, we may prefer at other times to deny it or make up another cause, such as "mental illness," genetic trans-mission and/or an abnormality of brain chemistry. Chu said, "It is hence not surprising to find that traumatized patients continue to engage others (including therapists) in repetitions of the most pow-erful interpersonal dynamics they have experienced. They reenact the roles of both abuser and victim because in their families one had to be one or the other [i.e., the defense-against-pain of *all-or-none thinking and behaving*]. For the therapist [or any other person] that becomes part of this [confusing] world and who is subject to the interpersonal struggles of the reenactments, the experience can indeed be intense and unpleasant. Yet the patient's dilemmas can be viewed as deficits in learning and deprivation concerning interpersonal experiences rather than as malicious or deliberate".[193]

Olivia worked on her painful feelings toward her father, but for those with her mother chose instead to act out conflict with women who she felt had some type of authority over her. It appeared that she did not want to face her mother, so instead she projected her feelings about her mother onto other women (reenactments or repetition compulsions).

*   *   *

People with personality disorders can be among the most difficult to assist in any kind of recovery program, and at any recovery stage. However, as the prior data and discussion show, a large percentage of them will have a history of childhood trauma. For these and other reasons, it is difficult to formulate an approach to best help them from a decision-making perspective. This is usually true whether or not they have any interest in healing their pain, which most do. A major problem is that they are usually able to progress only so far, in large part because most are not able to tolerate the emotional pain and grief work required in Stage Two recovery. In Figure 14.1 I illustrate a flowchart that may be helpful in some basic decision making when working with people with personality disorders. Of course, at the same time each person's individual problems, issues and needs should be addressed. To supplement this decision tree, I summarize some characteristics of people with personality disorders from a treatment and recovery perspective in Table 14.1. In this table, I give special attention to personality disordered people

Figure 14.1. Personality Disorder: Flowchart for Decision Making

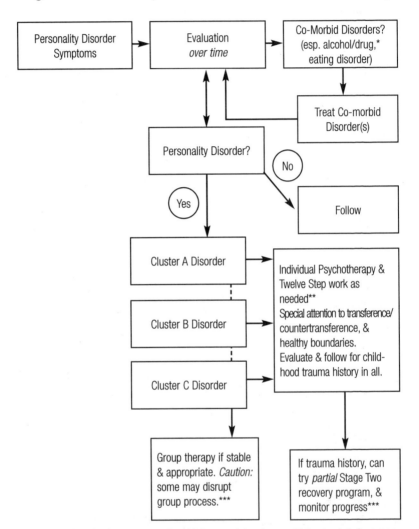

* Heavy alcohol or other drug use or an active addiction can mimic various mental disorders, including personality disorders. In this case it is useful to begin a Stage One abstinence-oriented recovery program & follow the person's progress.
** Twelve Step work is included here to address Stage One issues for anyone with an addiction.
See table 14.1 for summary guidelines & the references as needed.
***Most people with a PD are not motivated enough to begin, much less learn to tolerate the emotional pain required of trauma-focused recovery work & most with a cluster A or B PD will likely be disruptive & not work well in group therapy.

with an alcohol or other drug problem, or another addiction, since these are so common in this population.

The detrimental traits of personality-disordered people are usually so entrenched within their makeup that they are unable to get underneath them enough to change the very beliefs, attitudes and behavior patterns that so often get them into conflicts with others. Sometimes the best we can do as clinicians is to help them identify and adapt to their dysfunctional personality traits.[882] For example, when appropriate, we might say, "These are your traits. How can you handle them? How can you handle them without hurting others or disturbing your lifestyle? What do you want to happen with your traits? What are you willing to give up to get what you want to happen?" At the same time, as clinicians, we try not to be attached to helping them completely eliminate self-harming traits.

Some people with personality disorders, especially those with antisocial personality disorder, and to varying degrees other PDs, exhibit aggression and at times violence as one of their most detrimental personality traits. But aggression and violent behavior are not limited to people with personality disorders, which I will address in the chapter after next. The next chapter is about a commonly misdiagnosed and mistreated condition: ADHD in children and ADD in adults.

15 BEHAVIOR PROBLEMS, ADHD AND ADD

Behavior problems, aggression and violence have increased recently to become a more visible national and international problem. These toxic behaviors are often a component of various mental and behavioral disorders, including some personality disorders, as exemplified in the extreme by many with antisocial personality disorder, and in some people with alcohol or other drug addictions. They have also been further categorized as constituting a part of other clinical conditions such as conduct disorder, oppositional defiant disorder, ADHD and ADD. Disruptive behavior disorders are said to effect up to 10 percent of children and as many as a third who are referred for psychiatric treatment.[353-355]

ADHD AND ADD

Whether called attention deficit hyperactivity disorder (ADHD) in children or attention deficit disorder (ADD) in adults, this increasingly identified condition of children by teachers, parents and health-care workers has three main diagnostic criteria, any two of which are said to suffice for making the diagnosis: poor *attention* skills, decreased *impulse* control and *hyperactivity*. (For adults diagnosed with "ADD," usually only their attention is a problem, which may make the diagnosis suspect.) Yet critics have noted that there is *no valid laboratory* or *other test for* ADHD, and there is no convincing evidence that ADHD is caused by a primary brain malfunction or any other biological or genetic abnormality.[1023a] But another avenue may be more practical and help in prevention. What do we know about its connection to trauma?

History 15.1

John was a six-year-old boy who was diagnosed with ADHD by his schoolteacher and her referring pediatrician. He was prescribed the stimulant drug methylphenidate (Ritalin), which helped his symptoms minimally and intermittently. His parents had separated two years previously and were fighting for custody. John's mother came to me for assistance, describing John's symptoms and situation, which indicated that he may have been physically and/or sexually abused by his paternal grandfather. I reported John's symptoms and my concern to the appropriate local Child Protective Services, which on follow-up did not complete their investigation. His father continued to let John's grandfather see him alone, after which John would be upset, clingy and had nightmares.

John's frightening and sad story illustrates a common pattern among children diagnosed with ADHD and given Ritalin or other stimulants. The child's parents are often in conflict and may abuse or neglect the child. As a response, the child "acts out" or has a behavior problem in and out of school, and the teacher inappropriately labels the child with ADHD and refers him to a physician who prescribes a stimulant drug. Even if someone tries to intervene to protect the child from abuse or neglect, the dysfunctional parental–educational–health-care system in which he becomes stuck cannot or does not provide or allow the needed protection.

Substitute almost any other childhood mental disorder for ADHD and we may see that this same pattern is repeated for countless traumatized children. Many of the studies that I have described throughout this book have evaluated children with some of these "mental disorders" and found that a significant percentage of them had been abused or neglected. Their results indicate and their authors recommend that *all children with mental or behavioral symptoms, problems or disorders should be carefully screened* and *followed for* a history of past and present *childhood trauma.*

History 15.2

After 18 months into his participation in trauma-focused group therapy, Ralph (History 9.1 in chapter 9 on page 93) a successfully recovering alcoholic, thought he might have adult ADD and found a health professional who specialized in treating people with the disorder. As expected, the specialist diagnosed adult ADD and referred Ralph to a psychiatrist who worked in the same clinic and who prescribed a potent stimulant drug, which he tried for several weeks with no improvement in his symptoms of difficulty concentrating and occasional impulsiveness. He told us later in group, "I thought I had ADD and wanted to have it, in case a stimulant might help me calm down and focus on my work or whatever else I needed to do. But the drugs didn't help and now, a year later, I realize that I was looking for a short cut around my grieving. I had to try it anyway, to realize that I can do better without drugs, through my work on the effects of my past trauma here in group and in individual counseling and AA."

Ralph got off easy. Three other patients of mine did not. Also recovering chemical dependents, they went the same route as did Ralph, but got addicted to the Ritalin for two to five years, during which time it actually made their ADD symptoms of difficulty concentrating and low energy worse, instead of better. It took them more than two years of withdrawal to finally stop taking Ritalin. They were also severely psychologically abused as children, but elected not to confront their trauma wounds at that time.

CAUSAL FACTORS

These example case histories do not mean that: 1) all children and adults with symptoms and signs of ADHD/ADD do not have it, 2) they will become harmfully involved with the stimulant drugs in treatment, or 3) they have a history of childhood trauma. But many who are erroneously diagnosed with ADHD/ADD—and some who are accurately diagnosed with it—may have one or more of these crucial characteristics. I believe all people with symptoms or signs of ADHD/ADD should be evaluated for a history of trauma.

Other conditions can simulate the symptoms and signs of ADHD/ADD, including PTSD, heavy alcohol or other drug use and other mental illness—all of which should be excluded first. Poor to marginal nutrition, including eating many sugar products and other processed and junk food and caffeine, can cause and aggravate ADHD symptoms. Finally, a troubled or stressful environment can do the same. A primary question here is: How does childhood trauma relate to this only-recently described disorder?

Retrospective and Prospective Study Evidence

I found 77 published reports of a significantly higher incidence of ADHD among abused children. Fifteen of these were from *prospective* studies and 58 were *retrospective*, as shown in Tables A15.1 and 2 on pages 352 and 358 in the Appendix, and Table 15.3 on the next page. These investigations were conducted on a total of 168,801 traumatized children—and adults with a history of it—and their controls. Seventeen of these 77 studies looked for and found ADHD, and 49 of them did not look specifically for ADHD (for various reasons) but found behavior problems, school problems and delinquency, while seven found oppositional defiant disorder and eight found conduct disorder. Thus, most of these studies did not look specifically for ADHD but found *behavioral signs* of it, as these tables also show. In fact, most of the other studies on traumatized children referred to throughout this and the prior book *didn't look for ADHD,* possibly because this disorder was not as prominent at the time. I found *only one study* that looked for it that reported a negative association of ADD with trauma.[1119] These data are impressive enough to support including *trauma* as an *aggravating* or *causal* factor to be addressed clinically, and its extent warrants further research. Another factor, low self-esteem, is common, if not usual among people with ADHD/ADD, as I describe in chapter 7 of the prior book.

Index Cases

For index case studies, relatively fewer people with diagnosed ADHD and other problematic behavior, including violence, have been evaluated for a history of childhood trauma. I found four reports for children with ADHD, as summarized in Table A16.3 in

Table 15.3. ADHD, Behavior Problems & Childhood Trauma: Clinical, Community, Prospective, Index Case Studies, & Meta-Analysis/Literature Reviews

(see Tables A15.1–4 for details)

Year/Authors	Study	ADHD/Behavior Problems	Other Trauma Effects/ Full table Page
Clinical/ Community **58 studies** 1937–2003	153,185 people CT v. controls	↑ to 15x controls	↑ Co-morbidity Table on page 352
Prospective **15 studies** 1996–2003	15,227 people CT v. controls	↑ to 16x controls	↑ Co-morbidity Table on page 358
Index **4 studies** 1999–2002	389 children with ADHD & their controls	↑ to 73% with a CT history	↑ Co-morbidity Table on page 366
Meta-Analysis/ Literature Reviews 1989–2001	2 literature reviews & 1 meta-analysis	↑ association with CT among all	↑ Co-morbidity See Burgess & Conger 1975 and Johnson et al. 2001
Summary **77 studies by Independent International Authors** 1985–2003	**168,801 CT people and controls**	↑ **link between CT & ADHD/ behavior problems** ↑ **to 15x Clinical/ Community** ↑ **to 3.2x Prospective** **to 73% CT in Index Cases**	↑ **Co-morbidity** **All document CT link**

Key: CT = childhood trauma, ↑ = increased

the next chapter (page 366 in the Appendix). These involved 436 children and teens with ADHD, oppositional defiant disorder (ODD) and their controls. Those who had these disorders and behaviors had a significantly higher history of childhood trauma than their controls or the general population. There was also more associated PTSD and other co-morbidity. The authors concluded that there was a *need to address trauma* in most *children with behavior problems.*

Multiple co-morbidity is a marker of the advanced effects of child-hood trauma.[328, 867, 1090] The fact that children with ADHD are at high risk for multiple disorders and conditions, such as PTSD, depression, substance abuse, chemical dependence, school problems and dropout, low self-esteem, teen pregnancy, and others, further suggests that there may be a significant link between trauma and ADHD.

If a child or adult who is diagnosed with ADHD or ADD has experienced repeated trauma, they may also have PTSD. In fact, if their teacher, school counselor, physician or parent is not knowl-edgeable about PTSD, they may have misdiagnosed ADHD/ADD when they actually have PTSD or have it in addition to ADHD. The symptoms and signs or these two disorders are similar, and PTSD can easily be mistaken for ADHD/ADD, as shown in Table 15.4.

If a child or adult with PTSD is misdiagnosed as having ADHD or ADD and treated with stimulant drugs, their symptoms usually get worse, which I have observed among several of my patients. In such a case, the physician may erroneously try to increase the dose or switch to another stimulant drug. There are several other drawbacks. Such misdiagnoses and mistreatment may only retraumatize the per-son. As the family medicine physician Anna Kirkengen said, "Every time we deny a trauma survivor's reality, we revictimize them."[587]

Behavior problems in general are common among abused and

Table 15.4. Differential Diagnosis of ADHD & PTSD—Similarities*

ADHD Category	PTSD Diagnostic Criteria
Inattention	Acting or feeling as if the trauma were recurring.
	Distress at exposure to cues resembling the trauma.
	Reexperiencing trauma.
	Problems concentrating.
	Hypervigilant to perceived fear stimuli.
	Avoiding stimuli associated with trauma.
Hyperactivity/ Impulsivity	Acting or feeling as if the trauma were recurring.
	Distress at exposure to cues resembling the trauma.
	Inability to appropriately inhibit response due to hypervigilance.
	Psychological reactivity when exposed to cues symbolizing the trauma.
	Irritability/anger outbursts.
Externalizing Behaviors	Acting or feeling as if the trauma were recurring.
	Distress at exposure to cues resembling the trauma.
	Avoiding activities, people or places.
	Markedly diminished interest/participation in activities.
	Feeling detached/estranged.
	Restricted range of affect.
	Exaggerated startle response.
	Repetitive play with trauma themes.
	Irritability/anger outbursts.

*Compiled from Weinstein et al. 2002

neglected children. For example, Calam and colleagues (1998) reported a significant increase in *behavior* and *attentional* problems among 144 sexually abused children followed for two years (Table 15.5). The children were evaluated initially, and then at one, nine, and twenty-four months later. The research team found an increase of fifteen other problems over the two-year follow-up, as shown in Table 15.5. These findings are impressive, since they show how abused and neglected children are hurt by trauma, and yet are often *misdiagnosed* or even *blamed for having* these *trauma-induced results.*[163] Rather than address these effects appropriately as being caused by the trauma, many authority figures such as parents, teachers, law enforcement people, and some clinicians commonly label and blame the child, which revictimizes them and further decreases their already low self-esteem.

Table 15.5. Problems Found Among Sexually Abused Children (in Percentage)

Followed 2 years, in order of decreasing frequency *(from Calam et al. 1998)*

Disturbance/Problems	1 Month	9 Months	2 Years
School Difficulties	18	29	39
Attention Problems	11	20	33
Sleep Problems	20	34	33
Anger	10	34	33
Anxiety & Depression	19	36	31
Sexualized Behavior	11	28	23
Somatic Complaints	11	16	18
Eating Problems	7	9	17
Lack Peer Relations	3	25	15
Wetting and Soiling	11	18	15
Running Away	8	11	13
Substance Abuse	2	5	10
Suicide Attempts	0	4	8
Self-Mutilation		5	5
Speech Problems	5	5	2
Clumsiness	2	5	1

How helpful is it to label children with new "disorders" such as "ADHD" when, instead, the child's behavior may be a normal reaction to an abnormal environment? The child's dysfunctional educational system, teachers, parents and exposure to toxic media may be a major part of the problem. Child psychiatrist Sami Timimi and 33 co-endorsers (including myself) published a critique of the current party-line view of ADHD as espoused in an "International Consensus Statement" by long-time ADHD advocate Russell Barkley and co-endorsers.[1023a]

Citing the above concerns in our critique, we noted there were no valid diagnostic tests or brain abnormalities for this claimed disorder, and that there were no studies that showed that Ritalin/stimulants were helpful in the long-term.[275a] We also noted that ADHD is mostly a cultural construct to cover up our dysfunctional educational and parenting system.[1023a] Rather than engage us in a healthy debate, Barkley et al. answered with platitudes that essentially translated that they had the truth about ADHD, while we did not.[61a]

Pediatrician Lawrence Diller noted that: 1) over half of children receiving Ritalin do not have ADHD; 2) Ritalin/stimulants are not specific for ADHD. They increase *everyone's* ability to focus. But they do not help parents parent or teachers teach any better; 3) while our culture benefits from diversity, we train our children to think and behave the same, and if they don't, we give them Ritalin.[275a]

Psychologist Diane Willis said, "When we consider the reasons behind the current trend in medicating young children, parents, physicians, and even psychologists must bear some of the responsibility. Parents often do not choose psychological interventions over medications because of the extra demands on their time to participate in therapy or bring their child for therapy. The expense of psychological interventions is measured in terms of time demands as well

Figure 15.1. ADHD, ODD, CD: Flowchart for Decision Making

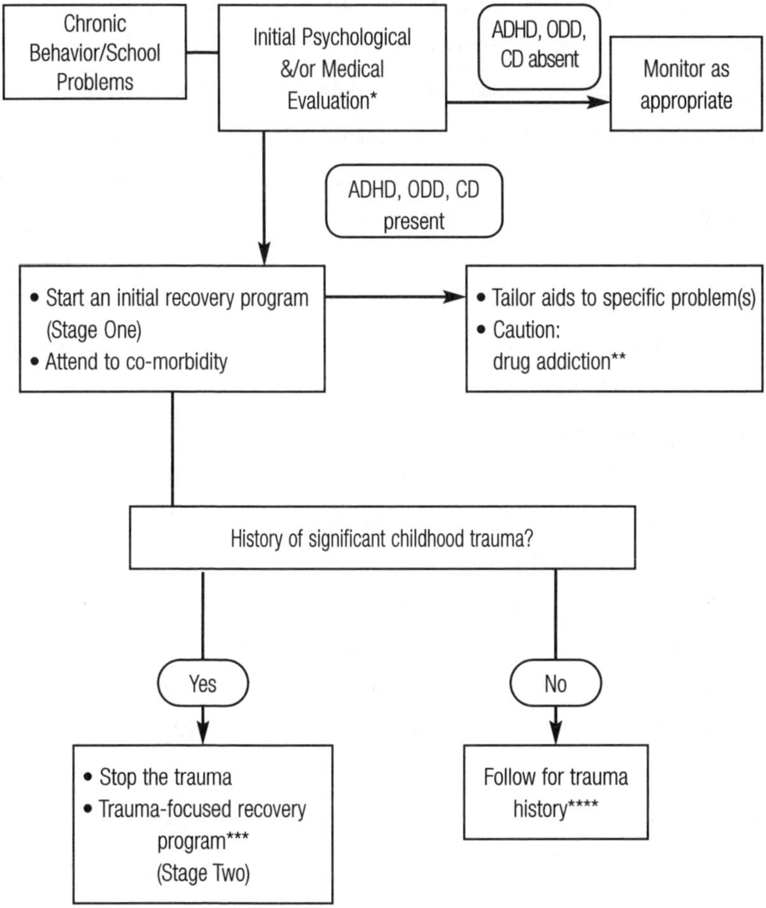

```
┌─────────────┐   ┌─────────────────┐   ┌─────────────┐
│  Chronic    │   │ Initial Psycho- │   │ ADHD, ODD,  │   ┌─────────────┐
│ Behavior/   │───│ logical &/or    │   │  CD absent  │   │ Monitor as  │
│ School      │   │ Medical         │   └─────────────┘──▶│ appropriate │
│ Problems    │   │ Evaluation*     │                     └─────────────┘
└─────────────┘   └─────────────────┘
```

ADHD, ODD, CD present

- Start an initial recovery program (Stage One)
- Attend to co-morbidity

- Tailor aids to specific problem(s)
- Caution: drug addiction**

History of significant childhood trauma?

Yes

No

- Stop the trauma
- Trauma-focused recovery program*** (Stage Two)

Follow for trauma history****

*Rule out more complex forms or causes of behavior/school problems, e.g., PTSD, addiction, dissociative disorder, serious physical problem & other effects of childhood trauma.
** Avoid using drugs to treat children, including stimulants, & especially benzodiazepine sedative drugs to treat anxiety, insomnia or depression. Buspirone is an acceptable, non-addicting antianxiety drug.
SSRIs are ineffective and dangerous for children and adolescents.
***Family therapy, group & individual therapy, self-help group attendance for parents
****Because many trauma survivors authentically forget the trauma (dissociative amnesia), or they may not be able to accurately name what happened to them as having been traumatic, or are embarrassed or want to protect the parents, keep an open mind that a substantial number of these people may eventually remember a serious trauma.

as professional and clinic fees, and busy parents may be unwilling to devote the effort to weekly sessions and/or practice new management techniques with their child. Parents may also consider a medically treatable diagnosis to be less of a personal reflection on their parenting skills or their own characteristics, and therefore less stigmatizing. When parents ask their child's physician for treatment suggestions, there is pressure on the physician to address the parents' concerns immediately, and prescribing medication is often the result. However, the least expensive approach to managing a young child's behavior (i.e., medication) may end up, in the long run, being the most costly. If we look at who is doing the medicating, it is often general practitioners and pediatricians rather than mental health professionals such as child psychiatrists."[1103]

In Figure 15.1 I outline an approach to recognizing and treating a child with behavior problems suggestive of ADHD, oppositional defiant disorder or conduct disorder.

In the next chapter I will continue this discussion on the more severe end of the spectrum of behavior problems: aggression, violence and other antisocial behavior.

16 AGGRESSION, VIOLENCE AND ANTISOCIAL BEHAVIOR

Most children and adults with ADHD and ADD are neither *harmfully aggressive, violent* nor *antisocial.* But these inappropriate behaviors may be part of a pattern, as explored and found in forty clinical and community studies and sixteen prospective ones that reported an association between these toxic behaviors and having a history of childhood trauma, shown in Tables A16.1 and 2 on pages 360 and 364 in the Appendix. I also found ten index case studies, four of which addressed ADHD, as shown on page 366 in the Appendix.

CAUSAL FACTORS

Retrospective Studies

I found forty clinical and community sample studies, conducted by independent research teams over the last three decades between the 1970s and 2003, that evaluated 45,088 traumatized children and adults with that history, and their controls. They all found a significant link between CT and subsequent aggressive and violent behavior, with odds ratios (risk factors) as high as four times that for the controls. These forty studies are but the tip of the iceberg regarding the firm link between childhood trauma and people's subsequent acting out of violence.

Prospective Studies

I found sixteen prospective studies that followed traumatized children and their controls for up to nineteen years. All showed a statistically significant link between having a history of repeated childhood trauma and subsequent aggressive behavior and violence, with odds ratios of up to twenty-two times that for the controls.

Index Case Studies

I found six studies of severely aggressive or violent people that reported a significantly high percentage (up to 100 percent) of them having had a history of repeated childhood trauma, as shown in Table A16.3 on page 366 in the Appendix. Four addressed ADHD.

SUMMARY

These add up to a total of 66 studies by independent researchers using multiple study designs on 54,242 people in different countries that show a highly significant relationship between repeated childhood trauma and later aggressive or violent behavior (Table 16.4). This is impressive evidence that clinicians, parents, teachers and others should take into account in their work, especially regarding prevention of further violence. In the next section I will review selected examples from these 66 studies, after which I will review some important dynamics relating to family and gender issues.

Table 16.4. Aggression, Violence and Childhood Trauma: Clinical & Community, Prospective, Index Case Studies*

Year/Authors	Study	Aggression/ Violence	Other Trauma Effects/ Full Table Page
Clinical/ Community **40 studies** 1977–2003	45,088 people CT v. controls	↑ aggressive &/or violent behavior	↑ Co-morbidity Table on page 360
Prospective **16 studies** 1990–2003	8,277 people CT v. controls	↑ to 22x	↓ Self-esteem ↑ Co-morbidity Table on page 364
Index Case **10 studies** 1982–2003	927 ADHD, ODD or violent children	↑ to 100% had CT history	↑ Co-morbidity Table on page 366
Summary **66 Studies by Independent International Authors** 1990–2003	**8,277 people** **CT v. controls**	↑ **link between CT & aggression &/or violence** ↑ **Clinical/Community;** ↑ **to 22x Prospective;** ↑ **to 100% CT in Index Cases**	↑ **Co-morbidity**

*Key: CT = childhood trauma, ↑ = increased

See also Table AX on page 351 for examples of violence induced by psychiatric drugs.

Example Studies

Whether treating children violently is likely to make them treat others violently later in life is of great social importance. In an attempt to sort out whether violence breeds violence across the generations, in 1989 researcher Cathy Widom analyzed eighteen reports on the topic published from 1970 to 1986 and said that there were not enough data to draw any firm conclusions at that time. But more recent studies have shown that maltreated children are at risk for many psychological, behavioral, and physical problems, including aggression and violence, as I have described throughout this book.[21, 127, 130, 272, 306, 328, 333, 496]

Three examples include: 1) Shields and Cicchetti (1998) measured the effects of childhood trauma on 141 abused, inner-city children who they compared with 87 controls. They found that the abused children exhibited increased levels of violent, aggressive behavior, especially those who were physically abused. Other effects of the trauma included increased emotional swings, dissociation, and difficulty focusing, all of which simulate ADHD.

2) Another research group looked at 4,790 middle- and high-schoolers and found higher levels of antisocial behavior, as well as more substance abuse and suicidal behavior, among those who self-reported having been abused, than was found among controls.[80, 81] 3) Widom and colleagues (1996–1999) followed 1,575 abused children long-term, and published their findings in five reports. They found that abused children had more aggression, violence, and antisocial behavior, as well as an increased risk of depression, suicide, anxiety, substance abuse and post-traumatic stress disorder than did the control children. Numerous others have found similar results, as summarized in the tables.

While there are not as many studies linking childhood trauma with subsequent aggressive, violent or antisocial behavior as those for most of the other mental disorders described in this book, they nonetheless provide firm evidence for such a link. These above-described 66 studies are also *independent of* and *in addition to* the seven reports that link trauma and antisocial personality disorder as summarized in chapter 13 in Table 13.5 on page 135, and in more detail in the corresponding tables in the Appendix.

FAMILY AND GENDER DYNAMICS

Research on the transgenerational transmission of family aggression and violence began forty years ago[667]. Multiple factors may be at play. These factors may include the *type* of abuse, and whether it was *experienced, witnessed* or both; its *severity* and *frequency;* the victim's *identification with* and *imitation of the abuser* and/or other victims; *enabling behavior* (co-abuse) *by others; gender* identification; the *overall impact* of the trauma(s); *self-esteem* (shame) of the victim; *memory* of the trauma; the use of *survival defenses;* and the *recovery* process itself.[31, 667, 1086, 1089] The abused person's *current adult relationships* add more factors: the *trauma history* of the partner, the *partner's current behavior,* the interpersonal *dynamics* and *boundaries* of the current relationship,[1094] and the abused person's *attachment history* in infancy and later.[662] Other factors, such as repeated viewing of TV and movie violence, contribute to and aggravate the cycle.

Women and men can be either victims or perpetrators of violence. [31, 32, 333, 334, 336, 476, 672, 990] Each gender appears to *initiate* the violence with equal frequency. However, women are more likely than men to suffer injuries as a victim and men are more likely to be perpetrators of the injuries.[31, 333] Archer (2000) did a meta-analysis of eighty-two separate reports of aggression among partners. He found that while women use physical aggression on men about as often as do men on women, more women than men reported having been injured (62 versus 38 percent, respectively). This process is often related to the phenomenon of subsequent *revictimization* as adults for people who were abused as children, as thirty-eight studies document (Table A19.2 on page 388).

Exposure to violence by *witnessing* it is also traumatic. For example, Hurt and colleagues studied 119 inner-city children who had a high exposure to violence by age seven years, and found significant signs of distress that frequently were not recognized by caregivers.[507] Among the children, 75 percent had heard gunshots, 60 percent had seen drug deals, 18 percent had seen a dead body outside, and 10 percent had seen a shooting or stabbing happen in the home. Higher exposure to violence in children was linked with poorer school performance, symptoms of anxiety and depression and lower self-esteem, some of which could be misdiagnosed and mistreated as having "ADHD."

These findings—that children exposed to abuse and violence are at increased risk of interpersonal violence later in life—have implications for personal recovery, clinical practice and prevention. Clinicians should screen for a history of violence and victimization in both men and women, as well as for a history of childhood trauma itself.[130, 223, 1085, 1089, 1090] By making these connections and offering effective treatment or referral, we can assist in all levels of prevention. We have to stop abusing and neglecting our children.

Becoming involved in violence either as a victim or a perpetrator is a high-risk behavior. In the ongoing adverse childhood experiences

(ACE) study, Rob Anda, Vince Felitti, and their colleagues have now evaluated over 17,000 adults as described in the first chapter of the prior volume, and referred to several times in this book.[21,328, 1085] Based on their findings, they have proposed and shown how repeated *childhood trauma* (ACEs) lead to a multitude of health and social problems that result from disrupted development of the brain and nervous system.[783–787] This disrupted neurodevelopment then is significantly related to impairment in the victim's *social, emotional and cognitive* (thinking and remembering) *functioning,* which causes or aggravates the adoption of *high-risk behaviors.*[328, 1085] These high-risk behaviors are many and varied such as overeating, heavy alcohol and other drug use (including nicotine), sexual promiscuity and other kinds of self-harm. Less commonly known, becoming involved in violence in any way is also highly risky, as are not wearing seat belts, not exercising or maintaining oral hygiene. These high-risk behaviors then lead to an *increase in disease, disability,* and *social problems,* which in turn can cause early death[21, 328] as shown in Figure 16.1. These detrimental effects of childhood trauma can be prevented in most of these levels in this pyramid by appropriate intervention by individuals or their clinicians.

While anyone can be aggressive and violent, among the most common disorders associated with them are alcohol and other drug addiction, antisocial personality disorder and psychoses. Cigarette smokers commonly use nicotine to help hold down their anger. Many of the hundreds of research reports linking CT to subsequent mental illness found inordinate anger to be a significant long-term effect of repeated CT.

Aggression and violence are the toxic end result of inordinate and unhandled anger. Clinical psychologist Ron Potter-Effron has written a helpful workbook on anger management,[804] and I have a

Figure 16.1. Mechanisms by Which Adverse Childhood Experiences Influence Health and Well-Being Throughout the Lifespan

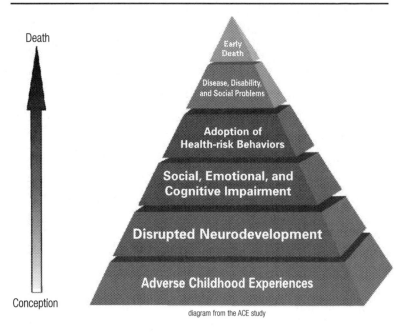

diagram from the ACE study

section that begins to address it in *A Gift to Myself.* It is useful to view anger as part of the normal and healthy process of grieving from childhood and other trauma, and to learn safe and effective ways to prevent it from escalating to aggression and violence.

In the next two chapters I address the uncommon mental illnesses known as the psychoses, the most common of which is the still enigmatic and complex schizophrenia.

17 PSYCHOSES AND SCHIZOPHRENIA

The fundamental nature of psychosis is an impaired ability to perceive reality, which clinicians call "reality testing." This impairment has many guises, from the transient confusion and disorientation of delirium that is sometimes associated with the stress of an acute severe physical illness, to the marked delusions and disturbing hallucinations of chronic schizophrenia.

SCHIZOPHRENIA

Schizophrenia affects just under 1 percent of people during their lifetime. Symptoms most often begin in the teens and twenties. The disorder involves three main areas of functioning: thinking, feeling and behaving, as outlined in Table 17.1. The psychotic disorders, also called psychoses, are *difficult to diagnose*. In spite of claims of disordered brain neurotransmitters as being their cause, like most mental disorders there are *no laboratory* or *other tests* that can positively identify a person as having schizophrenia or any other psychosis. Because physical illness and alcohol and other drug (legal

Table 17.1. Characteristics of Psychotic Disorders

Disorder/Code	Characteristics
Schizophrenia 295.0/x "x" = specify type: e.g., paranoid, catatonic, disorganized, undifferentiated or residual	Disorders of: 1. **Thinking** (orientation, content, concepts, abstraction, attention; mannerisms & posturing), 2. **Feeling** [so-called "negative" symptoms] (emotional or passive withdrawal, numbness, lack spontaneity; fear/anxiety, tension, anger/hostility, guilt, depression), 3. **Behaving** ["positive" symptoms] (delusions, hallucinations [often of voices], suspiciousness/persecution, grandiosity, body preoccupation, poor rapport, uncooperative, lack attention, judgment & insight; disorganized speech).* At least 2 of above categories; symptoms lasting for 6 months or more, and disrupt work, social life or self-care. A *criterion for all 6* of these psychotic disorders is that: *alcohol/drug & other disorders are ruled out* (see *DSM* for details).
Brief Psychotic Disorder 298.8	Any of: delusions, hallucinations, disorganized speech (e.g., frequent derailment or incoherence), grossly disorganized or catatonic behavior—lasting less than a month, with full return to normal functioning**
Schizophreniform Disorder 295.4	Two or more of: above symptoms of brief psychotic disorder, negative symptoms, i.e., affective flattening, alogia, or avolition—each present for a significant portion of time during a 1-month period; episode lasts at least 1 month but less than 6 months. (Dx = "Provisional" when recovery incomplete)
Delusional Disorder 297.1 Specify Type	Nonbizarre delusions (i.e., involving situations that occur in real life, such as being followed, poisoned, infected, loved at a distance, or deceived by spouse or lover, or having a disease) of at least 1 month's duration. Functions otherwise, not markedly impaired & behavior is not obviously odd or bizarre.
Schizoaffective Disorder 295.7	A cross between a thought and mood disorder. Both symptom clusters (depressive/manic and schizophrenic) must exist at the same time (co-morbid) to justify a diagnosis. Long & complex list of diagnostic criteria; see *DSM*.

Table 17.1. Characteristics of Psychotic Disorders *(continued)*

Disorder/Code	Characteristics
Shared Affective Disorder 297.3	A delusion develops during a close relationship with another person(s), who has an already-established delusion. The delusion is similar in content to that of the person who already has the established delusion. Partner shows same symptoms, e.g., buying into the belief of delusion.
Other Causes 293	Alcohol/drug & other medical & neurological diseases & disorders may cause psychotic symptoms & signs. Specify cause. See text for examples.

* Compiled from Lindenmayer et al. 1994 & *DSM-IV*
** **Specify if: With Marked Stressor(s)** (brief reactive psychosis): if symptoms occur shortly after and apparently in response to events that, singly or together, would be markedly stressful to almost anyone in similar circumstances in the person's culture, or **Without Marked Stressor(s):** if psychotic symptoms do not occur shortly after, or are not apparently in response to events that, singly or together, would be markedly stressful to almost anyone in similar circumstances in the person's culture, or **With Postpartum Onset:** if onset within 4 weeks postpartum.

and illegal) effects may cause psychotic symptoms, these must be ruled out. Having excluded these other causes, as well as mood disorders with psychotic features and dissociative disorders such as dissociative identity disorder (which may simulate schizophrenia, especially with schizophrenia's "positive" symptoms)[301] (Table 17.1) the clinician and the affected person are left with only the observed symptoms and signs, and those reported by family and friends. This paucity of information can cause delays in diagnosis, since many symptoms may not be obvious until the illness is advanced. Even so, the best diagnostic accuracy for a first episode of psychosis is in the range of 65 to 75 percent,[687] which translates to the probability that 25 to 35 percent are wrongly diagnosed. Such an error rate of one in three or four is high.

Physical Causes of Psychotic Symptoms

Many acute medical and drug-related conditions can cause a usually temporary psychotic state called *delirium*. Some common causes include: 1. brain trauma, infections and tumors; 2. temporal lobe epilepsy, multiple sclerosis; 3. hormonal imbalance (e.g., hyper-or hypothyroidism, hyper- or hypoadrenalism); 4. vitamin deficiency (B_{12}, folic acid or niacin); 5. acute severe infections such as pancreatitis and septicemia; and 6. drugs, especially alcohol, other drug intoxication or withdrawal from them, stimulants such as amphetamines and cocaine, phencyclidine (PCP), psychedelics, steroids, L-dopa and some anticholinergic drugs.[362]

BACKGROUND

In spite of countless research on schizophrenia over the past century, its cause remains unknown. There is no known single cause. Current conventional belief is similar to that for other mental illness: that it is caused by a genetically transmitted disorder of brain chemistry, here including the neurotransmitters dopamine, glutamate and serotonin. However, also similar to other mental disorders, the evidence for this theory is not strong.[97, 540–542, 768] For example, in people who have an *identical twin* with schizophrenia, if defective genes alone were to have caused it, we would expect a 100 percent chance that the twin would also have it. But the unaffected twin has only a 35 to 46 percent chance of developing the illness.[97, 539–542, 768, 1042] There is also no convincing evidence that neurotransmitters or neuronal receptor problems cause schizophrenia or any other mental disorder.[176, 190, 712, 1042]

One of the more telling studies that looked at the genetics of schizophrenia evaluated 322 children of schizophrenic mothers who were raised by either one of "healthy" adoptive families or "disturbed" adoptive families. Those raised by the disturbed families were diagnosed as severely psychotic 8.5 times more than those raised by the healthy families (34 versus 4 percent). The authors concluded that ". . . in healthy rearing families the adoptees have little serious mental illness, whether or not their biological mothers were schizophrenic".[1023] Further analyzing the data and somewhat complex statistics of this study, psychologist John Read and colleagues (2001) concluded, "Thus the dysfunction of the family and the maltreatment of the child implied thereby, had [over] seven times more explanatory power than genetic predisposition."

Since 1961, 33,648 research studies have looked for the cause of schizophrenia and, as expected, none has found it. Confident in their belief in a biogenetic cause, countless investigators looked high and low for evidence to prove their assumption. During this time they found a few biological defects and abnormalities among the schizophrenics that they tested and further assumed that these were biological "markers" for their theory, as shown in Table 17.2. However, for example, recently research psychiatrists Bruce Perry, Martin Teicher, J. Douglas Bremner, Michael De Bellis and their colleagues, and psychologist John Read and others have found that *these same defects* can also be *caused by childhood trauma.*[21, 783-788, 819-825, 1111-1115, 1090] They note that the accumulated research data indicate that a history of repeated *child abuse* is *significantly correlated* with psychosis in general, and schizophrenia in particular.[823] Even when abnormalities are found among schizophrenics, according to several comprehensive reviews and meta-analyses by independent authors, they appear to be nonspecific.[190, 542, 823, 1042, 1090, 1131]

Table 17.2. Deficits Assumed to Be Biological Markers for Genetic Predisposition/Transmission of Schizophrenia and Other Mental Illness (Compiled from Read et al. 2001)

Deficit	Characteristics and Comments	Example References
HPA axis*: Baseline **cortisol levels** high, DST response negative**	Childhood trauma can cause permanent HPA axis over-reactivity, which may reflect a neural-stress diathesis (see also Ensink 1992, De Bellis et al. 1999)	Walker & DiForio 1997, Heim et al. 2000
Cortical development: Cerebral atrophy/ ventricular enlargement	Childhood trauma can cause these serious & damaging structural brain abnormalities Childhood trauma causes this and other limbic system abnormalities	Ito et al. 1998, Read et al. 2001, Teicher et al. 1996, Bremner 1999
Left brain, reversed **cerebral** structural **symmetry,** EEG***	These defects are often found in "schizophrenics" and in victims of childhood trauma Non-specific EEG abnormalities are found to be 2–3x among childhood trauma survivors	Ito et al. 1993, Read et al. 2001
Neurotransmitter metabolism	Childhood trauma causes defects in dopamine & serotonin metabolism, receptors & sensitivity	Perry 1998, Read 2001
Verbal learning and **memory**	Abused children have 6 (for CPA/CSA) & 8 times more impairment. Decline in "intelligence" in schiz. stops by age 8, not in adulthood	Perry 1998, Read et al. 2001
Eye movement	Defects in smooth pursuit eye-movement tasks are significantly related to childhood trauma	Irwin et al. 1999
Resting heart rate	Increased in 29/34 children, indicating hyperarousal	Perry 1994

* HPA = hypothalamic-pituitary-adrenal axis. Activation of the HPA axis is one of the main manifestations of our response to stress. The adrenal cortex, stimulated by adrenocortropic hormone (ACTH) from the pituitary gland, releases glucocorticoids (including cortisol). The hippocampus contains a high density of glucocorticoid receptors and plays a vital role in the feedback system that regulates the activation of the HPA axis.
** DST = dexamethasone suppression test.   *** EEG = electroencephalogram
See also Tables 9.1, 9.2, 9.3, 9.4 on pages 106, 108, 112 & 116 of *The Truth About Depression*.

(For a further discussion on the neurobiology of trauma, see *The Truth About Depression,* chapters 7 and 8.)

Based on their experience and understanding of the literature, Read, Perry and colleagues believe that for some adults diagnosed as schizophrenic that their "diathesis," i.e., an underlying vulnerability to the well-documented high sensitivity and response to stress, is in fact a part of the *effects* of the abnormal neurodevelopmental process that evolves during *childhood trauma.* They believe that understanding that these trauma effects (the deficits and abnormalities listed in Table 17.2) are part of a pattern may improve our understanding of several crucial aspects of schizophrenia. These aspects include their *oversensitivity* to *stress, impairments* in *thinking* and *behaving,* and the *link between psychotic* and *dissociative* symptoms.[823]

Bias and Misunderstanding

In trying to sort out this information, a major problem has been that most of the researchers and their financial sponsors have not understood the important link here with trauma. In fact, they have, consciously or unconsciously, often taken any one or more of at least eight actions that lessen or invalidate the relationship between childhood trauma and psychoses, as shown in Table 17.3. The result of this process of denial has been to delay our understanding of the causes of the psychoses in general and schizophrenia in particular by a sizable degree. Indeed, regarding the above-mentioned 33,648 research studies conducted over the last forty years, for every *one* study that addressed the trauma-schizophrenia link there have been *forty-six* on the genetics and *thirty* on the biochemistry of schizophrenia.[823] This is a remarkable discrepancy that biases all results in favor of the biogenetic theory by a ratio 76 to 1.

Unfortunately, the process and results described in the above three paragraphs and two tables are not limited to investigations into the psychoses. Rather, they tend to reflect similar dynamics in our pursuit of knowledge about the causes of the other common and uncommon mental disorders, and some physical ones. Key in this erroneous thinking lies people's tendency to remain locked in a closed-circuit cycle that perpetuates their not considering all possible causes, which is the opposite of real science. In a strange kind of collective "thought disorder" themselves, they appear to be unable to think "outside of the box." In his classic book on the dynamics of scientific revolutions, science historian Thomas Kuhn (1960) described a key characteristic of believers in a dominant scientific paradigm (i.e., belief system): They ask only those questions which confirm the dominant paradigm's central assumptions.[605]

Currently, I see three levels of assumption and investigation about mental illness, as outlined in Table 17.4. Level 1 is the reigning, dominant paradigm today. It assumes that mental illness is predominantly caused by biogenetic origins, and thereby limits its search for them, which results in a limited range and success of treatment. Level 2 reflects a broader, although still somewhat conventional view, that adds the psychological and social to the prior bio-genetic assumption, resulting in a few more treatment and recovery options. Still a small part of the reigning paradigm, they represent the understanding of a sizable number of people, including many health professionals—especially psychologists, social workers and counselors—and people in general who ascribe to this view. Level 3 is represented by a smaller yet sizable and growing number of clinicians and people in recovery, who view the causes, treatment and prevention of mental illness as

Table 17.3. Actions that Lessen Understanding the Relationship Between Childhood Trauma and Psychosis

(Expanded from Read 1997)

Action	Characteristics	Example References
Exclude psychotic patients from trauma research	There is no evidence that psychotics lie about or imagine childhood trauma.	Darves-Bornoz et al. 1995, Read 1997
Don't ask trauma survivors about a history of psychosis	While a minority of researchers did ask, most don't ask this important question. Repeated CT can link with psychotic Sx	Whitfield & Stock 1996, Read 1997, Whitfield et al. 2004
Rely on clinical records only	Clinical records usually underestimate actual trauma histories, & records are not reliable for trauma history	Jacobson et al. 1987, Romanik 1988
Ignore the data	Most books, esp. on psychiatry & psychology, & some reviews (e.g., Beitchman et al. 1992) ignore the data*	Finkelhor 1984, Briere 1992
Reinterpret the data	Advantages & disadvantages here: can help person, but distort the truth re: causal factors in psychosis	Read 1997
Promote another factor	Propose & promote "genetic" or other biologic factors to invalidate/minimize the effect of the named trauma	Read 1997
Use biological model to exclude trauma as causal factor	Ignore fact that trauma causes biomedical changes & problems, claiming that these changes are causal*	Kuhn 1970
Political groups promote biological & ignore trauma	Most parent/family & academic/professional groups, & drug companies, promote & lobby the biological & ignore trauma as a possible important causal factor	Bremner 2002 Whitfield 2003 Stien & Kendall 2003

* Nearly every psychiatry, psychology or other health professional textbook that I have seen focuses on the biological and pays relatively little or no attention to the role of childhood trauma and its effects on psychosis.

involving not only the bio-psycho-social realms, but also as often being trauma-based. This view does not imply that childhood trauma is the only causal factor for the psychoses or other mental illnesses. Rather, it expands the biogenetic and the bio-psycho-social beliefs to consider and address, where it is found, the importance of a history of childhood trauma.

Schizophrenia and the other psychoses are complex illnesses that may be caused by any one or a combination of factors, including genetic or metabolic influences, brain injury at birth and childhood trauma. Unfortunately, we can't yet give someone new genes, nor can we reverse decades-old birth injuries. But for many people with schizophrenia or another psychotic disorder who experienced childhood trauma, we may be able to assist some of them in healing from many of their traumatic effects.

We know that many people with psychoses have one and often more co-morbid conditions, including depression and suicidality, PTSD, substance abuse and chemical dependence. People with these disorders have an increased history of childhood trauma, so that by association, as a kind of circumstantial evidence, we might infer that many people with psychoses may also have a history of childhood trauma. For this reason and from the trauma-illness link summarized in the next chapter, it is worth taking a careful history for the presence of childhood trauma in every person who has a psychotic process or disorder.

History 17.1

Bill was a forty-year-old married engineer, who at age twenty-two, after graduating from college and starting a job, had psychotic symptoms that led him to a psychiatrist who suspected schizophrenia. He lost his job and, in his mid-twenties, moved back with his parents, where he worsened

Table 17.4. Levels of Assumption & Inquiry About the Cause & Treatment of Mental Illness

Deficit	Assumptions and Questions	
3—**Expanded** Bio-psycho-social	What is the evidence for *trauma* in the assumed bio-psycho-social cause? What *relevant* physical, psychological & behavioral markers are present?	What bio-psycho-social interventions will *prevent* or *lessen* the symptoms?
2—**Conventional** Bio-psycho-social	What is the evidence for assumed bio-psycho-social cause? What measurable physical, psychological & behavioral markers are present?	What bio-psycho-social interventions will lessen the symptoms?
1—**Limited** Bio-genetic	What is the evidence for assumed bio-genetic cause? What measurable physical markers are present?	What physical interventions, esp. drugs, will lessen the symptoms?

and was hospitalized for a month on a psychiatric unit. There he was treated with major tranquilizers and "milieu" therapy (i.e., custodial care and brief supportive therapy sessions, still common in our age of "managed care"). The unit staff did not ask him about a possible trauma history, but did give him antipsychotic drugs. He improved enough to return home, only to worsen in a few weeks, necessitating his readmission.

He was again discharged a month later and began seeing a social worker who had an interest in working with schizophrenics. Here he explored his childhood and began to remember enough traumatic experiences that he was referred to me for further evaluation. At that time, he said that he had been physically abused by his father and psychologically abused by his mother and psychotic aunt who lived with his family. At first, he didn't want to believe that this was abuse. He believed that he deserved his father's beatings and his mother and aunt's shame and scorn. He also had a history of using LSD and other psychedelics, smoked cigarettes and at times drank heavily. He fulfilled most of the *DSM* diagnostic criteria for PTSD. I suggested that he stop drinking and smoking, and that he not use any more psychedelic drugs. I referred him to Alcoholics Anonymous and supported his continuation in weekly therapy with the social worker. Two years later he returned to see me and said that he had moved out of his parents' house and found a job, and although he had relapsed several times on alcohol and nicotine, that he had now had almost a year of abstinence from them. He was interested in doing some trauma-focused recovery work in our therapy group, but was conflicted about committing to it. Nonetheless, he joined the therapy group and has remained abstinent from alcohol and nicotine. He continues to take his previously prescribed 5 mg of haloperidol (Haldol) daily, and has begun to grieve about his childhood trauma memories. The group embraced him with his history of schizophrenia and wondered if the disorder was his way of adapting to his trauma and trying to control his pain. He is still working on trusting the group, which the members know and accept.

While not all people with schizophrenia and other psychoses will be so motivated or able to identify their past traumas and then work such a recovery program, some will. In addition to being effective in prevention, it is important that affected people and their clinicians understand the importance of the link between trauma and subsequent psychotic illness, which I will address in the next chapter.

18 PSYCHOSES AND SCHIZOPHRENIA
—CONTINUED

LINK WITH TRAUMA

In spite of the above reservations and difficulties, a fair number of published, peer-reviewed, databased research reports link the psychoses to a history of childhood trauma. I found 67 retrospective studies that were published between 1934 and 2003 that were conducted by independent, internationally dispersed investigators on diverse samples of people, as shown in Table A18.1 of the Appendix, page 368). These evaluated a total of 23,291 childhood trauma survivors and their controls from diverse international populations, which is a large number of people. Their results show the following.

1. Most (58) of the samples evaluated were from clinical populations. Nine were from community samples.
2. The kind and severity of the trauma varied among these studies.
3. Among this large number of people a history of repeated *childhood trauma* is *significantly associated* with *subsequent psychotic symptoms*. Only one study out of the 67 that looked for them did not find significant psychotic symptoms or signs

among survivors of childhood trauma. (Nearly every study that has looked for genetic causes has neglected to look for childhood trauma histories.)

4. Among the childhood trauma survivors, the amount of significant increase in psychotic symptoms, when compared to matched controls, varies and reaches numbers as high as 7.7[651] to 9 times those found among the control samples,[982] all of which indicate a *strong* and highly significant association.

5. While some of these 67 reports did not differentiate significant psychotic symptoms from the specific disorder of schizophrenia, 23 of them did. In addition, the number of studies that found a significant difference in various symptoms and/or signs of schizophrenia and other psychoses were: psychoticism* (13), schizophrenic symptoms (8), hallucinations (6), thought disorder (4), marked paranoia (3), schizoid (2), and delusions (1). There was also a large amount of co-morbidity found among the studies that looked for it.

Index Cases

I found 37 index case studies, wherein people with schizophrenia (mostly) and other psychoses were evaluated for having a history of childhood trauma. Like the retrospective studies above, these were conducted by independent, internationally based investigators on diverse *clinical* population samples (36 studies) and one *community*

---

* *Psychoticism* is a significant and disturbing disconnection from reality, such as bizarre or disoriented thinking, unrealistic expectations of harm or other strange beliefs or sensations that markedly differ from the family or society. At times, this definition can be contrasted with or weighed against creative thinking or behavior, such as Columbus' believing the world was round and not flat, or as Copernicus' and Galileo's believing that the earth was not the center of the universe, in spite of their persuasion to the contrary by reigning authority figures.

sample,[456, 457] and were published from 1963 through 2003. Evaluating 1,562 patients or subjects, all 37 showed a significant relationship between having a diagnosis of a psychotic disorder and a history of repeated childhood trauma, as shown in Table A18.2 in the Appendix on page 374. The findings showed that from 13 to 100 percent of people with schizophrenia or another psychosis reported a history of childhood trauma. While some have questioned it, schizophrenics do not tend to confabulate or lie about their trauma histories.[823] In fact, three example studies found that psychiatric inpatients, including those with psychoses, tend to *underreport* their childhood traumas.[825]

Prospective Studies

Prospective studies are among the most accurate and respected of all study designs, especially when they also use control samples for comparison of their findings. I found four such prospective studies (Table A18.3 on page 377 in the Appendix). One study showed a nine-fold increase in psychosis or significant psychotic symptoms among 52 children with highly critical or psychologically abusive parents, when compared with controls over a five-year follow-up period.[823] Another study compared 82 children who had been traumatized with 295 controls, all of whom were followed for 12 years—a long time for any longitudinal study.[53] The results showed that the traumatized group had significant, multiple psychiatric, psychological and behavioral symptoms and disorders. These disorders included: depression, suicidality, anxiety, self-harm, low self-esteem and psychotic symptoms (Table 18.3). This shows, as have well over 300 other scientific studies, that after their traumas, childhood trauma survivors tend to have multiple debilitating effects, disorders or co-morbidities.

The third study evaluated 5,362 children and followed them for forty years—an extremely long follow-up period. The authors found that those children whose mothers had poor parenting skills (and were also *not* schizophrenic) when the children were four years old were significantly more likely to be schizophrenic as adults.[536] The final one followed 585 children for twelve years and found that those who had been abused (CSA) had significantly more psychotic thinking problems than the controls.[619] These four long follow-ups of from five to forty years on 6,376 people, showed that both psychotic symptoms and schizophrenia are commonly associated with a history of repeated childhood trauma.

Family Studies

I found two studies that looked at the family dynamics of schizophrenia. While there are more, these are examples that show pertinent findings. In the second paragraph on page 173, I described the first of these, which showed that 322 *children* of *schizophrenic mothers* growing up in a *disturbed* or *traumatic* adoptive family were *8.5 times* more likely to develop schizophrenia than those simply having a schizophrenic mother.[1023] In the second, Rodnick and colleagues (1984) found that 65 disturbed (but not psychotic) adolescent children of *highly critical parents* (i.e. their parents were at least psychologically abusing them) were *nine times* more likely to be diagnosed with schizophrenia or a related disorder over the next five years than similarly disturbed adolescents whose parents were not so critical of them (91 percent v. 10 percent). I summarize these reports in Table 18.4 on the next page.

Table 18.4. Schizophrenia & Childhood Trauma:
2 Example Family Studies

Year/Author	Study Characteristics	Schizophrenia	Comments
1984 Rodnick et al.	65 disturbed teens of highly critical parents v. controls	9x more likely to have schizophrenia or related disorder (91% v. 10%)	Parents were at least psychologically abusing
1991 Tienari et al.	322 children of schizophrenic mothers into adoptive families: unhealthy v. healthy	8.5x (i.e., 34% in unhealthy & abusing, v. 4% in healthy adoptive families)	Family dysfunction & trauma had 7x the explanatory power than genetic predisposition. Discussed in Read 2001

Literature Reviews

I found eight literature reviews. Four of these reviewed the genetics and basic neuroscience of mental disorders, including the psychoses. For example, in the first, clinical and research psychologist Mary Boyle reviews the world literature on the genetic evidence for schizophrenia and other psychoses. Her analysis shows serious errors in the methods and data reported in most of these studies. For example, if identical (monozygotic) twins have the same defective genetic DNA material that is claimed to "cause" schizophrenia, we would expect 100 percent of both twin pairs where one twin has schizophrenia to develop it, but at the most, only 35 to 46 percent do. If fraternal (unidentical or dizygotic) twins have half of their twin's DNA material, we would expect 50 percent of their co-twins to develop schizophrenia, but at the most only 11 to 14 percent do. This is hardly convincing evidence in favor of genetic transmission.

In fact, the data argue as much against a genetic cause as they may argue for it. Apparently, few of the twin studies have looked for a childhood trauma history.[562]

In the next analytical review, research psychologist Alvin Pam reviews the literature on the genetic evidence for some of the most common mental disorders, including schizophrenia.[768, 769] He shows several errors in the research methods and data interpretations that have been used and made regarding claims for the genetic transmission of mental illness, which I summarize on page 38 and in Table 4.3 of the prior volume. He suggests that childhood trauma may be an important factor in the genesis of mental illness.

Third, in his book *Blaming the Brain,* neuroscientist Elliot Vallenstein carefully reviews the neuroscientific evidence for claims that mental illness such as depression and schizophrenia are caused by disordered brain chemistry, especially that of the neurotransmitters. When he started the project of extensively reviewing and describing the biological basis of mental illness he had planned to find positive results and to write a positive treatise. Neither happened. He said, "Along the way, I became convinced that it was . . . important to evaluate the evidence and arguments that support the now-prevailing theory that mental disorders are caused by chemical errors that are corrected by drugs. I have concluded that this theory, which is guiding much of clinical practice and our research efforts, is not supported by the evidence and may well be wrong. Yet for reasons that have little to do with science the theory is being pursued relentlessly on a path filled with many dangers."

After his long and thorough search as a neuroscientist, what Vallenstein further concluded was not what he had expected to say: "If . . . it could be convincingly demonstrated that a specific mental disorder is caused by an inherited malfunctioning of some part of the brain, there would be little justification for objecting to calling that condition a medical disease. On the other hand, there are good reasons for objecting if it could be proven that mental disorders are caused by a particular pattern of experiences—what are usually called 'psychosocial variables'—such as lack of nurturance and affection during some critical period of development, exposure to stress and trauma, growing up in a dysfunctional family, being abused, treated as a commodity in a highly competitive, capitalistic society, and an infinite number of other experiences that might adversely affect the developing psyche. Biological and psychosocial factors are so interrelated in mental disorders that they cannot be separated. It is unrealistic, therefore, to take an extreme position on either side of the debate. Moreover, most people recognize that biological and psychosocial factors may have a greater or lesser role in different mental disorders, so there is no logical reason that the same position has to be taken in regard to all such conditions. It is because *we really do not know the cause of any mental disorder* that the debate can be so heated" (my italics).[1042]

Clinical and research psychologist John Read has written extensively on the strong link between repeated childhood trauma and subsequent psychosis. He and his colleagues have carefully reviewed and analyzed the research and clinical literature and their findings agree with those reported by the other scholars summarizd here and in Table 18.5.

These eight extensive and critical literature reviews of the biogenetics of schizophrenia by diverse scientists conclude that there is no firm evidence of a specific or important genetic cause of schizophrenia, and four mention trauma as possible cause (Table 18.5).

Table 18.5. Schizophrenia, Other Psychosis & Childhood Trauma: Associations in Eight *Literature Reviews*

Year/ Author	Study Characteristics	Schizophrenia/ Psychosis	Other Effects of Trauma
1990 Boyle 2000 2nd ed	Literature review & analysis of genetic evidence	Shows errors in methods & data re- genetic claims	Of 15 twin studies (1928–75), for identical twins at best 46% had "schiz" & 11-14% of fraternal twins*
1995 Pam	Literature review & analysis of genetic evidence	Shows errors in methods & data re- genetic claims	Mentions trauma as a possible causal factor. (see Table 4.3 & text on page 40 of TTaD)
1997 Read	Literature review of 30+ articles	↑ association with childhood trauma	Critical analysis & review of bias factors (Table 17.3)
1998 Vallenstein	Literature review of neuroscientific evidence	Shows errors in methods & data re- neuroscientific claims	Mentions trauma as a possible causal factor (see text, page 184)
1999 Barondes et al.	Review of findings in the genetics of psychiatry	Bipolar disorder has a 10% or less genetic evidence	"genetically influenced psychiatric disorders have so far been resistant to analysis"
Joseph (see also book by Joseph 2003)	Overview of the genetic theory of schizophrenia	There is no firm evidence of a specific or important genetic component . . .	. . . Including that for other "mental illness." See page 257 for book overview
2001 Read et al.	Literature review of 230+ articles	↑ association with childhood trauma	Critical analysis & strong evidence for trauma factors
1990-2003 8 Studies	**Extensive, critical literature reviews of the bio-genetics of schizophrenia/ psychosis**	**No firm evidence of a specific or important genetic or other biological cause**	**4 mention trauma as possible cause. Most genetic & neuro-chemistry studies had methods problems**

* If identical (monozygotic) twins have the same genetic DNA material that "causes" schizophrenia, we would expect 100 percent of twin pairs to develop it, but at best 46 percent do. If fraternal (dizygotic) twins have half of the other's genetic DNA material, we would expect 50 percent of the twin pairs to develop schizophrenia, but at best 11–14 percent do. This is hardly convincing evidence in favor of genetic transmission, and in fact it argues as much *against* (as it may argue *for*) a genetic cause for schizophrenia. Apparently, none of the twin studies on psychoses looked for a childhood trauma history.

Summary of Studies

My clinical practice has focused on assisting adults who were traumatized as children, as they try to heal. In that capacity, for one reason or another I have been consulted by few people with a functional (i.e., non-drug or non-physical illness related) psychosis. Because of my lack of working directly with many people with psychoses, I did not expect to find the large amount of evidence that connected the psychoses with a history of childhood trauma. Yet, to my surprise I found what I have described above: 67 retrospective studies, mostly on clinical populations, 37 index case studies, two on the family and four prospective studies, for a total of 110 peer-reviewed and databased published reports on 31,551 people. These studies, in total, showed a strong relationship between psychotic symptoms, the psychoses, including schizophrenia in most cases, and having a history of childhood trauma. I summarize these study results in Table 18.6.

This is remarkable information. The eight example literature reviews strengthened this already impressive relationship, and argue against the predominance of the current biogenetic causal theory. From all of the above data we can estimate the relationships among the potential causal factors in schizophrenia, as shown in the pie chart, Figure 18.1.

These findings are especially important, since they confirm that people with childhood trauma histories commonly develop and manifest psychotic symptoms, and at times they may become schizophrenic or have other psychotic disorders. A lesson to be learned from these data is that *all people with psychotic* symptoms or signs should be initially *screened for a history* of *childhood trauma* and

Table 18.6. Psychosis & Childhood Trauma: Clinical & Community, Prospective, Index Case, Family Studies & Meta-Analyses/Reviews (see tables A18.1–3 on page 368 for details)

Year/Author	Study	Psychoses	Other Trauma Effects
Clinical & *Community* **67 Studies** 1934–2003	23,291 people CT v. Controls	↑ Psychotic symptoms, signs; psychoses, incl. schizophrenia	↑ Co-morbidity Table on page 368
Prospective **4 Studies** 1978–2003	6,376 people Ct v. Controls	↑ Psychotic symptoms & signs, to 5.8x schizophrenia	↓ self-esteem ↑ Co-morbidity Table on page 377
Index Case **37 Studies** 1982–2003	1,562 people with psychosis & their controls	↑ to 100% had CT history	↑ Co-morbidity Table on page 374
Family **Studies** 1984–1991	387 people 2 examples	Trauma is as or more likely to cause psychoses than genetics	Table on page 183
Literature **Reviews** 1990–2001	8 literature reviews & analyses	↑ 4 support trauma link. Little evidence for genetic theories.	↑ Co-morbidity Table on page 186
Summary **110 Studies by** **Independent** **International** **Authors** 1942–2003	**31,551** **CT people** **and** **controls**	↑ **to 7.7x** **Clinical/** **Community;** ↑ **to 5.8x** **Prospective;** ↑ **to 100% CT** **in Index Cases**	↑ **Co-morbidity**

Key: CT=childhood trauma, ↑ =increased

Figure 18.1. Potential Causal Factors in Schizophrenia: from Current Evidence* (see text for details)

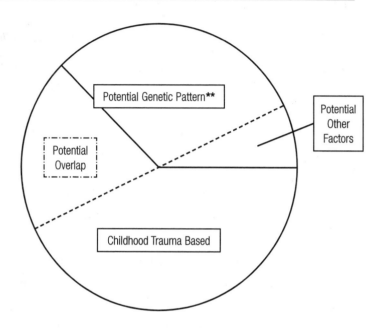

* Biological markers, such as neurotransmitter or structural abnormalities, may be the result of childhood trauma (see text, chapter 7 in the prior book & Table 17.2 in this book). There has been no definitive proof that any of these markers or abnormalities causes schizophrenia, another psychosis or any other common mental disorder.
** Both genes and childhood trauma run in families, and there has been no definitive proof that genetic transmission causes any common or major psychiatric illness.

then *monitored* for it in follow-up when they become more mentally stable. A second lesson may be that, if they are able to tolerate the emotional pain of the work, some people with a psychosis who have a history of childhood trauma *may benefit* from working a *trauma-focused program of recovery.*

RECOVERY AIDS

As health consumers and clinicians, how can we use this compelling information? These data are *as strong* for childhood trauma's being a likely factor, if not a cause, of psychoses—as they are claimed for genetics or a structural defect of the brain. Brain defects commonly *come from* repeated trauma, as I showed in the previous chapter and in more detail in chapters 7 and 8 of the prior volume. It is possible that these data may even be stronger for trauma than these other theories. Currently we assume that the biological model is true and limit our treatment to giving people potent and toxic drugs that often don't work well and that have a lot of uncomfortable and even disabling side effects.[109, 726-730]

Another problem is that most clinicians are not trained or experienced in working with childhood trauma survivors, so they may not know what questions to ask their patients and clients and how to respond to their answers. Treatment and recovery for the psychoses is complex and difficult, similar to that for most of the other disorders discussed throughout this book, but often to a greater degree. Therefore, any of the following statements should be taken with advisement and used only if the total context of the effected person's condition and circumstances may warrant it. For further information and guidelines see, e.g., the American Psychiatric Association treatment summary[17] and the recent Canadian summary.[458]

Drug Treatment

The first step in the process of recovery is to assure an accurate diagnosis, as outlined in Figure 18.2. If the person has schizophrenia or another psychotic illness, and is not functioning normally, they may want to do what they can to stabilize for a time before exploring or addressing any of their possible childhood trauma issues. This is *Stage One* in the total process of recovery (summarized in Table 2.3 on page 20).

There are two main ways to return to stable and normal functioning. The first—and the most commonly used today—is to take an antipsychotic drug in as low a dose as is effective in reducing the unwanted psychotic symptoms and behaviors. But there are *several key problems* here: 1. Most people with a psychosis deny that they have it, and commonly refuse to take the drugs; 2. Like most of the other psychiatric drugs, the anti-psychotics don't work very well, and when they do, they commonly have adverse, bothersome and often toxic effects; 3. These negative effects cause people to stop taking them; 4. Part of these effects are that the drugs numb the person's feelings and awareness of their inner and outer life to varying degrees; 5. These drugs primarily affect the so-called "positive" symptoms (delusions, hallucinations and the like), and not the "negative" ones (depression, fear [anxiety] and other emotional pain); and 6. There is evidence from at least twenty-five published studies that long-term use of these drugs may cause brain damage and disorders such as tardive dyskinesia.* By contrast, in the most severe cases these antipsychotic drugs may help some people by reducing *some* of their bothersome symptoms

---

* Mosher 2002 said, "It is generally held that the antipsychotic drugs are the mainstay of treatment and should, in most cases, be taken for a lifetime. In fact, the data indicate that neuroleptic drug treatment is not usually necessary (especially in persons newly identified as psychotic) if a proper interpersonal environment and social context is provided in alternatives to hospital care. It also appears that drug treatment has resulted in less favorable long-term outcomes than was the case before antipsychotic drugs were introduced. Furthermore, antipsychotic drug treatment is associated with the induction of irreversible brain pathology (resulting in reduced intellectual and abnormal motor functioning) and shortened life expectancy. Pre-neuroleptic drug era long-term follow-up studies indicate that [without drugs] *recovery can not only occur, but is to be expected in the majority of cases.*" (See Mosher's Web site for details: *http://www.moshersoteria.com/litrev.htm*)

Figure 18.2. Psychotic Symptoms:
Flowchart for Decision Making in Recovery

Note: Compassionate social support appears more efficacious long-term than drugs (see text).

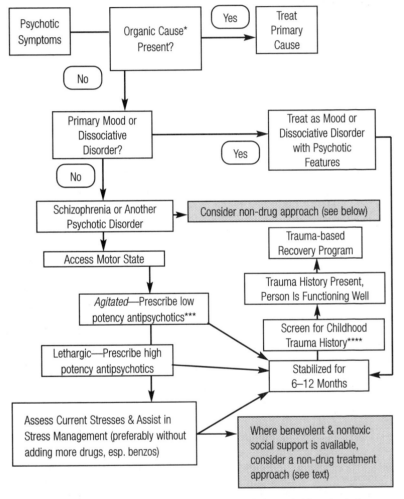

* Organic = a clear physical cause, e.g., alcohol/other drugs, neurological or medical illness (see text).
**Major depression or bipolar disorder, or a dissociative disorder, such as DID (dissociative identity disorder).
***See Table A18.10 on page 378.
****Many trauma survivors authentically forget trauma (dissociative amnesia), or may not be able to accurately name it as having been traumatic. A substantial number of them may eventually remember a serious trauma history.

and thereby may be worth trying in some cases, preferably under the evaluation and supervision of a psychiatrist experienced in using them. Like using antidepressant drugs, this process may take patience while different drugs are tried. While I am not recommending these toxic drugs, I summarize key aspects of the most common ones in Table A18.7 on page 378 of the Appendix.

SAFE SOCIAL SUPPORT, STRESS MANAGEMENT & LIFESTYLE

Non-Drug Treatment

The second way to stabilize is the most difficult and unusual: to help change the person's lifestyle, including their nutrition, drug use and stress management. Most people with a psychosis eat and live in an unhealthy way. A large part of this undertaking is to find what the nineteenth-century psychiatrists Emil Kraepelin and Adolph Meyer suggested for the treatment of depression. This included removal of the person from a negative human environment and submersion into the company of happy people (secure, upbeat, optimistic and safe). Meyer described a related "common sense" psychotherapy, characterized by "kindly, humane overtones and a searching practical use of the patient's life history and current situation . . . [giving] careful attention to the . . . [person's] milieu and how the patient might . . . best be served by it." Meyer also attended to sleep, nutrition, occupational therapy, hydrotherapy, and recreation, following a regime of work, rest and play, socialization and discussion with clinicians.[1090]

While this possibility may be taking a big leap from depression to psychosis, it bears some attention, since some controlled and prospective studies have shown that this kind of care works well for schizophrenics under certain circumstances. Without much difficulty, I found fourteen treatment studies and literature reviews that showed that alternative, non-drug treatment of people with schizophrenia is *as,* or *more* effective than conventional hospitalization and drug treatment, as shown in Table 18.8. For example, in the early 1970s, clinical and research psychiatrist Loren Mosher and colleagues began a social setting, compassionate, and mostly drug-free residential treatment program for schizophrenics who needed acute hospitalization. They found that this kind of treatment was as or more effective than conventional hospital care, and it was cheaper.[726–730] In 1986, psychiatrist John Weir Perry recounted the outcome of a three-year follow-up of eighty people with acute and chronic schizophrenia: ". . . persons on the medication had roughly the same rate of recurrence as the national average in mental hospitals, 73 percent; those off the medication and only on placebo showed only an 8 percent recurrence, a smashing statistic! To boot, the latter demonstrated a constantly upward curve in the profiles measuring their emotional development during that period, in contrast to the plateauing profiles of their counterparts. . . . What I learned from this principally was that one cannot satisfactorily conduct this mode of handling such episodes in a hospital setting, outcomes not withstanding".[789] Perry's subsequent work in a similar San Francisco project produced similar results. He said, ". . . [this second project] was a natural expression of the kindly and humane atmosphere of the culture of that era, one that lasted only a couple of decades or less".[789] The success of this social setting, non-drug approach has been replicated in numerous studies, as shown in Table 18.8. Unfortunately, the availability of these kinds of effective facilities are rare today.

Table 18.8. Alternative Treatments of Schizophrenia: 14 Example Study Results

Year/Author	Study	Result
1975, '78, '95, '99, 2000 Mosher	Prospective data from Soteria studies	Case-controlled: 85–90% of acute & chronic schizophrenics needing hospitalization were returned to community without drug treatment; better results than conventional methods
1981 Braun et al.	Review of outcome data	Alternative treatment programs are needed, as conventional ones are outmoded
1982 Straw	20 study literature review	19/20 found that alternate treatments were as or more effective than conventional hospital care, and were 43% cheaper
Keisler	Extensive review	Alternative care is better and cheaper
1984 Kresky-Wolff et al.	Data from Crossing Place	Showed equal results to hospitalization and drugs, requiring little or no drugs at a lower cost
1986 Perry	80 schizophrenics	Residential, non-drug treatment gave better results, including recurrence rates, than conventional hospitals and drugs (see page 194)
1992, '97 Ciompi et al.	Data from Soteria-Bern	$^2/_3$ of newly diagnosed schizophrenics recovered with little or no drug treatment in 2 to 12 weeks of residential care
1998 Fenton et al.	69 alternative v. 50 hosp. schiz.	Equivalent results, cheaper, much less drug exposure and toxicity
Tuori et al.	10 year follow-up	With comprehensive "need adapted" psychosocial care, drugs are usually unnecessary and may block recovery
2000 Alanen et al.	Finish model of treatment	Rapid in-home family and social network intervention to avoid hospitalization
Lehtinen et al.	2 yr. follow-up	Outcomes were comparable to or better than those treated with drugs. 44% of the randomly assigned received no drug treatment vs. 6% of the controls over 2 years.
1975–2000 14 Studies, International authors	**Data from diverse treatment studies**	**From international settings and authors, all 14 show alternative treatment to be as or more effective than conventional hospital and drug care, and less costly**

Over the course of the illness, many people with schizophrenia and other psychoses learn to control their symptoms, and some may try to explain them to others. Who among the unafflicted could imagine the shaming and threatening voices, inability to see things as real, and marked, disorienting fear and confusion? The truth may be that some other trauma survivors do—although in perhaps less severe and disorienting degrees, and through other manifestations of their wounds.

We can summarize this therapeutic experience as providing the affected person with acceptance, compassionate support and even an agape kind of love—what most psychotic and other mentally ill people have not usually experienced consistently. The movie *A Beautiful Mind,* based on the true story of Nobel laureate John Nash, briefly portrays a spectrum of approaches to assisting people with schizophrenia. Although Nash never loses his hallucinations, he is able to live a fairly full and productive life, including teaching at Princeton University. Nash was likely traumatized as a boy, and his own son developed psychotic symptoms (growing up with a mentally ill parent is a kind of childhood trauma in itself.[328])

Family Assistance

The above reminds us why it is important to pay attention to the *family* of the person with a psychosis, just as is true for other mental illness and addiction. Since there are few supports for family members, using recently published material and sharing of information from the Internet may be helpful (e.g., Health Canada 2002).[458] Also, if support groups for the family are not available in a community, attending Al-Anon meetings may be an unconventional but possibly useful aid, since it promotes a way of coping for the family and friends of alcoholics, who have a similar chronic illness that itself, with no recovery, commonly ends in insanity. Simply apply the psychotic symptoms for the alcoholic symptoms shared in the Al-Anon meetings. It can also be helpful for a family member or, if possible, the affected person to keep a diary of their illness and treatments.[458]

About a fourth of schizophrenics are said to stabilize with anti-psychotic drugs over time, with the remaining three-quarters suffering recurring psychotic symptoms. (This low "success" rate is not what would be expected if these drugs worked well.) Half of the latter 75 percent (i.e., 38 percent of the total) will develop chronic schizophrenia. It is unknown how the positive relating and support fits in this regard, since most communities and many families do not offer the kind of social support described above. Even so, *at best* some 58 percent of people with acute schizophrenia do *not* go on to develop the chronic disease. Ten percent may spontaneously improve after reaching old age. On balance, non-drug alternative treatment may offer as good or better results, since relatively benign long-term outcomes of from 50 to 75 percent full and social recoveries were reported before the neuroleptic drug era. John Modrow, a recovering schizophrenic, has written clearly on this topic.[713a]

Childhood Trauma Work (Stage Two Recovery)

Once the person is stabilized and functioning for a time, they may want to explore whether they experienced childhood trauma, as shown in Figure 18.2. How long their stable time should be may vary according to their individual recovery needs, as well as the facility and experience that the clinician has in assisting people in trauma effects recovery.

Trauma work is usually stressful, and one of its many goals is learning to tolerate emotional pain so that healthy grieving of the ungrieved trauma effects can be completed over time. Since people with schizophrenia are observed to have a greater-than-usual sensitivity and response to stress, this may raise doubts among them and some of their clinicians as to whether a trauma-focused recovery program would be a help and not a hindrance. I have seen countless people with all kinds of disorders—from depression to dissociative identity disorder—work through this kind of recovery. While it is difficult and time-consuming, the kind of stress experienced eventually transforms from *dis*tress to *eu*stress, since the healing grief work nearly always becomes a "good" and releasing form of grief. Based on my experience assisting a small number of people with psychotic disorders and on the literature,[789, 823] I believe that some people may be able to benefit from such healing work. For those clinicians who assist people in this way it may be helpful to all for them to report their results in the clinical literature.

Conventional belief has been that schizophrenia does not respond well to psychoanalysis. A problem here has been that classical psychoanalysis has so often viewed childhood trauma, especially child sexual abuse, as being only a fantasy in the mind of the patient. For a number of reasons, including that nine peer-reviewed, databased studies have shown retrospective reports of child abuse to be nearly always valid (as shown in Table 7.5 on page 70), even among schizophrenics,[823] a trauma-based recovery program generally sees the gist of the trauma as real. While trauma-based recovery uses some helpful techniques from psychoanalysis, it expands it and tends to work well in helping those survivors who have patience to stay engaged in the work. I have used this method for over twenty years with numerous recovering people and have found it to be successful for most who persist with it long term.

19   PHYSICAL ILLNESS

In this book I have focused on the important link between childhood trauma and mental illness. But, directly or indirectly, trauma also hurts the body and it can cause physical illness. In his recent book *Does Stress Damage the Brain?* psychiatrist J. Douglas Bremner said, "Our old distinctions—between mind and brain, psychology and biology, mental and physical—increasingly appear to have no meaning, as science deepens our understanding of how the mind and body function in health and disease."

Until recently, studies involving the effects of childhood abuse have focused on their *mental* health related effects. But researchers have also been attempting to discover what effect a history of child abuse may have on adult survivors' *physical* health. While these may be harder to prove in their association with the abuse, exploring this link can provide additional evidence of the harmful effects of repeated childhood maltreatment.

The results of these investigations have been striking. Since the mid-1980s, a large number of physical ailments have been identified in the medical literature, such as gastrointestinal, respiratory, gynecological, musculoskeletal and neurological problems, that may be related to having a history of abuse. In some cases, the chronic pain endured by some survivors may be the result of physical injuries sustained during childhood or later adult trauma. In others, medical conditions that appear to have no clear organic cause may be an indication of an unrecognized and unresolved trauma history. In still others, trauma causes organ damage indirectly, such as through inducing harmful behaviors, such as heavy drinking, drug using, including tobacco smoking, overeating, lack of exercise, poor nutrition, and other high-risk behavior or lack of self-care—all commonly associated with having a history of childhood trauma.

From a child development perspective, abuse and neglect can have a relatively detrimental effect on a child's body (e.g., height and weight) and its growth. For example, in a seven-year follow-up study, Olivan (2003) evaluated and monitored twenty emotionally abused and neglected toddler-aged boys and found that these traumas significantly inhibited their normal physical growth and development. What is more, *when these traumas were stopped,* their *normal growth resumed.* This is another example of how repeated trauma can harm the body. During the first three years of life, the factors that improve growth are nutrition, environmental conditions, and emotional treatment. Prolonged deprivation from repeated trauma gives rise to the pediatric problem called "failure-to-thrive," better defined as "growth and developmental delay of psychosocial origin." This delay of growth can be totally or partially reversible when the abuse stops.[761]

THE EVIDENCE

As well as damaging the nervous system, repeated childhood and subsequent trauma also seriously harms the body. There is current literature to fill several additional chapters on the toxic

Table 19.1. Physical Illness from Childhood & Later Trauma

Disease by Organ System	Example problems*	Example References** (see other tables)
Cardiovascular	Stroke 2.4x, coronary heart disease 2.2x, hypertension	Cunningham et al. 1988; Leserman et al.; Felitti et al. 1998, Mann 2000; Russek & Schwartz 1997
Gastrointestinal	Hepatitis/jaundice 2.4x, Psychosomatic pain Functional & organic	Kaufman et al. 1954; Felitti 1991; Cunningham et al.; Leserman et al.; Felitti et al. 1998; Baccini et al. 2003
Pulmonary	COPD 3.9x, Asthma	Felitti 1991; Cunningham et al.; Leserman et al.; Felitti et al. 1998
Endocrine	Diabetes 1.6x	Cunningham et al. 1988; Felitti et al. 1998
Infectious disease	Sexually transmitted disease 2.5x, urinary tract infections	Felitti et al. 1998; Springs & Fredrich 1992
Neurological/ Psychiatric	Seizures, headaches, mental illness	Shearer et al. 1990; Cunningham et al. 1998; Golding 1999; Scaer; Barber & Davis 2002. See also refs this & prior book
Orthopedic/ Rheumatologic	Broken bones 1.6x, chronic back, trunk, neck pain	Sarno 1991; Felitti et al. 1998; Krantz & Ostergren 2000; McCauley et al. 1997
Gynecological	Chronic pelvic pain, dysparunia, recurrent infections	Moeller et al. 1993; Walker et al. 1992; Cunningham et al. 1988; Leserman et al. 1998; Cameron 2000
Chronic pain	Chronic pain problems, headaches, jaw pain, acute chest pain	Felitti 1991; Walker et al. 1992; Goldberg et al. 1994; Cameron 2000
General medical problems/Other	Cancer 1.9x, severe obesity 1.6x, PTSD, fatigue, fibromyalgia, increased surgeries with no organic disease found, somatization	Browning & Boatman 1977; Beck & van der Kolk 1987; Arnold et al. 1990; Felitti 1993; McCauley et al. 1997; Moeller et al. 1993; Felitti et al. 1998; Duncan 1999; Hulme; Kendal-Tackett et al. 2000; Romans et al. 2002; Baccini et al.; Hastings & Kantor 2003

* "x" = times or odds ratios.
** Also see several other references in Tables 19.2 and 19.3.
The conclusion of the totality of these studies is to obtain a thorough childhood and later trauma history in all patients or clients who present with any medical or psychiatric complaints or problems.
Physical illness is also frequently co-morbid with mental illness.

effects of stress and trauma on the body. Here, I will summarize a few key findings. Either indirectly, through neurological and/or vascular damage, or directly on the various organs, undue stress and trauma in children and adults takes a significant toll (Table 19.1). It is especially harsh on the cardiovascular, hormonal and musculoskeletal systems, significantly contributing to heart disease, high blood pressure, arthritis and related illnesses. I have never seen a patient with chronic fatigue syndrome or a chronic pain condition (non-accident-related) who grew up in a healthy family. In his important book *The Body Bears the Burden,* clinical and research neurologist Robert Scaer has described the common link between chronic pain and other neurological problems and childhood trauma.[921]

Orthopedic surgeon John Sarno has suggested that through vaso-constriction of the microcirculation of blood to the ligaments, childhood trauma causes musculoskeletal pain syndromes of all sorts, including common back and neck pain problems. He calls this phenomenon "tension myositis syndrome" or TMS.[911, 912] Cardiologist Samuel Mann has shown that childhood trauma can be a major contributor to hypertension.[677] These clinicians and researchers and others have reported a statistically significant relationship between childhood and later trauma and subsequent physical illness. I summarize these according to diseases that involve organ systems in Table 19.1.

In the next two tables (A19.2 and A19.3 on page 380 in the Appendix) I list these links between trauma and physical illness in more detail. It is thus likely that many chronic illnesses, especially psychosomatic or functional ones, are closely tied to—if not often caused by—repeated childhood and sometimes ongoing trauma. What evidence is there for this link? A summary follows.

Retrospective Studies

I found 38 studies on 50,109 people that were published from 1984 to 2003 that documented a significant association between childhood trauma and physical illness (also called somatic illness or "somatization"). These 38 studies were retrospective ones conducted on clinical and community samples. They all showed a significant increase of somatic symptoms and medical problems among survivors of childhood trauma when compared with their matched controls. Indeed, these studies reported a risk factor for the trauma survivors as being from 1.6 to 23 times those for the controls for having physical symptoms and/or disorders (Table A19.2).

These risk factor figures are not just large. They vary from significant (1.6) to large (e.g., 3.9 in the Felitti and colleagues 1998 ACE study) to astounding (23 in the Walker and colleagues 1992 study). This means that these multiple and independent researchers, studying diverse samples of people using different study methods, came to the same or a very similar conclusion. That conclusion is that having a history of repeated childhood trauma is significantly and strongly associated with the likelihood of having serious physical or somatic symptoms and/or one or more physical or medical disorders subsequent to the trauma.

Prospective Studies

I also found eleven published prospective studies that reported similar results as the retrospective ones described above. Prospective studies are generally more reliable. Rather than representing a "snapshot" of associations among two or more variables, they instead provide us with a series of snapshots—almost like a primitive kind of movie—of the same variables. The time span over which these 11 studies were conducted ranged from two to thirty-five years, as shown in Table A19.3 in the Appendix. In epidemiological and medical research, this many years is a long time, and tells us much more than conventional retrospective one-time studies. Their sample size is also large. It totaled 8,264 childhood trauma survivors and their controls.

The results of these prospective studies were essentially the same as for those of the retrospective studies. They found a significant increase in somatic, physical, or medical problems among childhood trauma survivors when they were compared with people without such a history. They also found a significant increase of one or more mental illnesses to be present with the physical illnesses, as shown in Table A19.3. The common presence of PTSD in those studies, where it was looked for, also underscores the theory that childhood trauma (which usually caused the PTSD) can also result in later mental and/or physical illness.

Index Case Studies

I also found sixteen index case studies that were published between 1989 and 2003. These looked at 2,779 physically ill or somatizing patients and compared them with their controls. Every one of these showed a significant increase that linked them to having a history of repeated childhood trauma and physical illness, as shown in Table A19.4 in the Appendix on page 386.

Summary of Studies

These results are not from a small number of studies conducted on a small number of people. Rather, the 38 retrospective studies included 50,107 childhood trauma survivors and their controls. The

Table 19.5. Somatization, Physical Illness & Childhood Trauma: Clinical & Community, Prospective, Index Case Studies, & Literature Reviews*

(see Tables A19.2–4 on page 380–6 for details)

Year/Author	Study	Somatization	Other Trauma Effects/ Full table page
Clinical/ Community **38 studies** 1984–2003	50,109 people CT v. controls	↑ to 1.6 to 23x medical & surgical problems	↑ Co-morbidity Table on page 380
Prospective **11 studies** 1992–2002	8,264 people CT v. controls	↑ Somatic & medical problems	↑ Co-morbidity Table on page 384
Index **16 studies** 1989–2003	2,779 people with physical illness/ somatization & their controls	↑ to 3.8x	↑ Co-morbidity Table on page 386
Summary **65 studies by Independent International Authors** 1942–2003	**60,456 CT people and controls**	**↑ to 23x Clinical/Community** **↑ to 75% Prospective** **↑ to 3.8x CT in Index Cases**	↑ Co-morbidity

* **Key:** CT = childhood trauma, ↑ = increased, X = times (indicates risk factor)

11 prospective studies included 8,264 such people and the 16 index case reports included 2,779 people, for a total of 65 studies on 61,150 subjects. While these studies are not as large in number and sample size as the ones on, for example, depression, and on alcohol and other drug problems, they nonetheless are substantial, and their results call for more such investigations on people with physical disorders of all sorts. They also underscore the importance of taking a *careful trauma history,* initially and ongoing, *from every person* who comes for assistance with any mental, emotional or physical problem.

HOW TRAUMA MAY CAUSE PHYSICAL ILLNESS

How might childhood trauma cause physical illness? In chapters 8 and 9 on the neurobiology of trauma in the prior volume, I described how repeated childhood abuse and neglect causes brain damage and an associated disruption and dysregulation of the hormonal and neurotransmitter systems. Through these and other mechanisms, repeated childhood trauma also commonly causes PTSD, described in chapters 2 and 3. Thus, by direct and indirect damage to the brain and nervous system, hormonal and neurotransmitter systems, and ultimately the cardiovascular and other organ systems, combined with PTSD (which is a condition of disordered stress responses), these toxic effects of trauma eventually take their toll on the body.

We can conclude, possibly with a fair degree of accuracy, that repeated trauma brings about a chronically disordered stress response, often resulting in outright PTSD or complex PTSD. This then leads to the occurrence of a significant increase in mental and physical illness, which then feeds back upon and further aggravates the disordered stress response, as shown in Figure 19.1. Others and I believe that

Figure 19.1. The Psychobiology of Repeated Childhood Trauma

(adapted & expanded from De Bellis 2002)

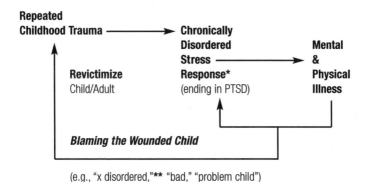

(e.g., "x disordered,"** "bad," "problem child")

* As described in De Bellis 2002, Bremner 2002 & others.
** e.g., "anxiety disorder," "bipolar disorder," "ADHD," or other psychiatric label(s)

repeated trauma in the form of *revictimization* or *retraumatization* plays a crucial role in the genesis of this physical illness.

THE ROLE OF REVICTIMIZATION

This pathogenic process is not limited to causing damaging physical changes. Rather, at its base the trauma process is carried out primarily through social and especially familial interactions. Without other humans to abuse and neglect children and each other, the only other traumas are accidents and events such as earthquakes and similar natural disasters. The *repetition* is not carried out through isolated or mysterious events. Rather, it occurs in the original traumas themselves—plus by two additional ways:

1. *intergenerationally* (a more likely explanation than "genetics" for the "runs in families" observation about mental and some physical illness), and 2. *psychodynamically* (since after the abuser is gone, the victim commonly continues unconsciously to inflict upon themself the same trauma as their abuser did).

This *repetition process* continues and builds as it takes on an insidious guise of *scapegoating* the *traumatized child* for having the very effects that the abusers have enacted or otherwise projected onto them. In a series of strange maneuvers, the parent-abusers blame the now-wounded child for having its problems—which they usually contend is also *causing* the family's problems. To survive, the child takes on this blame (discussed further on page 67 in the prior volume). And to punish the child for being "the problem," the parents and others then abuse and neglect the child again.

The regular repetition of the trauma conditions the nervous system and body to react abnormally—either in a *hypersensitive* or *hyperactive* manner or with *numbness,* which may fluctuate back and forth at any time. These two extremes are hallmark symptoms of PTSD.[247–249] Eventually, this entire toxic process results in neurological and other physical bodily damage. There is substantial documentation in the scientific literature for the existence and significance of this retraumatization.

The Evidence for Revictimization

I found thirty-eight published studies that document this egregious part of the toxic process of childhood trauma called revictimization or retraumatization (Table A19.6 on page 388 of the Appendix). Thirty-seven of these were retrospective studies and one was an eight-year prospective study, all conducted on clinical or community populations that totaled 12,694 childhood trauma survivors and controls. These thirty-eight independent researchers, or teams of them, each found a significantly increased incidence and prevalence of revictimization later in their life among the childhood trauma survivors. In addition, I found four reviews of the child abuse literature that also reported revictimization as being a significant and important effect of childhood trauma (Table A19.7). This increase in retraumatization was reported to have occurred from a moderate to a very high degree. There was also a high degree of co-morbidity, as shown in these tables.

Revictimization/retraumatization is usually experienced and learned inside the family, and is nearly always eventually associated with a low self-esteem, which comes from the repeated trauma. If I believe that I am bad and unworthy, then I will tend to more easily let others mistreat me. Whether the assaults are continued in childhood, adolescence or later in adulthood, the fact that they are *repeated* is what drives and continues the toxic and pathologic process of trauma and its hurtful and damaging effects on the victim's body, mind and spirit.

Stopping the Repeated Trauma

The first step in recovery is to stop the trauma and its repetitions. In the case of the *child* victim, usually an *adult has to intervene* for them. If no adult has intervened and yet they know of the abuse or neglect, they become part of the process of trauma. They are *co-abusers,* or *enablers* of the continued maltreatment.[1089, 1090, 1092, 1093] To intervene, the child or adult has to be able to *name* the assaults, whether psychological, physical or sexual, as constituting *abuse, trauma* or *neglect.* If they can't accurately name it, it may be hard to stop it. Once having named it, to stop it will likely require the setting of a healthy boundary between the abuser and the victim.[1094] For further dynamics, and treatment options and principles, please see references 1089, 1090 and 1094–1096).

*   *   *

The following history may serve as an example:

History 19.1

Jane was a forty-four-year-old woman who was referred to me by a gastroenterologist for a trauma psychology evaluation. Her chief complaint had been chronic intermittent difficulty swallowing (dysphagia) and occasional gagging. Over the past fifteen years, she had been evaluated with three complete medical histories and physical examinations, one of which was by her referring physician. Over the course of that time she also had two upper gastrointestinal barium X-ray series, a barium swallow and two gastroscopic examinations—the most recent also done by her referring physician. She had also been prescribed various medications over this time, including antidepressant and benzodiazepine sedative drugs. None had helped her symptoms of difficulty swallowing.

I took a trauma history, and within twenty minutes she began to cry. She said that as a child she had been forced to perform oral sex on her stepfather, and later, on her older brother. Both of her abusers had threatened to harm her if she told, and her stepfather said he would kill her mother if she told. She had never told anyone about this trauma, including her internists and her referring gastroenterologist. She said that her mother may have known about the abuse but didn't protect her from it. I saw her for several more psychotherapy sessions, and recommended that she join a trauma-focused therapy group to further process the effects of her trauma. She declined joining the group, but said that her symptoms had improved enough for her to live a more tolerable life.

Jane's story is an example of but one way that physical illness can develop from childhood trauma. It also illustrates how physical illness may represent a kind of disguised effect of childhood trauma. Most cases are not this simple. Indeed, often patients will prefer not to talk about these kinds of painful experiences, or through the process of dissociative (traumatic) amnesia may have forgotten that they happened.* Fortunately for her, her referring physician was also a trauma survivor whom I had treated in the past for the effects of severe physical and psychological abuse by his parents, and he was becoming more aware of the physical effects of trauma.

History 19.2

Jill was a sixty-year-old woman who has gone through several sequences of recovery (page 119). She was physically, emotionally and psychologically abused throughout her childhood by her mother (who was chemical dependent, depressed and anorexic). At age thirty-two, Jill was pushed into a swimming pool without warning and sustained an injury to her lumbar spine. She saw an orthopedist two weeks later for

---

*It is usually difficult to recognize a person from their *outward appearance* as having experienced repeated childhood trauma. Other than knowing that some 60–75 percent of people in general have endured such a history, there are few visible findings that suggest it. From the physical or mental illness perspective, I have found over the years some clues or "red flags" that may suggest a person's having had a significant history of childhood trauma: 1) the person has a chronic functional (non-organic) or psychosomatic illness, 2) they are obese, 3) they have a "thick" chart or medical record (exceptions: some with severe congenital debilitating diseases, such as cystic fibrosis, sickle cell anemia, etc. although these may also be abused or neglected as children), 4) they are a cigarette smoker, 5) they wear more than three rings on their fingers, 6) they have tattoos/body piercings (excluding ears), 7) they have any of the common mental disorders discussed in this book. These are only some of the outward manifestations of the effects of repeated childhood trauma. Even so, the presence of any of these findings raises the likelihood of the person's having a history of childhood trauma, for which taking a careful and patient trauma history is warranted. But most trauma survivors have none of these potential indicators, and we need to take a careful history over time to begin to discover this important finding.

increasing pain and over a three-year period was hospitalized five times for traction, nerve blocks and, finally, a spinal fusion surgery, after which she spent six months in a body cast.

She recently reviewed her experiences: "Five years ago I was assaulted, which was reminiscent of my push into the pool twenty years earlier. Both times I felt like I did when my mother used to push me—I lost control of my body and was forced to try to keep my legs below me and my body somehow balanced. I was flooded with the feeling of helplessness and knew that when my body landed I was about to be hit by my mother again (even though I knew she had been dead for four years).

"My first experience of being pushed into a swimming pool took me three catastrophic years to recover from. That second experience was some twenty years later after much therapy and healing work. I picked myself up and moved to safety. I spent four days recovering and it was an amazing process. I had flashbacks almost immediately. My heart raced and I heard a voice telling me that I was to blame and that I was worthless, which my mother had told me. My muscles became tight and my physician gave me a low dose of Valium, which I took for three days. I wrote down everything I was experiencing in the flashbacks, and many times my husband held my hand as I told him what I was feeling. On the fourth day I was able to do intense anger bat work, not only screaming at my assailant, but also at my mother, and my father for not protecting me. I believe I was able to recover so quickly the second time because I was more aware of my inner life and allowed my body to bring up and act out whatever was happening. As a child I had to hold it all in, and not react at all. Now I know enough about PTSD that I could honor my feelings and needs."

Commentary by Robert Scaer, M.D., author of *The Body Bears the Burden:* Jill's recovery from trauma shows some important examples of how the brain organizes, stores in memory and structures the physical responses of the body. These concepts include helplessness, cue-related conditioning and the recapitulation of old reflexive somatic responses to trauma.

The initial strain injury to her lower back occurred after having experienced repeated childhood trauma by her mother, which included physical abuse (hitting and pushing), and emotional abuse (making her feel worthless and helpless). When she was pushed into the pool, her body's natural defensive responses included bracing and self-protective postures that replicated similar defensive acts related to her own child abuse.

The post-operative placement in a body cast replicated Jill's basic sense of helplessness, a condition that promotes further traumas. This state no doubt perpetuated the post-traumatic spinal bracing response. When she was assaulted and robbed some twenty years later her response was again feeling helpless that evoked the memory of her mother's physical abuse, and again provided the physical cues already present in procedural memory for her to be revictimized.

Each of these sequential life events enhanced and solidified her conditioned motor response to the old somatic cue and promoted freeze-helplessness and chronic pain.

Fortunately, through her learning during the stages of recovery, she had learned about unconscious responses to threat. She became able to access her physical responses to these threats (racing heart, muscle bracing) as well as painful flashbacks without freezing or dissociating. Finally, through her anger bat work, she was able to gain empowerment and to dispel her chronic helplessness, leading to meaningful healing and insight. This in turn removed the necessity for the survival brain to protect her from threat by extinguishing the old, conditioned bracing reflex responses to threat, and resulted in disappearance of her spinal pain and the frequent reactivation of her PTSD.

CONCLUSION

All too often, health care professionals do not ask about a history of abuse, and for legitimate reasons, survivors do not mention it. When this happens, a series of diagnostic missteps are set into motion, resulting in additional visits to physicians' offices, emergency departments or hospitals, inaccurate or incomplete diagnoses, treatments that do not work, and frustration on the part of providers and the patients alike—that never seems to end or stop causing us pain, dysfunction and money. One analysis, for example, of the cost of health services provided to adult survivors of child sexual abuse notes that trauma survivors visit physicians' offices far more than those who haven't been abused. According to these data the costs associated with such additional office visits were estimated at $2.8 billion yearly in 1993. Just as occurs with addictions, it costs us a lot of energy, time and money *not* to treat and prevent child abuse and neglect.

20 THE DRUGS DON'T WORK WELL

Psychiatrist David Healy and his colleagues recently reported the first results of a study in North Wales on a population that has been stable for over 100 years regarding their numbers, age, cohorts, ethnic mix and rurality. It showed that since the introduction of the modern psychiatric drugs in psychiatry that there has been a fifteen-fold increase in the rate of admissions to psychiatric inpatient hospitals, and a three-fold increase in the rate of forced psychiatric hospital admissions. It also showed that people with bipolar disorders have relapsed sooner and more often. This is a remarkable study. Overall, patients with all psychiatric conditions now appear to spend a greater amount of time in a psych hospital than they would have fifty or 100 years ago. These conditions have worsened to these degrees despite the availability of supposedly effective and even prophylactic drug treatments. These findings are incompatible with drug treatments' being effective in practice for a majority of the patients.[468]

Most psychiatric drugs don't work well. For example, in the prior volume I reviewed a number of reasons why antidepressant drugs (ADPs) don't work adequately for most people with depression.

The success rate for these drugs ranges from one-third to two-thirds of all depressed people who take ADP drugs, although that success is too often short-lived. This means that for the other one-third to two-thirds, ADP drugs don't work sufficiently well for them, if at all. But it is not just ADPs. Other drugs that are commonly used to treat mental disorders tend not to work well either. Some of the reasons for their low success rates include the following clinical and political observations and concerns.

CLINICAL OBSERVATIONS

1) Antidepressant drugs are not specific for depression. They have a "shotgun" effect whereby other symptoms and neural systems are affected. This fact is also related to the next disadvantage.

2) Like most other psychiatric drugs, ADPs have a high number and frequency of toxic effects, which the drug industry has downplayed for decades by calling them "side effects."

3) Of those patients who are prescribed ADPs, 30 percent never get their prescription filled, and of those who do, another 40 percent stop taking the drug within from one to three months—primarily due to these toxic effects, such as weight gain, anorgasmia, oversedation or overstimulation.[56] Other psychiatric drugs often have similar drawbacks.

4) Drug companies tend to exaggerate the successes of their psychiatric drugs. Of course, the drugs that they promote are those for which they still hold the patent for exclusive rights to market and sell. Drug companies almost never market drugs for which they no longer hold a patent.

POLITICAL CONCERNS

5) To sell their drugs, they often first market the disease, for which they then have a more fertile field in which to promote their drugs. Drug companies have followed this pattern for decades with depression, and more recently with anxiety disorders (see page 220), bipolar disorder, ADHD/ADD, and for less common conditions as premenstrual dysphoric disorder (PMDD).

6) To help promote the acceptance of these disorders, drug companies have commonly hired psychiatrists, medical school faculty, and public relations firms to study, teach about and promote these disorders and their drugs (see also page 242). They have also financially subsidized seemingly independent mental health organizations, which then advocate for their disorders and drugs without disclosing the probable payola. Some of these conflicts of interest have been attributed to *Children and Adults with ADD* (CHADD), the *National Alliance for the Mentally Ill* (NAMI), the *National Institute of Mental Health* (NIMH), and the *American Psychiatric Association* (APA), to name a few.

7) In spite of all of the above, the required FDA-controlled clinical trials for their drugs' efficacy tend to be not only too short in duration (e.g., from only five to eight weeks), but the drug companies and their paid researcher/authors often manipulate the study design or research methods and their reporting to make their drugs look more successful. These distortions often end up providing the public and their clinicians with misinformation about both the disorders and the drugs,[461, 467–469, 888] which I detail below.

8) Part of the misinformation is to deny or minimize the toxic effects of many of their drugs. An example includes a long pattern of denying the fact that the benziodiazepine sedatives (e.g., those with trade names of Valium, Xanax, Ativan and the like) were *highly addicting,* including having an often severe and *prolonged withdrawal* syndrome. More recently they have denied and minimized the existence of similar bothersome withdrawal syndromes for ADPs[692, 697] and some of the antipsychotic drugs and "mood stabilizers," such as gabapentin (Neurontin).

9) The recently required financial disclosures by speakers and authors in psychiatry has revealed that most of these are paid by numerous drug companies for various reasons, which indicates a clear *conflict of interest* that is reflected in their imparted information.[73, 966a] The American Psychiatric Association also receives a substantial financial contribution from the drug industry, giving us a new slant on the term "drug money."

10) Finally, they routinely pay politicians for their votes on laws that increase their income and power. The drug industry's political lobbying power in Washington, D.C. and beyond has been especially influential in obtaining a number of pro "big-pharma" advantages, including the recent ability to market their drugs directly to the public over television. Such TV ads bypass the physician and invade and distort the integrity of the physician-patient relationship. The drug industry has also lobbied the close to $1 trillion Medicare drug entitlement law into existence. Now TV ads tell vulnerable seniors what drugs to take, big pharma gets richer, and we taxpayers foot the bill.

These observations and concerns may be only the tip of the iceberg.

Further Political Concerns: Drug Marketing

As a physician who has been both outside and inside the loop of drug politics, I have noticed several concerns about how the drug industry today is marketing and selling their wares. Drug companies are primarily in the business of making money, not saving lives. In that sense they're no different from the automotive, food or entertainment industries, which in general also have little interest in people's health or welfare. Their bottom line, too, is making money. A major problem is that today the drug industry has become inappropriately involved in educating and influencing physicians, other clinicians, and people in general about what mental illness is and how it is best treated. Some forty years ago medical education was given by medical schools, in post-graduate training, and by appropriately organized professional groups, all of which had little input from the drug industry. The basic and continuing medical education system was essentially independent. Since then there has been a gradual and subtle but strong encroachment by the drug companies, which have taken on a progressively increasing role of educating health professionals, especially psychiatrists and other physicians, about the nature of mental illness and how to treat it.

Because of the above, throughout this and the prior book, where appropriate, I have pointed out examples of the reasons that it is not only inappropriate for the drug companies to be "educating" us to this extent, but that it is also a clear and major conflict of interest that translates to a lack of trust and to a possible toxic monopoly (in the practice of law, this kind of behavior is sometimes called "undue influence"). A recent editorial in the medical journal *The Lancet* said, "[the drug] industry's ubiquitous influence has corrupted the integrity of medical research and the scientific literature upon which scientific research is built".[614] It has done so by paying or otherwise manipulating researchers and authors to speak in favor of their drugs. In addition, due to the fact that *government agencies* such as the FDA and its equivalents in other countries are commonly *enmeshed with the drug companies* and the *academics* that research and write about mental illness and its treatment, they are increasingly unable to objectively monitor and when necessary restrict the drug companies or restrain them to protect the public.[73, 215, 469, 697] Scientists who conduct the research are too often being unduly influenced by the drug industry, as are some bioethicists (who are supposed to watch and help them be honest).[652, 942] This escalating and precarious situation is similar to the fox guarding the hen house. Finally, many otherwise reputable professional associations, such as the American Psychiatric Association, are increasingly funded by drug companies, and thereby are possibly losing their objectivity.

This continuing stream of medical education, which includes the subtle influence of drug advertisements in medical and psychiatric journals and more recently in the popular press, keeps the clinicians' focus on prescribing their drugs. They also commonly influence the APA's diagnostic manual (the DSM) committees to include disorders so that their drugs can fit into their drug development and marketing plans. An example follows.

MARKET THE DISEASE, THEN THE DRUGS

In 1989, generalized anxiety disorder (GAD) was said to be uncommon, found in only about 1 percent of the population. To sell their drug, a frequent pattern is for a *drug company* to first *sell the disease* or disorder, which psychiatrist David Healy has documented to have happened with selling depression as a common disorder and then pushing antidepressant drugs[461, 467, 469] (see, e.g., pages 133–140 of *The Truth About Depression*). This is what GlaxoSmithKline appears to have done with GAD to help sell their drug Paxil (paroxetine).[597] Originally approved by the FDA as an antidepressant, Paxil still sold less than its major competitors Prozac (fluoxetine) and Zoloft (sertraline). To boost its sales, GSK hired the international public relations firm Cohn and Wolfe to help them market GAD as being a much more common and painful disorder (e.g., they upped the accepted 1 percent figure for GAD in the general population to 13 percent), while they ran clinical trials on their drug Paxil as an anti-anxiety agent.[597]

Typically, the drug company pays the PR firm and others to make and deliver a "disease awareness campaign," focusing on a mild psychiatric condition such as GAD, with a proposed large pool of potential sufferers. Then they pay prominent doctors to affirm the malady's proposed ubiquity to both the public and to clinicians at continuing medical education events.[597] They also pay organized "patient groups" to present patients who tell dramatic stories on TV spots and place ads promoting the disorder. Journalist Brendan Koerner gives us an example: "By early 1999 the PR firm [Cohn and Wolfe] had created a slogan, 'Imagine Being Allergic to People,' and wallpapered bus shelters nationwide with pictures of a dejected-looking man vacantly playing with a teacup. 'You blush, sweat, shake—even find it hard to breathe,' read the copy. 'That's what social anxiety disorder feels like.' The posters made no reference to Paxil or GlaxoSmithKline; instead, they bore the insignia of a group called the Social Anxiety Disorder Coalition and its three nonprofit members, the American

Psychiatric Association, the Anxiety Disorders Association of America, and Freedom from Fear. But the coalition was not a grassroots alliance of patients in search of a cure. It had been cobbled together by SmithKline Beecham and Cohn & Wolfe handled all media inquiries on behalf of the group".[597]

GlaxoSmithKline thus recently positioned Paxil as an antianxiety drug, even though drug makers already knew for decades that most *antidepressant* drugs also had *antianxiety* properties.[461, 469] But due to a more promising market for depression in the 1980s and fearful of associating their antidepressants with the addicting benzodiazepine antianxiety drugs, drug makers chose to market both depression and their new "antidepressant" drugs instead.[461, 469] Paradoxically, and not widely known, Paxil and other selective serotonin reuptake inhibitors (SSRIs) also can and often do cause or aggravate anxiety.

Originally approved only for the treatment of depression, the SSRIs are unfortunately now being marketed and prescribed for a wide array of previously obscure afflictions. Some of these include: GAD, social anxiety disorder, social phobia, premature ejaculation (drug companies hide this one, in part since it is the SSRIs' known *toxicity* on normal sexual functioning that delays ejaculation), premenstrual dysphoric disorder, obsessive compulsive disorder, as well as the more common PTSD. This strategy—marketing existing drugs for new uses—makes even more money for the drug companies, since they have fewer hoops to jump through in far less time than they would to get FDA approval for a new drug.[469, 470a, 597] And the health insurance industry, under the guise of managed "care," supports these kinds of drug treatments over the equally or more effective but often more expensive psychotherapy. A problem is that health insurance companies may also have inappropriate ties with the drug companies, which can be called a conflict of interest, as a recent expose uncovered.[363]

CONFLICTS OF INTEREST

The two forces that help sell drugs are thus 1) selling the disease first, then 2) vigorously marketing the drug.[469, 597] Unfortunately for the consumer, the drug industry does not always act in their best interest. In addition, drug companies pay experts to promote their drugs. For example, Dr. Robert Spitzer who headed the 1980 DSM committee that recommended GAD as a disorder was also paid by drug companies to research drug treatments for anxiety disorders,[597] a now-common pattern about which a growing number of people are also calling a *conflict of interest*. (This information is not intended to target Dr. Spitzer, but rather to inform about the dysfunctional system that enables such undue influence.) In this regard, researcher and author Justin Bekelman and his colleagues at Yale University School of Medicine conducted a meta-analysis on thirty-seven published studies on conflicts of interest in biomedical research. They found that these often unethical financial relationships are widespread among the drug industry, researchers, and medical schools. They reported that drug industry payments were *highly significantly associated* with *pro-industry conclusions* (by an odds ratio of 3.6 times, or increased by 360 percent over that from government or non-sponsored research). They also found restrictions on both data-sharing and the publication of negative results.[73] Other authorities have expressed similar concerns, some of which I discuss further on page 242 of this, and in the prior volume (on pages 20, 26–7, 122–8, 133–5 and 140–2).

These above kinds of reports and patterns have usually been kept from the public awareness, and they are just beginning to be published in the clinical literature, such as the *Journal of the American Medical Association, The Lancet* and the *New England Journal of Medicine,* in a limited fashion. Additional information that is often withheld or minimized includes that, just as for depression, SSRIs *don't work well* for many of these other mental disorders and that these drugs have bothersome and often *toxic side effects,* including a painful and often disabling withdrawal syndrome, similar to addicting drugs such as alcohol, opiates and the benzodiazepine sedatives.

Another conflict of interest may occur when physicians allow drug companies to place flyers that promote their drugs in their waiting rooms. This is an insidious and particularly invasive kind of marketing technique, and can be stopped if physicians don't allow it in their practices. And drug companies continue to pay physicians in indirect ways for this favor.[966a] An equally pernicious but farther-reaching behavior is the government's allowing drug ads, which are often inacurate and misleading, to be aired on television.[215]

One of the most harmful effects of focusing on the treatment of mental illness by using drugs alone is that doing so may distract the clinician and the patient from bringing to light a possible history of significant childhood and later traumas and stressors. But there is strong evidence in the clinical literature for the reality of a statistically significant link between trauma and anxiety disorders, which I summarize throughout this and the prior book.

I outline some of these common problems in the politics of psychiatric drug marketing and selling in Figure 20.1 on the next page.

Figure 20.1. Politics of Psychiatric Drug Marketing and Selling

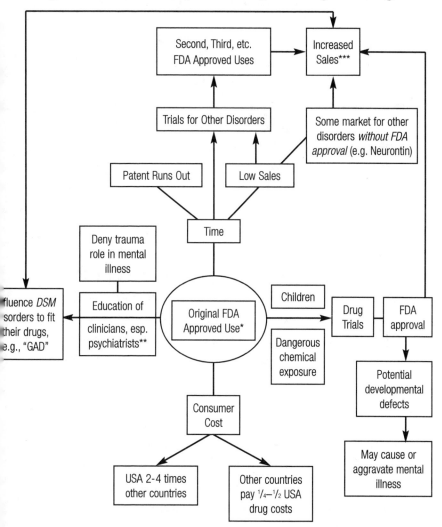

* FDA approval is based on short-term trials (usually from 5 to 8 weeks), yet drug companies recommend long-term use, often for life.

** Drug companies monitor physician prescribing data by buying it from pharmacies so their sales reps will know how to push physicians to prescribe their drugs.

*** Increased sales appears to be the bottom line, not drug effectiveness or patient care.

To keep negative publicity down, drug companies tend to hide the countless lawsuits against them over the toxic effects of their drugs. Many of these suits are settled out of court.

INFLATED DRUG PRICES

While drugs remain costly across the world, their prices in the U.S. are two to four times what they are in the other countries. This price inflation is true for most of the commonly marketed psychiatric drugs, which may cost the patient as much as $13 per pill (e.g., for antipsychotic Abilify). For a person who takes two or more psychiatric drugs, their daily cost may exceed $20, or over $600 each month. These drugs are not just toxic to our bodies and minds, but also to our financial well-being.

Not only has the drug industry infiltrated medicine and psychiatry to an inappropriate, dangerous and often alarming degree, but it has apparently been heavily behind the push for Medicare drug coverage. Through their massive lobbying money, the drug industry pays politicians to vote for Medicare drug payments, which then transfers multi-billions of our tax dollars into its own coffers. The drug lords have not only pushed their drugs onto children, but they have also long been promoting more drugging of seniors.

Time

Burdened by the constraints of minimal governmental authority, drug companies are especially concerned with time. Each new drug takes several years to complete animal and clinical human trials before the FDA may approve of its being marketed for a specific mental or physical illness. After that, the drug company has seventeen years during which it holds the patent exclusively to market and sell that particular drug. After that time, other companies can market and sell the drug, and through competition the price usually drops. Many drug companies have tried to extend the seventeen year limit so they can be its exclusive owner and keep the price up. For example, when the seventeen years was up for buspirone (Buspar), Bristol-Myers Squibb is reported to have threatened generic drug companies for almost two years, which kept their drugs cost at about $2 per pill, or up to $8 per day for many patients.

Drugging Our Children

To expand their market and sales, the drug industry has continued to promote giving these toxic psychiatric drugs to *children*, some as young as two to five years old. As is true for adults, it is highly likely that many of children's symptoms and signs are instead the effects of repeated childhood trauma (e.g., see Table 15.3 on page 152). This behavior by drug companies and clinicians who recommend or prescribe them is especially dangerous, since these already-toxic drugs are being given to children during the crucial growth and development of their brain and peripheral nervous system, as well as that for other organ systems. In addition, many of these drugs are not adequately tested upon and FDA-approved to treat children.

In her 2003 article, citing a recent *JAMA* report, psychologist Diane Willis said, ". . . the number of two- to four-year-old children on stimulant and antidepressant drugs (such as Ritalin, Prozac, etc.) increased 50 percent between 1991 and 1995. This report suggests to me at least four possible notions: 1) exceedingly poor judgment on the part of those writing the prescriptions; 2) desire for a "quick fix" by parents and daycare or preschool workers; 3) lack of knowledge about alternative ways to treat a young child's behavioral or emotional problems; and 4) a reflection of the current health-care mentality whereby rule-makers support the most inexpensive and expedient treatments (i.e., use of drugs) over brief psychological interventions that may be more expensive but offer more long-term benefits.[1103]

"The *JAMA* report notes that there is insufficient follow-up of young children while on medication. Little is known about the effects of early or long-term use of stimulant and antidepressant medications. As astounding as it sounds, the United States uses 80 percent of the world's methylphenidate (Ritalin), and the FDA does not approve giving the drug to children under six years of age!"[1103]

Finally, insurance companies pay psychiatrists three times more for a drug prescribing session than for a psychotherapy or family therapy session.[275a]

This disturbing information is just the tip of the iceberg. In June 2003, the British government's Medicines and Healthcare products Regulatory Agency (MHRA—the British equivalent of the U.S. FDA) issued a strong warning about the ADP drug paroxetine (Paxil, called Seroxat in Britain), saying that it "should not be used in children and adolescents under the age of 18 years to treat depressive illness." The MHRA evaluated nine recent studies of its use in children and concluded that in children it has higher risk and less benefit than previously thought. The main risk is that it can make depressed children suicidal. Those depressed children on the medicine were 1.5 to 3.2 times more likely than those taking placebo to engage in self-harm or episodes of suicidal or violent behavior. Paxil also showed a striking lack of benefit in children. Most of the psychiatric drugs used to treat children have not been adequately tested on them. Paxil's maker GlaxoSmithKline said the British authorities overreacted.

A week later, the FDA also said that Paxil should not be used in children and adolescents to treat depression. Three well-controlled trials in pediatric patients with major depression failed to show any advantage over placebo. Finally, the Alliance for Human Research Protection called for a moratorium on clinical trials that use children to test SSRI antidepressants.[13] As the FDA has pointed out, the drugs have shown no efficacy for children, but they do pose serious risks of harm. Unfortunately, the FDA has approved fluoxetine (Prozac) for depression in children. SSRIs have serious side effects in adolescents and children, including weight gain, sleep disturbances and problematic behavior changes. Moreover, no clear age and dosage guidelines exist for these drugs, since prescription practices are based on studies in adults and anecdotal experience with children. Most family doctors and pediatricians are now treating children with SSRIs for ADHD, despite a lack of scientific evidence to support their safety and effectiveness in youngsters. according to research pediatrician JerryRushton.[13]

DRUG TRIAL MANIPULATIONS AND DISTORTIONS

Psychiatrist Daniel Safer has shown how the drug industry has distorted the conduct and reporting of psychiatric drug trial results. In Table 20.1, I summarize the highlights of his observations. These include such observed manipulations as using *high* and/or more frequent *doses of a comparison drug to make their drug appear less toxic, changing study results in favor of their drug, masking* drug study *sponsorship,* and *withholding negative* or *unfavorable* drug study *results*. Safer concludes that these unsavory actions hurt us all by: 1) lowering the scientific quality of research reports, 2) influencing physicians to mis-prescribe the drugs, 3) corrupting drug researchers, 4) distorting our knowledge base, 5) limiting independent research, 6) discouraging generic drug prescribing, and 7) all of these thereby raising drug costs.[888]

Since 2002 at least one article each week has appeared in the popular news and often in medical journals that exposes more problems coming from within the drug industry (e.g., the reader can explore by an Internet search for "drug industry distortions," "drug industry manipulations," as well as for the *Alliance for Human Research Protection*[13] and the work of Vera Hassner Sharav). For further information on this topic, the reader may also refer to the works of researchers and authors as David Healy, M.D.; Elliot Valenstein, Ph.D.; Joseph Glenmullen, M.D.; Peter Breggin, M.D.; Loren Mosher, M.D.; Thomas Moore, M.D.; Charles Medawar; Irving Kirsch, Ph.D., and others.

Useful or Not?

This is not to say that some psychiatric drugs are not indicated and helpful for some conditions. As part of a full recovery program, some drugs help some people. I prescribe them for selected indications where, like most physicians, I consider the indications and the *risk-to-benefit ratio* for each drug (discussed on page 145 of the prior volume). Based on that R/B ratio, my knowledge of the literature and my clinical experience, I have estimated the effectiveness of frequently used psychiatric drugs for the most common mental disorders (Table 20.2). Note in the table that several drug types and sub-types have been used for depression, but that most do not work well to significantly lessen its symptoms, which I also discuss above and at length in the prior volume. Unfortunately, this same principle applies for most of the other psychiatric drugs and disorders. The beneficial and toxic *effects of these drugs* are *not as advertised.*

One drug, buspirone, does safely lessen anxiety in people with anxiety disorders and PTSD in about 80 percent of those who take it. While it was to have become available in generic form in 2001, its original maker, Bristol-Myers Squibb, fought to prevent that happening and thus keep its price high. Thus, becoming generic does

Table 20.1 Distortions in Drug Trial Study Design and Reporting (expanded from Safer 2002)

Possible Distortion	Example
Using dose & frequency outside the usual range for competitive advantage	e.g., Using high doses of a comparison drug e.g., Haldol at 20 mg/day (4 times the maximum effective dose) to make sponsored drug's side effects appear less in comparison
Using placebo washout to lower success of placebo results	e.g., starting all subjects on placebo during the first week, then dropping all from the study who improved
Using self-serving measurement scales and misleading conclusions	e.g., make risperidone appear to have no extra-pyramidal syndrome side effects; or make a stimulant drug appear more effective than placebo in ADHD when it was not
Selecting major findings & end-points after study is completed	Comparing drugs unfairly by reanalyzing results to make sponsored drug look better in effect & side effects
Masking toxic effects	Failing to ask specific questions. Saying sponsored drug has lower side effects than is true
Over-publishing the same or similar results	Repeating the same results in many different journals
Reporting only favorable results	e.g., ignoring high placebo responses when comparing 2 other ADP drugs' antianxiety effects
Editorializing for a sponsored drug in the abstract	Advocating for a sponsored drug without clear backup from collected study data
Withholding negative or unfavorable results	Drug company enforces not publishing negative or unfavorable results
Masking sponsorship	"Ghost" or hidden authorships that promote drug use[469, 470a]
Numerous other conflicts of interest	e.g., researchers' being paid by drug companies often prevents them from independent decisions and reports.[73, 469]

Table 20.2. Estimated Effectiveness of Psychiatric Drugs

Drug Type	Depression	PTSD	Anxiety Disorders	SA/CD	Eating Disorders
ADPs **Tricyclics SSRIs Other ADPs**	±	±	±	−	−
BZDs	−	Acutely only+	Acutely only+	−	−
Barbiturates Other sedatives	−	Acutely only+	Acutely only+	−	−
Buspirone	−*	+	+	−	−
Stimulants **Ritalin Other**	Rarely used, & acutely only ±	−	−	−	Rare. Brief effects only
Antipsychotics **Phenothiazines Newer**	Rarely used**	−	−	−	−
Anticonvulsants **Mood stabilizers**	±	±	−	−	−
Lithium	Bipolar only	−	−	−	−
B-blockers Clonidine	−	±	−	±	−
Miscellaneous	−	−	−	***	−
Summary **Most of the above drugs**	±	±	± to +	−	−

Effectiveness: − = not effective, ± = May or may not help, + = usually helpful.
Overall, these drugs are minimally effective and most have toxic consequences effects by the drug makers).
* Can help if anxiety present (occurs in about 80% of depressed people).
** For psychotic depression only.
*** Antabuse (disulfiram) only. SA/CD = substance dependence; PDs = personality disorsers; ‡ = dangerous.
BZD = benzodiazepine sedatives.

Table 20.2. Estimated Effectiveness of Psychiatric Drugs *(concluded)*

Dissociative Disorders	PDs	ADHD ADD	Aggressive Disorders	Schiz psychoses	Toxic Effects
−	−	−	±	−	++
−	−	−	−	−	++
−	−	−		−	+
−*	−	−	−	−	−
−/‡	−	±	−	−	++ to +++
Rare. Temporary only	−	−	−	±	++ to +++
−	−	−	−	±	− to ++
−	−	−	−	−	+ to ++
−	−	−	−	−	− to +
−	−	−	−	−	+ to ++
−	−	−	−	±	Most are + to +++

Toxic effects: − to + = none to minimal; + = minimal; ++ = moderate; +++ = marked.

not always guarantee an appropriately lesser cost. This is in addition to the fact, as mentioned above, that most drugs sold in the U.S. already cost two to four times what they do in most other countries.

Only one drug is useful in helping people with alcoholism—disulfiram (Antabuse), which can help to prevent impulse drinking. There are essentially no reliable or consistently effective drugs available to treat most of the other common mental illnesses, as Table 20.2 shows. I have described and summarized the indications and problems with *antidepressant* drugs above, and discuss them in more detail in the prior volume.

The *benzodiazepine sedatives* are especially useful for fearful acute medical and surgical conditions and procedures, but their down side is that they are usually mind-numbing and toxic when taken long term, with a commonly prolonged and painful withdrawal syndrome. Because of these drawbacks, they have almost no usefulness in treating any chronic mental illness.

While commonly prescribed, using methylphenidate (Ritalin) and other *stimulants* for ADHD in children and ADD in adults also remains controversial.[275a, 1023a]

Most of the so-called "mood stabilizers" are simply anticonvulsants, and except for phenytoin (Dilantin), they too are toxic and unproven for most of the symptoms and disorders for which they are prescribed, including "mood disorders" (see page 242 on the Neurontin controversy).

Advocates of the *antipsychotic* drugs, also called neuroleptics, have claimed that they are better than placebo for the so-called "positive" symptoms of psychoses (hallucinations, delusions and the like), which include schizophrenia. But studies when people are treated instead with social support and kindness but no drugs show as good or better results (Table 18.8 on page 195). Too, the drugs do not help their other symptoms, such as feeling fear, numbness and "depression." These drugs have serious toxic effects, as listed in chapter 18.

From a careful review of the literature and clinical experience over the decades of its use, research psychiatrist Joanna Moncrief and others found little evidence that lithium is effective for three of its commonly recommended uses: treatment of acute mania, prophylaxis of bipolar disorder, and helping treat depression that is unresponsive to ADP drugs.[718, 720] Although some people appear to benefit from it for a time, naturalistic follow-up studies fail to show that lithium has any beneficial effect on the course of bi-polar disorder. It has toxic consequences, including long-term physical complications and side effects. Taking lithium is often unpleasant, and there is a reasonable possibility that a manic state will be provoked by its withdrawal.[109, 720]

Many physicians use psychiatric drugs to treat symptoms, rather than or in addition to treating clearly diagnosed disorders. A problem is that some drug companies promote and many physicians tend to use these drugs for unproven or unapproved symptoms or disorders. On balance, these drugs are less helpful for psychiatric and psychological disorders than drug companies claim and advertise. The drug industry has thus overtaken a substantial part of the previous educational roles of medical schools, residency training programs, and professional medical organizations by delivering direct and indirect continuing medical education to physicians, nurses and other clinicians. Nowadays, far too much of their continuing education is delivered by the drug industry.

CONCLUSION

The take-home message from this chapter is to be skeptical and wary of using psychiatric, psychoactive drugs. Most of them are toxic, unpredictable and not specific in their action or effectiveness for any single symptom or disorder. Before taking any of them, do your homework. If you are already taking one or more of them, do not stop them suddenly, due to the probability that doing so (depending on the specific drug) will be associated with a painful withdrawal syndrome. If you decide to stop taking one, do so in gradually decreasing doses over weeks or months and under the supervision of a physician with expertise in this process.

On balance, while they are commonly prescribed, most psychiatric drugs are not only toxic, but with few exceptions, they don't work well to bring about significant improvement of most mental illnesses, and especially for improving a patient's quality of life. People with any of these disorders discussed throughout this book have more choices than using drugs alone to help them heal. I have described some of these often more effective recovery aids in each chapter and in chapter 12 of the prior volume, as well as in my book *My Recovery: A Personal Plan for Healing*.[1096] In the next chapter I address some of the evidence for using two potentially strong treatment methods: individual psychotherapy and group therapy for some of these disorders. I also describe the politics underlying conventional treatments.

21 A NOTE ON TREATMENT AND RECOVERY

I know that trauma-focused treatment and recovery works. So do many of you, especially clinicians who use this approach and survivors who have worked at it long-term. Our combined experiences of success, though mostly unpublished, probably total conservatively in the range of hundreds of thousands of people, if not more. I have personally assisted hundreds of trauma survivors, with a high success rate among those who were persistent and patient over the years of their recovery work.

Throughout this book I have commented on various aspects of treatment and recovery, and describe the recovery process in some detail in chapters of my prior books, *The Truth About Depression, A Gift to Myself, Boundaries and Relationships,* and *Memory and Abuse.* Other clinicians have described trauma recovery in their books (examples include: Judith Herman 1992, Davies and Frawley 1994, John Briere 1996, Christine Courtois 1998, James Chu 1998, McCann and Pearlman 1990, Sheldon Cashdan 1988, Steven Gold 2000, J. P. Wilson et al. 2001 and Richard Kluft 1993).

EVIDENCE

But what published databased evidence do we have that shows that trauma-focused treatment and recovery methods work? A problem is that these kinds of studies are expensive and time-consuming to conduct. There are also many variables among individuals, such as their personal motivations, preferences and ability to trust their therapist and recovery process. These variables and more compound and confound the capabilities of various research methods to provide an accurate measure of their progress. For these and other reasons, few research studies have been conducted on the efficacy of trauma-focused treatment.

I found thirteen studies, as summarized in Table 21.1. Since there are more, I offer these as but examples. While it does not address a trauma-focused approach, Seligman's study is one of many available that show that, in general, psychotherapy works for helping people recover from some mental illnesses. Others have shown that in treating depression, psychotherapy is as good or better than using antidepressant drugs, is cost effective, and its beneficial effects may last longer. For example, King and colleagues showed that among 464 depressed patients, psychotherapy was superior to antidepressant drugs at four-month follow-up, although they found no difference at one year (Table 21.1). Van Etten and Taylor's meta-analysis of numerous studies on patients with PTSD using various methods showed that psychotherapy and EMDR yielded clearly superior results than did antidepressant drugs (its results are expanded as Table 3.7 on page 32).

The two- and twelve-year follow-up studies by Ellason and Ross, and Cameron, show that for survivors with a spectrum of "mental disorders," a trauma-focused recovery approach is effective. The

Table 21.1 Treatment/Recovery Effectiveness for Trauma Effects: 13 Example Study Findings

Year/Author	Results	Study
1995 Seligman	Analysis of psycho-therapy results	Overall, psychotherapy worked well in efficacy studies for mental illness in general
1997 Ellason & Ross	2 year follow-up 54 DIDs in treatment & recovery	Trauma-focused treatment gave significant improvement, including of: depression, anxiety, SA/CD, dissociation, somatization, hospitalizations, & number of drugs needed
1998 Van Etten & Taylor	Meta-analysis of PTSD treatment effectiveness	Drugs overall less effective (.69) v placebo (.51), than psychotherapy (1.17), behavioral (1.27), EMDR (1.24), all v controls (.43) See also Table 3.7 on page 32
1999 Stevenson	Extensive literature review	45 studies & 8 meta-analyses show Tx of children is effective, as do 14 separate studies on Tx of abusing parents. Affirms strong trauma-effect link.
Maratta & Asner	Analysis of 21 of 35 studies	Provides some support that *group therapy* is effective in helping CSA survivors to heal from the effects. Said more controlled studies are needed.
2000 Cameron	72 CSA women	Trauma-focused treatment resulted in substantial improvement over time. 12-year prospective study.
King et al.	464 depressed patients	4-month follow-up showed superiority of 12 psychotherapy sessions vs. ADP drugs. No difference at 1 year. Cost effective.
2001 Wilson et al.	17 chapter PTSD Tx book, 23 int'l. authors	Describes studies that empirically (data based) validate a trauma-focused treatment approach using a variety of methods

(continued on next page)

Table 21.1 Treatment/Recovery Effectiveness for Trauma Effects *(concluded)*

Year/Author	Results	Study
2001 Pearlman	Describes treatment for complex PTSD	Describes an effective integration of developmental, cognitive, object relations, interpersonal and self-psychology methods to help people heal from trauma effects
Foy et al.	Compiles evidence for group Tx	General empirical support for *group therapy* effectiveness for people with PTSD
2002 Trowell et al.	71 CSA girls many with PTSD	Significant improvement using 30 individual psychotherapy sessions on some & 18 of (short-term) group therapy
2003 Wright et al.	132 CT adults with PTSD	Significant improvement at 1 year after a 6-week intensive inpatient treatment using frequent group therapy.
2002 Vaa et al.	54 CSA women	Significant improvement from group therapy on long-term follow-up of psychological & interpersonal functioning.
1995–2003 13 Studies	**International Authors & Patients**	**9 trauma-specific, 5 on group therapy, 3 on psychotherapy for mental disorders. All show positive and effective results.**

Key: Tx = treatment; ADP drugs = antidepressant drugs; PTSD = post-traumatic stress disorder

comprehensive book by J. P. Wilson and colleagues has seventeen chapters that describe some of the current state of the art in the treatment of people with psychological trauma effects, including PTSD.

My experience has been that long-term participation in a trauma-focused therapy group is a treatment of choice for helping heal from the effects of trauma. Maratta and Asner, and Foy and colleagues, show data that long-term group therapy is an effective recovery method, and several of the other ones in the table also used it as part of the treatment regimen.

In all, these thirteen reports consist of nine studies and descriptions of trauma-specific treatment effectiveness, five are on group therapy, and three are on psychotherapy in general for mental disorders. All thirteen show positive and effective results (Table 21.1).

Evidence-Based Clinical Practice

Using evidence to diagnose and treat illness has long been a foundation of medicine. It is nothing new. *How* the evidence is *used* is the question. Most of the time, clinicians collect and use evidence constructively to help their patients or clients get better. I believe that the recent focus on evidence in medicine, psychiatry and psychology is a good idea. But the use of "evidence" here can have double-edged sword qualities, since evidence can also be manufactured and misused. For example, to start, is it useful to know exactly *who produces* the *evidence? Who decides exactly which data will be called "evidence"? Who decides how* it should best be *used?* These are crucial questions, as I will explain below.

Conflicts of Interest

Long ago, it took less time and money to produce evidence than it does today. Back then it took creativity, observation, and at times, risk taking. Today it takes these qualities, too, but it takes mostly *money, time* and *influence*. Who has the most of these? Drug companies, government agencies and the researchers they pay—these are the usual sources of the money, time and influence. Money and influence allow time. The more money, the more time one has to complete the hard and long work of serious research. Drug companies have some bias built into most of the research and development of their drugs.[238, 813] Some government agencies and academics who receive their legal drug money may too.[652] Some have described these three groups as being "in bed" with each other. With this kind of bias and conflict of interest, objectivity and truth are commonly lost, and we health consumers pay for it.

Can we trust this triangular system of drug company, government, and hired academics to determine which drug will be reliably safe and effective to treat a given mental illness? It is illegal for a drug company to advertise, market or promote a drug for indications that are not approved by the Food and Drug Administration (FDA), which requires successful clinical trial results for short-term effectiveness and safety to grant approval for use in a specific disorder. In 1996 the Warner Lambert drug company (WL), which made and sold gabapentin (Neurontin) for the FDA-approved indication of treating epilepsy only, appeared suddenly to overstep its bounds by marketing the drug for over twelve other disorders (e.g., ADHD, neurological pain, bipolar disorder, migraine headaches, alcohol and drug withdrawal, and restless leg syndrome, to name a few).[360, 792] And this is an expensive drug that commonly has toxic effects.

Apparently without first going through appropriate clinical trials for each disorder, WL hired non-physicians to write at least twenty scientific-appearing articles (for publication in medical and psychiatric journals) promoting these unproven uses for their drug Neurontin, and then paid physicians to use their names as the authors. WL then recruited community physicians to become its "consultants" to attend dinners and weekend retreats, where other paid speakers told them when and how to use Neurontin. As a result, WL made three billion dollars on Neurontin in 2000 and

2001, 78 percent of which was from these off-label indications, and millions of which were paid for by the federal government (e.g., through prescriptions paid for by Medicare and Medicaid). Surprisingly, the FDA has not taken action on WL, or on Pfizer, who recently bought WL. The U.S. attorney's office in Boston is investigating this apparently illegal marketing scheme. Dr. David Franklin, a former WL insider hired in 1996 to help market the drug, has filed a civil lawsuit against WL for putting the public in danger.[360, 792] This is but one example of apparent drug company dishonesty and a lack of integrity. On page 128 of the prior volume, I mentioned how Eli Lilly had published in 2002 that the antidepressant drug Prozac was no better than placebo, now that its patent had run out in late 2001, after it had made multi-billions of dollars for the company. Other similar examples abound (e.g., see Sharav 2002, and ongoing updates by the *Alliance for Human Research Protection* on *www.researchprotection.org*).[13]

A Matter of Trust

How common is this phenomenon? Even if it occurs only occasionally, how can we trust these groups to develop, license and deliver effective drugs to clinicians and the people that they serve? Finally, since managed care companies commonly forced the use of antidepressant drugs over psychotherapy for depression, sometimes citing "evidence-based" treatment as its reason, how can we trust any agency or group to decide what is true evidence?

Drug *licensing, acceptance* and *use* are based on often brief and inadequate clinical trials by researchers who are hired by the drug companies. Jonathan Quick (2001), Director of Drug Policy at the World Health Organization, said, "Clinical trials form the basis of effective research and development, but their reliability is currently imperiled by three major flaws: *conflicts of interest* on the part of the investigators; *inappropriate involvement of research sponsors* in their design and management; and *publication bias* in disseminating their results . . . [including] bias in publicizing positive results and underreporting negative results" (italics added).[813]

Arnold Relman (2001), former editor of the *New England Journal of Medicine,* said, "The entire system of clinical investigation is driven by profit. . . . We are seeing the corruption of a system of research that used to have high ideals and be clearly in the public interest."[829] Concerned about these disturbing trends, the editors of thirteen leading medical journals published a joint editorial in which they said, "[Research] contracts should give the researchers a substantial say in trial design, access to the raw data, responsibility for data analysis and interpretation, and the right to publish."[238]

Some university-based researchers hold stock, stock options or decision-making positions in companies that may be affected by the results of their clinical research—a clear conflict of interest that obviously should not be allowed.[652, 829, 1024] Angell and Relman (2001) said, "A growing number of drug trials are being managed by investor-owned businesses that are even more beholden to the drug companies because the companies are their only clients. Furthermore, in their contracts with academic researchers, drug companies now often insist on controlling how the research is done and reported, and whether the results will even be published at all. Recently, there have been several widely publicized instances of drug companies suppressing research results that were not favorable to their drugs."[27]

The term "evidence based" is often being misused in psychiatric continuing education as a way (or as a "sound bite") to help promote and sell drugs. I say "misused" in part because most of the clinical skills that are being taught to psychiatrists to help "mentally ill" people are, in most training programs, limited to drugs, with little or no mention of other recovery aids, such as psychotherapy, group therapy, self-help groups, lifestyle changes and other effective methods (such as selected acupressure techniques).[597a] To consult most psychiatrists today is usually limited to getting an opinion about psychopharmacology and taking toxic and expensive drugs, which may not be the best way to lessen emotional pain.

Following the money trail, we can begin to see why most such "evidence based" continuing psychiatric education is sponsored and financed by the drug industry. Each speaker is nearly always on the payroll of numerous drug companies (e.g., I regularly see and hear speakers who are *each* paid by from ten to twenty different drug makers). Groups and organizations that put on free continuing medical and psychiatric "evidence-based" education are also usually subsidized by drug companies, which is another clear conflict of interest. The topics presented commonly include recommending as treatment the drug(s) made by the sponsoring drug company.[966a]

Of those who write *clinical practice guidelines,* 87 out of 100 psychiatric speakers and authors recently surveyed had been paid by drug companies. An estimated over 90 percent of drug researchers and at least half of institutional review board (IRB) members receive drug money. The medical and psychiatric journals where their articles about the nature and treatment of mental illness are published are financially subsidized by countless drug advertisements. These continuing education programs and journals almost never address the evidence for using other approaches, including those that help ameliorate the painful effects of trauma. In this context, when we see the term (or sound byte) "evidence based," we can take these facts and dynamics into consideration.* Its misuse has generated so much concern that objective authors in a recent *British Medical Journal* article on the topic called it "evidence b(i)ased" medicine and psychiatry.[699]

There is something wrong with the scientific process when bias and money control what is published and delivered. Will the coalition of *drug industry-paid researcher-managed care-government agency* continue to decide what is accepted as the best "evidence-based treatment"? Do medicine, psychiatry and psychology need to get out of bed with the drug and insurance industries?

                    *   *   *

Before we could effectively treat tuberculosis, we needed to identify its major cause, which we discovered was a germ that we named *mycobacterium tuberculosis*. Without that link as evidence —consistently finding the same germ in the lesions of those with the illness—we couldn't develop a cure, which turned out to be specific antibiotics. Likewise, before we can heal from mental illness, we need to find firmer evidence of its cause. Otherwise, all we can do is put on Band-Aids, which is what our current drug-and-custodial care mental health system appears to do.

Much of this book is about this evidence. Its central thesis—the reality of the trauma-disorder link—is evidence-based, but it considers kinds of evidence that are commonly ignored by conventional assumptions and encourages the development of an expanded scientific paradigm. My focus has been to present and summarize the large number of studies that document the link

---

Sound byte is a media term that means a short statement that conveys a specific belief or idea, usually used to influence the audience or sell them something. Its repetition can become hypnotic. For example, "The little purple pill. . . ."

between childhood trauma and mental disorders. This link is the crucial first half of the needed evidence. The other half of the evidence addresses the effectiveness and success of the treatment or recovery methods that may best help people heal, for which I have here and in the prior volume provided an introduction.

Most serious illness needs an initial period of stabilization (Stage One) before the task of longer term healing can occur (Stage Two) (Table 3.2 on page 20). This stage- or phase-oriented sequence has long been an appropriate part of medicine, psychiatry, and psychology. Its usefulness has recently been documented, reviewed and validated by numerous people in the field of trauma psychology and psychiatry.[193, 486, 1090, 1096] Just what recovery methods and aids are most effective in each of these stages are open for exploration, since our treatment for mental illness has so far not worked very well. Enter "evidence-based treatment" (EBT).

A Double-Edged Sword

Here the double-edged sword quality of gathering and using evidence becomes clearer, as I summarize in Table 21.2. In the helping professions there have always been the two foundations of the *science* and the *art*. The science is based on the evidence for cause and cure. The art is more complex. It is based on the individuality of each person. It also has to do with each person's internal and external resources—what methods and aids may work best for them to recover and heal. Finally, the art of clinical work also involves the communication, rapport, safety, trust and understanding that evolves between the person-in-need and their clinician-assistant.

Evidence-based treatment early on was applied to physical medicine, which is usually more objective or "black and white" than psychology and psychiatry. While conventional EBT is also an

Table 21.2 Evidence-Based Treatment:
Advantages and Disadvantages

Advantages for EBT	Disadvantages
Works best for physical medical problems, where problems & decisions are simpler & individual differences are less pronounced	Works less well for mental disorders, where problems & decisions are more complex & individual differences are more pronounced
Research is simpler & easier to conduct & process than clinical work	Research on mental disorders is more complicated & difficult to conduct & process
We have to start somewhere to get as close to the truth about scientific & clinical issues	Even the cleanest appearing research can be erroneous or even bogus*
Research rarely measures the patient-clinician relationship	The patient-clinician relationship has been shown to be important in physical medicine, & crucial in psychological
When properly conducted, studies that provide data & appropriate statistics can supply useful information	Data may have limited usefulness and statistics can provide only so much useful information*
Research is an important source to give us data for potential tools and goals	Clinical awareness, experience & judgment are important to be able to integrate & apply research data when appropriate
What works well in a lab can help determine what may work in practice	What works in the lab with selected people may not work well in practice
Rigorous control is more possible in research situations	Rigorous control is much less possible in practice
Objectivity shown by researcher & funding sponsor	Bias is likely or shown by researcher & funding sponsor (e.g., some drug company research)

*e.g., see Darrell Huff's 1954 book *How to Lie with Statistics*; and how thalidomide, based on prior research, was approved by authorities as a safe drug.

appropriate touchstone for mental disorders, due to their more complex nature, it may not always be as useful or effective. To some extent EBT may be easier to apply to physical medicine, where problems and decisions are simpler and individual differences less pronounced. I describe some of EBT's major advantages and disadvantages in Table 21.2.

A final and crucial aspect of gathering and using evidence has to do with its politics. Politics is about power and trust in relationships. We would like to trust those to whom we have delegated certain of our own personal powers. These authority figures may include clinicians, professional groups, drug and insurance companies, and government agencies. We would like to believe that they will always act in our best interest. We would also hope that the drug researchers and the drug companies who support them are always objective and ethical. Finally, we would like to trust the researchers, journalists and reporters in scientific journals and the media to tell us the truth about health matters. However, bias is likely in most of these areas.

Clinicians have a fairly effective monitoring and correction system through professional societies and state licensing boards to which a consumer can complain. However, the rest of the authorities tend to have a minimal to nonexistent corrective system to police their wrongdoings. No one may hold them accountable for their actions. For example, recent reports of biased drug company research and contrived methods and results have been published.[27, 28, 375, 469, 652, 697, 813, 1024] It has also been reported by many on the "inside" of medical research that money and power is switching hands between the drug companies and the researchers. We have been led to believe that the drug companies evolved out of science and therefore their integrity is based on the scientific model. This is not always true and needs to be looked at by independent investigators that aren't having their salaries paid by a special interest group.

Another example of the mistrust of authorities and reporters is the rise and fall of the claim of a "false memory syndrome," widely publicized during the 1990s by the print and broadcast media. Twelve years after the coining of this bogus term by an organized group of parents accused by their adult children of having molested them, there has still not been any substantial proof of the existence of such a syndrome.[137, 138, 800, 1086, 1089] These parents have also manipulated the media into making *them* appear to be the victims. But they have never offered convincing evidence for their claims. Rather, they have commonly challenged the rest of us to prove them wrong. This type of convoluted thinking was embraced by the media because it is less painful to believe that there is no such thing as child sexual abuse. The "false memory" advocates have also tried to promote their own brand of evidence-based treatment, which excluded any trauma-based treatment. Just as these accused parents have tried to cover up their adult children's allegations of abuse, so, too, perhaps there are other parents who would rather see their children and their adult children medicated—instead of taking responsibility for the trauma that is at the least aggravating and at most causing their child's mental illness. Whether bias comes from drug companies, some parent groups, insurance companies, or government agencies, we cannot accept its corrupting influence on what we know is the truth.

What we read and hear in the media is not always so. This is why it is important for consumers, their clinicians, and even their "authority figures" to know what is being reported "behind the scenes" in professional meetings and clinical scientific journals. In this book and in *The Truth About Depression,* I have tried to summarize much of that crucial information that links trauma to mental disorders.

Epilogue

STRONG EVIDENCE

Does childhood trauma cause mental illness? If we had only a few studies that looked at a small number of research subjects which showed a link between childhood trauma and a particular mental disorder, the answer would be "No." But that is not what we have.

While many clinicians suspected it for decades, before 1980 we didn't have enough data to prove a significant link between repeated childhood trauma and subsequent mental illness. Now we do. The data are clear, and for most disorders, strong. We have accumulated the data mostly since the early 1980s. Today in early 2004, we have hundreds of published databased and peer-reviewed reports conducted on well over 200,000 trauma survivors and their controls.

What makes this evidence so strong is that the authors of these reports didn't focus on a limited population using a limited method of evaluation. Instead, we have 1) *a large number of studies* (well over 300), 2) that used *a large number* of research *subjects* (well over 200,000 people). These studies were conducted by 3) multiple and independent researchers who were 4) from *different countries,* and who 5) used several *different study designs* and methods (e.g., retrospective, prospective, index cases and meta-analysis) on 6) *diverse samples* of people (e.g., clinical, community and some forensic groups). Most of these also controlled for other possible influences, which academics call confounding variables. While they sometimes used inappropriate control groups (such as other psychiatric inpatients or outpatients instead of non-mentally disordered people), which appeared to underestimate the strength of the trauma-disorder link, they still found a significant relationship between trauma and subsequent mental illness. Had they all used healthy controls, the link would have been even stronger. Furthermore, the trauma-disorder link was 7) *replicated* by nearly every one of these over 300 peer-reviewed studies. The characteristics of this large number of scientifically conducted and published studies fulfill all of the criteria for quality research reports (as summarized in Table 4.2 on page 37 of *The Truth About Depression*), including 8) highly meaningful *odds ratio* results and 9) a *graded response* pattern reported in all of the studies that looked for it.

For depression (now 327 studies—I found 51 more since *The Truth About Depression* was published) and alcoholism and other drug dependence (153 studies), the link with trauma is powerful. For others, such as anxiety disorders, PTSD, eating disorders, psychoses and some personality disorders, the evidence is very strong. For still others, such as behavior problems, including ADHD in children and ADD in adults, and violence, and the occurrence of revictimization and somatization (which are not mental disorders, but happen commonly with them), it is strong. And for others, such as nicotine dependence, substantial evidence is present, but currently less convincing than for the other problems above—perhaps because most of the studies conducted on it have not looked for

Table E.1 Number of Studies that Document a Link Between Childhood Trauma & Mental Illness

Clinical Area	Clinical	Community	Prospective	Index/Meta-Analys/LitRev	Strength of Data/Total #
Depression	96	70	22	21/2*	**Overwhelming/** 327 (see p. 255)
Suicidality		22 (both)		7	**Strong**/29
Alcohol/Drug Probs (SA/CD)		90	21	42 Index, 11 M-A/LitRev	**Powerful/** 153
Eating Disorders		58	7	43 index 7 Lit	**Very Strong/** 108
PTSD	54	21	10	0/6	**Strong**/85
Anxiety Disorder	35	38	12	15/2	**Very Strong/** 100
Personality Disorders		35	5	36/1	**Very Strong/** 76
Psychosis		67	4 (& 2 strong family studies)	37 index 8 lit reviews	**Very strong/** 110
ADHD		58	15	4/3	**Strong**/77
Aggression & **Violence**		40	16	10	**Strong**/66
Low Self-Esteem	17	10	4	Only 1 of 31 didn't find it	**Strong**/31
Dissociative Disorders	30	16	3	11/2	**Strong**/57
Nicotine		10	1		**Suggestive to Firm**/11
Somatization		38	11		**Strong**/65
Revictimization		38	1	4	**Firm to Strong/** 38 (see p. 208)

* Plus bipolar (13), suicidality (29) and 51 newer-found studies (see bottom of Figure E.1, page 255).

childhood trauma. I show the number of these studies for each in the bar graph (Figure E.1) and as a table (Table E.1). I also show the firm to strong link with some of these other associated effects of trauma in Figure E.2.

So why are we not using this information to help people in our mental health treatment system? Why are we not using it to prevent common mental illnesses? I believe that several factors are most likely operating to block the optimal use of these strong data. First, the momentum of the focus on *biological psychiatry assumptions,* as opposed to a psychodynamic or trauma-based approach to help people heal, has been promoted by the drug industry, academics, the health insurance industry (under the guise of "managed care"), and organized professional and other groups, has become so strong in favor of using drugs alone that they have influenced society to believe their erroneous assumptions.* These assumptions are that most common mental illnesses are genetically transmitted disorders of brain chemistry that are best treated by their drugs. A problem is that there is no databased evidence that proves the genetic transmission theory as a cause of any common mental illness.

THE BIOGENETIC THEORY

Most textbooks of psychiatry and psychology, as well as journal articles, assume and suggest a genetic and biological origin for most mental illnesses. So do the theories of most drug companies

---

* When we had some 100 studies that linked smoking to lung cancer, the tobacco companies were still denying any connection. Today we have a similar scenario. We have over 300 studies that link trauma to subsequent "mental illness," and yet drug companies and other influential but biased special interest groups are either ignoring or denying the importance of that link.

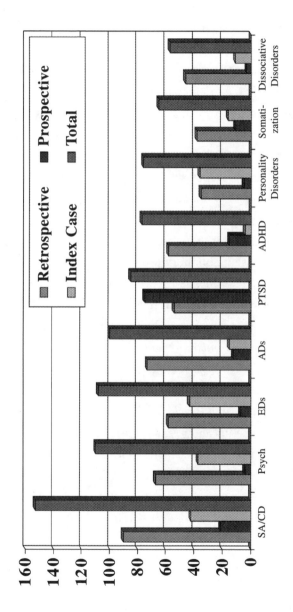

Figure E.1. Number of Studies Linking Common Mental Illness to Childhood Trauma

Key: SA/CD = substance abuse/chemical dependence, Psych = psychosis, EDs = eating disorders, ADs = anxiety & anxiety disorder, PTSD = post-traumatic stress disorder, ADHD = attention deficit hyperactivity disorder, CT = childhood trauma.

Also 276 studies on Depression (see TTaD, p. 55 & 193) + 51 new-found studies = 327 total linking CT with depression.

(which tend to be in bed with many who write journal articles and textbooks on psychiatry). But to date there remains no definitive evidence that proves such a claim. For example, in late 2003 a group of Ph.D. and M.D. clinicians and researchers challenged the American Psychiatric Association to identify one published study that proved the biogenetic theory of mental illness. The APA was unable to do so. In this regard, in Table E.2, I show some key statements from four authoritative sources (the Surgeon General's report, two major psychiatric textbooks, and the APA's response letter to the challengers) that are truthful about the lack of evidence for the biogenetic theory. None of these credible sources is able to provide any firm evidence for the existence of a biologic or genetic cause for any common psychiatric illness, nor for the existence of any biologically based laboratory test for any of them. In fact, they affirm the *absence* of evidence for all of these areas, in spite of the fact that psychiatry routinely advertises the opposite. Others and I believe that instead, most of the abnormal biology found is likely an *intermediary mechanism, which is* caused by the primary trauma, and not the cause of mental illness.

Another professional group (at the *International Center for the Study of Psychiatry and Psychology*) has for twenty-eight years opposed some of the untrue or inappropriate claims and actions of biological psychiatry. Their Web site (*www.ICSPP.org*) and that of other similar organizations (*www.mindfreedom.org*, with numerous links) and resources (e.g., Charles Medawar's rich antidepressant site: *http://www.socialaudit.org.uk/1.4.html*) provide more information about current psychiatric theory and practice.[692, 697]

GENETICS

Clinical and research psychologist Jay Joseph has extensively reviewed the genetic studies on psychiatric illness that have been reported over the last century.* After reanalyzing this large body of reports that favored a genetic origin for most mental illnesses, he concluded that this research is greatly flawed and that its conclusions are mostly invalid. As an example, he notes that the various *methods* used to look for possible genetic transmission are either invalid or methodologically flawed. These include foremost *the twin method* and *adoption* studies.[542] Research psychologist Alvin Pam, whose work I summarize on page 38 of the prior volume, has criticized the *pedigree* (family tree, "consanguinity," "clustering," or "runs in families") method as well. But "familial" is not the same as "genetic." Nearly all such pedigree studies are methodologically unsound for various reasons, including that almost all do not look for a trauma history among the evaluated subjects and their family members. There are only a few genetically oriented studies that do show a significant link between repeated childhood trauma and subsequent mental illness.[559–563, 747] Most genetic studies do not look for any mental-illness family history that goes back more than one generation, and most do not interview any past generation family members. These are serious flaws.

In a review of the state of the art of the genetic evidence for mental illness, the National Institute of Mental Health *Genetics Workgroup* led by psychiatrist Samuel Barondes said, ". . . only

---

* I critique the biogenetic theory of mental illness in more detail in chapter 4 on page 29 of *The Truth About Depression*. Dr. Joseph's book was published after that prior volume went to press, and it is timely now that I summarize some of his current findings here.

Table E.2. No Evidence of Specific Biological Cause for Mental Illness

Source →	*Mental Health: A Report of the Surgeon General* (1999)	*American Psychiatric Association* Statement 26 September 2003	Andreasen & Black *Introductory Textbook of Psychiatry* (2001); Hales & Yudofsky *Textbook of Clinical Psychiatry* 3rd edition (1999)
Area Evaluated ↓			
Cause Unknown	"The precise causes (etiology) of mental disorders are not known." p. 49	See **Genetic Evidence** on next page	"In the areas of patho-physiology and etiology, psychiatry has more uncharted territory than the rest of medicine." p. 23 A&B
Abnormal Biology Is Not Necessarily the Cause	"All too frequently a biological change in the brain (a lesion) is purported to be the 'cause' of a mental disorder . . . [but] The fact is that any simple association— or correlation— cannot and does not, by itself, mean causation." p. 51 "Few lesions or physiologic abnor-malities define the mental disorders, and for the most part their causes remain unknown." p. 102	"[There are no] biological markers for mental disorders . . ." "[There is] no diagnostic labora-tory test capable of confirming the presence of a mental disorder"	"[In] identifying the patho-physiology and etiology of major mental ill-nesses, ...this goal has been achieved for only a few disorders (Alzheimer's disease, multi-infarct dementia, Huntington's disease, and substance-induced syndromes such as amphetamine-related psychosis or Wernicke-Korsakoff syndrome)." p. 23 A&B

Table E.2. No Evidence of Specific Biological Cause for Mental Illness *(concluded)*

Genetic Evidence	The report offers or cites no proof of genetic evidence.	". . . Brain science has not advanced to the point where [we] can point to readily discernible pathologic lesions or genetic abnormalities that [are] reliable or predictive biomarkers of a given mental disorder or mental disorders as a group."	"Most of these [genetic studies] examine candidate genes in the serotonergic pathways, and have not found convincing evidence of an association [between genes and mental illness.]" p. 51 H&Y
Diagnosis Is Often Difficult	"The diagnosis of mental disorders is often . . . more difficult than diagnosis of somatic medical disorders, since there is no definitive lesion, laboratory test, or abnormality in brain tissue that can identify the illness." p. 44	"[There may be] 'triggering' by certain adverse environmental influences. Here, 'environment' may refer to traumatic events. . . ."	"Although reliable criteria have been constructed for many psychiatric disorders, validation of the diagnostic categories as specific entities has not been established." p. 43 H&Y
Summary	None of these 3 mainstream psychiatry & 1 highest U.S. Government medical sources is able to provide any proof for the existence of a biologic or genetic cause for any common psychiatric illness, nor for the existence of any biologically based laboratory test for any of them. In fact, they affirm the *absence* of evidence for all of these areas, in spite of the fact that psychiatry routinely claims and advertises the opposite. (*Any abnormal biology* found is likely the intermediary ***mechanism,*** caused by the primary trauma, and not the cause of most mental illness.)		

Table E.2. Notes—concluded

"It is not always easy to establish a threshold for a mental disorder, particularly in light of how common symptoms of mental distress are and the lack of objective, physical symptoms." p. 48 Surgeon General Report

"In the absence of visible lesions and known pathogens, investigators have turned to the exploration of models that could explain the diversity of symptoms through a single cognitive mechanism." p. 231 A&B

See also Valenstein 1998; Pam 1995; Boyle 1990; Joseph 2003; Whitfield 2003

Figure E.2. Number of Studies Linking Common Findings in Mental Illness to Childhood Trauma *(continued)*

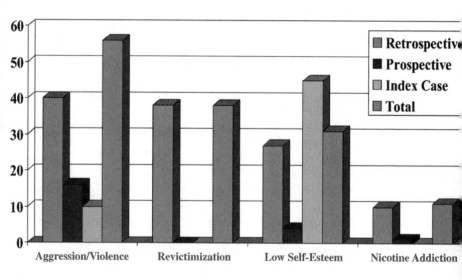

about 1 of 10 children of parents with either schizophrenia or bipolar disorder develops the full-blown disorder."[64] This is not the kind of summary evidence that would prove a genetic cause. In fact, in the rest of the article he is unable to cite any proof of a genetically transmitted cause for any mental disorder.

Joseph said, "The results of behavior genetic and psychiatric genetic research can be plausibly explained on the basis of methodological error, bias and environmental factors. Still, the authors of secondary sources (such as textbooks) typically endorse the conclusions of original researchers at the expense of critical analysis. Not surprisingly, genetically oriented researchers tend to conclude that they found evidence supporting the genetic position. This leads to a reasonable proposal: society should be skeptical about the conclusions reached by human genetic researchers, since these conclusions are heavily influenced by their reductionistic views. Let them collect and publish data, but we should rely on others to help us determine what conclusions should be drawn from this data."[542]

He cites psychologist George Albee who concluded that *his early belief* that social scientists discover facts in order to build theories is wrong, and that *instead*, ". . . it is more accurate to say that [they] select theories that are consistent with their personal values, attitudes, and prejudices, and then go out into the world, or into the laboratory, to seek facts that validate their beliefs about the world and human nature, neglecting or denying observations that contradict their personal prejudices."[542]

In summary, according to Joseph, 1) **Family tree or pedigree studies:** "Familial does not mean genetic" (see above and my discussion on page 29 of the prior volume), 2) **Twin research:** in part due to the erroneous "equal environment assumption," the twin method should be discarded, 3) **Adoption research:** like reared-apart twin studies, these are fraught with problems that have not been seriously addressed in most of the studies published. 4) Because of its vagueness, the term **"heritability"** in genetics should be discarded, 5) **Mental illness:** there is little evidence supporting a genetic basis for mental illness, including especially for ADHD and schizophrenia. Most psychiatric diagnosis describes behaviors and mental states, not diseases. 6) **Molecular genetic research** (looking for abnormal genes), for several reasons, is a waste of time, energy and money, and thus: 7) **The genome:** genes are not destiny, any more than sheet music is the essence of a concert performance.[542] Geneticist Dave Curtis agrees that no abnormal genes have been found associated with any functional (non-organic) mental illness.[233]

I challenge any skeptical reader to find one data based published report that definitively proves the genetic transmission theory of mental illness.

Joseph concludes "in contrast to the bleak view of humans and their future laid out by behavior and psychiatric genetics, there exists a radically different perspective. Human psychological distress, to the extent that it goes beyond people's normal reactions to life events, is primarily the result of well-known and well-documented psychologically traumatic environments and events, and social conditions such as racism, sexism, homophobia, unemployment, economic inequality, war and societal alienation [unfortunately, he does not mention childhood trauma]. Future societies lacking these conditions will see a dramatic reduction of human suffering, as well as a flourishing of human ability and innovation, and the possible role of genetic influences in shaping human differences will be of interest only to historians."[542]

CONCLUSION

Does childhood trauma cause mental illness? From the results of the reports summarized in this and the prior book, the answer is "Yes, repeated childhood trauma causes some mental illnesses in a sizable number of people." Depending upon the amount of available evidence, for some disorders, such as depression and alcohol and other drug abuse and dependence, the evidence is overwhelming. For others, such as anxiety disorders, PTSD, eating disorders, psychoses, and some personality disorders, the evidence is strong. For still others, such as behavior problems, including violence, and the occurrence of revictimization and somatization (which are not mental disorders, but happen commonly in association with them), it is firm. And for others, such as ADHD in children and ADD in adults, some evidence is present, but currently less convincing—perhaps due to the fewer studies published and the fact that most of the ones conducted on these disorders did not look for associated childhood trauma. I show a summary of the number of studies published to date that I found and an estimate of the strength of the evidence in Table E.1. A more graphic way to look at these data is shown in the bar graph in Figures E.1 and E.2.

As an example, the ongoing adverse childhood experiences (ACE) study results—from 17,421 people evaluated and then followed prospectively—are correlated with previously and independently demonstrated *effects* of the repeated trauma which, as others have shown, damages the developing child's brain and nervous system, as (summarized in Table E.3.) Rather than being caused by "genetic" defects, these are the *neurobiological effects* of the trauma, and are thus in part, instead, *mechanisms* of the origin of most mental illness.

Table E.3. Relationships Among Neurobiological Defects Associated with Childhood & Later Trauma & ACE Study Epidemiological Findings

Area of Function & Dysfunction	Demonstrated neurobiological defects from trauma	ACE Study findings: Graded relationship of ACE score to—
Mood & other: **Anxiety & panic,** **depression,** **hallucinations,** **& SA/CD**	Repeated stress & childhood trauma → hippocampus, amygdala & medial prefrontal cortex atrophy & dysfunction that mediate anxiety & mood problems	Unexplained panic, depression, hallucinations, & alcohol & other drug problems
Sexual & **aggressive** **behavior**	Repeated stress & childhood trauma → amygdala defects; role in sexual & aggressive behavior	Risky sexual behavior, anger control & risk for perpetrating & receiving intimate partner violence
Memory storage **& retrieval**	Hippocampus role in memory storage & retrieval; hip. & amygdala size reduction in childhood trauma; memory expression less on [if need] neuropsych. testing	Impaired memory of childhood (i.e., impaired memory of childhood increases as ACE score)
Body weight **& obesity**	Repeated stress & distress, via glucocorticoid pathways, leads to increased intra-abdominal & other fat deposits	Increased obesity
Other physical **problems**	Repeated stress & distress, via several pathways, leads to increased other physical problems	Increased somatic symptoms & disorders, including sleep problems
Co-morbidity/ **Trauma** **spectrum** **disorders**	Multiple brain & nervous system structure & function defects, including for monoamine neurotransmitter systems	Multiple co-morbidity
Summary **Psychiatric &** **physical symptoms** **& disorders**	**Repeated stress & childhood** **trauma → Multiple nervous** **system structure & function** **defects**	**Graded relationship of** **ACE score to psychiatric** **& physical symptoms &** **disorders, including** **multiple co-morbidity**

*   *   *

Having accumulated all of this information, what can we do with it? As a reader, you may already have some ideas. Perhaps we can explore them together. Feel free to modify these in any way that might best suit you. From my thirty-five-year experience as a physician (the last twenty-five years of which has been as a psychotherapist) and my research in the areas of mental illness and childhood trauma, I offer the following conclusions and recommendations.

1) Every person who has any of the mental disorders described in this book should be screened by a properly trained, experienced and licensed clinician who is knowledgeable about the effects of childhood trauma.

2) If there is a trauma history, the clinician can consider offering assistance to the person in a stage-oriented sequence, as described in chapter 11 of the prior volume, and summarized in Table 3.2 on page 20 in this book.

3) The concerned person and their clinician may consider using the flowcharts or decision trees shown throughout this book as possible guidelines.

4) A history of repeated childhood trauma may be appropriately considered to be an aggravating, if not possibly causal factor in the genesis of the mental illness. This consideration can have meaningful implications for the person's treatment and recovery.

5) Among several of these implications, the practice of connecting the two experiences of childhood trauma and mental illness now and in subsequent therapy and recovery-oriented situations can be healing. (It is usually easier to heal from

childhood trauma than it is to be labeled lifelong as mentally ill, with no way out.)

6) This healing process may occur most successfully by using a trauma-focused and stage-oriented treatment and recovery program. Trauma-focused treatment is an empirically based art and science that has slowly and carefully evolved over the last century, and especially since about 1980 (see chapter 21 and other works [e.g., as listed at bottom of page 239]).

7) In it, over time, the recovering person gradually identifies, accurately names, addresses and grieves the trauma and its painful effects.

8) It is useful to lower our expectations that psychoactive drugs will be of much help, and be aware of drug toxicities (which the drug industry and most clinicians call "side effects").

9) Consider improving nutrition and getting regular exercise. When possible, avoid caffeine and sugar. Address any sleep problems, which are common among trauma survivors. Doing these will likely help the recovery process go more smoothly and successfully. Reviewing these and other aids in chapter 12 on page 147 of the prior volume can also help.

10) The program is usually best facilitated by using a supplemental, written personal recovery plan, ideally accomplished by the concerned person and reviewed with them by their clinician. To facilitate this process, see *My Recovery: A Personal Plan for Healing.*[1096]

11) This whole process cannot be rushed, and usually takes a long time, i.e., at least a few years.

12) I and countless others, including my several group therapy co-leaders over the years, have seen that for people who are patient and persistent about their recovery work, that

recovery works and healing happens. They are usually eventually able to realize peace and gratitude in their lives.

I wish you the best in your recovery, and/or if you are a clinician, in your helping others to heal.

Charles L. Whitfield, M.D.
Atlanta, GA, January 2004

Trauma Spectrum Disorders

With this strong evidence that repeated childhood trauma is significantly associated with (at the least) and likely in large part causal for several of the most common mental disorders, we can now consider a rational re-classification of how we look at mental illness, especially with reference to the *DSM's* structure. This more accurate and clinically appropriate and useful classification would have a large part of the *DSM* subsumed under the heading of *Trauma Spectrum Disorders,* as suggested by several independent researchers and clinicians (e.g., Vermetten, Charney & Bremner 2002, Ross 2000, Briere 1996). Rather than separating various trauma-effect disorders into symptom-related categories (e.g., calling depression a mood disorder, anxiety disorder and PTSD as anxiety disorders, dissociative identity disorder and related disorders as only dissociative disorders, and perhaps even alcoholism and other chemical dependence as simply addictions), it appears that from a treatment and prevention perspective it would be more accurate and useful to classify them as follows.

Trauma Spectrum Disorders

PTSD (acute or chronic)	Dissociative identity disorder (& other dissociative disorders)
Anxiety disorders	
Depression (major or minor, & suicidality)	Borderline personality disorder
	Somatization disorder
Chemical dependence (alcohol, other drugs)	Disorders of violence & re-victimization
Eating disorders	Some psychoses

(continued)

Exclusions can be made when, over time and after a careful and objective search, no trauma has been found to have been associated with any of these above conditions (with a reservation that dissociative amnesia may be present and the person therefore may not remember any or all aspects of their trauma).

The other disorders and conditions that I have found reports for and which link them to childhood trauma include the psychoses, some personality disorders other than BPD and ADHD/ADD. Since these have also been shown to be commonly linked to childhood trauma, whenever they are diagnosed, a trauma history should be taken initially and, as appropriate, in follow-up.

A problem is that the *DSM* has traditionally avoided addressing the causes of the mental disorders that it classifies. Combined with the long tendency of psychology and psychiatry to discount childhood trauma as an important causal factor for mental illness, such a tradition is unlikely to be broken.

To see that the above changes will advance the treatment and prevention of mental illnesses requires that we remain objective and open to the large amount of data reported by numerous researchers, which I summarize throughout this and the prior book. A marker of an authentic truth seeker or scientist is openness to explore and go where the data leads them.

READER/CUSTOMER CARE SURVEY

BB1

We care about your opinions. Please take a moment to fill out this Reader Survey card and mail it back to us.
As a special **"thank you"** we'll send you exciting news about interesting books and a valuable **Gift Certificate.**

Please PRINT using ALL CAPS

Name [_____] [__] [_____]
First   MI.   Last
                                        Name

Address [_____]

City [_____] ST [__] Zip [_____]−[___]

Phone # ([___]) [___]−[____]   Fax # ([___]) [___]−[____]

Email [_____]

(1) Gender:
____ Female   ____ Male

(2) Age:
____ 12 or under   ____ 40-59
____ 13-19   ____ 60+
____ 20-39

(3) Marital Status
____ Married
____ Single
____ Divorced/Widowed

(4) Did you receive this book as a gift?
____ Yes   ____ No

(5) How many Health Communications books have you bought or read?
____ 1   ____ 2-4   ____ 5+

(6) How did you find out about this book?
Please fill in ONE.
1) ____ Recommendation
2) ____ Store Display
3) ____ Bestseller List
4) ____ Online
5) ____ Advertisement
6) ____ Catalog/Mailing
7) ____ Interview/Review (TV, Radio, Print)

(7) Where do you usually buy books?
Please fill in your top TWO choices.
1) ____ Bookstore
2) ____ Religious Bookstore
3) ____ Online
4) ____ Book Club/Mail Order
5) ____ Price Club (Costco, Sam's Club, etc.)
6) ____ Retail Store (Target, Wal-Mart, etc.)

(9) What subjects do you enjoy reading about most? Rank only **FIVE**. Use 1 for your favorite, 2 for second favorite, etc.

	1	2	3	4	5
1) Parenting/Family	O	O	O	O	O
2) Relationships	O	O	O	O	O
3) Recovery/Addictions	O	O	O	O	O
4) Health/Nutrition	O	O	O	O	O
5) Christianity	O	O	O	O	O
6) Spirituality/Inspiration	O	O	O	O	O
7) Business Self-Help	O	O	O	O	O
8) Teen Issues	O	O	O	O	O
9) Sports	O	O	O	O	O

(14) What attracts you most to a book?
(Please rank 1-4 in order of preference.)

	1	2	3	4
1) Title	O	O	O	O
2) Cover Design	O	O	O	O
3) Author	O	O	O	O
4) Content	O	O	O	O

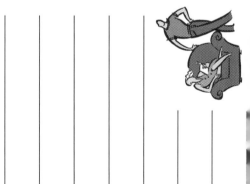

Comments:

Appendix

Table A 3.1. PTSD and Childhood

Year/Author	Study Characteristics	PTSD
1985 Lindberg & Distad	17 CSA	All (100%)
1986 Donaldson & Gardner	26 ♀ in Tx for CSA	25/26 (96%)
1987 Burgess et al.	34 CSA children, 34 controls	↑
1988 McLeer et al.	31 children CSA 25 girls, 6 boys	38x when F. abuser 25% when trusted adult
1989 Deblinger et al.	58 CS/PA, 29 controls 49 CS/PA, 40 CS/PA	3.8x (38%) 10% controls
1989 Coons et al.	26 PTSD women (Index cases)	72% had a CT history
1990 Davidson & Smith	54 new psych patients, 44 CT	↑
1991 Kiser et al.	10 CSA children (severe CT)	90%
1991 Brown & Anderson	1.019 psych inpatients CT v. controls	↑
1992 Pribor & Dinwiddie	52 women	25x
Famularo et al.	61 CT 5-10 yo 35 controls	20–46.4x
1993 Rowan & Foy	CT subjects	69% PTSD
1993 Famularo et al.	101 CT children 39% PTSD	
1994 Pelcovitz et al.	27 CPA teens 27 controls	3/27 (due to CSA)

Trauma: 54 Clinical Studies

Other Effects of Trauma	Comments
100% depressed, 47% suicidal, 12% SA/CD	
↑ anxiety, SA/CD antisocial behavior	↑ insomnia, somatization
29x depression ↑ anxiety	DSM criteria alone often → false negative
↑ depression, anxiety, behavior problems	
co-morbidity	Men veterans had a 20% CT history
↑ depression, anxiety, SA/CD, PD, bulimia	
CTS without PTSD tend to show other disorders	
↑ Co-morbidity	
6x SA/CD, 9x depession 6-15x anxiety d.	
↑ ADHD, conduct, oppositional, depression, SA/CD	↑ anxiety, PD, bedwet/soil, psychosis, adjustment disorder
↑ depression, behavior problems, thought disorder	Used non-clinician grad students as interviewers

Table A 3.1 PTSD and Childhood Trauma: 54 Clinical Studies *(continued)*

Year/Author	Study Characteristics	PTSD
1994 Famularo et al.	109 CT children	36% PTSD CT at younger age more PTSD
1994 Famularo & Fenton	117 severe CT children	35% PTSD
1994 Roesler & McKenzie	188 CT adults (20 men, 168 women)	↑ PTSD
1994 De Bellis et al.	12 CSA 8-15 yo girls, 9 controls	↑
1995 Grice et al.	100 SA/CD 66 CT	↑
1996 Davidson et al.	67 CSA (1/3 < 16 yo)	3-4x
1996 Ellason et al.	106 SA/CD inpts (69 CT)	↑
1997 Pillay & van der Veen	2,851 controls 100 children	↑
1997 Roth et al.	234 CT adults	↑ complex PTSD
1998 Alexander et al.	92 white women well-educated	↑
Ackerman et al.	127 CSA, 43 CPA, 34 both, 7-13 yo	↑
1998 Carlson et al.	187 psych inpatients CT v. controls	↑

Table A 3.1 PTSD and Childhood Trauma: 54 Clinical Studies *(continued)*

Other Effects of Trauma	Comments
Lower birth weight & illness—more PTSD	
Depression, dissociation, sexual dysfunction & self-esteem	Showed CSA was a significant factor
↑ depression/suicide, ADHD	↑ with catecholamines
	From Southeast USA catchment area study
↑ depression, dissociation, PD	
↑ depression	More were depressed who delayed disclosure
	More CT → more PTSD
↑ PTSD	Associated attachment disorders
↑ depression, bipolar, anxiety, phobia	Behavior problems: ADHD, OD, conduct dis, OCD, avoidant
↑ dissociation, amnesia	Control sample bias likely

Table A 3.1 PTSD and Childhood Trauma: 54 Clinical Studies *(continued)*

Year/Author	Study Characteristics	PTSD
1999 Fondacaro & Holt	86 CSA prisoners 125 controls	↑
1999 Dickinson et al.	552 women CSA v. controls	↑
2000 De Bellis et al.	11 CT children 11 controls	100% PTSD
2000 Elhai et al.	64 CSA adults	100% PTSD
2000 Messman-Moore et al.	633 women CT/AT v. controls	↑
2000 Gurvitz et al.	21 CSA women	
2000 Hefferman & Cloitre	71 CSA survivors	100%
2001 Ford et al.	50 ADHD, 270 DD, 40 both, 48 adjustment disorder controls	↑
2001 De Bellis et al.	53 CTs & family 46 controls & family	85% PTSD
Johnson et al.	89 CSA women	78% PTSD
2002 Saigh et al.	151 CT children	↑ PTSD
2002 Martinez et al.	47 women CT v. controls	64% PTSD
2002 Taylor & Jason	18,675 people CT v. controls	↑
2002 Runyon et al.	98 CT children	↑

Table A 3.1 PTSD and Childhood Trauma: 54 Clinical Studies *(continued)*

Other Effects of Trauma	Comments
↑ depression, OCD, ASPD, psychosis	41% CSAs thought they were not molested
↑ depression, anxiety, bulimia, somatization	Medical clinic patients
Brain damage evidence	
↑ depression, anxiety, somatization	observation that is similar to combat PTSD
↑ anxiety	
↑ 57% ADHD symptoms	
↑ borderline personality	Compared BPD & PTSD
↑ behavior problems in CS/PA	
↑ depression/suicidally anxiety, ADHD,ODD	Shows trauma is transgenerational
68% depression, 22% DDs	Shows trauma is transgenerational
↑ depresson, anxiety	↑ somatization, thought dis
↑ revictimization	
	All were HIV positive
↑ anxiety disorders	Among those with chronic fatigue
↑ depression	

Table A 3.1 PTSD and Childhood Trauma: 54 Clinical Studies *(continued)*

Year/Author	Study Characteristics	PTSD
2002 Simpson	SA/CD women CSA severe v. less severe	↑
2002 Cloitre	58 women with PTSD	All had CSA histories
2002 Mestin & Mohr	56 CT children	↑
2002 Yen et al.	455 people with PD, 76-92% CT	↑
2002 Brady & Caraway	41 CT children 7 to 12 yo	24 to 58%
2002 Lewis- Fernandez et al.	11 PTSD patients	↑ CT
2002 Mertin & Mohr	56 CT children	↑
2002 Kennedy et al.	50 BDs, 30 Schiz 57 & 65 CT	1/3 to 1/2
2002 Levetich et al.	631 bipolar outpatients (45% with CT)	↑
2003 McLean & Gallop	65 CSA women	↑ complex PTSD
2003 Wright et al.	132 adults with PTSD	all had CT history
2003 Grossman et al.	52 PD pts	↑
54 studies 1985 to 2003	**28,894**	**↑ to 46x controls**

Table A 3.1 PTSD and Childhood Trauma: 54 Clinical Studies *(concluded)*

Other Effects of Trauma	Comments
More severe CSA → more mental health care & less SA/CD care	
Index case study & phases of treatment	
↑ anxiety, depression, dissociation	
94 depressed people had 78% CT histories	Trauma severity → disorder severity
↑ depression, anxiety, dissociation, anger	
	Index case study
↑ depression, anxiety, dissociation	
↑ SA/CD, anxiety, EDs	Earlier onset, more severe & co-morbidity among CT
↑ BPD, revictimization (55-91%)	Both parents neglected (22-71%)
Group therapy helped heal	Index cases
↑ revictimization	DST: Cortisol suppression assoc with PTSD
↑ co-morbidity: SA/CD depression, suicide, anxiety, aggression, violence, psychosis, antisocial behavior	**Overly strict reliance on DSM criteria may cause false negatives for PTSD** (Physical problems not looked for in most)

Table A 3.2. PTSD and Childhood

Year/Author	Study Characteristics	PTSD	Other Effects of Trauma	Comments
1987 Kilpatrick	126 CSA survivors	10% incidence 36% prevalence		
1990 Greenwald & Lutenberg	54 ♀	4% incidence 17% prevalence		
Winfield et al.	1,157 women CSA v. controls	↑	↑ depression, panic, SA/CD, OCD	Adult trauma assessed
1991 Bagley	750 women CT v. controls	↑ PTSD symptoms	↑ depression ↓ self-esteem	ages 18–27
1992 Saunders et al.	122 CS/PA 137 controls	↑	↑ depression	
Wind & Silvern	259 women CT v. controls	↑ PTSD symptoms	↑ depression adult neg. experience*	Uses trauma Checklist 33
1994 Bagley et al.	750 college men CT v. controls	↑	↑ depression, suicidality, anxiety, pedophilia	
Rosler & McKenzie	188 CT survivors	↑	↑ depression, dissociation ↓ self-esteem	no control group
1995 Boney-McCoy & Finkelhor	2,000 10–16 yo national sample, CSA	↑ PTSD symptoms	↑ school problems	Controlling for family dysfunction, CSA still assoc.
Elliott & Briere	116 CSA 385 controls	↑	↑ depression, dissociation	Further data in Fig. 7.2 on page 76
1996 Duncan et al.	4,008 women, national survey	5x (incidence) 10x prevalence	Depression 2/4x MHTx 2 + x SA/CD 2–3 + x	Problems: Legal 4x, job 1.5/11x, Rel'ns probs 10–25x Tx for SA 1.2–7.4x

Trauma: 21 Community Studies *(concluded)*

Year/Author	Study Characteristics	PTSD	Other Effects of Trauma	Comments
1997 Dansky et al.	3,006 women CSA/adult rape v. controls	↑	↑ bulimia nervosa & binge eating	
1998 Mulder et al.	1,028 people CT v. controls	7.7x	↑ depression, anxiety, SA/CD, dissociation	Several CT factors involved
1998 Alexander et al.	92 CSA	↑	↑ depression	Attachment disorder focus
Schaaf & McCanne	475 women college students CT v. controls	↑	↑ revictimization, anxiety, depression, dissociation	↑ self-esteem ↑ sexual problems
1999 Saunders et al.	2,008 young women CSA/rape v. controls	3.1–3.4x	↑ depression, SA/CD	
Duncan	210 college students Ct v. controls	↑	↑ depression, anxiety, somatization, psychoticism	used SLC-90-R survey
2001 Reynolds et al.	45 5–11 YOs who witnessed domestic violence	↑	ADHD, conduct & hyperactivity problems	No control group
Hanson et al.	4,008 women	↑	↑ depression	National probability sample
2002 Ullman & Brecklin	national sample women, CT v. controls	↑	↑ depression, suicidality, SA/CD	
2001 Taylor & Jason	18,675 adults CT v. controls	↑	↑ anxiety, chronic fatigue	
1987–2002 21 Studies	**39,344 CTs and controls**	**↑ to 7.7x**	**↑ co-morbidity: SA/CD, depression, suicidality, anxiety, aggression, ADHD**	**↑ legal, job problems ↓ self-esteem**

Table A 3.3. PTSD and Childhood Trauma:

Year/Author	Study Characteristics	PTSD
1996 Silverman et al.	375 to 519 children 17 yr. follow-up at ages 5, 9, 15, 18, 21 at 21, retrospective abuse assessment	3 to 16x
Boney-McCoy & Finkelhor	1,433 10–16 yos, national, 15 month follow-up	↑ (reinterviewed 1995 sample 15 mos. later)
Famularo et al.	526–12 yos with PTSD 1,575 children followed 20 yrs* (5 reports)	100% traumatized
Duncan	210 college students Ct v. controls	↑
1998 Epstein et al.	2,994 women CT v. controls	↑
1996–1999 Widom et al.	3,579 CTs and controls	↑
2000 Cameron	72 women, 51 for the full 5 surveys over 12 years follow-up	63% had PTSD
2002 Lansford et al.	585 children CT v. controls	↑
Feiring et al.	80 CT children 57 CT teens	↑
2003 Breslau et al.	899 people CT v. controls	↑
Hawke et al.	446 SA/CD teens with ↑ CT	↑
1996–2003 10 Studies	**7,221 CT people & controls**	**↑ to 16x**

Associations from 10 Prospective Studies

Other Effects of Trauma	Comments
Other co-morbidity	
↑ depression	Trauma appears causal of psychological symptoms
After 2 years, 1/3 still had PTSD	PTSD is a chronic debilitating disorder
↑ depression, anxiety, somatization, psychoticism	used SLC-90-R survey
↑ SA/CD	PTSD possible factor in SA/CD
↑ depression/suicide, anxiety, SA	↑ aggression, violence, antisocial behavior
↑ depression/suicide, anxiety, sexual & somatic problems, ↑ self-esteem	With trauma-focused treatment there was substantial improvement over time
↑ depression, aggression, social problems	↑ thought disorder
↑ depression ↓ self-esteem	
↑ SA/CD nicotine use	10-year follow-up
↑ co-morbidity	5-year follow-up
↑ depression/suicide, anxiety, SA, ↓ self-esteem	**↑ aggression, violence, antisocial behavior**

Table A 3.6. PTSD and Childhood Sexual Trauma: Meta-Analyses/Literature Reviews of 300+ Studies*

Year/Author	Study Characteristics	PTSD	Other Effects of Trauma	Comments
1993 Kendall-Tackett et al.	45 study literature review	↑	Co-morbidity	Evidence for PTSD as a CT central effect
Rowan & Foy	Literature review	↑	↑ Co-morbidity	PTSD = core features of CSA effects
1996 Newmann et al.	38 study meta-analysis CSA/ depression/ other disorders, 11,162 subjects	↑	↑ Association with co-morbidities	Symptoms were effects of trauma, not character defects
1999 Gershuny & Thayer	Literature review of over 200 articles	↑	↑ dissociation, bulima, BPD	
2001 Rosenberg et al.	Literature review	↑		PTSD is often undiagnosed & untreated
2002 Paolucci et al.	37 study meta-analysis CSA/depression/ suicide	↑	↑ association with co-morbidities	High difficulty to disprove these results
Summary of Reviews 1993–2002	**4 Literature Reviews, 2 Meta-analyses**	**↑ association with CT**	**↑ Co-morbidity**	**Need to diagnose & treat PTSD**

*Other literature reviews include references 72, 144, 343 and 556.

Table A 4.1. Anxiety and Childhood

Year/Author	Study Characteristics	Anxiety/Disorder
1972 Lukianowicz	26 CSA girls	↑
1982 Adams-Tucker	28 CSA children	↑
1985 Kroll et al.	31 CT alcoholics 31 non-CT alcoholics	↑
1986 Friedrich et al.	85 CSA 3–12-year-old children clinical, forensic	↑
1989 Stein et al.	51 women	↑ + phobia
1990 Metcalfe et al.	100 men psych patients	↑
Davidson & Smith	54 new psych patients (44 CT)	↑
1991 Bagley & Shewchuck Dann	60 CSA pre-teens 320 controls	↑
1992 Pribor & Dinwiddie	52 women	6–15x + phobia
Scott	167 CSA survivors v. 2,964 controls, from general population	phobia 3.4x
1992 Kinzl & Biebl	33 CSA women psych patients	↑ , plus OCD
Friedrich et al.	42 CSA boys	↑ anxiety & OCD
1993 Moeller et al.	354 abused ♀ (CSA, PA, EA) v. 314 controls in a GYN practice	1.5x
Swett & Halpert	71 of 88 psych unit hosp. women CS/PA v. 17 "no abuse"	↑

Trauma: 35 Clinical Studies

Other Effects of Trauma	Comments
↑ depression, PDs	
↑ ODD, suicidality, psychosis	
Depression, somatization, aggression, delinquency, hyperactivity, etc.	Evaluated by Child Behavior checklist
Depression & SA/CD	
Depression, bipolar, psychosis	
↑ depression, SA/CD, DD, bulimia, PTSD	
↑ depression, ADHD symptoms, SA/CD, ↓ self-esteem	All had also offended
4–9x depression 6x SA/CD	
SA 2.1–5.2x, Depression: 3.5x for contact CSA; 5.2x for intercourse; any affective disorder 2.4x	
↑ depression, SA/CD, BPD, MPD	Traumas triggered illness
SA (2.5x alc, 28x drug), depression 2x/6.4x 2x obesity	Found 26 dysfunctional char's. of abused's parents [8% of perps were women]
↑ hostility & psychoticism, plus BPD, APD, S–D, PD & schizoid PD	"Controls" were also psych inpatients = hi risk & control bias

Table A 4.1. **Anxiety and Childhood Trauma: 35 Clinical Studies** (continued)

Year/Author	Study Characteristics	Anxiety/Disorder
1995 Yaryura Tobias et al.	19 women CT v. controls	↑ OCD
Menne & Meadow	135 girls 6–18 with CSA evaluated	↑
Lanz	77 CSA v. 164 controls, all pregnant single adolescents	↑
Walker et al.	43 CT women 46 controls	3.5x anx. dis. 2.3x panic dis. 16.2x OCD
1997 McCauley et al.	424 of 1,931 ♀ CS &/or CPA	↑
Ferguson & Dacy	55 women CSA 55 controls	↑
Jarvis & Copeland	130 CSA	↑
1999 Thompson & Kaplan	75 CT children	↑
Duncan	210 college students CT v. controls	↑
Dickinson et al.	552 women CSA v. controls	↑ GAD phobia
2000 Marshall et al.	74 people with panic disorder	↑ CT
Sadowski & Friedrich	32 CSA teens	↑
Hulme	91 CSA women 304 controls	↑
2001 Kirkengen	34 CSA survivors	↑

Table A 4.1. Anxiety and Childhood Trauma: 35 Clinical Studies *(continued)*

Other Effects of Trauma	Comments
Self-harm	Index Case OCD's
↑ depression, ↓ self-esteem	Force & penetration = more symptoms
↑ depression, SA, delinquency ↓ self-esteem, support family rel'ns	Controls not being normals may bias the degree of difference
↑ somatization	
1.6x depression, ↑ SA & medical disorders	Half also abused as adults
↑ depression & dissociation	
↑ co-mobidity	
↑ ADHD, disruptive behavior	
↑ depression, PTSD, somatization, psychoticism	Used SLC-90-R survey
↑ depression, PTSD, bulimia, somatization	Medical clinic patients
↑ co-morbidity (highest were excluded)	Index case study
↑ depression, PTSD	↑ dissociation, anger
↑ co-morbidity	
↑ depression, SA/CD, EDs, somatization, revictimization, hospitalization	From a general practice study

Table A 4.1. Anxiety and Childhood Trauma: 35 Clinical Studies *(concluded)*

Year/Author	Study Characteristics	Anxiety/Disorder
2002 King et al.	140 CSA men 191 "consensual" sex as child, 2,357 controls	1.7x
2002 Menton & Mohr	56 CT children	↑
Paul	376 ED women CT v. controls	↑ OCD
Brady & Caraway	41 CT children 7 to 12 yo	46% anxiety
2003 Salmon et al.	125 GI patients CT v. controls	↑
Callahan et al.	17 CSA adults 34 psych clinic controls	↑ anxiety & phobia
Walrath et al.	759 CSA children 2,722 controls 5–17 yo	3.5x
Total 35 Studies 1972–2003	**13,212 survivors & controls**	**↑ to 15x 5 found phobia 4 OCD**

Table A 4.1. Anxiety and Childhood Trauma: 35 Clinical Studies *(concluded)*

Other Effects of Trauma	Comments
↑ co-morbidity	
↑ PTSD, depression, dissociation	
↑ depression, PTSD, dissociation	
↑ dissociation, revictimization	
↑ personality disorders	↓ self-esteem
↑ depression, somatization, aggression, self-harm	2x psych hospitalization, ↓ functioning
↑ Co-Morbidity	Diverse samples showed same results linking anxiety and anxiety disorders to history or repeated CT

Table A 4.2. Anxiety/Anxiety Disorder

Year/Author	Study Characteristics	Anxiety/Disorder
1986 Bagley & Ramsay	82 CT woman v. 285 controls	11x
1987 Briere & Runtz	152 adult women at a health crisis center (67 CSA [44%] v. 85 controls)	2x
1986 Gorcey et al.	41 CSA survivors,* 56 controls	↑ *(Some clinical subjects)
1988 Briere & Runtz	41 undergrad. ♀ v. 237 controls	↑
Stein et al. (LA Epid. Catchment Area study)	2,683 random sample CSA v. controls	2–10x
Burnam et al. (above follow-up)	432 CSA v. 2,693 controls	↑ , plus OCD
Scott	167 CSA survivors v. 2,964 controls, from general population	↑ (as 3.4x phobias)
1989 Fromuth & Burkhart	582 college men CT v. controls	↑ OCD symptoms
1990 Greenwald et al.	54 CSA nurses 54 controls	↑ anxiety phobia, OC symptoms
Winfield et al.	1,157 women CSA v. controls	↑ panic disorder, OCD
1992 Yama et al.	college students; 42 CSA, 67 ACoA, 70 controls	↑
1993 Yama et al.	139 college students: (46 CSA women v. 93 controls)	↑

and Childhood Trauma: Community Studies

Other Effects of Trauma	Comments
↑ depression, 7x psychosis	2–3x ↓ self-esteem
↑ depression, SA (2.6x alcsm, 9x drug), 2x anxiety, 2x anger, self-harm, sexual problems, muscle tension	Control group also in crisis may have minimized the differences
↑ depression, sexual problems	Difficulty trusting men
↑ depression, dissociation, medical disorders	
3 + x depression, 2x SA, 9x schiz., 5x OCD, 3.8x APD	2.2x any mental disorder
↑ substance abuse No ↑ mania, schiz., APD	Younger age abused → later more mental disorders
Depression 3.5–5.2x, SA 2.1–5.2x, any affective disorder 2.4x	
↑ psychoticism, hostility, depression	
↑ depression, somatization	
↑ depression, SA/CD, PTSD	Assault as adult included
↑ depression	Family may mediate some effects
↑ depression and family dysfunction	

Table A 4.2. Anxiety/Anxiety Disorder and Childhood Trauma: Community Studies *(continued)*

Year/Author	Study Characteristics	Anxiety/Disorder
1994 Bagley et al.	750 men CT v. controls	↑
Collings	284 college men CT v. controls	↑ plus phobias & OCD
1995 Romans et al.	252 CSA women v. 252 controls	↑
1996 Golding et al.	6,025 people CT v. controls	↑
1997 Fisher et al.	665 9–17 YOs 26% (172) PA	↑
Ferguson & Dacey	55 ch. psych. abused women* v. 55 controls	↑
Ferguson & Lynskey	1,265 children surveyed; PA, some CSA	↑
Ellason & Ross	144 psych inpatients all CT	↑
1998 Mulder et al.	1,028 people CT v. controls	5x
Schaff & McCanne	475 college women CT v. controls	↑
1999 Duncan	210 college freshman	↑
Kent et al.	236 college women CT v. controls	↑
Armsworth et al.	36 women CSA v. 35 controls	1.9–5x
2000 Messman-Moore et al.	633 women CT/AT v. controls	↑

Table A 4.2. Anxiety/Anxiety Disorder and Childhood Trauma: Community Studies *(continued)*

Other Effects of Trauma	Comments
↑ depression, suicidality PTSD, pedophilia	
↑ depression, somatization, psychoticism	May underestimate findings
↑ depression, SA eating disorders	These esp. ↑ among self-harming
↑ depression, somatization	↓ functioning
↑ anxiety, conduct, defiant & impairment	↓ social skills
↑ depression & dissociation	*2/3 denied having been psych. abused
↑ depression & suicide in a graded fashion	
↑ SA/CD, depression, BPD	
↑ depression, SA/CD, dissociation	6% of gen pop dissociative
↑ depression, PTSD, dissociation, revictimization	↓ self-esteem
↑ depression, PTSD, somatization, psychoticism	Used SLC-90-R survey
↑ depression, EDs, dissociation	
3–9x depression, 2x suicide 13x psych. hosp. admissions 2–11x eating disorders	↓ self-esteem, ↑ adult victimization
↑ PTSD, revictimization	

Table A 4.2. Anxiety/Anxiety Disorder and Childhood Trauma: Community Studies *(concluded)*

Year/Author	Study Characteristics	Anxiety/Disorder
2000 Harder & Vanecek	651 college students CT v. controls	↑
2001 MacMillan et al.	7,016 people CT v. controls	2x
Lipman et al.	1,471 mothers, trauma Hx v. controls	2.1x
2002 Harkness & Wildes	76 depressed women, CT v. controls	↑
Nelson et al.	1,991 twin pairs CT v. controls	↑ social anxiety
Taylor & Jason	18,675 adults CT v. controls	↑
2003 Krause et al.	127 adults CT v. controls	↑
Levitan et al.	6,597 people CT v. controls	↑
1999, 2000 & 2003 Kendler et al.	1,411 ♀ twin pairs 30% CSA	↑ anxiety & phobia
2000 Krantz & Ostergren	128 P/CSA v. 263 controls all Swedish ♀ random	↑
Harter & Taylor	333 college students, age 18–29, median 19, 59% ♀	↑
1987–2003 38 Studies	**63,223 people CT v. controls**	↑ **to 11x**

Table A 4.2. Anxiety/Anxiety Disorder and Childhood Trauma: Community Studies *(concluded)*

Other Effects of Trauma	Comments
↑ depression, somatization	
↑ co-morbidity	Women more affected
2.1x depression, 3.2 SA	Child abuse Hx consistent & significant assoc. with adult problems, when controlled for
↑ co-morbidity	
↑ fatigue, PTSD	↑ adult trauma
↑ depression	↑ emotional inhibition
↑ depression (common co-morbid)	Co-morbidity marked with CSA
↑ depression, SA, panic, bullimia	CSA is causal of diverse psychiatric disorders
↑ depression & somatic symptoms, esp. musculoskeletal	16% abused as adults
↑ depression, paranoia, psychosis, hostility	Parental alcoholism had no independent effects when controlled for abuse history
↑ **Co-Morbidity**	**Confirms clinical samples**

Table A 4.3. Anxiety/Anxiety Disorder and

Year/Author	Study Characteristics	Anxiety/Disorder
1986 Baglay & Ramsay	82 CSA 285 controls	6x
1996 Silverman et al.	375–519 children 17-yr. follow-up ages 5, 9, 15, 18, 21 at 21, retrospective abuse assessment	↑
Boney-McCoy & Finkelhor	1,433 10–16 yos, national, 15-month follow-up	↑ as PTSD (see text)
Fergusson et al.	1,000 children, sexually abused v. controls, followed yearly to 18 yo	↑
1998 Putnam et al.	164 girls: 77 CSA, 15 other abuse, 77 controls; followed ↑ 2 yrs x 20 yrs to young adulthood	↑
1996–99 Widom et al.	1,575 children followed 20 yrs** (5 reports)	↑
2000 Cameron	72 women, 51 for the full 5 12 year follow-up surveys	77% anxiety
2000 & 2002 Fergusson et al.	1,265 CSA & CPA, children followed yearly to 21 yo	↑
2002 Johnson et al.	167 children, CT v. controls	↑
Lansford et al.	585 children, 12-year follow-up	↑
2003 Hawke et al.	446 teens, CT v. controls	↑
2000–03 Johnson et al.	593 families	3x
12 Studies Long-term	**7,593 subjects & 593 families**	↑ **to 6x**

*Developmental effects: self-pathology, affect dysregulation, and developmentally delayed effects.
**Court-documented: 520 cases of neglect, 110 cases of physical abuse, 96 cases of childhood sexual abuse, and 543 control subjects.

Childhood Trauma: 12 Prospective Studies *(concluded)*

Other Effects of Trauma	Comments
↑ depression, suicidality, psychosis ↓ self-esteem	Cold & punitive parents, lack of support
↑ depression, suicidality, anxiety, SA, aggression, violence, antisocial behavior	High co-morbidity
(Other problems not screened for)	Trauma appears causal of psychological symptoms
↑ depression, suicidality, SA, aggression, violence, antisocial behavior	Effects had a graded relationship to severity of trauma
↑ depression, SA, dissociation, somatization, ADHD, hypersexual behavior, older partners, developmental problems*	Co-morbidity (multiple)
↑ depression, SA, aggression, violence, antisocial behavior, PTSD	
7x (60% depressed); 32% somewhat depressed; 47% suicidal) 88%, 77% ↓ self-esteem; 82% ED; 78% sexual problems; 63% PTSD, 75% GYN; 67% headaches/jaw pain	With trauma-focused treatment there was substantial improvement in these disorders & symptoms over time
↑ depression, SA/CD, behavior	Significant false negatives may underestimate effects
↑ depression, aggression	
↑ depression, PTSD, behavior, thought	
↑ depression, PTSD, conduct disorders	↑ ADHD, violence
3x SA, 4x depression, 7.1x disruptive disorders	7.5x personality disorders, 3x any disorder
↑ depression, suicidality, SA, dissociation, somatization, ADHD, sexual probs, developmental & med problems	**Strong evidence that CT causes anxiety disorders**

Table A 4.4. Anxiety/Anxiety Disorder & Childhood

Year/ Author	Study Characteristics	Childhood Trauma	Other Effects of Trauma
1995 Mancini et al.	205 anxiety disordered	↑	
1996 Garfinkel et al.	8,116 people 62 bulimics with ↑ anxiety, phobia & panic disorder	↑	↑ depression, SA/CD
Berenbaum	21 anxiety disordered	↑	↑ alexithymia (feelings problems)
Portegijs et al.	40 anxiety disordered	1.2 to 2.3x	
1999 Thompson et al.	9 anxiety disordered	↑	↑ co-morbidity including ADHD
2002 Roy	532 SA/CDs with ↑ anxiety (neuroticism)	↑	
Simpson	72 SA/CD women with ↑ anxiety & depression	↑	↑ PTSD
2001 Taylor & Jason	222 chronic fatigue with ↑ anxiety disorders 74 controls	↑	↑ PTSD

Trauma: 15 *Index Case* Studies (concluded)

Year/ Author	Study Characteristics	Childhood Trauma	Other Effects of Trauma
2002 Leverich et al.	631 bipolars with ↑ anxiety	↑	↑ PTSD, SA/CD, EDs
Friedman et al.	159 anxiety disordered	↑ (CPA16-40%; CSA 13–43%)	More CT = more severe disorder
2002 Striegel-Moore et al.	47 anxiety disordered 251 controls	↑	
2002 Hexel & Sonneck	42 anxiety disordered	64%	
2002 Safren et al.	149 anxiety disordered	↑	↑ depression
Lewis Fernandez et al.	8 anxiety disordered	↑	↑ depression, PTSD
Lochner et al.	74 OCD patients 31 controls	↑	
15 Studies 1995–2002	**10,609 anxiety disordered or affected**	↑	↑ **Co-morbidity**

Table A 7.1. Dissociative Disorders and

Year/Author	Study Characteristics	Dissociation/Disorder
1985 Lindberg & Distad	17 CSA women	↑
Lindberg & Distad	27 CSA teens	↑
1988 Briere et al.	133 women, 61 controls average age 27	2x
Briere	40 CSA 40 controls	↑
1989 Herman et al.	55 adults (half men) CT v. controls	↑
Deblinger et al.	29 CP/SA 3–13, 29 CPA, 29 psych inpatients	↑
1990 Goodwin et al.	20 CT women (severe abuse)	100%
1991 Sanders & Giolas	47 psych unit teens	↑
1993 Nash et al.	56 CSA women v. 49 controls	↑
Pribor et al.	99 women, CT v. controls	↑
Anderson et al.	51 CSA women	55% DID, 88% some kind DD
1994 Waldinger et al.	99 consecutive psych outpatients 65 (2/3) CSA v. 34 controls	↑
Roesler & McKenzie	188 CSA adults, mean age 40 (20 men)	↑
Ross et al.	83 adults with ↑ CT	↑ on DES
1995 Brodsky et al.	60 BPD inpatient women, 60% CT	↑
1996 Engeland & Susman	24 women CT history 14 dissociators, 10 non	↑ on DES

Childhood Trauma: 30 Clinical Studies

Other Effects of Trauma	Comments
↑ SA/CD, depression, suicidality	
4–9x SA/Cd, 2x suicide, 8x self-harm, 8x revictimization	↑ sleep & sexual problems
↑ depression/suicidality, anxiety, insomnia, anger	Crisis center clients, men equally affected
BPD, traits, other psych disorders	
↑ inappropriate sexual behavior, ± PTSD	Used psych inpatients as controls: bias favors negative results
↑ co-morbidity	
Found a graded relationship between childhood trauma & degree of dissociation	
↓ self-esteem (feel damaged & inadequate)	Dissociation may be due to toxic family &/or CSA
All somatizers	
94% depression, 84% BPD, 65% SA, 45% somatization disorder	
More dissociation if abused younger	↑
↑ depression, PTSD, sexual dysfunction ↓ self-esteem	Showed CSA a significant factor in these
All schizophrenic	
↑ depression, psychiatric treatment, 52% self-harm	
The 14 idealized, avoided, and were inconsistent in their childhood descriptions	

Table A 7.1. Dissociation, Dissociative Disorders & Childhood Trauma: Clinical *(concluded)*

Year/Author	Study Characteristics	Dissociation/Disorder
1997 Jarvis & Copeland	310 women CT v. controls	↑
Ferguson & Dacey	55 women CSA 55 controls	↑
1998 Carlson et al.	187 psych inpatients CT v. controls	↑
Putnam et al. *Prospective*	164 girls: 77 CSA, 15 other abuse, 77 controls	↑
2001 Kisiel & Lyons	114 10–18 YO wards of state, 87 CSA/PA v. 27 controls	↑ Significant with CSA, not PA
Macfie et al.	198 preschoolers, 155 maltreated, v. 43 controls	↑
1999 Gold et al.	118 women CSA v. controls	
2000 Sadowski & Fredrich	32 CSA v. 87 psych disordered teens	↑
2001 Steiger et al.	60 women Ct v. controls	↑
2002 Hart & Waller	23 women bulimics with ↑ CT	↑
Mertin & Mohr	56 CT children	↑
2003 Nijenhuis et al.	52 chronic pain patients CT v. controls	↑ dissociation
Salmon et al.	125 GI patients CT v. controls	↑ dissociation
Total 30 Studies 1985–2003	**2,961 CTs and controls**	**↑ dissociation & dissociative disorders**

Table A 7.1. **Dissociation, Dissociative Disorders & Childhood Trauma** *(concluded)*

Other Effects of Trauma	Comments
↑ co-morbidity	
↑ depression & anxiety	
↑ PTSD dissociative amnesia	
↑ depression, anxiety, SA, somatization, ADHD, hypersexual, older partners, developmental problems	Followed every 2 yrs x 20 yrs to young adulthood. Study is ongoing.
↑ suicide, sexual aggression, self-mutilation, psychiatric symptoms	Severity of CSA not assoc. with psychiatric symptoms Neglected children also had signif dissoc.
↑ PTSD, depression, anxiety, anger	
Core issues found	
↑ depression, anxiety, PTSD	
↑ anxiety, revictimization	
↑ **multiple co-morbidity**	

Table A 7.2. Dissociation and Childhood

Year/Author	Study Characteristics	Dissociation
1988 Briere & Runtz	41 undergrad. ♀ v. 237 controls	↑
1989 Sanders et al.	#1: 309 college students	↑
Sanders et al.	#2: 337 college students (2/3 ♀)	↑
1994 Irwin	121 college students CT v. controls	↑
1995 Becker-Lausen et al.	301 college students	↑
Elliot & Briere	113 CSA 385 controls	↑
1998 Shields & Cicchetti	141 abused inner-city children v. 87 controls	↑
Schaff & McCanne	111 CT college students 211 controls	↑
Mulder et al.	1,028 people, CT v. controls	1.7–5.4x
1999 Sacco & Farber	259 college, 174 CSA/PA 85 controls	↑
Sanders & Moore	30 CSA/PA college women 133 controls	↑
Kent et al.	236 CT women v. controls	↑
1999 Startup	224 college students, CT v. controls	↑
2001 Banyard et al.	167 poor black women, CT v. controls	↑
2002 Lansford et al.	585 children CT v. controls	↑
Romana et al.	354 women, CT v. controls	↑
Total 16 Studies 1988–2002	**5,502 CTs and controls**	**Increased in all**

Trauma: 16 *Community* Studies

Other Effects of Trauma	Comments

↑ depression, anxiety, medical disorders

Both studies found a graded relationship between childhood trauma
& degree of dissociation

↑ depression, various negative life events*	
↑ depression, anxiety, anger, irritability, sexual problems	↓ self-esteem (see also Figure 7.2)
↑ emotional liability, attention deficits	↑ aggression esp. among physically abused
↑ depression, anxiety, PTSD	↑ revictimization
↑ depression, PTSD, SA/CD	
Both kinds of abuse showed dissociation	No significant perceptual distortions
↑ anxiety, depression, dysfunctional sexual behavior	↑ revictimization e.g., date rape (related to ↑ dissociation)
↑ depression, anxiety, ED symptoms	Emotional abuse a strong factor
↑ schizotypy	
↑ mental health problems	
↑ depression, anxiety, PTSD behavior problems	12-year follow-up
↑ medical problems	6-year follow-up
↑ **co-morbidity, revictimization**	

*Supports a pattern in which the dissociation, depression, and other effects caused by childhood
trauma and themselves the cause of various negative life events, such as relationship difficulties,
work problems, and being fired from a job.

Table A 7.3. Dissociation and Childhood

Year/Author	Study Characteristics	Childhood Trauma
1984 Bliss	70 MPDs	78–90% CSA 27–60% CPA
1986 Putnam et al.	100 MPDs	97% had severe (86% CSA)
Coons & Millstein	20 MPDs 20 controls	85% CS/PA (11–15x controls)
1988 Coons et al.	50 DD patients	68% CSA 60% CPA
1989 Coons et al.	6 atypical DDs 11 dissociative amnesia, 20 DID	100% CT 82% 95%
Schultz et al.	355 DD patients	86% CSA 82% CPA
1995 Ross	236 MPDs	88% CS/PA 75% CPA
1990 Ross et al.	102 MPDs	95% CS/PA (97/102)
1995 Ellason & Ross	108 DID patients	Nearly all
1997 Ellason & Ross	2-year follow-up 54 DIDs in treatment	Most had CT history
1998 Honig et al.	15 dissociative disordered	86%
Total 11 Studies 1984–1998	**1,167 DDs & controls**	**60–97%**

Trauma: 11 *Index Case* Studies

Other Effects of Trauma	Comments
23–38 conversion paralysis/ anesthesia	32–48% visual hallucinations
15x fugue, 20x visual hallucinations, 5x conversion paralysis/anesthesia	5.5x headaches, 2x organic seizures, 30x raped (revictimized)
	Cited in Ross 1989
↑ headaches, 61% somatization, 64% prior Dx BPD	27% diagnosed schizophrenic, 27% history of ECT
↑ "positive" Sx of schizophrenia	

Trauma-focused treatment gave significant improvement, including ↓ hospitalization & number of drugs needed

↑ Co-morbidity	↑ psychotic & neurologic symptoms

Key: MPD = multiple personality disorder; DD = dissociative disorder; DID = dissociative identity disorder; CSA = childhood sexual abuse; CPA = childhood physical abuse

Table A 8.1. Substance Abuse/Chemical Dependence & Childhood Trauma: 90 Clinical & Community Studies

Year/Author	Study	SA/Chemical Dependence	Depression/Suicide Anxiety/Other
1942 Sloane & Kapinsky	5 CSA ♀ (incest)	8x (40% = 8x gen pop.)	↑ ; all 5 promiscuous. One of earliest CT reports
1972 Lukianowicz	26 CSA (incest) girls	3x	↑ personality disorders ↑ promiscuity, prostitution
1974 NIAAA, by Booz, Allen, Hamilton	Detailed interviews of 50 CoAs	↑	↑ , ↑ promiscuity, teen pregnancy, etc.
1980 Sowder & Burt	365 CT children 369 controls	↑	↑ school & behav. prob's Heroin addicted families
1981 Herman	Clinical, CT v. controls	7x	
1984 Briere	CSA survivors v. controls	2.4–10.5x	
Burgess et al.	66 CSA children	↑ alcohol & drug use	↑ somatization
1985 Lindberg & Distad	17 CSA women (incest)	2x (12% = 2x gen pop.)	↑ (100%) (47% suicidal) ↑ PTSD (100%)
1986 Putnam et al.	100% DIDs 96% CT	50%	90/97%, 18–20% schiz. Sx, 15/25% bulimia/anorexia
Baumgraber	21 CSA women incest	↑	↑ hyperactive, somatization
1987 Briere & Runtz	67 CSA 85 controls	↑	↑ suicide, anxiety, anger, insomnia, sexual & self-destructiveness
Bryer et al.	48 CS/PA 27 controls	56–63%	↑ anxiety, PDs
Dembo et al.	145 troubled youth CT v. controls	↑	↑ violence 69 of 145 were girls

Table A 8.1. Substance Abuse/Chemical Dependence & Childhood Trauma *(continued)*

Year/Author	Study	SA/Chemical Dependence	Depression/Suicide Anxiety/Other
Burgess et al.	34 CSA (23 boys) 34 controls	↑	↑ anxiety, PTSD, somatization ↑ antisocial behavior, violence
Beck & van der Kolk	12 ♀, psych unit	3x controls	3-6x
1988 Steth et al.	3,132 adults CT v. controls	↑	↑ depression, co-morbidity
Peters	71 CSA women 48 controls	4x (17 v. 4%)	
Craine et al.	105 ♀, psych hospital	↑	2x 2x sexual dysfunction
Briere	133 CSA 61 controls	4–9	↑ 2x dissociation, 8x self-harm, ↑ revictimization
Dembo et al.	145 teens, troubled 46–76% CT	↑ + ↑ nicotine	↓ self-esteem
Burnam et al.	432 CSA 2,693 controls	2–4x (LA Catch Area)	↑, + ↑ OCD, Younger abuse → more illness
Caviola & Schiff	150 CS/PA teens 350 controls	↑	3/4 parental SA/CD
1989 Seng	70 CSA children 35 child prostitutes	↑	↑ depression, runaways
Stein et al.	51 women	↑	↑
Krug	8 CSA men	↑ (5/8)	↑ depression, teen problems
Caffaro-Rouget et al.	240 CSA children v. 57 controls	↑ (2.1–3.7x)	↑ physical illness & trauma in all teen treatment units
Briere & Zaidi	35 CSA 15 controls	2x	↑ sexual problems

Table A 8.1. Substance Abuse/Chemical Dependence & Childhood Trauma *(continued)*

Year/Author	Study	SA/Chemical Dependence	Depression/Suicide Anxiety/Other
1989 Hart et al.	38 CT teens 23 controls	1.4x SA	↑ health & legal probs ↓ self-esteem SA/CDs
1990 Shearer et al. clinical	40 BPD women (27 CSA, 17 PA)	12x	↑ EDs, ASPD, seizures ↑ hospitalizations
Brown & Garrison	132 CSA (incest), 250 controls	30–38x	↑ depr/suicide, ↑ + obesity, sexual probs, ↓ focusing ability
Winfield et al.	1,157 women CSA v. controls	↑	↑ depression, PTSD, anxiety, OCD
1991 Goodwin et al.	20 CT women severe	80%	↑ co-morbidity
1991 Brown & Anderson	166 CT 781 controls	↑	↑ , ↑ PDs, esp BPD 2x eating disorders
Rose et al.	89 psych patients CT v. controls	↑	↑ hospitalization, health care use
1991 Bagley & Shewchuck-Dann	60 CSA youth 320 controls	↑	↑ co-morbidity
Swett et al.	189 psych outpatients	↑	
1992 Pribor & Dinwiddie	52 women	6x	4–9x, 6–15x 25x PTSD
Hernandez	311 CSA 2,867 controls	4x alcohol, ↑ drugs/nicotine	2.4–3.4 CSA/ ↑ SA/CD in parents
Scott et al.	166 CSA 2,965 controls	2.1–5.2x	3.4x 3.8 any disorder
Frazier & Cohen	82 women, college clinic	↑	↑ ↑ revictimization
1993 Sibthorpe et al.	155 CT youth	↑	

Table A 8.1. Substance Abuse/Chemical Dependence & Childhood Trauma *(continued)*

Year/Author	Study	SA/Chemical Dependence	Depression/Suicide Anxiety/Other
1993 Mullen et al.	252 CSA 535 controls	2.4–9x	2.6–5.2x, 2.4–3x 3.2-6.7x ED 16x psych inpatient
Hussey & Singer	174 teens	↑	↑
Muenzenmaier et al.	78 psych outpatients (2/3 CT)	↑	↑ psychosis ↑ revictimization
Moeller et al.	354 CT 314 controls	1.8–2.5x	↑ , 2x obesity, PMS, GYN probs, High co-morbidity
Anderson et al.	51 CSA women	↑	↑ dissociation, BPD
1994 Bennett & Kemper	733 women CT v. controls	1.58x	
Bennett & Kemper	733 women CT v. controls	↑	
McKenna & Ross	79 men CT v. controls	↑	
1995 Polusney & Follette	N	3.5x****	↑ ↑ eating disorders
Widom et al.	611 CT youth 657 controls	↑ (in women)	control bias?
Walker et al.	43 CT ♀, 46 controls	3.2–7.3x (all lifetime figs)	↑ depr, anxiety/panic OCD, ↑ somatization, revictim- ization, GI clinic patients
Lanz	77 CSA teens 164 controls	↑	↑ , ↑ delinquency ↓ self-esteem All were single & pregnant
Ellason et al.	135 DIDs (96% CT)	6–12x (65%)	↑ depr/bipolar, anxiety, EDs, ↓ psychosis, soma- tization, High co-morbidity

Table A 8.1. Substance Abuse/Chemical Dependence & Childhood Trauma *(continued)*

Year/Author	Study	SA/Chemical Dependence	Depression/Suicide Anxiety/Other
1996 Garfinkle et al.	8,116 people CT v. controls BN v. controls	↑	↑ ↑ anxiety, phobia, BN
Wurr & Partridge	120 psych inpatients CSA v. controls	↑	↑ depression, PD, schiz
1997 McCauley et al.	424 of 1,931 ♀ CS/PA v. controls	↑	1.6x (↓ self-esteem) ↑ ↑ 1/2 also abused as adults
Ellason & Ross	144 CT psych inpatients	↑	↑ ↑ anx, BPD, psychoticism
Newmark-Sztainer et al.	123,132 teens CT v. controls	↑	↑ depr, suicidality ↑ delinquency
Walker et al.	1,000 HMO women	↑	↑ ↑ risk taking, DOV, illness
Felitti et al.	9,508 patients (ACE study)	4.7–10.3x	4.6–12.2x, 2–10.3x ↑ 1.6–3.9x
Robin et al.	129 CSA (246 controls)	2.4–4.9x	3–7x 2.3–6x school/behavior/ runaway probs 1.3–4x violence & crime
Briere et al.	93 ♀ psych ER patients (80+% CT/± adult trauma)	2 + x	2 + x, 3–8x violence 2x psychosis 42% revictimization
Pharrs et al.	1,157 teens	↑	↑ ED, behavior problems
1998 Roberts et al.	335 women in ED, abused v. controls	↑	↑ ↑ + domestic violence
Wilsnack et al.	278 CSA 690 controls women	1.6–3x	2.5x depression 1.6x anxiety, sexual problems National sample

Table A 8.1. Substance Abuse/Chemical Dependence & Childhood Trauma *(continued)*

Year/Author	Study	SA/Chemical Dependence	Depression/Suicide Anxiety/Other
1998 Kaplan et al.	99 CT teens 99 controls	↑	↑ nicotine, conduct disorder
Mulder et al.	1,028 people CT v. controls	5.2x	↑ depression, anxiety, PTSD, dissociation
1999 Fondacaro et al.	86 CSA prison inmates, 125 controls	↑ in both groups (83% = 8.3x gen population)	↑ ↑ anxiety, panic, PTSD ↑ OCD, OSPD, psychosis
Gladstone et al.	40 CSA women, 130 depressed "controls"	1.9–4.7x	2.5–26x +, ↑ BPD, self-harm, ↑ psych visits, ↓ self-esteem Not using normal controls may underestimate results
Saunders et al.	2,008 young women, CSA v. controls	↑	↑ depression, PTSD,
Grilo et al.	70 CT teens 93 controls	↑	↑ violence All on psych unit
Bensley et al.	4,790 teens CT v. controls	3–12x, plus ↑ nicotine	
2000 Bensley et al. Phone survey	518 ♀, 254 ♂ CS/CPA 2,701 controls	1.8–3.2x	HIV risk behavior ♀ 5–7x ♂ 3–8x
Hulme et al.	91 CSA women 304 controls	↑	↑ co-morbidity, somatization
Barnes et al.	506 teens CT v. controls	↑	
Kendler et al.	1,411 women twin pairs	1.9–5.7x	↑ depression, anxiety, ED
Clark & Foy	41 CVSA 37 controls	↑ alcohol use	↑ domestic violence, All treated for domestic violence

Table A 8.1. Substance Abuse/Chemical Dependence & Childhood Trauma *(concluded)*

Year/Author	Study	SA/Chemical Dependence	Depression/Suicide Anxiety/Other
2001 Dube et al.	17,337 people CT v. controls	↑	↑ co-morbidity
MacMillan et al.	1,858 CT 5,158 controls	1.8–3.8x	2.5x depression, 1.9 and psych disorder, 2x, 3.7 ASD Risk more in women
Lipman et al.	1,471 mothers, trauma Hx v. controls	3.2x	2.1x depr., 2.1x anxiety, CT consistent & significant...assoc. with adult prob's, even when controlled for
2002 Dohm et al.	215 ED women CT v. controls	↑	↑ self-harm, co-morbidity high association with CT
Fals-Stewart et al.	Children of 112 SA/CD fathers	↑	
Dube et al.	9,508 CT v. controls	↑	↑ , marry SA/CD Further ACE study data
King et al.	341 CSA men 2,357 controls	2.4x	↑ depression, anxiety, self-harm
Leverich et al.	631 bipolars (half CT)	↑	↑ co-morbidity
Diaz et al.	3,005 teen girls CT v. controls	↑	↑ depression, nicotine
Nelson et al.	3,982 adult twins	↑	↑ depression, anxiety, conduct disorder, ↑ nicotine, revictimization
2003 Lau et al.	489 teens CT v. controls	↑	↑ self-harm
Kendler et al.	5,600 twins CT v. controls	↑	↑ depression, anxiety, PD Prospective arm of prior report
Total 90 studies 1942–2003	**237,886 people CT v. controls**	**↑ to 2–38x**	**4–12x depression ↑ to 15x anxiety, other Multiple co-morbidity Common**

Key: CT = childhood trauma; SA/CD = substance abuse/chemical dependence; CSA = child sexual abuse; CPA = child physical abuse; CoA = child of an alcoholic; DOV = doctor office visit; ED = emergency department; ↑ = Increased, ***See refs below, ****Community and clinical samples. Where blanks are left, these problems were not reported as having been evaluated.

Table A 8.2. Substance Abuse/Chemical Dependence

Year/Author	Study	SA/Chemical Dependence
1978 Kroth 14 Months	70 CSA teens	4% admitted SA; thought most denial
1990 Riggs et al.	81 CS/PA 544 controls	2–3x, 3x nicotine
1992 Bushnell et al.	301 CSA women	1.2x
1996 Fergusson et al. 18 years	1,000 children	↑
Silverman et al. 17 years	63 CS/PA v. 479 controls	↑
1996–9 Widom et al. 20+ years	726* CS/PA, Neglect v. 543 controls	↑
1997 Russek & Schwartz 35 years	126 college men CT v. controls	↑
Lynskey & Fergusson to 18 years	107 CSA 918 controls	↑
1998 Putnam	77 CSA 72 controls	↑
Fergusson & Horwood 18 years	1,265 children followed yearly***	Alcohol 1.5–2.9x MJ 1.2–3X Nicotine 1.2–2.7x Other 1.2–6.1x
Epstein et al. 1 year	2,994 women community	2x (among the 291 raped as child)

& Childhood Trauma: 21 Prospective Studies

Depression/Suicide/Anxiety	Medical Disorders
	Followed 14 months FT → improved
↑ depression, mania, bulimia ↑ anxiety, conduct dis, ± APD ↑ co-morbidity	Asked "family context" a factor in found effects
↑ depression, ↑ anxiety (↑ ADHD)	↑ PTSD, dissociative disorders, somatization disorder, sexual problems, ↓ self-esteem** & affect control See also Table 8.3 on p. 87
↑ depression	↑ PTSD, dissociative disorders, somatization disorder, sexual problems, ↓ self-esteem** & affect control See also Table 8.3 on p. 87
↑ somatization	
↑	↑ conduct disorder; 1/4 appeared "normal"
↑ depression, ↑ anxiety (↑ ADHD)	↑ PTSD, dissociative disorders, somatization disorder, sexual problems, ↓ self-esteem** & affect control See also Table 8.3 on p. 87
Depression 1.2–x Suicidality 1.2–2.6x 1.1–3.3x	Conduct disorder 1.2–4.6x; Repeated Crime: Violent 1.1–3x Property 1.4–3.5x
↑ PTSD	PTSD from the CSA = a factor in alcohol abuse

Table A 8.2. Substance Abuse/Chemical Dependence & Childhood Trauma *(continued)*

Year/Author	Study	SA/Chemical Dependence
1998 Calam et al.	144 CSA 13–16 YOs	10x
Wilsnack et al. 15+ years	696 women CSA v. controls	↑
2000 Fergusson 21 years	1,265 children CT v. controls	↑
2000 Kendler et al. 4–10 years	1,411 ♀ adult twin pairs	3.2–6.6x in abused
Jasinski et al. 20 years	113 CSA (55% PA) children reinterviewed	2.5–8.7x heavy drinking
2001 Johnson et al. 18 years	593 families CT v. controls	3x
Schuck & Widom	582 children/women CT v. controls	↑
2000–2003 Sussman et al. study ongoing	115 CT teens 158 controls	↑ alcohol, MJ, nicotine
2003 Breslan et al.	899 people CT v. controls	↑
Ehrensaft et al. 20 years	543 youths CT v. control	↑
Total **21 studies** **1978–2003**	**15,873** **CT v. controls**	**1.2–10x, incl other** **drugs & nicotine**

Table A 8.2. Substance Abuse/Chemical Dependence Childhood Trauma *(concluded)*

Depression/Suicide/Anxiety	Medical Disorders
↑ depression, self-harm ↑ anxiety, ADHD Sx, EDs	See Table 15.5 on page 158 for full list of CSA effects
	20–24% of 696 had CSA in this ongoing prospective study
↑ co-morbidity	completion of prior study
1.1-2.8x GAD 1.2–2.6x	Bulimia 1.3–4.2x "Genetic transmission unlikely" ↓ self-esteem
4x depression 3x anxiety (7.1x disruptive disorders)	7.5x personality disorders 3x any disorder ↓ self-esteem
	Childhood trauma is prevalent & associated with ↑ drug use
↑ PTSD, nicotine use	SA/CD associated with PTSD
↑ violence, conduct disorder	Followed from childhood
↑ , 1.1–4x+ PTSD, ADHD, conduct dis, ED, ± APD	**Multiple Co-morbidity Common ↓ self-esteem**

PTSD = post-traumatic stress disorder; ADHD = attention deficit hyperactivity disorder; ED = eating disorder; APD = antisocial personality disorder
*Analysis of data on severe child neglect is in process; **Called decreased self-sense by authors;
***Traumas = witnessing extreme fighting between parents, some CSA, COA & other family dysfunction.

Table A 8.3. Chemical Dependence/Substance Abuse & Childhood Trauma: 29 *Index Case* Studies

Year/Author	Study Characteristics	Childhood Trauma	Other/ Comments
1975 Benward & Densen-Gerber	118 CD women inpatients	44% (52) CSA	1.5x depressed (CSA v. non-CSA), One of the earliest databased reports
1982 Cohen & Densen-Gerber	178 CD people	84% CT	Cited in Bernstein et al. 1998
1984 Harrison & Lumry	SA/CD ♀ in psych Dx clinic	74% CPA 29% CSA	Peer-reviewed presentation of data, cited in Jasinski et al. 2000
1985 Kroll et al.	31 CT alcoholic men 31 non-CT alc. men	CPA	↑ suicide & medical/ physical consequences Cited in Malinowsky-Rummel & Hansen 1993
1986 Herman	19 SA/CDs	53%	↑ BPD, violence, CTs had 2x SA/CD & 4x BPD
Covington	35 ♀ alcoholics 35 controls	↑ 2 + x CSA CPA	Cited in Langland & Hartgers 1998
1987 Jacobson & Richardson	17 SA/PDs	81% of total had major CT	
Downs et al.	45 ♀ alcoholics 40 controls	↑ CPA	
Miller et al.	45 ♀ alcoholics 40 controls	2.4x CSA	Same sample as Downs et al.
1988 Schaefer et al.	100 alcoholics	33% CPA (2.3x general pop.)	
Rohsenow et al.	753 SA/CDs CT v. controls	♀ 75–90% CT ♂ 16–42 CT	Routine inquiry is important
Caraiola & Schiff	500 SA/CD teens	30%	Dissociative amnesia likely in many

Table A 8.3. Chemical Dependence/Substance Abuse & Childhood Trauma *(continued)*

Year/Author	Study Characteristics	Childhood Trauma	Other/ Comments
1989 Jacobson	8 SA/CDs	↑	↑ revictimization as adult, ↑ alcohol/drug use during trauma
1990 Davidson & Smith	4 SA/CD patients	↑	↑ PTSD, anxiety, depression
Wallace	61 SA/CD patients	↑	
Lacy	112 bulimics SA/CD v. controls	↑	
1990 Jacobson & Herald	17 SA/CD	↑	44% perps used alc/drugs
1991 Rose et al.	49 SA/CD patients	↑	↑ self-harm
1992 Downs et al.	142 alcoholics	↑	↑ domestic violence
Wallen & Berman	217 SA/CD	↑	↑ parental violence
1993 Miller et al.–1	180 alcoholic women 82 controls	2–3x CSA ↑ CPA	
Miller et al.–2	178 ♀ alcoholics 174 controls	↑ CSPA	
1994 Loftus et al.	105 ♀ outpatients in drug treatment	59% CSA (62/105)	Dissociative amnesia common
Bernstein et al.	286 SA/CDs	↑	Cited in Higgens & McCabe 1994
1995 Windle et al.	302 ♀, 481 ♂ alcoholic patients	59% for ♀ 30% for ♂	↑ depression/suicide, anxiety disorder & APD. FH of alcoholism associated with higher trauma
Triffleman et al.	46 men SA/CD inpatients	77% had severe childhood trauma	58% PTSD. "Strong positive association"

Table A 8.3. Chemical Dependence/Substance Abuse & Childhood Trauma *(continued)*

Year/Author	Study Characteristics	Childhood Trauma	Other/ Comments
Grace et al.	100 SA/CDs	66%	↑ PTSD, anxiety disorder
1996 Moncrieff et al.	126 alcoholics CSA v. controls	↑ (26–54%)	↑ treated with psych drugs
1997 Fleming et al.	124 SA/CD women's opinions of rel'n to CSA	↑ % CT, NS relation SA/CD to CSA	↑ EDs, sexual probs, DV. Limited usefulness separating CSA from other traumas in outcome.
Jarvis & Copeland	131 SA/CD women	↑	↑ anxiety, dissociation, somatization
Clark et al.	183 SA/CD teens 73 controls	6–21x	
1998 Kunitz et al.	434 alcoholics v. 300 non-alcoholics	↑ physical abuse	↑ conduct disorder in abused. ↑ domestic violence in PA & alcoholism
2000 Heffernan et al.	137 opiate CDs 618 psych inpatients	2.7x among opiate users	Opiate use highest among physical and/or CSA survivors
Anderson et al.	10 SA/CD women	↑	↑ personality disorders, depression
2001 Boyer	60 CD women (40 in MMTP)	50% (30 of 60) had a history of CSA	All had current/prior depression. Many were suicidal. Half said drug use was for unresolved CSA. Unknown how many were amnesic for CSA.
2002 DeBernardo et al	24 SA/CDs 35 with co-morbidity	↑	
Shoemaker et al.	62 SA/CD patients	↑	↑ co-morbidity
Kang et al.	432 opiate addicts	64–71%	↑ depression

Table A 8.3. Chemical Dependence/Substance Abuse & Childhood Trauma *(concluded)*

Year/Author	Study Characteristics	Childhood Trauma	Other/ Comments
2003 Crowley et al.	98 SA/CD teens	67%	↑ depression
2003 Hawke et al.	446 SA/CD teens	↑	↑ depression, anxiety, ADHD, PTSD, violence. 5 years prospective
Titus et al.	214 SA/CD teens	↑	
Grella & Joshi	803 SA/CD teens	↑	↑ depression, conduct disorder, ADHD. 1 year prospective
Total 42 studies 1975–2003	**7,836 people with CD & their controls**	**30–90% CT**	**Multiple co-morbidity Numerous other findings**

CD = chemical dependence (alcohol/drug dependence); CT = childhood trauma; SA/CD = substance abuse/ chemical dependence; CSA = child sexual abuse; CPA = child physical abuse; CoA = child of an alcoholic; FH = family history; PD = personality disorder; APD = antisocial personality disorder; BPD = borderline personality disorder; MMTP = methadone maintenance treatment program; Dx = diagnosis

Table A 9.1. Effects Found Among Survivors of

(2 meta-analyses and 9 literature reviews

Year/Author	Study	SA/Chemical Dependence
1966 Browne & Finkelhor	Literature review of 27 early studies	↑
1990 Shetky	Literature review of 86 studies & articles	↑
1993 Kendall-Tackett et al. (Reviewed from 1984–91)	Review 45 retrospective studies on abused children v. controls	2–46% (Since these figures are on children, they are very high)
Malinosky & Hansen	Literature review of physical abuse effects	↑
Glod	Literature review	↑
1996 Neumann et al. (Reviewed from 1974–92)	Meta-analysis of 38 studies of CSA effects on women	↑
Dhaliwal et al.	Review CSA affects in men	↑
1998 Simpson & Miller	Meta-analysis of x studies	2x
Langeland & Hartgers	Review of 13 index case studies	Significant assoc. of SA/CD with CT
2000 Harper	Review of 150+ studies	↑
2003 Putnam	Literature review of over 100 CSA studies	↑
1966–2003	**2 Meta-Analyses 8 Literature Reviews**	↑

Child Sexual &/or Physical Abuse

of studies with SA/CD as an effect)

Depression/Suicide/ Anxiety/Other	Medical Disorders/Others
↑ depression, isolation stigma, self-harm ↑ anxiety, revictimization	↑ social & sexual function
↑ depression, DD, running away, prostitution, revictimization ↑ PTSD	↑ somatization, psych hospitalization ↑ parenting, self-esteem
↑ . . . a wide range of symptoms found. No one symptom characterized most CSA survivors ↑ PTSD	↑ sexual behavior, 1/2–2/3 appear better early
↑ depression ↑ anxiety	↑ aggression & violence
↑ violence, crime, ↑ psychosis	↑ medical disorders
↑ (plus ↑ anger, sexual & relationship problems, ↑ anxiety	↑ somatization, DDs,* revictimization, PTSD ↓ self-esteem
↑ anxiety	↑ co-morbidity
↑ ↑ anxiety	↑ co-morbidity
↑ co-morbidity	
↑ depression, sexualized behavior	
↑ **Co-morbidity** ↓ **self-esteem**	**All support trauma link**

*DD = dissociative disorders; PTSD = post-traumatic stress disorder

Table A 11.1. Eating Disorders and Childhood Trauma:
58 *Clinical* & *Community* Studies

Year/Author	Study Characteristics	Eating Disorders	Other Trauma Effects/Comments
1986 Putnam et al.	100 MPDs (96% CDT)	15 + x BN 25 x AN	Depression/suicidality, hallucinations/delusions/ thought disorder
1989 Calam & Slade	130 college women age 18–40 year olds	↑ among those with CSA & adult SA	None measured. Used Eating Attitudes Test & Sexual Events Questionnaire.
Bailey & Gibbons	276 college women CT v. controls	↑ BN	
1990 Smolak et al.	298 college students; 60 abused, 229 not	↑ EAT scores among abused	None measured
Shearer et al.	40 BPD women, nearly all CS/PA	60% BN, 8x gen. population, AN 4x, Mixed 3x	↑ SA/CD, seizures, hospitalizations
Beckman et al.	340 college students CT v. controls	↑	
1990 Goodwin et al.	20 CSA women	75%	multiple co-morbidity
1991 Felitti	131 CSA v. 100 controls	1.6–4.2x	2.6x depression, 3.7x DOV,* 1.6x GI probs, 1.8x headaches
Brown & Anderson	166 patients PA & CSA v. inpatient controls	2x	↑ SA/CD & suicide (Most suicidal inpatients have the same high incidence of childhood trauma . . . control bias?
1992 Bushnell et al.	39 F CSA v. 262 controls	1.5x	2.1x depression, 1.2 SA. New Zealand women 18–44 yo

Table A 11.1. Eating Disorders and Childhood Trauma *(continued)*

Year/Author	Study Characteristics	Eating Disorders	Other Trauma Effects/Comments
Williams et al.	21 CSA women	↑	
Pribor & Dinwiddie	52 CSA women, 23 controls	↑ BN (23%)	↑ violence link
Frazier & Cohen	82 CSA women CT v. controls	↑	↑ SA/CD, depression, revictimization. ↓ self-esteem
1993 Moeller et al.	354 abused, 314 controls GYN practice	↑ obesity	↑ depression, anxiety, SA/CD, fatigue & PMS, GYN problems, tension, ↓ 2.3x self-esteem, ↑ family dysfunction
Mullen et al.	298 CSA (252 covert, 191 overt) 298 controls	3.2–6.7x	↑ depression/suicide, anxiety, psych. in- & outpatient
Reto et al.	183 college students CT v. controls	↑	
1994 Kinzl et al.	200 college students CT v. controls	↑	Link is not with CSA alone
1995 Byram et al.	100 college students CT v. controls	↑	Other factors involved
Vize & Cooper	180 psych. in or outpatients	3x bulimia, 4.4x anorexia	3x depression
Brewerton & Dansky	3,006 women CSA/ adult rape v. controls	↑ BN	↑ PTSD (correlated with BN). See also Dansky et al. 1997
Romans et al.	252 CSA women v. 225 controls	↑	↑ depression, SA, anxiety. These esp. ↑ among self-harming
Mallinkrodt et al.	154 women CT v. controls	↑	Several factors involved

Table A 11.1. Eating Disorders and Childhood Trauma *(continued)*

Year/Author	Study Characteristics	Eating Disorders	Other Trauma Effects/Comments
1996 Mullen et al.	107 abused (53 SA, 39 PA, EA 57) v. 390 controls	3.2x	3.7x depression, 5–18x suicide attempt, 2–3x SA, 3x sex problems & early preg; 7.2x ever hospital- ized for mental disorder*
Wonderlich et al.	157 CSA v. 497 controls	2–2.6x bulimic behavior	CSA survivors were signif. more likely to have bulimic behavior. In 1/6–1/3, could be caused by bulimic behavior CSA
Zlotnick et al.	92 CSA v. 42 control psych inpatients	↑ ED Sx by EDI survey	Conclusion: CSA survivors are likely to have ED symptoms
1996 Whitfield & Stock	100 adult CSA 88 ♀, 12 ♂	2.6x	7x PTSD, 6x SA, 14x DID, 1 1/3 self-harm, 7x (57%), over half had been depressed. 3x psychosis, 1/3 sex. dysf., 22% molested a child
Chandy et al.	3,051 CSA teens	↑ EDs	↑ suicidality, school & behavior problems
Baldo et al.	390 college women CSA v. controls	↑	↑ revictimization (follow-up report)
Ellason & Ross	135 DIDs (96%)	27x BN 27x AN	Multiple & high co-morbidity
1997 Pharris et al.	1,157 teens CT v. controls	↑ purging	↑ SA/CD, behavior problems
Kinzl et al.	301 college men CT v. controls	↑	

Table A 11.1. Eating Disorders and Childhood Trauma *(continued)*

Year/Author	Study Characteristics	Eating Disorders	Other Trauma Effects/Comments
Moyer et al.	65 CSA teens 136 controls	↑ BED	↑ depression ↓ self-esteem
Neumark-Sztainer et al.	123,132 teens, CT v. controls	↑ ED symptoms	↑ SA/CD, suicidality delinquency
Javis & Copeland	180 SA/CD &/or 130 CSA women	↑	↑ co-morbidity
Andrews	20 CT women, 49 controls	↑ BN	↑ bodily shame, may be a mediating factor
Jarvis & Copeland	94 CSA women, ± SA/CD 37 SA/CD only	67% EDs 38% EDs	
1998 Felitti et al.	9,508 patients CT v. controls	1.6x	4.6–12.2x depression/suicide 2–10.3 self-destruc, 4.7–10.3x SA/CD
Kemardy & Ball	469 women, CT v. controls	↑ EDs	
1998 Dembo et al.	145 delinquent teens (CT 46%, CSA 68% CPA)	↑	SA/CD self-esteem
1998 Shirer et al.	7,884 teens, CSA v. controls	↑ bulimic behavior	↑ suicidality, risky sex, violence
1999 Armsworth, et al.	36 women CSA v. 35 controls	2–11x	3–9x depression, 2x suicide 1.9–5x anxiety, 13x psych hosp, ↓ self-esteem, ↑ adult victimization
Kent et al.	236 women CT v. controls	↑ ED Symptons & attitudes	↑ anxiety, dissociation. Emotional abuse a strong factor

Table A 11.1. Eating Disorders and Childhood Trauma *(continued)*

Year/Author	Study Characteristics	Eating Disorders	Other Trauma Effects/Comments
Kent et al.	236 college women	↑	↑ depression, dissociation anxiety
Perkins & Luster	7,903 teens, CT v. controls	1.8x purging	
Dickinson et al.	252 women, CSA v. controls	↑ bulimia	↑ co-morbidity. Graded relationship to abuse severity
2000 Neumark-Sztainer et al.	9,943 students surveyed	2–5x for CSA/PA	
Kendler et al.	1,411 ♀ twins, 30% CSA	↑ bulimia 1.8–5.6x	↑ depression, anxiety, panic. CSA is *causal* of diverse psychiatric disorders
Wonderlich et al.	20 CSA children (10–15 yos) v. 20 controls	↑	↑ SA & impulsive behaviors. First controlled study in children
2001 Wonderlich et al.	26 CSA, 21 rape, 25 both, 25 controls	↑	↑ multiple self-destructive behaviors clinical sample
Romans et al.	254 CSA women, 223 controls	↑ (incl. AN & BN)	Maternal neglect a factor in AN
Thompson et al.	5,681 teen girls, CS/PA (11–21%) v. controls	↑ weight control behaviors 0.86–2.5–3.9x	Excluding physical abuse lowered results
2001 Ackard et al.	6,728 teens CT v. controls	Girls 2.4–4.2x Boys 1.2–8.2x	Discussing the abuse lessened bulimic behaviors
Wonderlich et al.	20 CSA 10–15 yos 20 controls	↑ ED Sx	↑ drug use, impulsiveness. Expansion of 2000 data

Table A 11.1. Eating Disorders and Childhood Trauma *(concluded)*

Year/Author	Study Characteristics	Eating Disorders	Other Trauma Effects/Comments
2002 Leverich et al.	631 bipolars, CT v. controls	↑	↑ anxiety, PTSD, SA/CD
Fonseca et al.	9,042 teens CT v. controls	↑ ED behaviors 1.5–2.8x	
Johnson et al.	717 teens & their mothers	↑	↑ co-morbidity
Murray et al.	214 college women CT v. controls	↑ BN	↓ self-esteem (shame) = mediator from CSA
2003 Thompson et al. (in press)	97 women CTs v. controls	4.3x–6.5 ED	↑ SA/CD, depression 2.3, PTSD, 7.05, anxiety 2.9–3.3
Total 1986–2003 58 Studies	**201,092 subjects (childhood trauma survivors v. controls)**	**1.6 to 11x, including ↑ bulimia ± anorexia**	**2.6–12.2x depression/ suicide, 2–10.3x SA/CD, 1.9–5x anxiety, 3x sex probs & early preg, ↑ DOV, GI probs, headaches, hospitaliza- tions, self-destructive, ↓ self-esteem ↑ adult victimization**

Table A 11.2. Eating Disorders and Childhood

Year/Authors	Study Characteristics	Eating Disorders
1992 Bushnell et al.	301 women CSA v. controls	↑ bulimia
1993 Dubowitz et al.	93 CSA children 80 controls	↑ obesity
Waller et al.	20 AN 30 BN	↑ CSA/CT
1994 Miller et al.	72 BN 72 controls	↑ CSA
Waller et al.	115 ED women	↑ CSA & BPD
1996 Welch et al.	102 BN women 204 controls 102 other psych dis	↑ CSA/SA
1997 Swanston et al.	68 CSA children v. 84 controls	2.3x bingeing, 11x vomiting
1998 Calam et al. Followed 2 years	144 CSA children 1.3–16 yos	↑
2000 Cameron 21 years	72 women, 51 for the full 5 surveys	82% ED
2000 Kendler et al.	1,411 twin pairs	↑ bulimia nervosa
2002 Johnson et al.	782 mothers & children CT v. controls	↑ EDs
Summary 11 Studies 1992–2002	**4,374 CT & controls**	**↑ EDs**

Trauma: 11 Prospective Studies

Other Effects of Trauma	Comments
↑ co-morbidity	2-year follow-up
↑ co-morbidity, behavior problems	4 months
Esp if abused in family & with force	
	High correlation
	Other factors involved
↑ depression, suicide, SA/CD, nicotine, anxiety, behavior problems ↓ self-esteem	↑ other traumas during 5-year follow-up
Several, as shown in Table x.	2 years
Depression, suicidality, anxiety; ↓ self-esteem; ↑ SA/CD	Substantial improvement with trauma-focused treatment over time
↑ co-morbidity (see other reports)	18-year follow-up
↑ **Co-morbidity**	**4 mos to 21 years follow-up**

Table A 11.3. Eating Disorders and Childhood Trauma:
43 *Index Case* Studies

Year/Author	Study Characteristics	Childhood Trauma	Other Findings	Comments
1986 Finn et al.	87 ED women CT v. controls	No difference		
1989 Coons et al.	20 BN 10 AN	30% 40%	15% Revictimized 20%	Most had PTSD symptoms
Ross et al.	20 EDs	30% (6x)	80% MDD	Cited in Glod 1993
Hall et al.	72 BN/AN, 86 other psych inpats.	1.8x		
Folsum et al.	102 ED inpats. 49 psych inpats. 44 nl. controls	69% CSA 81% CSA Not found		Control bias. Cited in Glod 1993.
1990 Palmer et al.	80 AN 78 BN	58% CSA		Clinical
Stuart et al.	30 BN 15 depressed 100 controls	↑	↑ school problems & truancy	
Davidson & Smith	3 BN	↑		
1990 Lacey	112 bulimics	↑ CSA	↑ SA/CD	
Steiger & Zanko	73 ED patients 21 psych pats. controls 24 normal controls	3.3x (30% CSA) 3.6x (33%) (9%)		Control bias.
1991 McClelland et al.	50 ED patients	30% CSA	↑ PD	
1992 DeGroot et al.	184 AN, BN or mixed	↑ CSA		

Table A 11.3. Eating Disorders and Childhood Trauma *(continued)*

Year/Author	Study Characteristics	Childhood Trauma	Other Findings	Comments
1993 Rorty et al.	80 bulimic females v. 40 controls	↑ physical, sexual & emotional	Not measured	PA, EA & multiple abuse more common than CSA alone
1994 Welch et al.	100 BN 100 controls	↑ CSA		
Rorty et al.	80 BN women 40 controls	↑ CT (incl. CSA)		
1995 Vize & Cooper	40 AN, 60 BN 40 controls 40 depressed	53% CSA, 35% CSA, 12% CSA, 42% CSA	67% BPD	
Garfinkel et al.	77 BN 4,208 controls	↑ CT	↑ co-morbidity	
Andrews et al.	76 BN daughters 59 BN mothers	6.9 to 13.7x .25 to 3.5x	↑ depression	
1997 Favaro et al.	283 EDS	↑ CSA (other CT not looked for)	↑ self-harm & suicidality	Suicidality assoc. with ADP use
Friedman et al.	37 BN, 37 BED, 10 Fat, 38 controls	↑	↑ family hostility	↑ self-directed hostility
Brown et al.	117 EDs 39 controls	↑ (45–51% CSA (16-34% CPA)		
Mangweth et al.	110 men, EDs v. controls	↑	↑ depression, SA/CD	Researcher negative bias?
1998 Felitti & Williams	190 severely obese (47 men)	11–23% had a Hx of CSA &/or PA*; 24% home ED, 23% early parental loss, 17% COA	66% chronic depression* Failure to lose & keep weight off was highly correlated with	Hx of child abuse.** Crucial to take a child-hood trauma his-tory in severely overweight.

Table A 11.3. Eating Disorders and Childhood Trauma *(continued)*

Year/Author	Study Characteristics	Childhood Trauma	Other Findings	Comments
Favaro et al.	69 BN, 86 AN, 81 controls	↑	↑ self-harming	
1999 Nagata et al.	136 AN/BN women 99 controls	No ↑ CT v. controls	2x dissociation & self-harm	Confounded by common public touching (called *Chikan* in Japan)
Deep et al.	26 AN women 20 BN & SA/CD 27 BN 44 controls	23% (3+x) CSA 65% CSA 37% CSA 7% CSA	67–82% CSA preceeded onset of CSA	
Cachelton et al.	31 BED women	↑ CSA	High relapse	High drop-outs
2000 Anderson et al.	45 bulimic inpatients (6 AN, 3 binge EDs)	100% CSA	84% depressed 22% SA/CD, 55% PD	CSA details were neither significant nor helpful
2001 Streiger et al.	35 AN women 25 controls	↑	↑ co-morbidities	
Laporte & Gutman	34 BN women 33 controls	↑ CT		
Grilo & Masheb	116 BED adults both genders	83% CT	↑ depression ↓ self-esteem	
Walker et al.	61 BN women	21/61 CSA		
Forman et al.	2 AN teens	Both CT		
2001 Kirkenger	20 severe EDs	↑	Multiple co-morbidity	
2002 Paul et al.	376 ED women	↑		

Table A 11.3. Eating Disorders and Childhood Trauma *(concluded)*

Year/Author	Study Characteristics	Childhood Trauma	Other Findings	Comments
Shoemaker et al.	38 BN, 1350 healthy controls	1 to 8x		
Fonseca et al.	9,042 teens extreme weight controlers v. controls	↑	↓ family communication	
Dohm et al.	53 BN women 162 BED	↑	↑ SA/CD, self-harm	
2002 Striegel-Moore et al.	162 BED women 251 controls	↑		
1986–2002 43 Studies	**20,518 EDs alone or v. controls**	**11–100% 1.8–3.6x (2=NS)**	**Multiple co-morbidity in 4**	**5 of these studies show can't use psych patients as normal controls (control bias)**

*Of those more than 100 patients who each lost over 100 lbs
**Compulsive overeating in these patients was an attempt to manage the dysphoria related to childhood trauma.
BN=bulimia nervosa, AN=anorexia nervosa, BED=binge eating disorder, ED=eating disorder,
psych=psychiatric, PA=physical abuse, EA=emotional abuse, CSA=child sexual abuse,
SA/CD=substance abuse/chemical dependence, BPD=borderline personality disorder

Table A 11.5. Eating Disorders and Childhood Trauma:

Year/Author	Study Characteristics	Childhood Trauma
1992 Pope & Hudson	Selected 14 studies on bulimia only. Evaluated these for a history of CSA only, not other CT	"No significant differences"
1993 Connors & Morse	Reviewed 10 databased reports, mostly on bulimia & AN from 1986–90	↑ association in 5, no difference in 3, "NA" in 2
1994 Everill & Waller	Analyze 16+ databased studies	11 positive correlations, 5 negative (for 3 give no data)
1997 Wonderlich et al.	2 independent teams evaluated 53 controlled studies on CSA and EDs	In 66% CSA was related to BN, 83% CSA related. ↑ co-morbidity in EDs
2000 Kent & Waller	Literature review of 75 references on CEA* & EDs	Emotional abuse is a causal factor
2001 Smolak & Murmen	Meta-analysis of 53 studies	↑ to 2.1x controls
2002 Klump et al.	Review of 9 twin studies of BN & AN	Environment is a factor
Summary 7 Reports 1992-2002	**6 Reviews 1 meta-analysis**	**Vast majority show significant trauma— ED links**

* CEA = childhood emotional abuse

7 Multiple-Study Analysis/Literature Reviews

Other Findings	Comments
None assessed. "CSA is not a risk factor for bulimia." The authors excluded at least 4 positive studies and appeared to misinterpret at least another 2.	Methodological flaws. See discussion in text. Their conclusions and opinions are in the distinct minority.
Generally not measured. Concluded that 1/3 of ED pts had CSA—one part of the causal puzzle. Did not assess physical or emotional abuse as possible factors	
Borderline PDs correlated. Negative reports made "inappropriate levels of analysis." Five mediating factors observed**	
	"CSA is a risk factor for BN" & AN. A more thorough and updated analysis than Pope & Hudson's
	Emotional abuse is a strong mediating factor
Discuss genetic interface	More research needed
Co-morbidity not generally evaluated	**These 7 reviews covered all CT-ED reports to about 2001**

** Five mediating factors were observed between CSA and bulimic symptomatology, including: dissociation, shame (low self-esteem), borderline PD, invalidating disclosure experiences, and cognitive/thinking errors. Concluded that a child sexual abuse history is highly likely to be associated with and relevant to the development of and maintenance of bulimic symptoms.

Table A 13.2. Personality Disorders and

Year/Author	Study	Personality Disorders
1972 Lukianowicz	26 CSA survivors	14/26 (54%)
1979 Rosenfeld	18 ♀ psych pts. w/mixed disorders, including PDs	10 of 18
Tsai et al.	Chart review 90 women (30 each: clinical, non-clinical, controls)	↑ Paranoid, psychopathic deviate on MMPI only
1981 Gross et al.	25 GYN patients chronic pelvic pain; CT	18/25 (72%) BPD or HPD
1985 Barnard & Hirsch	30 CSA incest psych patients	57% BPD
1986 Putnam et al.	96 CT MPD patients	50%
1988 Stein et al.	34 CSA children 34 controls	↑ antisocial behavior
1989 Zanarini et al.	2,683 overt CSA only	3.8x BPD
Briere & Zaidi	100 women, CT controls	↑ BPD
1990 Goodwin et al.	20 women severe CT	95% (19 of 20)
1990 Ross et al.	97 CT inpatients	↑ BPD
1991 Brown & Anderson	194 CS/PA v. 853 "control" psych unit patients	↑ PDs esp. BPD
McClelland et al.	50 EDs 30% CSA	↑
1992 Raczek	16 abused v. 34 "controls" military—age 22	2 + x BPD & APD
Kinzl & Biebl	33 CSA (incest) psych patients	↑ BPD

Childhood Trauma: 35 *Clinical* Studies

Other Findings	Comments
↑ promiscuity & prostitution	one of earliest studies
No objective assessmet beyond psychiatric clinical interactions	Published before PTSD became an accepted diagnosis in psychiatry
↑ Depression; hypochondriasis, shcizophrenia* on MMPI	↓ social skills, family & sexual function
Other psych disorders found in remaining 28%	60% had normal pelvic exams, 40% minor findings
90% depression 50% SA/CD	
↑ SA/CD, anxiety, PTSD, somatization, insomnia	(LA Epi. demiological Catchment Area study)
3 + x2–10x anxiety disorder, 2x SA schiz, 5x OCD	2.2x any mental disorder
↑ SA/CD	Abuse predicted later disorders
40% (8) antisocial	↑ co-morbidity
↑ somatization	Abuse predicted disorders
↑ SA/CD, suicidality	Military population Control bias possible
	"Controls" also referred for psychiatric evaluation
↑ SA/CD, anxiety, MPD, OCD	

Table A 13.2. Personality Disorders and Childhood Trauma *(continued)*

Year/Author	Study	Personality Disorders
1992 Pribor & Dinwiddie	52 CSA women 23 controls from self-help group	7x ASPD
1993 Swett & Halpert	71 of 88 women, CS/PA v. 17 "no abuse" all on psych unit	↑ PDs: BPD, APD, S-DPD & Schizoid PD
Anderson et al.	51 CSA women	↑ BPD
1997 Quimette et al.	52 women Vietnam veterans	↑ BPD among those with alcohol problems and CSA history
Ellason & Ross	144 CT inpatients	↑ BPD
1998 Bernstein et al.	339 CD (85% men) (54–80% CT)	↑
1998 Ackerman	127 CSA only 43 CPA only; 34 both, 7–13 years old	↑ obsessive, compulsive, avoidant
1999 Grillo et al.	70 abuse Hx v. 93 controls	1.9x BPD symptoms
Gladstone et al.	40 CSA women v. 130 controls (all depressed)	↑ borderline personality style
Fondacaro et al.	211 men inmates, 86 CSA v. 125 controls	↑ ASPD
2000 Kendler et al.	1,411 ♀ twin pairs, 30% CSA v. controls	↑
Anderson et al.	45 CSA women	58%
2001 Wonderlich et al.	26 CSA; 21 rape; 25 both; 25 controls	↑ BPD-like symptoms ↑ other PD symptoms
Steiger et al.	38 CT women	↑ BPD

Table A 13.2. Personality Disorders and Childhood Trauma *(continued)*

Other Findings	Comments
↑ co-morbidity	
↑ anxiety, hostility & psychoticism	"Controls" were psych inpatients = high risk for CT. One of many examples of control bias.
↑ SA/CD, dissociative disorders	
Those with PTSD & alcoholism had more sexual assault in . . .	. . . childhood & wartime, PTSD, dissociation & BPD
↑ depression, anxiety	↑ co-morbidity
High co-morbidity among CDs & PDs	
↑ depression, anxiety, phobia, PTSD, ADHD, behavior problems	
3.5x depression, 2.5x suicidal, 2.1x SA	1.8x violent
↑ SA/CD, depression, self-harm, suicidality, psych visits	CSA likely *causal* of BPD features
↑ depression, SA/CD, anxiety, panic, PTSD, OCD, schizoaffective	41% of CSA did not believe that they were sexually abused
↑ depression, SA/CD, anxiety, panic, bulimia	CSA is *causal* of diverse pcychiatric disorders
↑ depression, SA/CD	
↑ PTSD, depression	

Table A 13.2. Personality Disorders and Childhood Trauma *(concluded)*

Year/Author	Study	Personality Disorders
2001 MacMillan et al.	1,858 CTs v. 5,158 controls	3.7–4.3x ASPD
2002 Grilo & Masheb	95 CT 21 controls (all EDs)	30% (esp from cluster C)
2003 McLean & Gallop	65 CSA women	↑ BPD
Callahan et al.	17 CSA 34 psych clinic v. patients	53% 35%
2003 Leverich et al.	648 bipolar outpatients with ↑ CT	↑ cluster BPDs
Kendler et al.	5,600 twins CT v. controls	↑ antisocial
Total **35 Studies** **1972–2003**	**21,596 CT & Controls**	**↑ to 95% PD** **Link with CT**

Table A 13.2. **Personality Disorders and Childhood Trauma** *(concluded)*

Other Findings	Comments
↑ depression, SA/CD	Community sample
↑ PTSD (complex), revictimization	↑ neglect by both parents
↑ anxiety & phobia	
↑ co-morbidity	
↑ co-morbidity	
Co-morbidity common	**2 said CSA is *causal* of BPD**

*MMPI codes: Hs = Hypochondriasis, Pd = Psychopathic deviate, Pa = Paranoia, Pt = Psychasthenia, Sc = Schizophrenia
Key: BPD - borderline personality disorder, ASPD = antisocial personality disorder, PD = personality disorder, Hx = history, CSA = child sexual abuse, CT = childhood trauma, SA/CD = substance abuse/chemical dependence, ♀ = female, W/ = with, GYN = gynecology.

Table A 13.3. Personality Disorders and

Year/Author	Study Characteristics	Childhood Trauma
1981 Stone	12 BPD patients in hospital	75% (9/12)
1982 Bemporad et al.	24 BPD patients in hospital	41–91%, child physical abuse
1986 Herman	12 BPD patients	67% (8/12) v. 22% in entire outpatients
1987 Bryer et al.	14 BPD patients in hospital v. entire hospital population	86% (12/14) v. 21% of entire hospital population
Nelson et al.	14 BPD inpatients 86 controls	86% CSA v. 34% = 2.5x entire 100%
1989 Herman et al.	21 BPD patients v. 11 with B traits v. 23 "controls"	81% childhood trauma among BPD v. 73% & 52% for traits & "controls"
1989 Coons et al.	13 BPDs	77%
1990 Ogata et al.	24 BPD v. 18 depressed controls	↑
Ludolph et al.	27 BPDs v. 23 psych inpatients	2–4.5x CT
Byrne et al.	15 BPDs	87% CSA, high family trauma
Shearer et al.	44 BPD women	All CSA
Davidson & Smith	9 PD psych outpatients	↑
1991 Famularo et al.	19 7–14 YO BPD patients	80% trauma 37% PTSD
1991 Nigg et al.	29 BPDs, 15 controls	↑ (48–72%)
1992 Carlin & Ward	18 PD psych inpatient women	35% CSA
1992 Hurlburt et al.	32 BPDs 32 controls	5x CSA (31.2% v. 6.3) 23x CPA (21.9 v. 9)
Palmer et al.	26 PD psych inpatients	58%

Childhood Trauma: 36 Index Case Studies

Other Findings	Comments
BPD figures included in controls	Cited in Herman & van der Kolk 1987, page 118 (unpublished data)
	Controls were schizotypal, APD & bipolar
27% adult trauma (retraumatization)	
↑ dissociation & derealization	Control group known to have ↑ trauma Hx
↑ major psych disorders among close relatives	Controls underestimate differences
↑ SA/CD, anxiety, suicide, behavior problems	Controls underestimate differences
↑ SA/CD, ED, seizures	↑ hospitalization
↑ PTSD, depression, anxiety	
4/19–ADHD, 6/19—conduct disorder/oppositional defiant	
repressed sample also had ↑ CT	
DSM–III, MMPI, others	

Table A 13.3. Personality Disorders and Childhood Trauma *(continued)*

Year/Author	Study Characteristics	Childhood Trauma
Goldman et al.	44 BPD children 100 psych clinic children	4 + x
1993 Bernstein et al.	339 chemical dependents (85% men) with ↑ personality disorders	54–80% trauma
Steinberg et al.	43 PD patients	50% CT
1994 Paris et al.	61 BPD men v. 60 with other PDs	↑ CSA/PA, severe
1995 Brodsky et al.	60 BPD women psych inpatients	↑ 60% (36/60) CSA/PA
Windle et al.	244 APD adults	44–81%
1995 Norden et al.	90 PD adults	↑
Norden et al.	90 PD outpatients	↑
1996 Berenbaum	23 PDs of 60 oupatients	↑ CT
Wurr & Partridge	5 PDs	3/5 = 60% CSA
New et al.	66 PDs	↑ CT, especially CSA
1997 Modestin et al.	90 PD inpatients	↑
2000 Hefferman & Cloitre	26 BPDs with PTSD	All CSA
2001 LaPorte & Guttman	35 BPD women, 33 controls	↑
2002 Zlotnick et al.	149 BPDs	32% had PTSD
2002 Hexel & Sonneck	41 BPDs	39%
2003 Grossman et al.	52 PDs	42% (22/52)
2003 Rinne et al.	30 BPD women	56%
Total **36 Studies** **1981–2003**	**2,674 people with PDs** **& their controls**	↑ **to 87%**

Table A 13.3. **Personality Disorders and Childhood Trauma** *(concluded)*

Other Findings	Comments
	CT contributes to high % PDs in CD
Abnormal prolactin & MHP/cortisol	
	Trauma important in the genesis of BPD in males
↑ depression, dissociation & self-mutilation →	Those with dissociation had more depression & self-mutilation
↑ depression, suicide & anxiety	Need to address trauma in treatment
ASD—CPA, BPD—CSA , Others PDs—CSA	Poor parental relationships important
Alexithymia comon among CTs	
↑ suicide	
↑ MHPG/cortisol levels	
↑ co-morbidity	
BPD & PTSD are independent . . .	. . . and comorbid CT effects
	PTSD cause not disclosed
30% revictimization, ↑ PTSD, depression	↑ abnormal cortisol tests
HPA axis disruption	
↑ depression, suicide, anxiety, dissociation, self-mutilation	**Control groups known to have ↑ trauma history: control bias**

Table A 13.4. Personality Disorders and Childhood Trauma: 5 Prospective Studies

Year/Author	Study Characteristics	Personality Disorders	Comments
1980 Surtees & Ingram	71 psychiatric patients	↑	Followed life stress model (Brown & Harris 1978)
1992 Bushnell et al. 2 years	301 women (community v. controls)	↑ ASPD symptoms	
1994 Luntz & Widom Forensic in Community	416 SA v. 283 controls 18–35 yo, mean age 27	2x APD (13.5 v. 7.1%)	Controls were screened for severe, legally documented abuse only
1996 Silverman et al. 17 years	23 CSA 164 controls	↑ APD	↑ SA/CD, multiple co-morbidity
1999 Johnson et al. 18 years Community	31 abused v. 608 controls followed over 16–19 years	4 to 6 + x any PD among abused (except schzoid & O-C PD) see Figure 13.1	Significant even after controlled for childhood & parental disorders & education
Summary 5 Studies 1980–1999	**1,897 people CT v. controls**	**↑ to 6x**	**Up to 18 years follow-up**

*Another prospective study (Yen et al. 2002) showed a significant link (see Table A 13.3).

Table A X. Suicidal and Homicidal Behavior from Psychiatric Drugs: 10 Examples

(variously published in media). There are countless others.

Name	Crime	Drugs	Comments
Andrea Yates 2002	Drowned her 5 children	Effexor (WD*), Wellbutrin, Remeron, Haldol	Was recently withdrawing from Effexor
Columbine, 1999 Colorado Eric Harris	Murdered 12 students and 1 teacher	Luvox	Reputation of being good boy until this episode
Other school killers 15 yo Kip Kinkel 1998 14 yo Eliz Bush 18 yo Jason Hoffman 16 yo Cory Bradsgaard	Murder	Prozac Paxil Effexor, Celexa Effexor, Paxil (WD)	Most were not widely publicized
Breyn Hartman 1998	Shot and killed husband Phil Hartman and then self	Luvox	Lawsuit settled out of court
Donald Schell 1998	Shot and killed wife, daughter and granddaughter	Paxil 2 days	Jury found drug 80% responsible.
Henri Paul 1997 Princess Di's driver	Car crash killed 3 people	Prozac, with likely manic reaction	Prozac likely aggravated heavy drinking
Michael Hutchence 1997	Suicide by Australian rockstar	Prozac	Received little publicity in the USA

* WD = withdrawal from the drug; These are but a few examples of how many psychiatric drugs can be associated with or induce extreme violence (suicide or homicide). Since the early 1990s the drug companies have had countless law suits filed against them for this and other toxic effects of their drugs.[469.] [470] Unfortunately, most of this information is kept quiet and unpublished. This denial by the drug industry and the FDA has misinformed clinicians and consumers about these potentially dangerous drugs, resulting in otherwise preventable toxic drug effects.

Table A 15.1. ADHD, ADD & Behavior Problems & Childhood Trauma: 61 Studies (including a meta-analysis & 2 reviews)

Year/Author	Study Characteristics	ADHD/ Symptoms	Other Effects of Trauma	Comments
1937 Bender & Blau	16 CSA 5–12-year-olds	6/16 (38%)	↑ behavior problems	These symptoms described before ADHD concept.
1977 Browning & Boatman	14 CSA (incest)	↑ runaways & hypersexual	↑ depression, anxiety	Several other similar reports
Burgess & Conger	30 families, 20 CT, 10 controls	↑ behavior problems		
1978 Burgess & Conger	34 families, with CT, 19 controls	↑ behavior problems		
1979 George & Main	20 CT, 1–3 years old	↑ abnormal behavior & aggression		
1981 Alfaro	6,428 CT children	↑ delinquency, behavior		
1982 Adams-Tucker	28 CSA children	↑ behavior & oppositional		
1983 Wolfe & Mosk	71 CTs 35 controls 6–16 years old	↑ hyperactive, aggressive, delinquent	↑ depression, somatization, schizoid	
1984 Hoffman-Plotkin & Twentyman	28 CT 3–6 years old, 14 controls	↑ behavior problems		
Rosenthal & Rosenthal	16 suicidal pre-schoolers (most CT), 16 controls	↑ hyperactive		
Salzinger	64 CT, 48 controls, mean age 11 years	↑ hyperactivity, behavior problems, conduct disorder		

Table A 15.1. ADHD, ADD & Behavior Problems & Childhood Trauma *(continued)*

Year/Author	Study Characteristics	ADHD/ Symptoms	Other Effects of Trauma	Comments
1986 Bradley et al.	39 CT 2–5 years old	↑ hostility, anxiety, hyperactivity		
Brichngraber	21 CSA women, incest	↑ hyperactive	↑ SA/CD, somatization ↓ self-esteem	Community sample
Freidrich et al.	85 CSA 3–12 years old	↑ hyperactivity, aggression, delinquency	↑ depression, anxiety, somatization	
1987 Tong et al.	49 CSA children v. controls	↑ behavior, aggression & school problems	↓ self-esteem	
Conte & Scheurman	369 CSA children 318 controls	↑ behavior problems	↓ depression, anxiety, SA/CD	Community sample
Sansonnet-Hayden et al.	17 CSA children 37 controls	↑ behavior problems		Control group bias (psych inpatients)
Janus et al.	89 teen boy runaways CT v. controls	↑ school problems	↑ depression ↓ self-esteem	
Livingston	28 CT children v. 72, all on psych unit	↑ CD, ODD	↑ depression, anxiety, somatization	
1989 Conaway & Hansen	Lit Review 23 Studies of CPA & neglected children	↑ behavior problems, aggression, ↓ social skills & compliance		Excellent review. Noted study design problems
Seng	105 teens most CSA	↑ behavior, school problems	↑ depression	

Table A 15.1. ADHD, ADD & Behavior Problems & Childhood Trauma *(continued)*

Year/Author	Study Characteristics	ADHD/ Symptoms	Other Effects of Trauma	Comments
Hast et al.	38 CT teens 23 controls	↑ conduct disorder	↑ legal problems, health problems	↓ self-esteem
1990 Byrne et al.	15 BPD, 14 schiz. most CT	↑ behavior problems, delinquency	↑ SA/CD, suicidality, anxiety	Clinical
Brown & Garrison	132 CSA 250 controls	poor concentration	↑ co-morbidity	
Stuart et al.	45 BN/dept women 100 controls	↑ school problems & truancy		↑ CT among index cases
1991 Famularo et al.	19 7–14 yos BPD, 80% trauma, 37% PTSD	4/19—ADHD	6/19—conduct disorder/ oppositional defiant	
Bagley & Shewchuck -Dann	60 assaultive & CT youth 320 controls	↑ hyperactivity & behavior problems	↑ depression, anxiety, SA/CD	
1992 Famularo et al.	61 CT children 35 controls	↑ ADHD, behavior problems, ODD, CDD	↑ depression, anxiety, SA/CD, PTSD, PD	
Sanford et al.	3,294 children	↑ ADHD, behavior school problems	↑ depression	Community sample
1993 Dubowitz et al.	93 CSA children, 80 controls	↑ hyperactivity & behavior problems	↑ depression ED (obese)	
1994 Manly et al.	145 CTs, 90 controls, 5–11 years old	↑ behavior problems, aggression, other		Proportional to CT severity & frequency

Table A 15.1. ADHD, ADD & Behavior Problems & Childhood Trauma *(continued)*

Year/Author	Study Characteristics	ADHD/ Symptoms	Other Effects of Trauma	Comments
Pelcovitz et al.	27 CPA teens 27 controls	↑ behavior problems	↑ depression, thought disorder	Commmunity sample
1995 Stern et al.	84 CSA children 84 controls	↑ behavior & sexual problems	↑ depression ↓ self-esteem	
Moss et al.	99 CT children 78 controls	↑ behavior & school problems	↓ IQ	CT=CoAs
1996 Glod & Teicher	19 CT children 15 controls	↑ ADHD symptoms	↑ PTSD, depression	
Famularo et al.	117 CT children	↑ ADHD	↑ PTSD, anxiety disorders, psychosis	
Cohen et al.	70 CT teens 35 controls	↑ school & behavior problems		Control group bias (psych inpatients)
Chandy et al.	3,051 teens	↑ behavior, school problems	↑ suicidality, EDs	
1997 Kessler et al.	5,877 people CT v. controls	↑ behavior problems	↑ depression, anxiety, SA/CD	
Saig et al.	151 CT children	↑ school/academic problems	↑ PTSD	Cited to show difficulty focusing
Newmark-Sztainer et al.	123,132 teens CT v. controls	↑ delinquency, behavior probs	↑ depression, suicidality	↑ EDs
Robin et al.	129 CSA adults 246 controls	↑ behavior & school problems	↑ co-morbidity	
Pharris et al.	1,157 teens CT v. controls	↑ behavior problems	↑ SA/CD, purging	

Table A 15.1. ADHD, ADD & Behavior Problems & Childhood Trauma *(continued)*

Year/Author	Study Characteristics	ADHD/ Symptoms	Other Effects of Trauma	Comments
1998 Ackerman et al.	127 CSA only 43 CPA only; 34 both. All 7–13 years old	↑ ADHD ↑ op-defiant, conduct disorder	↑ defiant, conduct dis, PTSD, OCD, avoidant	↑ depression, phobia, anxiety
Kaplan et al.	99 teen patients v. 99 controls	2–3x	2.9–9x depression 13–15 SA/CD	
1999 Thompson & Kaplan	75 CT children	↑ ADHD, disruptive behavior	↑ anxiety	Listed in Table A16.3 also as index cases
Pelletier & Handy	40 CT 20 controls	↑ behavior problems	↑ depression	
2000 Ruggiero et al.	80 CSA children/teens	↑ attention problems	↑ PTSD, sexual behavior	↓ global functioning
Carrion & Steiner	64 teens 97% CT	↑ behavior problems	↑ aggression, dissociation	Detention sample
Dembo et al.	164 v. teens CT	↑ behavior problems	↑ SA/CD, delinquency	physical abuse significant
Gurvitz et al.	21 CSA women	↑ ADHD symptoms	↑ PTSD	
2001 Reynolds et al.	45 5–11 year olds, no controls	↑ ADHD, conduct & hyperactivity problems	↑ depression, PTSD, ↓ self-esteem	
Paolucci et al.	Meta-analysis of 37 CSA studies	Poor school performance	↑ depression, PTSD, suicidality	↑ promiscuity, violence cycle
2002 Beers & De Bellis	14 CT children with PTSD 15 controls	↓ attention & abstract reasoning/executive functioning		

Table A 15.1. ADHD, ADD & Behavior Problems & Childhood Trauma *(concluded)*

Year/Author	Study Characteristics	ADHD/ Symptoms	Other Effects of Trauma	Comments
Simmel	808 children CT v. controls	↑ ADHD	↑ ODD	Adopted youth
Kernic et al.	153 children witnessed family violence	↑ behavior, school & emotional problems		
Cohan et al.	99 CT teens 99 controls	15x ADHD	↑ depression, conduct disorder, nicotine	Parent marital disruption a factor
2002 Nelson et al.	3982 twins CT v. controls	2.5–6.6 conduct disorder	↑ comorbidity	
Greene et al.	643 ODDs 262 ODDs & CD	↑ conflicted family functioning	↑ comorbidity	Index case study
2004 Becker-Blease & Freyd	13 CT children 15 controls	↑ ADHD		Community sample (in process)
Total 58 Studies & 2 literature reviews, 1 meta-analysis 1937–2004	**153,185 CTs & controls**	**↑ Behavior problems, ADHD symptoms or ADHD itself**	**↑ comorbidity**	**All behavior & focusing problem children should be evaluated for CT**

Key: CD = conduct disorder; ODD = oppositional-defiant disorder; CT = childhood trauma; CoAs = children of alcoholics; SA/CD = substance abuse/chemical dependence; ADHD = attention deficit hyperactivity disorder

Table A 15.2. ADHD, ADD & Behavior Problems

Year/Authors	Study Characteristics	ADHD/Symptoms
1983 Ageton	2,221 teen girls, CSA	↑ behavioral problems & delinquency
1995 Leifer & Shapiro	64 CSA girls, 1-year follow-up	↑ behavioral problems*
1996 Silverman et al.	375 children CT v. controls	↑ ADHD symptoms, delinquency, aggression
1997 Tebutt et al.	84 children, CT v. controls	↑ behavior problems
1998 Putnam et al.	164 girls, 77 with CSA, 15 other CT, 77 controls	↑ ADHD
Calam et al.	144 CSA children	↑ attention, behavior and school problems
1998 & 2000 Fergusson & Horwood	1,265 children	↑ conduct disorder
1999 Bagley et al.	565 children & teens CT v. controls	↑ behavior, conduct problems
Wozniak et al.	260 boys & teens ADHD v. controls	↑ CT (when bias corrected)
2001 Johnson et al.	593 families, CT v. controls	↑ADHD, ODD, CD
Cornelius et al.	73 CT teens, 123 controls	3.2x ADHD
2002 Egeland et al.	140 high-risk children CT v. controls	↑ behavior problems, conduct disorder
Shepherd et al.	411 boys, CT v. controls	↑ behavior problems
2002 Lansford et al.	585 children, CSA v. controls	↑ behav. & school prob's
2003 Hawke et al.	446 SA/CD teens most with CT	↑ ADHD & conduct disorder
Grella & Joshi	803 SA/CD teens most with CT	↑ ADHD & conduct disorder
15 Studies 1983–2003	**15,227 children CT v. controls**	**↑ ADHD, behavior, conduct problems**

Childhood Trauma: 15 *Prospective* Studies

Other Trauma Effects	Comments
↑ depression revictimization	3 years
↑ depression, anxiety	↓ symptoms with treatment
↑ depression, PTSD	17 years
↑ depression, ↓ self-esteem	5-year follow-up
↑ depression, suicidality, SA, dissociation, somatization, hypersexual	20-year follow-up every 2 years, ongoing
Multiple co-morbidity (See Table 15.5)	2-year follow-up
	21 years
↑ depression, anxiety	followed from birth. "Calgary Study"
↑ depression, mania	observer bias included accidents among controls
↑ depression, anxiety, PD, SA/CD	prospective 1975–93
4.7x ODD	4 years (ongoing)
Alienation as path	17.5 years
↑ violence, lung disease	8-year follow-up
↑ depression, anxiety, PTSD, thought problems	12-year follow-up
↑ anxiety, depression	5 years
↑ depression	1 year
Multiple co-morbidity	**1- to 30-year follow-up**

*No difference between foster care v. not foster care bases.
Most of these studies that reported behavior problems did not look for ADHD specifically.
SA = substance abuse, ADHD = attention deficit hyperactivity disorder, ODD = oppositional defiant disorder,
CD = conduct disorder, SA/CD = substance abuse/chemical dependence, CT = childhood trauma,
CSA = child sexual abuse

Table A 16.1. Aggressive Behavior, Violence and Childhood Trauma: 40 Clinical & Community Studies

Year/Authors	Study Characteristics	Violent/Agg. Behavior	Other Effects of Trauma	Comments
1997 Reidy	36 CT 22 controls	↑ aggression		
1983 Wolfe & Mosk	71 CT children 35 controls	↑ aggression, delinquency	↑ depression, hyperactive	↑ schizoid, somatization
1984 Bousha & Twentyman	24 CT, 12 controls, 2–8 years old	↑ aggression	reports verified	
Carmen et al.	80 CT 108 controls	↑ aggression, abusive, criminal behavior	↓ self-esteem	90% abused by family
Burgess et al.	66 CSA children & teens	↑	↑ somatization	
1985 Kroll et al.	31 ALC men CT 31 ALC controls	↑ violence	↑ anxiety, suicidality	
1986 Friedrich et al.	85 CSA children 3–12 years old	↑ aggression, delinquency, hyperactivity, etc.	↑ depression, anxiety, somatization	Evaluated by Child Behavior Checklist
1987 Burgess et al.	34 CSA (23 boys) v. 34 controls	↑ aggression & violence	↑ SA/CD, anxiety, PTSD, antisocial, somatization, insomnia	
Tong et al.	49 CSA children v. controls	↑ aggression	↑ behavior & school problems	↓ self-esteem
Dembo et al.	145 teens CT v. controls	↑ violence		
1988 Kunitz et al.	352 SA/CD ↑ CPA	↑ conduct disorder & domestic violence		

Table A 16.1. Aggressive Behavior, Violence and Childhood Trauma *(continued)*

Year/Author	Study Characteristics	Violent/Agg. Behavior	Other Effects of Trauma	Comments
Becker	27 CSA teens	↑ sex offending & deviance		
1989 Einbender & Friedrich	46 CSA girls 46 controls	↑ aggression	↑ behavior & school problems	↑ depression, somatization
1990 Briere & Runtz	227 college ♀ CT v. controls	↑ aggressive behavior		
Pollock et al.	131 CTs 70 controls	↑ aggression & violence		Physical abuse strong factor
Goodwin et al.	20 CT women (severe)	55% violent		
1991 Kiser et al.	40 CSA/PA	↑ aggression & delinquency		
1992 Toth et al.	153 children; 46 abused, 35 neglected v. 72 controls	↑ aggressive behavior	↑ depression	Children lower SES
Friedrich et al.	42 CSA boys	↑ aggressive, delinquency	↑ depression, anxiety, somatization	
Shields & Cicchetti	141 abused inner-city children v. 87 controls	↑ esp. among physically abused	↑ emotional liability, attention deficits & dissociation	
Randall et al.	50 children 248 teens CT v. controls	↑ conduct problems	↑ depression adjustment dis.	Chart review under bias
1995 Moss et al.	34 Ct 10–12 YOs, 39 controls	↑ aggression & ODD		

Table A 16.1. Aggressive Behavior, Violence and Childhood Trauma *(continued)*

Year/Author	Study Characteristics	Violent/Agg. Behavior	Other Effects of Trauma	Comments
1998 Thompson & Braaten	2,358 6–12th graders CT v. controls	↑ –4x gang membership & gang fights (2x)		
Song et al.	3,735 children CT v. controls	↑ violence		Community sample
Schreier et al.	7,884 teens CT v. controls	↑ violence	↑ bulimia, suicidality, sexual risking	Community sample
1999 Gold et al.	187 adults CSA	↑ aggression & impulsiveness	↑ depression, anxiety, psychoticism, somatization	Used SLC-90-R
Bensely et al.	4,780 students CT v. controls	↑ antisocial behavior	↑ SA & suicidal behavior	(The SA was reported in a 2nd paper)
Grilo et al.	70 CT teens 93 controls	↑ violence	↑ depression, SA/CD, impulsivity	
2000 Carrion & Steiner	64 teens 97% CT	↑ aggression	↑ dissociation, behavior problems	Detention sample
2001 Shields & Cicchetti	169 abused inner-city children v. 98 controls	↑ esp. among physically & sexually abused	↑ emotional liability marked bullies & victims	Bullies also tended to be victims
Merrill et al.	CT v. controls	↑ sexual assault		Sample: men Navy recruits
Shields & Cicchetti	169 CT children 98 controls	↑ aggression & bullying	↑ revictimization	Middle childhood
Kisiel & Lyons	114 CT children	↑ sexual aggression	↑ dissociation, suicidality	

Table A 16.1. Aggressive Behavior, Violence and Childhood Trauma *(concluded)*

Year/Author	Study Characteristics	Violent/Agg. Behavior	Other Effects of Trauma	Comments
Cold et al.	1,207 children CT v. controls	↑ abusers/ victims of domestic violence	↑ revictimization	
2002 Nelson et al.	3,982 twins CT v. controls	↑ conduct disorder	↑ co-morbidity	
2003 Whitfield et al.	8,629 adult HMO patients, CT v. controls; ACE study	↑ spouse abuse or being a victim	2–10.3x self-destructive 4.7–10.3x SA/CD	↑ Childhood trauma
Baldry	1,059 children CT v. controls	↑ aggression (bullying)	↑ victimization	
Guerra et al.	4,458 children CT v. controls	↑		Acts through imitation & thinking
Walrath et al.	759 CSA children, 2,722 controls 5–17 yo	1.7X	↑ anxiety, depression, somatization	↑ psych hospitalization, general impairment
Total 40 Studies 1977–2003	**45,088 CTs & controls**	**↑ Violent &/or Aggressive Behavior**	**↑ co-morbidity**	**Significant link with childhood trauma**

Key: See end Table A 15.1

Table A 16.2. Aggressive Behavior, Violence and Childhood Trauma: 16 Prospective Studies

Year/Author	Study Characteristics	Aggression Behavior	Other Effects of Trauma	Comments
1990 Dodge et al. 6+ months	46 CPA children 258 controls	↑ aggression		
1994 Paradise 6 months	154 CSA children v. 53 controls	↑ behavior & school problems	Family dysfunction may be contributing factors	
1996 Silverman et al., 17 years	375–519 children	↑	↑ depression, suicidality, anxiety, SA	↑ co-morbidity
1996 Fergusson et al.	1,000 CSA children followed yearly to 18	↑ aggression, violence	↑ depression, suicidality, anxiety, antisocial	Graded relationship to trauma severity
1997 Fergusson et al.	1,265 PA children followed yearly to 18	↑ aggression, violence	↑ depression, suicidality, anxiety, antisocial	Graded relationship to trauma severity
1998 Calam et al. 2 years	144 CSA children 1.3–1.6 yos	↑	Several, as shown in Table 18.4	Most CSA was substantiated
2000 Frothingham et al. 7 years	140 CSA children v. 83 controls, 1990 to 1997	22x; + 32x more use of mental health services	35x further abuse, 19x sexualized, 15x surname changes, 10x genital problems, 3.3x enuresis . . .	. . . 3x growth problems, 2x address changes, 1.5x chronic health problems
Bagley & Mallick 12 years	290 CT girls	↑ conduct disorder	↑ emotional problems (esp. linked to CSA)	High proverty + other risk factors

Table A 16.2. Aggressive Behavior, Violence and Childhood Trauma *(concluded)*

Year/Author	Study Characteristics	Aggression Behavior	Other Effects of Trauma	Comments
2001 Herrenkohn & Russo 12 years	80 (?) CT 294 control children	↑ aggressive behavior		Increased in a graded relationship
2002 Johnson et al. 8 years	167 children CT v. controls	↑ aggression	↑ depression, anxiety	
Lansford et al.	585 children CT v. controls	↑ aggression	↑ depression, anxiety, PTSD, thought disorder	12 year follow-up
Shepherd et al.	411 boys CT v. controls	↑ violence, behavior problems	↑ APD, lung disease	8 years
2003 Salfer et al. 7–19 years	224 CSA boys	↑ violence		3x women perps
Ehrensaft et al.	543 adults CT v. controls	↑ violence & conduct disorder	↑ SA/CD	20 years
Hawke et al.	446 SA/CD teens most with CT	↑ violence	↑ depression, anxiety, PTSD	5 years
Total 16 Studies 1990–2003	**8,277 CT children & controls**	**↑ to 22x**	**↑ Co-morbidity**	**6 months (one study) to 20-year follow-up**

Table A 16.3. ADHD/ODD/Violence and

Year/Author	Study Characteristics	Childhood Trauma
1975 Sendi & Blonigren	10 murderer teens, 10 attempted murderers, 10 hospitalized controls	↑ CT
1985 Lewis et al.	9 teen murderers v. 24 controls, all incarcerated	↑ CPA (8/9)
1988 Herman	19 violent people (6 were women)	100%
1990 Della Femina et al.	69 imprisoned youth high violence	↑
1999 Thompson & Kaplan	22 ADHD children	↑ CT (esp. emotional abuse)
1999/2001 Ford et al.	27 ODD only 40 ODD/ADHD children v. 48 adjustment disorder controls	48% CPA/18% CSA 73% CPA/31% CSA 10% CPA/0% CSA
2001 Ford et al.	50 ADHD children v. 48 adjustment disorder controls	26% CPA 11% CSA
2002 Lee	64 sex offenders 33 property thieves*	↑
Hinshaw	93 ADHD girls, 47 inattentive type 88 controls	↑ CT among the 93
2003 Crowley et al.	98 conduct disordered SA/CD teens 102 controls	2/3
Total 10 Studies 1975–2003	**927 ADHD/ODD/violent children/teens & controls**	**↑ Childhood Trauma**

Childhood Trauma: 10 *Index Case* Studies

Other Trauma Effects	Comments
All murderers had personality disorders or schizophrenia	
↑ psychotic symptoms (all) (2x controls)	↑ mental illness among & abuse by parents
	Need to address trauma
22–24% PTSD (0% in controls)	Need to address trauma in behavior problems
	Need to address trauma in behavior problems
↑ co-morbidity	
↑ depression	
↑ PTSD, Co-morbidity	Need to address trauma in all behavior problems

Table A 18.1. Psychosis and Childhood Trauma: 58 Clinical & 9 Community Studies

Year/Author	Study Characteristics	Psychosis/ Schizophrenia	Other Trauma Effects/Comments
1934 Rasmussen[1*]	54 CSA children	5.5x	
1979 Tsai et al.	90 women (30 each: clinical, non-clinical, controls)	↑	MMPI: ↑ Hs, Pd, Pa, Pt & Sc.** ↓ social skills, family & sexual function
1980 Meiselman	16 CSA psych pt's 16 psych patients	↑ both	Control bias?
1983 Wolfe & Mosk	71 CT children 35 controls	↑ schizoid	↑ depression, behavior, somatic
1984 Belkin et al.	105 CSA v. 849 controls	↑	↑ interpersonal discord, social alienation, psychopathic deviant
Livingston et al.[3]	28 CT v. 72 6–12 children on psych unit	7.7x (77% CSA Dx'd psychotic v. 10% of controls)	P<.0005
Rodnick et al.[3]	65 teens of hostile parents	↑ schizophrenic	
1985 Ellenson[3]	40 women CSA	↑ psychotic symptoms, including hallucinations	
Lewis et al.	9 murderers (8/9 CPA) v. 24 controls, all incarcerated	100% psychotic symptoms (2x controls)	↑ mental illness & abuse by parents
1986 Fromuth	383 ♀ college CSA v. controls	↑ psychoticism & paranoia	↑ depression, anxiety, somatization ↓ parental support a major factor

Table A 18.1. Psychosis and Childhood Trauma *(continued)*

Year/Author	Study Characteristics	Psychosis/ Schizophrenia	Other Trauma Effects/Comments
Scott & Stone	22 CSA incest	↑	↑ somatization
Putnam et al.	96 CT patients all have MPD	30% hallucinations 20% delusions	↑ co-morbidity
1987 Sansonet -Hayden et al.[3]	29/54 teens CT v. controls	↑	↑
1987 Jacobson & Richardson[2]	50 psych inpatients CT v. controls	↑	
Livingston	13 CSA children mean age 10	↑ psychotic symptoms	
Bryer et al.	66 women psych inpatients, CT v. controls	↑ psychoticism	↑ depression, anxiety, revictimization, paranoia
Bryer et al.	66 ♀ psych inpatients, CT v. controls	↑ psychotic symptoms, paranoia	↑ depression, anxiety, revictimization
1988 Stein et al.	2,683, overt CSA only (LA Epidem. Catchment Area study)	9x	3 + x depression, 2–10x anx. dis, 2x SA, 5xOCD, 3.8x APD, 2.2x any mental disorder
Burnam et al.	432 CSA v. 2,693 controls	No increase (Younger age abused, → more mental dis.)	↑ depression, SA, anxiety disorders, OCD No ↑ mania, APD
Goodwin et al.[2]	40 psych inpatients CT v. controls	↑ psychotic symptoms	
Schaefer et al.	36 CT 64 controls	↑ psychoticism, paranoia	↑ depression, anxiety, OCD
1989 Fromuth & Bukhart	582 college students CT v. controls	↑ psychoticism	↑ depression, OCD, hostility

Table A 18.1. Psychosis and Childhood Trauma *(continued)*

Year/Author	Study Characteristics	Psychosis/ Schizophrenia	Other Trauma Effects/Comments
1990 Swett et al.[3]	65 abused men 65 controls	↑ on psychoticism scale	
Shearer et al.	40 BPD psych inpatients CT v. controls	↑ psychotic symptoms	
Chu & Dill[3]	98 inpatients	Common, esp. auditory hallucinations	
Greenwald et al.	54 CSA nurses v. 54 controls	↑ on psychoticism scale	↑ depression, anxiety, phobia, OC, paranoid, somatization
1990 Jacobson & Herald[3]	100 psych inpatients 23 CT v. 76 controls	↑	
Gold et al.	187 adult CSAs	↑ psychoticism	↑ depression, aggressive & impulsive behavior, somatization
Metcalf et al.	100 men psych patients, 23 CSA v. 76 controls	↑	↑ "bipolar"
1991 Heins et al.	10 CSA survivors	↑ hallucinations & voices (3 of 10)	
Hunter	52 CSA adults 52 controls	↑ psychotic symptoms	Co-morbidity; 12.5% of molesters were women
1992 Lundberg -Love et al.[3]	107 women, CSA v. controls	↑ on psychoticism scale	Used SLC-R-90
Carlin & Ward[3]	149 women psych pts 51% CSA	↑ Sc MMPI scale	
Famularo et al.	61 CT 5–10 yos 35 controls	↑	
Ensink[2]	100 incest survivors	↑ hallucinations	More trauma was associated with ↑ Sx

Table A 18.1. Psychosis and Childhood Trauma *(continued)*

Year/Author	Study Characteristics	Psychosis/ Schizophrenia	Other Trauma Effects/Comments
Ross & Joshi[2]	502 adults CT v. controls	5x schiz. symptoms	Community sample
Label	502 psych inpatients CT v. controls	↑	
1993 Dubowitz et al.	93 CSA children 80 controls	↑ schizoid	↑ depression, hyperactive, ED
Swett & Halpert	78 CT women 17 inpt. "controls"	↑ psychoticism	↑ anxiety, PDs, hostility
1994 Ross et al.[3]	CT v. controls	↑ positive psychotic symptoms	
1994 Pelcovitz et al.	27 CPA/CSA teens v. 27 controls	3x thought disorder	↑ depression, behavior problems, PTSD (3); Non-clinician grad stud. interviewers
Collings	284 college men CT v. controls	↑ psychoticism	↑ depression, anxiety, phobia, OCD ↑ Somatization
Bellan et al.	105 CSA patients 105 controls	↑	Used MMPI. Record review
1995 Ellason & Ross	108 DID pts. (nearly all with CT history) v. 240 schizophrenics	↑ positive symptoms of schizophrenia	Beware false positive diagnosis of schiz in DID; DID & complex PTSD may show psychotic features
Goodman et al.[2]	99 patients CT v. controls	↑	
Belliveau & Stoppard	118 ACoAs, 307 controls college students	↑ psychoticism (men only)	↑ depression, maladjustment

Table A 18.1. Psychosis and Childhood Trauma *(concluded)*

Year/Author	Study Characteristics	Psychosis/ Schizophrenia	Other Trauma Effects/Comments
1996 Whitfield & Stock	100 adult survivors of CSA, 88 ♀, 12 ♂	3x	7x (57%) depression, 7x PTSD, 6x SA, 14x DID, 40% ED; 1/3 self-harm, sex, dysfunction, 22% molested a child
Ellason et al.	135 DID patients (96% CT)	74% (prior psychosis diagnosis)	↑ co-morbidity
Silverman et al.	23 CSA 164 controls	↑ thought disorder	
Cohen et al.[3]	73 teen psych inpts. CT v. control		
Davies-Netzley et al.[4]	120 psych patients	↑	
1997 Briere et al.	77/93 ♀ psych ER admissions abused	↑ psychoses (non manic)	↑ SA/CD, anxiety, dep./suicide, assaults as adults; Multi-ethnic, poor, ↑ hospitalizaiton
Ellason & Ross	144 CT survivors	↑ psychosis	↑ depression, dissociation
1997 Cairns	88 college women CT v. control	↑ schiz (on MMPI)	↑ depression
1998 Muser	153 outpatients CT v. controls	↑	
1999 Read & Argyle	22 CS/PA v. 88 control acute psych inpatients	↑ psychotic symptoms	Medical records only, known to underestimate
Fondacaro & Holt	85 CSA, 125 controls, prison inmates	↑ schiz, schizoaffective	↑ depression, SA/CD, PTSD, anxiety, panic, OCD, ASPD; 41% of CSAs believe they weren't abused

Table A 18.1. Psychosis and Childhood Trauma *(concluded)*

Year/Author	Study Characteristics	Psychosis/ Schizophrenia	Other Trauma Effects/Comments
Duncan	173 CT teens 73 controls	↑ psychoticism	↑ depression, PTSD, anxiety; ↑ somatization
Saigh et al.	151 children CT v. controls	↑ thought disorder	↑ depression, anxiety, somatization
Gold et al.	187 CSA adults	↑ psychoticism	↑ depression, behavior probs, anxiety, somatization
Lipschitz et al.	35 teen inpatients CT v. controls	↑	
Startup	224 college students CT v. controls	↑ schizotypy	↑ dissociation
2000 Harter & Taylor	333 college students, age 18–29, 59% ♀	↑ psychosis	↑ depression, anxiety, Pa, hostility. Parental alcoholism alone had no independent effects
Lipschitz et al.	57 teen inpatients CT v. controls		
2001 Read[2]	CSA/CPA	↑ psychotic Sx, hallucinations	
Felon et al.	71 teen inpatients CT v. controls	↑	
2004 Whitfield et al.	171 trauma survivors v. 8,353 controls	↑ hallucinations	Multiple co-morbidity; Graded relationship to traumas
Total 67 Studies 1934–2003	**23,291 Childhood trauma survivors & controls**	**↑ Psychotic symptoms/ signs, psychoses, incl. schizophrenia**	**↑ Co-morbidity; Only one study that looked for it did not find psychotic symptoms**

Key: * 1 = cited in Bendr & Blau 1937; 2 = cited in Read 2001; 3 = cited in Read 1997; 4 = cited in Read & Ross 2003. ** MMPI codes: Hs = Hypochondriasis, Pd = Psychopathic deviate, Pa = paranoia, Pt = Psychasthenia, Sc = Schizophrenia.

Table A 18.2. Schizophrenia & Childhood Trauma:
37 *Index Case* Studies

Year/Author	Study Characteristics	Childhood Trauma	Other Effects of Trauma/Comments
1963 Gleuck	4 schizophrenics + 3 suspected	all CT	
1980 Surles & Ingham	40 affective psychotics	↑ total life stress	
1981 Walker et al.	45 w/schizophrenic symptoms	Parent loss, institutionalized	
1984 Friedman & Harrison[2]	20 schizophrenic women	60% CSA	
Livingston[2] et al.	100 6–12 yos on a psych unit	7.7x (77% CSA in psychotic v. 10% of controls)	$P > .0005$
1987 Beck & van der Kolk	26 actively psychotic women, Tx refractory	46% CSA	Incest only, no eval. for other CSA or PA, thus under-biasing
Carlin & Ward[2]	149 women psych patients, many schiz	51% CSA, Sc MMPI scale	
Jacobson & Richardson[1]	100 psych inpatients	81% CT+/or revictimized	
1988 Craine et al.	50 schiz (psychotic inpatients)	48% CSA	↑ depression, SA/CD
Herman	38 psychotics	100%	co-morbidity
1989 Coons et al.	15 schizophrenics	7 to 33% CT and adult trauma	↑ PTSD 33% adult trauma
1990 Byrne et al.	14 schizophrenics	21–64% high family trauma 27% CSA	↑ SA/CD, anxiety, suicide, behavior problems

Table A 18.2. Schizophrenia & Childhood Trauma *(continued)*

Year/Author	Study Characteristics	Childhood Trauma	Other Effects of Trauma
1991 Golf et al.	61 chronic psychotics	27/61 (44%) CT	↑ dissociation & relapse
Rose et al.[1,3]	39 predom. psychotic Dxs	38–50% CT	
1992 Palmer et al.	5 schizophrenics	40%	
1993 Muenzen-Maier et al.	36 schizophrenics 9 dchizoaffective	65% CT	↑ depression, SA/CD, adult victimization, homelessness
1994 Ross et al.	83 schizophrenics	45% CT (37/83)	↑ dissociation, BPD Sx
Greenfield et al.[3]	19 predom. psychotic patients	53% CSA/PA	
1994 Trojan	48 predom. psychotic patients	25–27% CSA	
Darves-Barnoz et al.[3]	89 predom. psychotic patients	34% CSA	
Darves-Barnoz et al.	64 schizophrenics	36% CSA	↑ SA/CD, suicidality revictimization
1996 Teicher et al.	253 adult outpatients	↑ psychotic symptoms	
Wurr & Partridge	34 schizophrenics	38% CSA	
1996 Miller & Finnerty	44 schizophrenics	36% CSA	Cited in Read & Ross 2000
1997 Heads et al.	102 schizophrenics	48% CSA, 28–52% CPA	Community sample

Table A 18.2. Schizophrenia & Childhood Trauma *(concluded)*

Year/Author	Study Characteristics	Childhood Trauma	Other Effects of Trauma
Honig et al.	18 schizophrenics	83% CSA, CPA or EA	
Griese et al.	29 psychotic inpatients	↑	
1999 Goodman et al.[3]	29 schizophrenics	78% CSA	
Agid et al.[3]	76 schizophrenics 76 controls	3.8–4.3x	
2001 Lysaker et al.	31 schizophrenic men 12 schizoaffective	35% CSA (very high for men), 33% CSA	↓ psycho-social functioning ↓ neuro-cognitive functioning in CSA groups
2002 Lysaker et al.	36 schizophrenics or schizoaffective	↑ CPA	predicted hostility
Friedman et al.	22 schizophrenics	↑ CT, esp early parent loss	
2003 Resnick et al.	47 schizophrenics	38–66%	↑ revictimization
2003 Holowaka et al.	26 schizophrenics	↑	↑ dissociation
Lysaker et al.	38 schizophrenic men (new sample)	38% CT	↑ relationship difficulties
Resnick et al.	47 schizophrenics	↑ CT & adult trauma	↑ PTSD
Total 37 Studies 1963–2003	**1,562+ patients with schiz/ psychosis**	**↑ to 100% had childhood trauma history**	**↑ Co-morbidity. Evaluate all for trauma Hx.**

*MMPI codes: Sc=Schizophrenia. 1=cited in Read 2001; 2=cited in Read 1997; 3=cited in Read & Ross 2003

Table A 18.3. Psychosis & Childhood Trauma:
4 Prospective Studies

Year/Author	Study Characteristics	Schiz./ Psychosis	Other Effects of Trauma	Comments
1982 Norton (dissertation)	52 children, with highly critical parents v. controls	9x		5-year follow-up
1986 Bagley & Ramsay	82 abused children v. 285 controls	7x psychosis/ psychotic symptoms	↑ depression, suicidality, anxiety, self-harm. ↓ self-esteem	12-year follow-up
1994 Jones et al.	5,362 births children of poor-skilled v. control mothers	5.8x schizo-phrenia among children of poor-skilled		40 year prospective
2002 Landsford et al.	585 children CSA v. controls	↑ significant thought problems	↑ depression, anxiety, PTSD, behavior, school, dissociation	12-year follow-up
Total 4 Studies 1982–2002	**6,376 people, CTs v. controls**	**↑ psychotic symptoms to 5.8x schizophrenia**	**↑ co-morbidity**	**5- to 40-year follow-ups**

Table A 18.10. Example Antipsychotic Drugs,

Drug	Trade Name	Daily Dose	Sedation
"Low Potency"			
Chlorpromazine	Thorazine	25-1500 mg.	+++
Thioridazine	Mellaril	20–800	+++
"High Potency"			
Haloperidol	Haldol	0.5–20	+
Trifluoperazine	Stelazine	4–50	+
Fluphenazine	Prolixin	0.5–20	+
"Atypicals"*			
Risperidone	Risperdal	0.25–6	++
Ziprazidone	Geodon	40–160	++
Olanzapine	Zyprexa	5–20	++
Sertindole	Serlect	6–24	+++
Quetiapine	Seroquel	100–800	+
Clozapine	Clozaril	slow ↑ to 300–450	+++
Aripiprazole	Abilify	2–30	±

Summary of "atypicals"—These drugs are very expensive and are too new to know their full toxicity. Most have toxic effects: weight gain, diabetes, higher blood lipids, cardiovascular toxicity, sedation, etc. As is true for all drugs, these are all toxic and potentially dangerous chemicals that should be used with caution and only under the ongoing supervision of a physician who is knowledgable and experienced in their use. On balance, most of the new "atypicals" may be as or more toxic than the older ones, and are much more expensive. See ref. 56 for details.

Some Adverse Effects and Comments

EPS*	ACH Effects	Comments
+++	++++	This and next 3 have strong hypotensive effects
++		
++++	+	*High potency* means fewer mg. are needed for similar effect
++++	++	
++++		
++	0 (?)	Caution for all these drugs' claims, as for any new drug. Diabetes, cardiotoxic, etc.
+	+	Geodon claims helps pos & neg symptoms, with claimed less weight gain
+	++	Claims helps pos & neg symptoms, but causes weight gain & diabetes
+	(?)	Caution: Heart arrhythmias, other toxicities
+	±	Caution: cataracts, diabetes, thyroid toxic, other
+	++++	Highly toxic to bone marrow & CNS; diabetes. Blood dyscrasias (1–2%), seizures (1–5%) cardiotoxic; doesn't lower suicide attempts
+	++	Claims less weight gain; toxicity still a concern. Most expensive.

*Acute extrapyramidal symptoms (EPS): Parkinson's dystonias, akathisia. Does not reflect risk for tardive dyskinesia (see footnote). All these and other neuroleptics may cause tardive dyskinesia except clozapine.
**ACH (anticholinergic) effects include dry mouth, constipation, difficult urination, and blurred vision.
***These newer "atypicals" may be used when the other drugs do not work. Some recommend them as primary treatment, although they may not have a better risk-benefit ratio.

The risk of developing tardive dyskinesia and the chance of it becoming irreversible are believed to increase as the duration of treatment and the cumulative dose of antipsychotic drugs increase, although it can develop after brief treatment at low doses. There is no known treatment for TD. It may remit, partially or completely, if antipsychotic drug treatment is withdrawn. Antipsychotic drug treatment may suppress its signs and symptoms, masking the underlying TD process.

Table A 19.2. Somatization and Childhood Trauma: Results from 38 Example Peer-Reviewed, Databased *Clinical* & *Community* Studies

Year/Author	Study Characteristics	Somati-zation	Other Effects of Trauma	Comments
1984 Burgess et al.	66 CSA children	↑	↑ alcohol & drug use	
1986 Friedrich et al.	85 CSA 3- 12-year-old children clinical, forensic sample	↑	↑ depression, anxiety, aggression, delinquency, hyperactivity, etc.	Evaluated by Child Behavior Checklist
Scott & Stone	22 CSA (incest)	↑		
Fromuth	383 college CSA v. controls	↑		↓ family support a major factor
1987 Burgess et al.	34 CSA children 34 controls	↑	↑ PTSD, anxiety, SA/CD, antisocial behavior, insomnia	
Livingston	28 CT children v. 72 on inpt. psych unit	4x	↑ phobia, behavior problems	Control bias may under-estimate differences
Kashani & Carlson	9 CT 3-6 year olds 18 controls	↑	all 9 depressed	
Breyer et al.	48 CS/PA 27 controls	↑	↑ depression, anxiety, paranoia, psychoticism	
Beck & van der Kolk	12 CT chronic psychotics	6x medical disorders	3x depression, SA/CD	3x CSA
1988 Briere & Runtz	47 CSA 237 controls	↑	↑ depression, anxiety, dissociation	Did not look for SA/CD

Table A 19.2. **Somatization and Childhood Trauma** (continued)

Year/Author	Study Characteristics	Somati-zation	Other Effects of Trauma	Comments
Einbender & Friedrich	46 CSA girls 6-14 yo 46 controls	↑	↑ aggression, school & behavior problems	
1990 Knowles & Schroeder	199 ACoAs 601 controls	↑	↑ depression, family problems	
Goodwin et al.	20 CT women	↑	↑ co-morbidity	Trauma severe
Arnold et al.	7 CT medical patients	↑ med probs & surgery		
1991 Felitti	131 CSA 100 controls	↑	↑ DOVs, EDs, depression	1.6x GI probs, 1.8x headaches
1992 Walker et al.	14 ♀ severe CSA v. 86 controls	23x, 7.6x chronic pelvic pain	5-10x depression, 47x panic, 6x pho-bia, 1.7-5.9x SA/CD, 2-2.5x sexual dysf.	All scheduled for diagnostic laparoscopy, 50 for chronic pelvic pain, 50 for tubal ligation
Friedrich et al.	42 CSA boys	↑	↑ co-morbidity	
1993 Moeller et al.	354 CP/S/EA 314 controls in gyn clinic	↑ Gyn problems, 2x, 2x obesity, fatigue	6x revictimization, 1.5-6x anxiety, 2x low self-esteem, 3x pessimism, depression	Found 16 char's of parents; (8% perps women)
Anderson et al.	51 CSA women	↑ somati-zation disorder	↑ SA/CD, PDs, dissociation	↑ traumatic amnesia
1994 Goldberg et al.	201 patients	↑ chronic pain problems	↑ depression	Depression an expected result of chronic pain

Table A 19.2. Somatization and Childhood Trauma *(continued)*

Year/Author	Study Characteristics	Somati-zation	Other Effects of Trauma	Comments
Collings	284 college men CT v. controls	↑	↑ depression, anxiety, disorders, psychoticism	
1995 Walker et al.	43 CT women 46 controls	5.7x	↑ depression, SA/CD, anxiety, panic, OCD, revictimization	GI clinic patients
Ellason et al.	135 DIDs (96% CT)	↑	↑ depr/bipolar, SA/CD, anxiety, EDs, psychosis	High co-morbidity
1996 Golding	6,024 adults CT v. controls	↑	↑ depression, anxiety	General population
1997 Moisan et al.	60 boys SA (30 black, 30 Latino)	↑	↑ depression, anger, hopelessness	30% molesters were women
McCauley et al.	424 of 1,931 CS/PA women	↑	↑ depression, SA/CD	Half revictim-ized as adults
Jarvis & Copeland	94 CSA women 37 controls	↑	↑ SA/CD, anxiety, dissociation	
1998 Felitti et al.	9,508 patients ACE study CT v. controls	1.6-3.9x medical probs	↑ depression/ suicidality, SA/CD, co-morbidity	Study is ongoing in follow-up
1999 Gold et al.	287 CSA adults	↑	↑ depression, anxiety, aggressive, impulsive behavior, psychoticism	

Table A 19.2. Somatization and Childhood Trauma *(concluded)*

Year/Author	Study Characteristics	Somati-zation	Other Effects of Trauma	Comments
Walker et al.	527 CT women 698 controls	↑	1.5x SA/CD	
2000 Hulme	91 CSA women 304 controls	↑	↑ depression, SA/CD, anxiety	↑ Doctor office visits
Harter & Vanecek	651 college students CT v. controls	↑	↑ anxiety	
2002 Taylor & Jason	18,675 adults CT v. controls	↑ (chronic fatigue)	↑ anxiety	community
Greenwald et al.	54 CSA nurses v. 54 controls	↑	↑ depression, anxiety, phobia, OC, paranoid, psychoticism	No ↓ self-esteem/sexual dysfunction
2003 Stevens et al.	378 teens CT v. controls	↑	↑ depression, anxiety, revictimization	All had SA/CD
Summary 38 Studies 1984-2003	**50,127 CTs & Controls**	**1.6-23x medical & surgical problems**	**↑ Depression, SA/CD, Anxiety, Behavior Problems**	**↑ Revictim-ization, co-morbidity**

Table A 19.3. Somatization and Childhood Trauma:
11 *Prospective* Studies

Year/ Author	Study	Somati- zation	Depression, Suicide, Anxiety/Other	Medical Disorders/ Other
1992 Bushnell et al. 2 years	39 CSA women 362 controls	↑	Depression, SA/CD/ ED, PD	
1993 Lundberg 13 years	4,216 people v. controls	1.3-7.7x	1.8-10.2x mental illness	1.2-2x early death
1997 Russek & Schwartz 35 years	126 college students v. controls	2x	↑ SA/CD	heart disease, hypertension, ulcers
1996 Silverman et al. 17 years	63 CS/PA v. 479 controls		↑ (+ ↑ ADHD, SA/CD)	↑ PTSD, dissociative disorders, sexual problems
1996-9 Widom et al. 20+ years	726 CS/PA, N v. 543 controls	↑	↑ Co-morbidity	↓ self-esteem & affect control
1998 Putnam 8 yrs, ongoing	77 CSA 72 controls	↑	↑ (+ ↑ ADHD, SA/CD)	
Calam et al. 2 years	144 CSA children 1.3-16 yo	↑	Several, as shown in Table 15.5 on page 158	

Table A 19.3. **Somatization and Childhood Trauma** (concluded)

Year/ Authors	Study	Somati- zation	Depression, Suicide, Anxiety/Other	Medical Disorders/ Other
2000 Cameron 2 years	72 women, 51 for the full 12 years	75% gyn problems; 67% had headaches, jaw pain	7x depression; 77% anxiety; 82% EDs, 78% sexual problems; 63% PTSD ↓ self-esteem	Trauma-focused treatment → substantial improvement over time
Frothingham	140 CSA 83 controls	1.5-10x	↑ co-morbidity	3x growth problems
2002 Johnson et al.	717 teens & their mothers CT v. controls	↑	↑ co-morbidity	Authors' other reports on same sample (Brown et al. 1998, Johnson et al. 1999, 2000, '01)
Romans et al.	354 women CT v. controls	↑ medical problems	↑ dissociation	
Summary 11 Studies 1992-2002	**8,264 CTs & controls**	**Significant ↑ in Somatic/ Medical Problems**	**↑ Depression, Anxiety, EDs, PTSD, SA/CD, ADHD ↓ Self-esteem**	**Multiple co-morbidity common**

Table A 19.4. Somatization and Childhood Trauma: 16 Example Index Case Studies

Year/Author	Study Characteristics	Childhood Trauma	Other Effects of Trauma
1989 Morrison	60 somatization disordered women 31 depressed	↑	
1991 Felitti	231 medical patients	↑ (131 CSA)	↑ doctor office visits
1992 Walker et al.	Chronic pelvic pain women, 21 controls	↑	↑ dissociation
1993 Pribor et al.	99 somatizing women	↑	↑ dissociation
1994 Barsky et al.	60 hypochondriacs 60 controls	↑	
1996 Portegijs et al.	51 somatization 39 depression	2.8x	
1998 Leserman et al.	139 GI clinic patients	↑ 51%	↑ office visits, somatization
1999 Nijenhuis	52 women with pelvic pain	↑	↑ depression, dissociation, revictimization
2002 Hexel & Sonneck	22 somatizing patients	68%	
2002 Yucel et al.	41 chronic headache & 32 backache patients	↑ in both	
Sundbom et al.	13 chronic fatigue, 19 conversion disorders, 13 controls	↑ (life trauma)	

Table A 19.4. Somatization and Childhood Trauma *(concluded)*

Year/Author	Study Characteristics	Childhood Trauma	Other Effects of Trauma
Taylor & Jason	222 chronic fatigue patients 74 controls	3.8x CSA	↑ PTSD, anxiety disorders
2003 Salmon et al.	64 irritable bowel syndrome 64 ulcerative colitis or Crohn's disease	55% CSA 31% CSA	↑ anxiety, dissociation, revictimization
2003 Baccini et al.	226 GI clinic patients	↑ (32% in organic & functional)	
Preschers et al.	1,075 gyn patients	↑	↑ revictimization & later trauma
2003 Nijenhuis et al.	52 chronic pain patients	↑	↑ dissociation
Summary 16 Studies 1989-2003	**2,779 Somatizing Patients**	**↑ to 3.8x Childhood Trauma Histories**	**↑ Co-morbidity**

Table A 19.6. Revictimization and Childhood Trauma: 38 Example Studies

Year/Author	Study Characteristics	Revictimization	Other Trauma Effects/ Comments
1978 Miller et al.	341 sexual assault victims	4.5x	↑ among CSA survivors
1984 Bryer et al.	66 women, psych inpatients	50+% as adult	↑ psychoticism
Friedman & Harrison	20 schizophrenics (6x CSA); 15 controls	3x	↑ sexual dysfunction
Bagley & McDonald 8-year prospective	57 abused girls (20 CSA) separated from mother v. 30 non-abused	Repeated abusive relationships (without recovery work)	↑ depression, sexual problems neurosis-related to separation from M, physical abuse & neglect, ↓ self-esteem
1986 Coons & Millstein	20 MPDs, 20 controls 85% CS/PA (11-15x controls)	30x raped as adult (revictimized)	15x fugue, 20x visual hallucinations, 5x conversion paralysis/ anesthesia, 5.5x head-aches, 2x organic seizures
1987 Bryer et al.	48 CS/PA 27 controls	50+% as adult	↑ depression, anxiety, SA/CD, somatization. Likely underestimated trauma %
Alexander & Lupfer	149 CSA ♀ college students v. 437 controls	↑ vulnerability to sexual assault	↓ self-esteem. ↓ family concept, empathy & support
Jacobson & Richardson	50 women psch inpatients	↑ (38-64%)	↑ co-morbidity
1988 Briere	133 CSA, 61 controls	3x as adult	↑ dissociation, SA/CD, self-harm, suicide
Mullen et al.	314 women CT v. controls	3.6-26.6x	↑ co-morbidity

Table A 19.6. Revictimization and Childhood Trauma *(continued)*

Year/Author	Study Characteristics	Revictimization	Other Trauma Effects/ Comments
1989 Jacobson	8 SA/CDs most CTs	↑	↑ alcohol/drug use during trauma. Index cases
Gottman & Katz	56 4–5-year-olds + their families	↑	"Negative parenting" a factor
Muenzen -Maier et al.	78 psychiatric outpatients (2/3 CT)	↑	↑ depression, SA/CD, psychosis, homelessness
1992 Wallen & Berman	217 SA/CDs, 31 CSA, 186 no CSA history	↑	↑ suicidality Control bias likely
1993 Moeller et al.	354 abused ♀ (CSA, PA, EA) v. 314 controls in a gyn practice	6.2x more likely to be a crime victim	↑ depression, anxiety, SA/CD, obesity, fatigue & PMS, GYN problems, tension, pessimistic; ↓ self-esteem, Found 16 dysfunctional char's. of parents of abused
Fullilove et al.	104 CT women	↑	↑ SA/CD, PTSD
1994 Fox & Gilbert	253 people	↑	↑ depression, partner conflicts, ↓ self-esteem
1995 Walker et al.	43 CT women 46 controls	↑	↑ depression, SA/CD, anxiety/panic, OCD, somatization. GI clinic patients
Goodman et al.	99 psych patients, most CT	↑ (76-87%)	↑ co-morbidity
1997 Pettigrew Burcham	72 CSA 73 controls	↑	↑ anxiety

Table A 19.6. Revictimization and Childhood Trauma *(concluded)*

Year/Author	Study Characteristics	Revictimization	Other Trauma Effects/Comments
1997 Briere et al.	93 ♀ psych ER patients (80+% CT/± adult trauma)	42% revictimized	2+x depression, SA/CD 3-8x violence, 2x psychosis
McCauley et al.	424 CS/PA women of 1,931	Half revictimized as adults	↑ depression, SA/CD, somatization
Whiffin & Clark	167 people CSA v. controls	↑	↑ depression
Jarvis & Copeland	94 CSA women 37 controls	↑	↑ anxiety, SA/CD, somatization, dissociation. ↑ co-morbidity
1999 Armsworth et al.	36 CSA (incest) 35 controls	2-8x	↑ depression, anxiety, eating disorders
Sanders	30 CSA/PA college women, 133 controls	↑ date rape (related to ↓ dissociation)	↑ anxiety, depression, dysfunctional sexual behavior, dissociation
Duncan	210 college fresh, CT v. controls	↑	↑ depression, anxiety, PTSD, psychoticism
2000 Clark & Foy	41 CSA 37 controls	↑ later domestic violence	↑ alcohol use in CSA group
Frantz & Ostergren	128 CT women 363 controls	↑ (16%)	↑ anxiety
1992 Frazier & Cohen	82 college women CT v. controls	↑	↑ co-morbid
Pribor & Dinwiddie	52 CSA (incest) v. 23 psych patients	7x	↑ co-morbid

Table A 19.6. Revictimization and Childhood Trauma *(concluded)*

Year/Author	Study Characteristics	Revictimization	Other Trauma Effects/ Comments
1996 Lipshitz et al.	120 psych patients CT v. controls	↑	↑ somatization, depression, anxiety. All had SA/CD
Baldo & Baldo	390 college women CT v. controls	↑	↑ EDs
1998 Schaff & McCanne	111 CT women 211 controls	↑	↑ co-morbidity; Community sample
2002 Swanston et al.	183 CSA children	↑	2-year prospective
2003 Grossman et al.	52 PD pts. Most CT	30%	
Resnick et al.	47 schizophrenics with ↑ CT	↑	
Stevens et al.	378 teens CT v. controls	↑	
Total 1978-2003 38 Studies	**6,116 CTs & controls**	**↑ to 30x Revictimization**	**↑ Multiple co-Morbidities**

Table A 19.7. Revictimization and Childhood Trauma: 4 Literature Reviews

Year/Author	Study Characteristics	Revictim- ization	Other Effects of Trauma	Comments
1990 Shetky	Literature review of 86 studies & articles	↑	↑ depression, DD, PTSD running away, prostitution, somatization	↑ somatization, psychiatric hospitalization ↓ parenting, self-esteem
1992 Beitchman et al.	Literature review of CSA long-term effects	↑	↑ depression, suicidality, anxiety/fear, personality disorders	
2001 Roodman & Clum	Review of 19 studies	↑ rape as adults in CSA survivors		
2002 Arata	Review of over 100 articles & over 30 studies	2–3x	↑ dissociation, PTSD	Extensive review & analysis of CSA
Summary 4 Reports 1990–2002	**4 Literature Reviews**	**↑ to 3x revictim- ization**	**↑ co-morbidity**	**Need to prevent original traumas**

References

A ──

1. Abbasi K, Smith R (2003). No more free lunches: patients will benefit from doctors & drug companies disentangling. BMJ 326: 1155–7.

2. Abraham J (2002). The pharmaceutical industry as a political player. Lancet 360: 1498–502.

3. Ackard DM, Neumark-Sztainer D, Hannan PJ, French S, Story M (2001). Binge and purge behavior among adolescents: associations with sexual and physical abuse in a nationally representative sample: the Commonwealth Fund survey. Child Abuse Negl 25(6):771–85

4. Ackerman PT, Newton JE, McPherson WB, Jones JG, Dykman RA (1998). Prevalence of post-traumatic stress disorder and other psychiatric diagnoses in three groups of abused children (sexual, physical, and both) Child Abuse & Neglect 22:759–74

5. Adams-Tucker C (1982). Proximate effects of sexual abuse in childhood: a report on 28 children. Am J Psychiatry. 1982 Oct;139(10):1252–6

6. Ageton SS (1983). Sexual assault among adolescents. Lexington Books, Lexington MA

7. Agid O, Shapira B, Zislin J, Ritsner M, Hanin B, Murad H, Troudart T, Bloch M, Heresco-Levy U, Lerer B (1999). Environment and vulnerability to major psychiatric illness: a case control study of early parental loss in major depression, bipolar disorder and schizophrenia. Molecular Psychiatry 4(2):163–72

8. Alanen YO, Ugelstad E, Armelius BA, Lehtinen K, Rosenbaum B, Sjostrom R, Eds. (1994) Early treatment for schizophrenic patients: Scandinavian psychotherapeutic approaches. Oslo, Norway: Scandinavian University Press.

9. Alanen YO, Lehtinen V, Lehtinen K, Aaltonen J, Rakkolainen V (2000) The Finnish model for early treatment of schizophrenia and related psychoses. In: Martindale et al, (eds): Psychosis: Psychological approaches and their effectiveness. London: Gaskell

10. Alexander P, Lupfer S (1987). Family characteristics and long-term consequences associated with sexual abuse. Archives of Sexual Behavior 16: 235–245

11. Alexander PC, Anderson CL, Brand B, Schaeffer CM, Grelling BZ, Kretz L (1998). Adult attachment and long-term effects in survivors of incest. Child Abuse & Neglect 22:45–61

12. Alfaro JD (1981). Report on the relationship between child abuse and neglect and later socially deviant behavior. Published as Chapter 15 of a report from the Select Committee on Child Abuse, State of New York, page 175–219

13. Alliance for Human Research Protection (2004). [Archives of documents on the politics and dangers of psychiatric and medical drugs] Found on Web site *http://www.ahrp.org*

14. American Medical Association, Council on Scientific Affairs (1993). Mental health consequences of interpersonal and family violence: implications for the practitioner. CSA Report (BCA-93). Chicago

15. American Psychiatric Association (1980). Diagnostic and statistical manual of mental disorders (*DSM-III*) Washington, DC. *DSM-II-R* published years later.

16. American Psychiatric Association (1994). Diagnostic and Statistical Manual of Mental Disorders (*DSM-IV*) Washington DC

17. American Psychiatric Association (1997). Practice guideline for the treatment of patients with schizophrenia. Am J Psychiatry 154(4 Suppl):1–63

18. Ammerman RT, Cassisi JE, Hersen M, Van Hasselt VB (1986). Consequences of physical abuse and neglect in children. Clinical Psychology Review 6:291–310

20. Anda RF, Whitfield CL, Felitti VJ, Chapman D, Edwards VJ, Dube SR, Williamson DF (2002). Adverse childhood experiences, alcoholic parents, and later risk of alcoholism and depression. Psychiatric Services 53: 1001–9

21. Anda RF, Felitti VJ, Walker J, Whitfield CL, Bremner JD, Perry BD. Dube SR, Giles WH (2004). The enduring effects of childhood abuse and related experiences: a convergence of evidence from neurobiology and epidemiology (in submission, 2004)

22. Anderson CM, Teicher MH, Polcari A, Renshaw PF (2002). Abnormal T2 relaxation time in the cerebellar vermis of adults sexually abused in childhood: potential role of the vermis in stress-enhanced risk for drug abuse. Psychoneuroendocrinology 27(1–2):231–44

23. Anderson G, Yasenik L & Ross CA (1993). Dissociative experiences and disorders among women who identify themselves as sexual abuse survivors. Child Abuse & Neglect 17 (5): 677–686

24. Anderson KP, LaPorte DJ, Crawford S (2000). Child sexual abuse and bulimic symptomatology: relevance of specific abuse variables. Child Abuse Negl. 24(11):1495–502

25. Andrews B, Valentine R, Valentine JD (1995). Depression and eating disorders following abuse in childhood in two generations of women. British Journal of Clinical Psychology 34: 37–52

26. Andrews B (1997). Bodily shame in relation to abuse in childhood and bulimia: a preliminary investigation. Br J Clin Psychol. 36 (Pt 1):41–9

27. Angell M, Relman AS: Prescription for Profit. The Washington Post June 20, 2001

28. Angell M (2000). Is academic medicine for sale? New England Journal of Medicine 342:1516–8

29. Anthenelli RM, Schuckit MA (1997). Chapter 5. Genetics. In Lowinson JH et al (eds). Substance Abuse: A comprehensive textbook. 3rd ed, Williams & Wilkins, Baltimore, p 41–51

30. Anxiety Disorders Association of America, 8730 Georgia Avenue, Suite 600, Silver Spring, MD 20910

30a. Arata CM (2002). Child sexual abuse and sexual revictimization. Clin Psychol Sci Prac 9:135–64

31. Archer J (2000). Sex differences in aggression between heterosexual partners: a meta-analytic review. Psychological Bulletin 126:651–680

32. Archer J, Ray N (1989). Dating violence in the United Kingdom: a preliminary study. Aggressive Behavior 15:337–43

33. Armsworth MW, Stronck K, Carlson C (1999). Body image and self perceptions of women with histories of incest. In J. Goodwin, R. Attias, Eds., Splintered Reflections: Images of the body in trauma. New York: Basic Behavioral Science

34 . Arnold RP, Rogers D, Cook DA (1990). Medical problems of adults who were sexually abused in childhood. British Medical Journal 300:705–8

B ———————————————————————————————

35. Bachman G et al (1988). Childhood sexual abuse and the consequences in adult women. Obstetrics and Gynecology 71:631–42

36. Baccini F, Pallotta N, Calabrese E, Pezzotti P, Corazziari E (2003). Prevalence of sexual and physical abuse and its relationship with symptom manifestations in patients with chronic organic and functional gastrointestinal disorders. Dig Liver Dis. 35(4):256–61

37. Bagley C (1988). Daycare, mental health, and child development: evidence from a longitudinal study. Early Child Development and Care 39:134–61.

38. Bagley C, McDonald M (1984) Adult mental health sequelae of sexual abuse, physical abuse and neglect in maternally separated children. Canadian Journal of Community Mental Health. 3(1): 15–26

39. Bagley C (1989). Prevalence and correlates of unwanted sexual acts in childhood: evidence from a national Canadian survey. Canadian Journal of Public Health 80:295–6.

40. Bagley C (1991). The prevalence and mental health sequels of child sexual abuse in a community sample of women age 18–27. Canadian Journal of Community Mental Health 10:103–16

41. Bagley C, Shewchuk-Dann D (1991). Characteristics of 60 children & adolescents who have a history of sexual assault against others: evidence from a controlled study. Journal of Child and Youth Care special issue: 43–52

42. Bagley C (1992). Psychological dimensions of poverty and parenthood. International Journal of Marriage and the Family 1:37–49.

43. Bagley C (1992). The urban setting of juvenile pedestrian injuries: a study of behavioral ecology and social disadvantage. Accident Analysis and Prevention 24:673–8

44. Bagley C, Wood M, Young L (1994). Victim to abuser: mental health and behavioral sequels of the sexual abuse of males in childhood. Child Abuse and Neglect 18:683–97

45. Bagley C (1996). A typology of sexual abuse: the interaction of emotional, physical, and sexual abuse as predictors of adult psychiatric sequelae in women. Canadian Journal of Human Sexuality 5:101–112.

46. Bagley C, Bolitho F, Bertrand L (1995). Mental health profiles, suicidal behavior, and community sexual assault in 2112 Canadian adolescents. Crisis: Journal of Crisis Intervention and Suicide Prevention 16:126–31.

47. Bagley C, Mallick K (1997). Temperament, CNS problems, and maternal stressors: interactive predictors of conduct disorder in 9-year-olds. Perceptual and Motor Skills 72:287–8.

48. Bagley C, Mallick K (2000). Prediction of sexual, emotional, and physical maltreatment and mental health outcomes in a longitudinal cohort of 290 adolescent women. Child Maltreatment 5 (3): 218–226

49. Bagley C, Young L (1998). Long-term evaluation of group counseling for women with a history of child sexual abuse: focus on depression, self-esteem, suicidal behaviors, and social support. Social Work with Groups 21:63–74.

50. Bagley C, Young L (1999). Chapter 5. Long-term evaluation of group counseling for women with a history of child sexual abuse In Bagley C, Mallick K (eds.) Child Abuse in Adult Offenders: New Theory and Research (pp 143–158). Brookfield, VT: Ashgate International

51. Bagley C, Young L (1989/90). Depression, self-esteem, and suicidal behavior as sequels of sexual abuse in childhood: research and therapy. In M. Rothery, G. Cameron (eds.), Child Maltreatment: Expanding Our Concept of Healing. (pp 183–209) Hillsdale, NJ Earlbaum

52. Bagley C, Young L, Mallick K (1999). The interactive effects of physical, emotional, and sexual abuse on adjustment in a longitudinal study of 565 children from birth to 17. In Bagley C, Mallick K (eds.) Child Sexual Abuse in Adult Offenders: New Theory and Research (pp 143–158). Brookfield, VT: Ashgate International

53. Bagley C, Ramsay R (1986). Sexual abuse in childhood: Psycho-social outcomes and implications for social work practice. Journal of Social Work and Human Sexuality 4(1–2): 33–47

54. Bailey JM, Gibbons SG (1989). Physical victimization and bulimic-like symptoms: Is there a relationship? Deviant Behavior 10:335–52

55. Bailey JM, Shriver A (1999). Does childhood sexual abuse cause borderline personality disorder? J Sex Marital Ther. 25:45–57

56. Baldessarini RJ (1996). Chapters 18 & 19. Drugs and the treatment of psychiatric disorders. (p 399–459). In Hardman JG & Limbird LE (eds.) Goodman and Gilman's The Pharmacologic Basis of Therapeutics 9th ed., McGraw Hill, NY

57. Baldo TDB, Baldo AJ (1996). Intrafamilial assaults, disturbed eating behaviors, and further victimization. Psychological Reports 79:1057–8

58. Baldry AC (2003). Bullying in schools and exposure to domestic violence. Child Abuse Negl. 27(7):713–32

59. Banyard V (1999). Childhood maltreatment in the mental health of low-income women. American Journal of Orthopsychiatry 69:161–71

60. Barber MA, Davis PM (2002). Fits, faints, or fatal fantasy? Fabricated seizures and child abuse. Arch Dis Child. 86(4):230–3

61. Barker LR, Whitfield CL: Chapter 21. Alcoholism. In Barker LR, Burton JR, Zieve PD (eds): Principles of Ambulatory Medicine, 3rd Edition, Williams & Wilkins, Baltimore, 1991

61a. Barkley RA et al. (2004). Critique or misrepresentation? A reply to Timimi et al. Clinical Child & Family Psychology review 7(1), March

62. Barnes GM, Reifman AS, Farrell MP, Dintcheff BA (2000). The effects of parenting on the development of adolescent alcohol misuse: A six-wave latent growth model. Journal of Marriage and the Family 62:175–86

63. Barnett A (2003). Revealed: how drug firms "hoodwink" medical journals: Pharmaceutical giants hire ghostwriters to produce articles—then put doctors' names on them. The Observer, Sunday December 7 ADD

64. Barondes S et al (1999) An agenda for psychiatric genetics. Arch. Gen. Psych. 56: 549–552

65. Barsky AJ, Wool C, Barnett MC, Cleary PD (1994). Histories of childhood trauma in adult hypochondriacal patients. Am J Psychiatry. 1994 Mar;151(3):397–401

66. Beck JC, van der Kolk B (1987). Reports of childhood incest and current behavior of chronically hospitalized women. American Journal of Psychiatry 144 (11): 1474–76

67. Becker JV (1988). Chapter 11 The effects of child sexual abuse on adolescent offenders. In G Wyatt & G Powell (eds) The Lasting Effects of Child Sexual Abuse (pp193–207). Sage, 1000 Oaks, CA

68. Becker-Blease KA, Freyd JJ (2004). (in prep) Attention deficit hyperactivity disorder and child abuse: a comparison of abused and non-abused children who have difficulty with inattention and hyperactivity

69. Becker-Lausen E, Sanders B, Chinsky JM (1995). Mediation of abusive childhood experiences: depression, dissociation, and negative life outcomes. Am J Orthopsychiatry. 65(4):560–73

70. Beckman KA, Burns GL (1990). Relation of sexual abuse and bulimia in college women. Int'l J Eating Disorders 9:487–92

71. Beers SR, De Bellis MD (2002). Neuropsychological function in children with maltreatment-related posttraumatic stress disorder. Am J Psychiatry 159(3):483–6

71a. Beilke R (1986). Behavioral problems in sexually abused young children. J Pediatr Psychol 11:47–57

72. Beitchman JH, Zucker KJ, Hood JE, daCosta GA, Akman D, Cassivia E (1992). A review of the long-term effects of child sexual abuse. Child Abuse & Neglect 16:101–118

73. Bekelman JE, Li Y, Gross CP (2003). Scope and impact of financial conflicts of interest in biomedical research: a systematic review. JAMA 22–29;289(4):454–65

74. Belkin DS, Greene AE, Rodrigue JR, Boggs SR (1994). Psychopathology and history of sexual abuse. Journal of Interpersonal Violence 9:535–47

75. Bell D, Belicki K (1998). A community-based study of well-being in adults reporting childhood abuse. Child Abuse Negl. 22(7):681–5

76. Bemporad JR, Smith HF, Hanson G, Cicchetti D (1982). Borderline syndromes in childhood: criteria for diagnosis. Am J Psychiatry 139(5):596–602

77. Bemporand JR, Romano S (1993). Childhood experience and adult depression: a review of 17 European] studies. American Journal of Psychoanalysis 53(4):301–315

78. Bemporand JR, Smith HF, Hanson G et al (1982). Borderline syndromes in childhood; criteria for diagnosis. American Journal of Psychiatry 139:596–602

79. Bender L, Blau A (1937). The reaction of children to sexual relations with adults. American Journal of Orthopsychiatry 7:500–18

80. Bensley LB, Speiker SJ, van Eenwyck J, Schoder J. (1999). Self-reported abuse history and adolescent problem behaviors. I. Antisocial and suicidal behaviors. Journal of Adolescent Health, 24, 163–172

81. Bensley LS, Eenwyk JV, Simmons KW (2000). Self-reported childhood sexual and physical abuse and adult HIV-risk behaviors and heavy drinking. American Journal of Preventive Medicine. Vol 18(2):151–158

82. Berger AM, Knutson JF, Mehm JG, Perkins KA (1988). The self-report of punitive childhood experiences of young adults and adolescents. Child Abuse Negl 12(2):251–62

83. Bennett EM, Kemper KJ (1994). Is abuse during childhood a risk factor for developing substance abuse problems as an adult? J Dev Behav Pediatr. 15(6):426–9

84. Benward J, Densen-Gerber J (1975). Incest as a causative factor in anti-social behavior: an explorative study. Contemporary Drug Problems 4: 322–340

85. Berenbaum H (1996). Childhood abuse, alexithymia and personality disorder. J Psychosom Res. 41(6):585–95

86. Berkowitz CD (1998). Medical consequences of child sexual abuse. Child Abuse & Neglect 22:541–50

87. Bernstein DP, Cohen P, Velez CN, Schwab-Stone M, Siever LJ, Shinsato L (1993). Prevalence and stability of the *DSM-III-R* personality disorders in a community-based survey of adolescents. Am J Psychiatry 150(8):1237–43

88. Bernstein DP, Fink L, Handelsman L, Foote J, Lovejoy M, Wenzel K, Sapareto E, Ruggiero J (1994). Initial reliability and validity of a new retrospective measure of child abuse and neglect. Am J Psychiatry 151(8):1132–6

89. Bernstein DP, Stein JA, Handelsman L (1998). Predicting personality pathology among adult patients with substance use disorders: effects of childhood maltreatment. Addictive behaviors 23:855–68

90. Biederman J, Faraone SV, Hirshfield-Becker DR, Friedman D, Robin JA, Rosenbaum JF (2001), Patterns of psychopathology and dysfunction in high-risk children of parents with panic disorder and major depression. Am J Psychiatry 158(1): 49–57.

91. Bifulco A, Brown GW, Lillie A, Jarvis J (1997). Memories of childhood neglect and abuse: corroboration in a series of sisters. J Child Psychol Psychiatry 38(3):365–74

92. Bleuler, M. (1968). A 23 Year Follow-up Study of 208 Schizophrenics. In Rosenthal and Kety (eds) The Transmission of Schizophrenia. Oxford: Pergamen Press.

93. Blount HR, Chandler TZ (1979). Relationship between childhood abuse and assaultive behavior in adolescent male psychiatric patients. Psychological Reports 44:1126

94. Bliss EL (1984). A symptom profile of patients with multiple personalities, including MMPI results. J Nerv Ment Dis.172(4):197–202

95. Blumenthal DR, Neeman J, Murphy CM (1998). Lifetime exposure to interparental physical and verbal aggression and symptom expression in college students. Violence Vict 13:175–181

96. Bombard J, Trosclair A, Schooley M, Husten C (2004). State-specific prevalence of current cigarette smoking among adults—United States, 2002. CDC MMWR Weekly Vol 52, No. 53 January 9, Office of Smoking and Health, National Center for Chronic Disease Prevention and Health Promotion, CDC

97. Boyle M (1990). Schizophrenia: A Scientific Delusion. Routledge, NY [2nd Edition 2003]

98. Boney-McCoy S, Finkelhor D (1995). Prior victimization: a risk factor for child sexual abuse and for PTSD-related symptomatology among sexually abused youth. Child Abuse Negl. 19(12):1401–21

99. Boney-McCoy S, Finkelhor D (1996). Is youth victimization related to trauma symptoms and depression after controlling for prior symptoms and family relationships? A longitudinal, prospective study. J Consult Clin Psychol. 64(6):1406–16

100. Boseley SD (2002). Bitter pill. The Guardian, London, 21 May

101. Bower P, Richards D, Lovell K (2001).The clinical and cost-effectiveness of self-help treatments for anxiety and depressive disorders in primary care: a systematic review. Br J Gen Pract 51(471):838–45 [Bibliotherapy]

102. Boyer AM (2001) Treating substance abuse in women with untreated childhood sexual abuse: are we treating the symptom but not the cause? Presented at the 32nd Annual Medical-Scientific Conference of ASAM, Los Angeles, 20 April

103. Boudewyn AC, Liem JH (1995). Childhood sexual abuse as a precursor to depression and self-destructive behavior in adulthood. Journal of Traumatic Stress 8:445–59

104. Bousha DM, Twentyman CT (1984). Mother-child interactional style in abuse, neglect, and control groups: naturalistic observation in the home. Journal of Abnormal Psychology 93:106–14

105. Bradley RH, Caldwell BM, Fitzgerald JA, Morgan AG, Rock SL (1986). Experiences in day care and social competence among maltreated children. Child Abuse & Neglect 10:181–9

106. Bradley RG, Follingstad DR (2001). Utilizing disclosure in the treatment of the sequelae of childhood sexual abuse: A theoretical and empirical review. Clin Psychol Rev 21(1):1–32

107. Brady KL, Caraway SJ (2002). Home away from home: factors associated with current functioning in children living in a residential treatment setting. Child Abuse & Neglect 26:1149–63

108. Braun PB, Kochansky G, Shapiro R., Greenberg. S, Gudeman JE, Johnson S, Shore MF (1981) Overview: Deinstitutionalization of psychiatric patients: A critical review of outcome studies. American Journal of Psychiatry, 138, 736–749.

109. Breggin PR, Cohen D (1999). Your Drug May Be Your Problem: How and why to stop taking psychiatric drugs. Perseus Publishing, Cambridge MA

110. Breggin PR (1998). Electroshock: scientific, ethical, and political issues The International Journal of Risk and Safety in Medicine 11(1): 5–40

111. Breggin PR (2000). The NIMH multimodal study of treatment for attention-deficit/hyperactivity disorder: a critical analysis. Int'l J Risk & Safety in Medicine 13:15–22

112. Bremner JD, Southwick SM, Darnell A, Charney DS (1996). Chronic PTSD in Vietnam combat veterans: Course of illness and substance abuse. Am. J. Psychiatry 153:369–375

113. Bremner JD, Randall P, Vermetten E, Staib L, Bronen RA, Capelli S, Mazure CM, McCarthy G, Innis RB, Charney DS (1997): MRI-based measurement of hippocampal volume in post-traumatic stress disorder related to childhood physical and sexual abuse: A preliminary report. Biol. Psychiatry 41:23–32.

114. Bremner JD (1999). Does stress damage the brain? (review article). Biological Psychiatry 45:797–805

115. Bremner JD (2002). Does stress damage the brain? Understanding trauma based disorders from a neurological perspective. Norton, NY

116. Breslau N, Davis GC, Schultz LR (2003).Post-traumatic stress disorder and the incidence of nicotine, alcohol, and other drug disorders in persons who have experienced trauma. Arch Gen Psychiatry 60(3):289–94

117. Breslau N (2002). Epidemiologic studies of trauma, post-traumatic stress disorder, and other psychiatric disorders. Can J Psychiatry 47(10):923–9

118. Brewerton TD, Dansky BS (1995). Bulimia nervosa, victimization, and PTSD. Eating Disorders Review 6:1–4

119. Brewin, C.R., Andrews, B., & Gotlib, I.H. (1993). Psychopathology and early experience: A reappraisal of retrospective reports. Psychological Bulletin, 113, 82–89

120. Bridges KW, Goldberg DP (1985). Somatic presentation of DSM III psychiatric disorders in primary care. Journal of Psychosomatic Research 29:563–9

121. Briere J (1984, April). The effects of childhood sexual abuse on later psychological functioning. Paper presented at the 3rd Nat. Conf. on Sexual Victimization of Children, Washington, DC [cited in Browne & Finkelhor 1986]

122. Briere J, Runtz M (1987). Post sexual abuse trauma: Data and implications for clinical practice. Journal of Interpersonal Violence 2(4): 367–379

123. Briere J (1988). The long-term clinical correlates of childhood sexual victimization. Journal of the New York Academy of Sciences 528:327–334

124. Briere J, Runtz M (1988). Symptomatology associated with childhood sexual victirnization in a non clinical adult sample. Child Abuse and Neglect, 12, 51–59

125. Briere J, Evans D, Runtz M, Wall T (1988). Symptomatology in men who were molested as children: a comparison study. American Journal of Orthopsychiatry 58:457–61

126. Briere J, Runtz M (1990). Differential adult symptomatology associated with three types of child abuse histories. Child Abuse & Neglect 14:357–64

127. Briere J, Runtz M (1991). The long-term effects of sexual abuse: A review and synthesis. New Directions for Mental Health Services 51:3–13

128. Briere J, Woo R, McRae B, Foltz J, and Sitzman, (1997). Lifetime victimization history, demographics, and clinical status in female psychiatric emergency room patients. Journal of Nervous and Mental Disease 185:95–101

129. Briere J (1992). Methodological issues in the study of sexual abuse effects. J Consult Clin Psychol. 60(2):196–203

130. Briere JN (1996). Treatment of adults sexually molested as children: Beyond survival (Rev. 2nd ed.). New York: Springer

131. Briere J, Runtz M (1987). Post sexual abuse trauma. Journal of Interpersonal Violence, 2(4): 367–379

132. Briere J, Zaidi L. (1989). Sexual abuse histories and sequelae in female psychiatric emergency room patients. American Journal of Psychiatry, 146, 1602–1606

133. Brodsky BS, Cloitre M, Dulit RA (1995). Relationship of dissociation to self-mutilation and childhood abuse in borderline personality disorder. American Journal of Psychiatry 152:1788–1792

134. Brook DW, Brook JS, Rosen MS, Dela Rosa M, Montoya ID, Whiteman M (2003). Early risk factors for violence in Columbian adolescents. Amer J Psychiatry 160:1470–8

135. Brown B (1999). Soul Without Shame: A guide to liberating yourself from the judge within. Shambhala Boston, MA

136. Brown BE, Garrison CJ (1990). Patterns of symptomatology of adult women incest survivors. Western Journal of Nursing Research 12(5):587–600

137. Brown D, Scheflin A, Whitfield CL (1999): Recovered memories: the current weight of the evidence in science and in the courts. The Journal of Psychiatry and Law 26:5–156, Spring 1999

138. Brown D, Scheflin AW, Hammond C: Trauma, Memory, Treatment & Law. WW Norton, NY, 1997

139. Brown D (2001). (Mis) reprensations of the long-term effects of childhood sexual abuse in the courts. Journal of Child Sexual Abuse 9:79–107

140. Brown GR, Anderson (1991). Psychiatric morbidity in adult inpatients with childhood histories of sexual and physical abuse. American Journal of Psychiatry 148 (1) 55–61

141. Brown L, Russell J, Thornton C, Dunn S (1997). Experiences of physical and sexual abuse in Australian general practice attenders and an eating disordered population. Aust N Z J Psychiatry 31(3):398–404

142. Brown J, Cohen P, Johnson JG & Salzinger S (1998). A longitudinal analysis of risk factors for child maltreatment: Findings of a 17-year prospective study of officially recorded and self-reported child abuse and neglect. Child Abuse and Neglect 22(11):1065–1078

143. Brown GW, Moran P (1994). Clinical and psychosocial origins of chronic depressive episodes. I: a community survey. British Journal of Psychiatry 165:447–56

144. Browne A, Finkelhor D (1986). Impact of child sexual abuse: a review of the research. Psychological Bulletin 99(1):66–77

145. Browne KD, Hamilton CE (1999). Police recognition of the links between spouse abuse and child abuse. Child Maltreatment 4(2): 136–147

146. Browning DH, Boatman B (1977). Incest: children at risk. American Journal of Psychiatry 134:69–72

147. Brunngraber LS (1986). Father-daughter incest: immediate and long-term effects of sexual abuse. ANS Adv Nurs Sci 8(4):15–35

148. Bryer JB, Nelson BA, Miller JB, Kroll PA (1987). Childhood sexual and physical abuse as factors in adult psychiatric illness. American Journal of Psychiatry 144: 1426–1430

149. Bulik CM, Sullivan PF, Rorty M (1989).Childhood sexual abuse in women with bulimia. J Clin Psychiatry 1989 Dec;50(12):460–4

150. Burgess AW, Hartman CR, McCausland MP, Powers P (1984). Response patterns in children and adolescents exploited through sex rings and pornography. American Journal of Psychiatry 141: 656–662

151. Burgess AW, Hartman CR, McCormack A (1987) Abused to abuser: Antecedents of social deviant behaviors. American Journal of Psychiatry 144:1431–6

152. Burgess A, Hartman CR, Baker T (1995). Memory presentations of childhood sexual abuse. Journal of Psychosocial Nursing 33(9), 9–16

153. Burgess RL, Conger RD (1977). Family interaction patterns related to child abuse and neglect: some preliminary findings. Child Abuse & Neglect 1:267–77

154. Burgess RL, Conger RD (1978). Family interaction in abusive, neglectful, and normal families. Child Development 49:1163–73

155. Burnam MA, Stein JA, Golding JM, Siegel JM, Sorenson SB, Forsythe AB, Telles CA (1988). Sexual assault and medical disorders in a community population. J Consult Clin Psychol. 56:843–850

156. Burton B, Rowell A (2003). Unhealthy [drug company] spin. BMJ 326:1205–7

157. Bushnell JA, Wells JE, Oakley-Brown MA (1992): Long-term effects of intrafamilial sexual abuse in childhood. Acta Psychiatria Scandavia 85:136–142

158. Byram V, Wagner HL, Waller G (1995). Sexual abuse and body image distortion. Child Abuse Negl. 19(4):507–10

159. Byrne CP, Velamoor VR, Sernovsky ZZ, Cortese L, Losztyn S (1990). A comparison of borderline and schizophrenic for childhood life events and parent-child relationships Canadian Journal of Psychiatry 35:590–5

C

160. Caffaro-Rouget A, Lang RA, van Santen V (1989): The impact of child sexual abuse on victims' adjustment. Annals of Sex Research 2: 29–47

161. Cairns S (1997). MMPI-2 and Rorschach assessments of adults physically abused as children. Unpublished doctoral dissertation. University of Manitoba. [Cited in Read & Ross 2003]

162. Calam RM, Slade PD (1989). Sexual experience and eating problems in female undergraduates. International Journal of Eating Disorders, 8, 391–397

163. Calam RM, Horne L, Glasgow D, Cox A (1998). Psychological disturbance in child sexual abuse: a follow-up study. Child Abuse & Neglect 22:901–13

164. Callahan KL, Price JL, Hilsenroth MJ (2003). Psychological assessment of adult survivors of childhood sexual abuse within a naturalistic clinical sample. J Pers Assess. 80(2):173–84

165. Cameron C (1994). Women survivors confronting their abusers: issues, decisions and outcomes. Journal of Child Sexual Abuse 3(1), 7–35

166. Cameron C (2000). Resolving Childhood Trauma: a long-term study of abuse survivors. Sage Publications, Thousand Oaks, Ca

167. Campbell EG, Weissman JS, Clarridge B, Yucel R, Causino N, Blumenthal D (2003). Characteristics of medical school faculty members serving on institutional review boards: results of a national survey. Acad Med. 78(8):831–6

168. Caplan PJ (1995). They Say You're Crazy: How the world's most powerful psychiatrists decide who's normal. Addison-Wesley, NY

169. Carlin AS, Ward NG (1992). Subtypes of psychiatric in-patient women who have been sexually abused Journal of Nervous and Mental Disease 180:392–7

170. Carlin AS, Kemper K, Ward WG, Sowell H, Gustafson B, Stevens N (1994). The effect of differences in objective and subjective definitions of childhood physical abuse on estimates of its incidence and relationship to psychopathology. Child Abuse Negl;18:393–399 ADD

171. Carlson B (1984). Children's observations of interparental violence. In AR Roberts (ed.), Battered women and their families (pp. 147–167). NY: Springer

172. Carlson M, Earls F (1997). Psychological and neuroendocrinological sequelae of early social deprivation in institutionalized children in Romania. Ann N Y Acad Sci 807:419–28

173. Carlson EB. Armstrong J, Lowenstein R, Roth D (1998). Chapter 7. Relationships between traumatic experiences and symptoms of PTSD, dissociation, and amnesia. In JD Bremner & CR Marmar (eds) Trauma, Memory, and Dissociation. APA Press, Washington, DC

174. Carlson EB, Dalenberg C (2000). A conceptual framework for the impact of traumatic experiences. Trauma, Violence & Abuse 1:4–28

175. Carlsson A (1995). Neurocircuitries and neurotransmitter interactions in schizophrenia. Int Clin Psychopharmacol. 10 Suppl 3:21–8

176. Carlsson A, Hansson LO, Waters N, Carlsson ML (1997). Neurotransmitter aberrations in schizophrenia: new perspectives and therapeutic implications. Life Sci. 1997; 61(2):75–94

177. Carlsson A (2001). A half-century of neurotransmitter research: impact on neurology and psychiatry. Nobel lecture. Biosci Rep. 21(6):691–710

178. Carmen E, Rieker PP, Mills T (1984). Victims of violence and psychiatric illness. American Journal of Psychiatry 141:378–383

179. Carrion VG, Steiner H (2000). Trauma and dissociation in delinquent adolescents. J Am Acad Child Adolesc Psychiatry 39(3):353–9

180. Cashden S (1988). Object Relations Therapy: Using the relationship. WW Norton, NY

181. Cavaiola AA, Schiff M (1988). Behavioral sequelae of physical and/or sexual abuse in adolescence. Child Abuse & Neglect 12:181–8

182. Cecil H, Matson SC (2001). Psychological functioning and family discord among African-American adolescent females with and without a history of childhood sexual abuse. Child Abuse Negl 2001 Jul; 25(7):973–88

183. Centers for Disease Control and Prevention (2003). Cigarette smoking among adults—United States, 2001. MMWR 52:953–56

184. Chaffin M, Kelleher K, Hollenberg J (1996). Onset of physical abuse and neglect: psychiatric, substance abuse, and social risk factors from prospective community data. Child Abuse & Negl 20(3):191–203

185. Chalmers I (1990). Underreporting research is scientific misconduct. Journal of the American Medical Association 263:1405–8

186. Chandy JM, Blum RW, Resnick MD (1996). Gender-specific outcomes for sexually abused adolescents. Child Abuse & Negl. 1996 Dec; 20(12):1219–31

186a. Chapman DP, Whitfield CL, Felitti VJ, Dube SR, Edwards VJ, Anda RF (2004). Adverse childhood experiences and the risk of depressive disorders in adulthood. J Affective Disorders (in press)

187. Cheasty M, Clare AW, Collins C (1998). Relation between sexual abuse in childhood and adult depression: case control study. British Medical Journal 316: 198–201

188. Chefetz RA (2004). Personal communication, Washington, DC, March

189. Choudhry NK, Stelfox HT, Detsky AS (2002). Relationships between authors of clinical practice guidelines and the pharmaceutical industry. JAMA 287: 612

190. Chua SE, McKenna PJ (1995). Schizophrenia—a brain disease? A critical review of structural and functional cerebral abnormality in the disorder. Br J Psychiatry 166(5):563–82

191. Chu, JA, Dill DL (1990). Dissociative symptoms in relation to childhood physical and sexual abuse. American Journal of Psychiatry, 147:887–892

192. Chu JA, Dill DL (1991). Dissociation, borderline personality disorder, and childhood trauma. Am J Psychiatry. Jun; 148(6):812–3

193. Chu JA (1998). Rebuilding Shattered Lives: The responsible treatment of complex post-traumatic and dissociative disorders. John Wiley, NY

194. Ciompi L, Duwalder HP, Maier C, Aebi E, Trutsch K, Kupper Z, Rutishauser C (1992). The pilot project "Soteria Berne": Clinical experiences and results. British Journal of Psychiatry 161 (suppl.18):145–153

195. Ciompi L. (1980) Catamnestic long-term study of the life course and aging of schizophrenics. Schiz. Bull. 6, 606–618

196. Ciompi L (1997). The concept of affect logic: an integrative psycho-socio-biological approach to understanding and treatment of schizophrenia. Psychiatry 60(2):158–70

Clark DB, Lesnick L, Hegedus A (1997). Traumas and other adverse life events in adolescents with alcohol abuse and dependence. Journal of the American Academy of Child and Adolescent Psychiatry 36:1744–51

197. Clark AH, Foy DW (2000). Trauma exposure and alcohol use in battered women. Violence Against Women, January vol. 6(1):37–48(12)

198. Classen C, Field NP, Atkinson A, Spiegel D (1998). Representations of self in women sexually abused in childhood. Child Abuse & Neglect 22:997–1004

199. Clayton P, Ernst C, Angst J (1994). Pre-morbid personality traits of men who develop unipolar or bipolar disorders. Eur. Arch. Clin. Neurosci. 243, pp. 340–346

200. Clennell A (2003). Threat of suicide leads to ban of major antidepressants for children. The Independent, London, 10 Dec.

201. Cloitre M, Cohen LR, Edelman RE, Han H (2001). Post-traumatic stress disorder and extent of trauma exposure as correlates of medical problems and perceived health among women with childhood abuse. Women Health. 34(3):1–17.

202. Cloitre M, Koenen KC, Cohen LR, Han H (2002). Skills training in affective and interpersonal regulation followed by exposure: a phase-based treatment for PTSD related to childhood abuse. J Consult Clin Psychol. 70(5):1067–74.

203. Cohen FS, Densen-Gerber J (1982). A study of the relationship between child abuse and drug addiction in 178 patients: preliminary studies. Child Abuse & Neglect 6:383–7

204. Cohen Y, Spirito A, Sterling C, Donaldson D, Seifer R, Plummer B, Avila R, Ferrer K (1996). Physical and sexual abuse and their relation to psychiatric disorder and suicidal behavior among adolescents who are psychiatrically hospitalized. J Child Psychol Psychiatry 37(8):989–93

205. Cohen AJ, Adler N, Kaplan SJ, Pelcovitz D, Mandel FS (2002). Interactional effects of marital status and physical abuse on adolescent psychopathology. Child Abuse & Negl 26(3):277–88

206. Cold J, Petruckevitch A, Feder G, Chung W, Richardson J, Moorey S (2001). Relation between childhood sexual and physical abuse and risk of revictimization in women: a cross-sectional survey. Lancet, 258:450–454

207. Cole C (1988). Routine comprehensive inquiry for abuse: A justifiable clinical asessment procedure. Clinical Social Work Journal 16:33–42

208. Cole CE, Paterson RM, Craig JB, Thomas WE, Ristine LP, Stahly M, Pasamanick B (1959). A controlled study of efficacy of ipronazid in treatment of depression. Archives of General Psychiatry 1:513–8

209. Cole P, Putnam FW (1992). Effect of incest on self and social functioning: a developmental psychopathology perspective. Journal of Consulting and Clinical Psychology, 60, 174–184

210. Collings S, King M (1994). Ten-year follow-up of 50 patients with bulimia nervosa. Br J Psychiatry 164(1):80–7

211. Collings SJ (1994). The long-term effects of contact and noncontact forms of child sexual abuse in a sample of university men. Child Abuse & Neglect 19:1–6

212. Conaway LP, Hansen DJ (1989). Social behavior of physically abused and neglected children: a critical review. Clinical Psychology Review 9:627–52

213. Connor S (2003). Glaxo chief: our drugs do not work on most patients. The Independent, London, 8 Dec

214. Connors ME, Morse W (1993). Sexual abuse and the eating disorders: A review. International Journal of Eating Disorders, 13:141

215. Consumer Reports (2003). Free regin for drug ads? February, pages 33–37

216. Conte JR, Schuerman JR (1987). Factors associated with an increased impact of child sexual abuse. Child Abuse & Negl. 11(2):201–11

217. Conte JR (1996) [Reliability of self reports of abuse] Presented at the National Conference on Trauma & Memory, Univ. of New Hampshire.

218. Coons PM, Millstein V (1986). Psychosexual disturbances in multiple personality: characteristics, etiology, and treatment. J Clin Psychiatry. 47(3):106–10.

219. Coons PM, Bowman ES, Milstein V (1988). Multiple personality disorder. Journal of Nervous and Mental Diseases, 176, 519–527

220. Coons PM, Bowman ES, Pellow TA, Schneider P (1989). Post-traumatic aspects of the treatment of victims of sexual abuse and incest. Psychiatric Clinics of North America, 12, 335–338

221. Copeland ME (1994). Living without Depression and Manic Depression. New Harbinger, Oakland CA

222. Cornelius JR, Pringle J, Jernigan J, Kirisci L, Clark DB (2001). Correlates of mental health service utilization and unmet need among a sample of male adolescents. Addict Behav. 26(1):11–9

223. Courtois C (1991). Theory, sequencing, and strategy in treating adult survivors. In. J. Briere, ed., Treating Victims of Child Sexual Abuse. Jossey-Bass,

224. Courtois C (1979). The incest experience and its aftermath. Victimology: An International Journal 4:337–47

225. Courtois CA (1998). Recollections of sexual abuse. Norton, New York

226. Covington SS (1986). Facing the clinical challenge of women alcoholics: physical, emotional and sexual abuse. Focus on the Family and Chemical Dependence 9:10–11,37, 42–4

227. Cox T (1979). Stress. University Park Press, Baltimore, MD

228. Coxell A, King M, Mezey G, Gordon D (1999). Lifetime prevalence, characteristics, and associated problems of non-consensual sex in men: cross-sectional survey. British Medical Journal 318:846–50

229. Craine LS, Henson CE, Colliver JA, MacLean DG (1988). Prevalence of a history of sexual abuse among female psychiatric patients in a state hospital system. Hospital and Community Psychiatry 39 (3) 300–304

230. Crowley TJ, Mikulich SK, Ehlers KM, Hall SK, Whitmore EA (2003). Discriminative validity and clinical utility of an abuse-neglect interview for adolescents with conduct and substance use problems. Am J Psychiatry 160(8):1461–9

231. Culhane C (2002). Favor of the month—Did the White House give the drug industry veto power over FDA appointments? The New Republic, March

232. Cunningham J et al. (1988). Childhood sexual abuse and medical complaints in adult women. Journal of Interpersonal Violence 3:131–44

233. Curtis D. Genetics of functional psychiatric disorders. Lecture notes, Royal London School of Medicine, July 2002, posted at Web site: *http://www.mds.qmw.ac.uk/statgen/dcurtis/lectures/pgen func.html* (Although he was strong and clear in 2002, as of January 2004 he had changed his clear statement to confusing genetic language.)

D

234. Dallam SJ (2001). The long-term medical consequences of childhood trauma. In K Franey, R Geffner, R Falconer (eds.), The cost of child maltreatment: Who pays? We all do. (pp. 1–14). Family Violence & Sexual Assault Institute, San Diego, CA

235. Dansky BS, Saladin ME, Coffey SF, Brady KT (1997). Use of self-report measures of crime-related posttraumatic stress disorder with substance use disordered patients. J Subst Abuse Treat. 14(5): 431–7

236. Dansky BS, Brewerton TD, Kilpatrick DG, O'Neil PM (1997). The National Women's Study: relationship of victimization and post-traumatic stress disorder to bulimia nervosa. Int J Eat Disord. 21(3):213–28

237. Darves-Bornoz JM, Lemperiere T, Degiovanni A, Gaillard P (1995). Sexual victimization in women with schizophrenia and bipolar disorder. Social Psychiatry and Psychiatric Epidemiology 30:78–84

238. Davidoff F et al. (2001). Sponsorship, authorship, and accountability. Lancet 325:854–856 (published simultaneously in 12 other medical journals)

239. Davidson S, Smith R (1990). Traumatic experiences in psychiatric outpatients. Journal of Traumatic Stress Studies 3:459–75

240. Davidson J (1993). Issues in the diagnosis of PTSD. In Pynoos RS (ed): PTSD: A Clinical Review. Sidran Press, Lutherville, MD

241. Davidson J, Foa EB, Blank AS, Brett EA, Fairbank J, Green BL, Herman JL, Keane TM, Kilpatrick D, March JS, McNally RJ, Pitman RK, Resnick HS, Rothbaum BO (1994). Post-traumatic stress disorder. In *DSM-IV* Sourcebook, vol. 2. Washington, D.C., American Psychiatric Press 577–605

242. Davidson JR, Hughes DC, George LK, Blazer DG (1996). The association of sexual assault and attempted suicide within the community. Arch Gen Psychiatry 53(6):550–5

243. Davies JM, Frawley MG (1994). Treating the Adult Survivor of Childhood Sexual Abuse: A psychoanalytic perspective. Basic Books, San Francisco

244. Davies-Netzley S, Hurlburt MS, Hough RL (1996). Childhood abuse as a precursor to homelessness for homeless women with severe mental illness. Violence Vict. 11(2):129–42

245. DeAngelis CD (2000). Conflict of interest and the public trust. Journal of the American Medical Association 284:2237–8

246. De Bellis M., Lefter L., Trickett P, and Putnam F (1994). Urinary catecholamine excretion in sexually abused girls. Journal of the American Academy of Child and Adolescent Psychiatry 33:320–27.

247. De Bellis MD (1997). PTSD and acute stress disorder. In RT Ammerman & M Hersen (eds). Handbook of prevention and treatment with children and adolescents. (p 455–94) Wiley, NY

248. De Bellis MD, Keshavan MS, Frustaci K, Shifflett H, Iyengar S, Beers SR, Hall J (2002). Superior temporal gyrus volumes in maltreated children and adolescents with PTSD. Biol Psychiatry Apr 1;51(7):544–52

249. De Bellis MD (2002). Developmental traumatology: a contributory mechanism for alcohol and substance use disorders. Psychoneuroendocrinology 27(1–2):155–70

250. De Bellis MD, Keshavan MS, Harenski KA (2001). Anterior cingulate N-acetylaspartate/creatine ratios during clonidine treatment in a maltreated child with post-traumatic stress disorder. J Child Adolesc Psychopharmacol 11(3):311–6

251. De Bellis MD, Broussard ER, Herring DJ, Wexler S, Moritz G, Benitez JG (2001). Psychiatric comorbidity in caregivers and children involved in maltreatment: a pilot research study with policy implications. Child Abuse & Neglect 25(7):923–44

252. De Bellis MD (2001). Developmental traumatology: the psychobiological development of maltreated children and its implications for research, treatment, and policy. Dev Psychopathol 13(3): 539–64

253. De Bellis MD, Casey BJ, Dahl RE, Birmaher B, Williamson DE, Thomas KM, Axelson DA, Frustaci K, Boring AM, Hall J, Ryan ND (2001). A pilot study of amygdala volumes in pediatric generalized anxiety disorder. Biol Psychiatry 1; 48(1):51–7

254. De Bellis MD, Clark DB, Beers SR, Soloff PH, Boring AM, Hall J, Kersh A, Keshavan MS (2000). Hippocampal volume in adolescent-onset alcohol use disorders. Am J Psychiatry 157(5):737–44

255. De Bellis MD, Keshavan MS, Clark DB, Casey BJ, Giedd JN, Boring AM, Frustaci K, Ryan ND (1999). A.E. Bennett Research Award. Developmental traumatology. Part II: Brain development. Biol Psychiatry 15; 45(10):1271–84

256. De Bellis MD, Baum AS, Birmaher B, Keshavan MS, Eccard CH, Boring AM, Jenkins FJ, Ryan ND (1999). A.E. Bennett Research Award. Developmental traumatology. Part I: Biological stress systems. Biol Psychiatry 15; 45(10):1259–70

257. De Bernardo GL, Newcomb M, Toth A, Richey G, Mendoza R (2002). Comorbid psychiatric and alcohol abuse/dependence disorders: psychosocial stress, abuse, and personal history factors of those in treatment. J Addict Dis. 21(3):43–59. Hospitalizations.

258. Deep AL, Lilenfeld LR, Plotnicov KH, Pollice C, Kaye WH (1999). Sexual abuse in eating disorder subtypes and control women: the role of comorbid substance dependence in bulimia nervosa. Int J Eat Disord. 25(1):1–10

259. deGroot JM, Kennedy S, Rodin G, McVey G (1992). Correlates of sexual abuse in women with anorexia nervosa and bulimia nervosa. Can J Psychiatry 37(7):516–8

260. Deblinger E, McLeer SV, Atkins MS, Ralphe D, Foa E (1989). Post-traumatic stress in sexually abused, physically abused and non-abused children. Child Abuse & Neglect 13:1403–8

261. Dembo R, Dertke M, La Voie L, Borders S, Washburn M, Schmeidler J (1987). Physical abuse, sexual victimization and illicit drug use: a structural analysis among high risk adolescents. J Adolesc. 10(1):13–34

262. Dembo R, Dertke M, Borders S, Washburn M, Schmeidler J (1988). The relation between physical and sexual abuse to tobacco, alcohol, and illicit drug use among youths in a juvenile detention center. The International Journal of the Addictions 23:351–78

263. Dembo R, Schmeidler J, Pacheco K, Cooper S, Williams LW (1997). The relationships between youths' identified substance use, mental health or other problems at a juvenile assessment center and their referrals to needed services. Journal of Child and Adolescent Substance Abuse 6:23–54

264. Dembo R, Pacheco K, Schmeidler J, Ramirez-Garnica G, Guida J, Rahman A (1998). A further study of gender differences in service needs among youths entering a juvenile assessment center. Journal of Child and Adolescent Substance Abuse 7:49–77

265. Dembo R, Wothke W, Seeberger W, Shemwell M, Pacheco K, Rollie M, Schmeidler J, Klein L, Hartsfield A, Livingston S (2000). Testing a model of the influence of family problem factors on high-risk youths' troubled behavior: a three-wave longitudinal study. Journal of Psychoactive Drugs 32(1):55–65

266. Dembo R, Williams L, Wothke W, Schmeidler J (1994). The relationships among family problems, friends' troubled behavior, and high risk youths' alcohol/other drug use and delinquent behavior: a longitudinal study. International Journal of the Addictions 29(11):1419–42

267. Dembo R, Williams L, Wothke W, Schmeidler J, Brown CH (1992). The role of family factors, physical abuse, and sexual victimization experiences in high-risk youths' alcohol and other drug use and delinquency: a longitudinal model. Violence and Victims 7(3):245–66

268. Dennis ML, Stevens SJ (2003). Maltreatment issues and outcomes of adolescents enrolled in substance abuse treatment. Child Maltreatment 8(1):3–6

269. Deykin EY, Alpert JJ, McNamarra JJ (1985). A pilot study of the effect of exposure to child abuse or neglect on adolescent suicidal behavior. Am J Psychiatry 142(11):1299–303

270. Dhaliwal GK, Gauzas L, Atonowicz DH, Ross RR (1996). Adult male survivors of childhood sexual abuse: prevalence, sexual abuse characteristics, and long-term effects. Clinical Psychology Review 16(7):619–39

271. Diaz A, Simantov E, Rickert VI (2002). Effect of abuse on health: results of a national survey. Arch Pediatr Adolesc Med 156(8):811–7

272. Dietz TL (2000). Disciplining children: characteristics associated with the use of corporal punishment. Child Abuse & Neglect 24(12):1529–42

273. Dickinson LM, deGruy FV, Dickinson WP, Candib LM (1999). Health-related quality of life and symptom profiles of female survivors of sexual abuse. Archives of Family Medicine 8:35–43

274. Dierker LC, Avenevoli S, Stolar, Merikangas KR (2002). Smoking and depression: an examination of mechanisms of comorbidity. American Journal of Psychiatry 159:947–53

275. Dill DL, Chu JA, Grob MC, Eisen SV (1991). The reliability of abuse history reports: a comparison of two inquiry formats. Compr Psychiatry 32(2):166–9

275a. Diller LH (2002). Prescription stimulant use in American children: ethical issues (PCBE, 12 Dec)

276. Dimock PT (1988). Adult males sexually abused as children: characteristics and implications for treatment. Journal of Interpersonal Violence 3:203–21

277. Dodge KA, Bates JE, Pettit GS (1990). Mechanisms in the cycle of violence. Science 250(4988):1678–83

278. Dohm FA, Striegel-Moore RH, Wilfley DE, Pike KM, Hook J, Fairburn CG (2002). Self-harm and substance use in a community sample of black and white women with binge eating disorder or bulimia nervosa. Int J Eat Disord 32(4):389–400

279. Donaldson MA, Gardner R, Jr (1986). Diagnosis and treatment of traumatic stress among women after childhood incest. In CR Figley (ed), Trauma and Its Wake: the study and treatment of Posttraumatic stress disorder. Brunner/Mazel, NY

280. Double DB (2001. Integrating critical psychiatry into psychiatric training. (This and several other excellent papers at www.uea.ac.uk/~wp276/homepage.htm)

281. Downs WR, Miller BA, Gondoli DM (1987). Childhood experience of parental physical violence for alcoholic women as compared with a randomly selected household sample of women. Violence and Victims 2:225–40

282. Downs WR, Miller BA, Testa M, Panek D (1992). Long-term effects of parent-to-child violence for women. Journal of Interpersonal Violence 7:365–82

283. Driessen M, Hermann J, Stahl K, Zwaan M, Meier S, Hill A, Osterheider M, Petersen D (2000). Magnetic resonance imaging volumes of the hippocampus and the amygdala in women with borderline personality disorder and early traumatization. Archives of General Psychiatry 57:1115–22

284. Drossman DA, Leserman J, Nachman G, Li Z, Gluck H, Toomey TC, Mitchell M: Sexual and physical abuse in women with functional or organic gastrointestinal disorders. Annals of Internal Medicine 113: 828–833, 1990.

285. Dube SR, Anda RF, Felitti VJ, Chapman DP, Williamson DF, Giles WH (2001). Childhood abuse, household dysfunction, and the risk of attempted suicide throughout the life span: findings from the Adverse Childhood Experiences Study. JAMA 286(24):3089–96

286. Dube SR, Whitfield CL, Felitti VJ, Brown DW, Dong M, Anda RF (2004). Childhood sexual abuse and the risk of health behaviors and outcomes among men and women. (in process)

287. Dubowitz H, Black M, Harrington D, Verschoore A (1993). A follow-up study of behavior problems associated with child sexual abuse. Child Abuse & Neglect 17:743–54

288. Duff G (2003). [The un]safety of paroxetine [Paxil/Seroxat] in children & adolescents. 10 June *http://medicines.mhra.gov.uk/*

289. Duncan RD, Saunders BE, Kilpatrick DG, Hanson RF, Resnick HS (1996). Childhood physical assault as a risk factor for PTSD, depression, and substance abuse: findings from a national survey. American Journal of Orthopsychiatry 66:437–48

290. Duncan RD (1999). Maltreatment by parents and peers: the relationship between child abuse, bully victimization, and psychological distress. Child Maltreatment 4:45–55

E

291. Effect Size (2004). [Explanation of effect size as a measure of treatment effect.] From internet search *http://cem.dur.ac.uk/ebeuk/research/effectABE/*

292. Egeland B, Susman-Stillman A (1996). Dissociation as a mediator of child abuse across generations. Child Abuse & Neglect 20(11):1123–32

293. Egeland B, Yates T, Appleyard K, van Dulmen (2002). The long-term consequences of maltreatment in the early years: a developmental pathway model to antisocial behavior. Children's Services 5:249–60

294. Ehrensaft MK, Cohen P, Brown J, Smailes E, Chen H, Johnson JG (2003). Intergenerational transmission of partner violence: a 20-year prospective study. J Consult Clin Psychol. 71(4):741–53

295. Ehrle LH (2002). Partnerships between universities and industry. JAMA 287(11):1398–9; discussion 1399–400

296. Einbender AJ, Friedrich WN (1989). Psychological functioning and behavior of sexually abused girls. Journal of Consulting and Clinical Psychology 57(1):155–7

297. Elhai JD, Frueh BC, Gold PB, Gold SN, Hamner MB (2000). Clinical presentations of post-traumatic stress disorder across trauma populations: a comparison of MMPI-2 profiles of combat veterans and adult survivors of child sexual abuse. J Nerv Ment Dis. 188(10):708–13

298. Ellason JW, Ross CA (1997). Two-year follow-up of inpatients with dissociative identity disorder. Am J Psychiatry 154(6):832–9

299. Ellason J, Ross C (1997). Childhood trauma and psychiatric symptoms. Psychological Reports 80:447–50

300. Ellason J, Ross C, and Fuchs D (1996). Lifetime axis I and II comorbidity and childhood trauma history in dissociative identity disorder. Psychiatry 59:255–66.

301. Ellason J, Ross C (1995). Positive and negative symptoms in dissociative identity disorder and schizophrenia:A comparative analysis. Journal of Nervous and Mental Disease 183:236–41

302. Ellason JW, Ross CA, Sainton K, Mayran LW (1996). Axis I and II comorbidity and childhood trauma history in chemical dependency. Bulletin of the Menninger Clinic 60:39–51

303. Ellason JW, Ross CA (1997). Two year follow-up of inpatients with dissociative identity disorder. American Journal of Psychiatry 154, 832–839

304. Ellenson G (1985). Detecting a history of incest: A predictive syndrome. Social Casework Nov: 525–32

305. Elliott DJ, Tarnowski KJ (1990). Depressive characteristics of sexually abused children. Child Psychiatry Hum Dev 21(1):37–48

306. Elliott DM, Briere J (1995). Post-traumatic stress associated with delayed recall of sexual abuse: A general population study. Journal of Traumatic Stress 8: 629–647

307. Ensink B (1992). Confusing Realities: A study on child sexual abuse and psychiatric symptoms. Amsterdam: Vu University Press.

308. Epstein JN, Saunders BE, Kilpatrick DG, Resnick HS (1998). PTSD as a mediator between etiology, and treatment. Journal of Clinical Psychiatry 47:106–10

309. Everill JT, Waller G (1995). Reported sexual abuse and eating psychopathology: a review of the evidence for a causal link. Int J Eat Disord 18(1):1–11

F

310. Fals-Stewart W, Kelley ML, Cooke CG, Golden JC (2002). Predictors of psychosocial adjustment of children in households of parents in which fathers abuse drugs. Addictive Behaviors 27:1–19

311. Famularo R, Kinscherff R, Fenton T (1991).Post-traumatic stress disorder among children clinically diagnosed as borderline personality disorder. J Nerv Ment Dis 179(7):428–31

312. Famularo R, Kinscherff R, Fenton T (1992). Psychiatric diagnoses of maltreated children: preliminary findings. Journal of the American Academy of Child and Adolescent Psychiatry (1992) 31:863–67

313. Famularo R, Kinscherff R, Fenton T (1992). Parental substance abuse and the nature of child maltreatment. Child Abuse & Neglect 16: 475–83 [Increased association between alcohol abuse and physical maltreatment, and cocaine abuse and sexual maltreatment

314. Famularo R, Kinscherff R, Fenton T (1992). Psychiatric diagnoses of abusive mothers. A preliminary report. J Nerv Ment Dis 180(10):658–61

315. Famularo R, Kinscherff R, Fenton T (1992). Psychiatric diagnoses of maltreated children: preliminary findings. J Am Acad Child Adolesc Psychiatry 31(5):863–7

316. Famularo R, Fenton T, Kinscherff R, Ayoub C, Barnum R (1994). Maternal and child post-traumatic stress disorder in cases of child maltreatment. Child Abuse & Neglect 18(1):27–36

317. Famularo R, Fenton T, Augustyn M, Zuckerman B (1996). Persistence of pediatric post traumatic stress disorder after 2 years. Child Abuse & Neglect 1996 Dec: 20(12):1245–8.

318. Fava GA , Tomba E (1998). The use of antidepressant drugs: some reasons for concern. The International Journal of Risk and Safety in Medicine 11(4): 271–274

319. Fava GA (2002). Long-term treatment with antidepressant drugs: the spectacular achievements of propaganda. Psychotherapy and Psychosomatics 71:3:2002, 127–132

320. Favaro A, Santonastaso P (1997). Suicidality in eating disorders: clinical and psychological correlates. Acta Psychiatr Scand. 95(6):508–14.

321. Favaro A, Dalle Grave R, Santonastaso P (1998). Impact of a history of physical and sexual abuse in eating disordered and asymptomatic subjects. Acta Psychiatr Scand. 97(5):358–63

322. Fehon DC, Grilo CM, Lipschitz DS (2001). Correlates of community violence exposure in hospitalized adolescents. Compr Psychiatry. 42(4):283–90

323. Fehon DC, Grilo CM, Lipschitz DS (2001). Gender differences in violence exposure and violence risk among adolescent inpatients. J Nerv Ment Dis. 189(8):532–40.

324. Felitti VJ, Williams SA (1998). Long-term follow-up and analysis of more than 100 patients who each lost more than 100 pounds. The Permanente Journal 2 (3):17–21

325. Felitti V (1991). Long-term medical consequences of incest, rape, and molestation. Southern Medical Journal 84 (3): 328–331

326. Felitti VJ (1993). Childhood sexual abuse, depression, and family dysfunction in adult obese patients: a case control study. Southern Medical Journal 86 (7):732–736

327. Felitti VJ (2000). Adverse childhood experiences and the leading causes of death in America. Videotape presentation from Kaiser Permanente, San Diego

328. Felitti VJ, Anda RF, Nordenberg D, Williamson DF, Spitz AM, Edwards V, Koss MP, Marks JS (1998). Relationship of childhood abuse and household dysfunction to many of the leading causes of death in adults. American Journal of Preventive Medicine,14, 245–258

329. Feiring C, Taska L, Chen K (2002). Trying to understand why horrible things happen: attribution, shame, and symptom development following sexual abuse. Child Maltreatment 7(1):26–41

330. Feiring C, Taska L, Lewis M (2002). Adjustment following sexual abuse discovery: the role of shame and attributional style. Dev Psychol. 38(1):79–92

331. Femina DD, Yeager CA, Lewis DO (1990). Child abuse: adolescent records versus adult recall. Child Abuse & Neglect 14:227–231

332. Fenton WS, Mosher LR, Herrell JM, Blyler CR (1998). Randomized trial of general hospital and residential alternative care for patients with severe and persistent mental illness. Am J Psychiatry 155(4):516–22

333. Fergusson DM, Horwood LI (1998). Exposure to interparental violence in childhood and psychological adjustment in young adulthood. Child Abuse & Neglect 22:339–57

334. Fergusson DM, Horwood LI, Lynskey MT (1996). Childhood sexual abuse and psychiatric disorder in young adulthood: II. Psychiatric outcomes of childhood sexual abuse. Journal of the American Academy of Child and Adolescent Psychiatry 34(10):1365–74

335. Fergusson DM, Lynskey MT (1997). Physical punishment/maltreatment during childhood and adjustment in young adulthood. Child Abuse & Neglect 21:617–630

336. Fergusson DM, Horwood LI, Woodward LJ (2000). The stability of child abuse reports: a longitudinal study of the reporting behavior of young adults. Psychological Medicine 30:529–44

337. Fergusson DM, Swain-Campbell NR, Horwood LJ (2002). Does sexual violence contribute to elevated rates of anxiety and depression in females? Psychol Med. 32(6):991–6

338. Ferguson KS, Dacey CN (1997). Anxiety, depression and dissociation in women health care providers reporting a history of childhood psychological abuse. Child Abuse & Neglect 21(10): 941–52

339. Figueroa C, "Malarcher A, Sharp D 2002" Anda R, Whitfield CL, Felitti V, Nordenberg D, Edwards V, Malarcher A, Sharp D: Sexual abuse as a risk factor for smoking, substance abuse, and attempted suicides for boys and girls. (in process) 2004 check with Rob

340. Figley CR (1986). Trauma and Its Wake: the study and treatment of post-traumatic stress disorder. Brunner/Mazel, NY

341. Figley CR (1999). Traumatology of Grieving: Conceptual, theoretical, and treatment foundations. Brunner-Routlege, London

342. Finlay-Jones R, Brown GW (1981). Types of stressful life events and the onset of anxiety and depressive disorders. Psychological Medicine 11:803–15

343. Finkelhor D (1984). Child Sexual Abuse: New theory & research. Free Press, NY

344. Finkelhor D, Hotaling G, Lewis IA, Smith C (1990). Sexual abuse in a national survey of adult men and women: prevalence, characteristics, and risk factors. Child Abuse & Neglect 14:19–28

345. Finn S, Hartinan M, Leon G, Lawson L (1986). Eating disorders and sexual abuse: Lack of confirmation for a clinical hypothesis. International Journal of Eating Disorders, 5, 10:1060.

346. Flisher AJ, Kramer RA, Hoven CW, Greenwald S, Alegria M, Bird HR, Canino G, Connell R, Moore RE (1997). Psychosocial characteristics of physically abused children in adolescence. Journal of the American Academy of Child and Adolescent Psychiatry 36:123–31

347. Fleming J, Mullen P, Bammer G (1997). A study of potential risk factors for sexual abuse in childhood. Child Abuse & Neglect 21(1):49–58

348. Fleming J, Mullen P, Sibthorpe B, Bammer G (1999). The long-term impact of childhood sexual abuse in Australian women. Child Abuse & Neglect 23:145–59

349. Flitter JMK, Elhai JD, Gold SN (2003). MMPI-2F scale elevations in adult victims of child sexual abuse. J Traumatic Stress 16:269–74

350. Folsom V, Krahn D, Nairn K, Gold L, Demitrack M, Silk K (1993). The impact of sexual and physical abuse on eating disordered and psychiatric symptoms: A comparison of eating disordered and psychiatric inpatients. International Journal of Eating Disorders, 13, 249–257.

351. Fondacaro KM, Holt JC, Powell TA (1999a). Psychological impact of childhood sexual abuse on male inmates: the importance of perception. Child Abuse & Neglect 23:361–9

352. Fonseca H, Ireland M, Resnick MD (2002). Familial correlates of extreme weight control behaviors among adolescents. Int J Eat Disord 32(4):441–8

353. Ford JD, Racusin R, Daviss WB, Ellis CG, Thomas J, Rogers K, Reiser J, Schiffman J, Sengupta A (1999a). Trauma exposure among children with oppositional defiant disorder and attention deficit-hyperactivity disorder. J Consult Clin Psychol 67(5):786–9

354. Ford JD, Racusin R, Ellis CG, Daviss WB, Reiser J, Fleischer A, Thomas J (2000). Child maltreatment, other trauma exposure, and post-traumatic symptomatology among children with oppositional defiant and attention deficit hyperactivity disorders. Child Maltreatment 5:205–217

355. Ford JD (2002). Traumatic victimization in childhood and persistent problems with oppositional-defiance. Journal of Trauma, Maltreatment, and Aggression 11:25–58.

356. Fox KM, Gilbert BO (1994). The interpersonal and psychological functioning of women who experienced childhood physical abuse, incest, and parental alcoholism. Child Abuse & Neglect 18:849–58

357. Foy DW et al. (2001). Chapter 8. Group therapy for PTSD. In Wilson JP, Friedman MJ, Lindey JD (eds.) Treating Psychological Trauma and PTSD. Guilford, NY

358. Frank E, Turner SM, Stewart BD, Jacob M, West D (1981). Past psychiatric symptoms and the response to sexual assault. Comprehensive Psychiatry 22:479–87

359. Frank E, Kupfer DJ, Perel JN, Comes C, Jarrett DB, Mallinger AG, Thase ME, McEachran AB, Grochocinski VJ (1990). 3-year outcomes for maintenance therapies in recurrent depression. Archives of General Psychiatry 47:1093–9

360. Franklin D, Hockenberry J (2003). Drug giant accused of false claims. Dateline NBC [interview], 3 July

361. Frazier PA, Cohen BB (1992). Research on the sexual victimization of women: implications for counselor training. The Counseling Psychologist 20(1):141–58

362. Freedman, Kaplan & Sadock's (1995) Comprehensive Textbook of Psychiatry. Lippincott Williams & Wilkins, NY

363. Freudenheim M (2003). Lawsuit documents detail drug makers paying big bucks to sway sales. New York Times, 14 March

364. Friedman S, Harrison G (1984). Sexual histories, attitudes and behavior of schizophrenic and Norman women. Archives of Sexual Behavior 13:555–67

365. Friedman MA, Wilfley DE, Welch RR, Kunce JT (1997). Self-directed hostility and family functioning in normal-weight bulimics and overweight binge eaters. Addict Behav 22(3):367–75

366. Friedman S, Smith L, Fogel D, Paradis C, Viswanathan R, Ackerman R, Brian Trappler R (2002). The incidence and influence of early traumatic life events in patients with panic disorder: A comparison with other psychiatric outpatients. Journal of Anxiety Disorders 16:259–272

367. Friedrich WN, Urquiza AJ, Beilke RL (1986). Behavior problems in sexually abused young children. J Pediatr Psychol. Mar; 11(1):47–57

368. Friedrich WN (1998). Behavioral manifestations of child sexual abuse. Child Abuse & Neglect 22 (6): 523–31

369. Friedrich WN, Luecke WJ, Beilke RL, Place V (1992). Psychotherapy outcome of sexually abused boys: an agency study. Journal of Interpersonal Violence 7(3):396–409

370. Fromuth ME (1986). The relationship of childhood sexual abuse with later psychological and sexual adjustment in a sample of college women. Child Abuse & Neglect 10:5–15

371. Fromuth ME, Burkhart BR (1989). Long-term psychological correlates of childhood sexual abuse in two samples of college men. Child Abuse & Neglect 13:533–42

372. Frothingham TE, Hobbs CJ, Wynne JM, Yee L, Goya A, Wadsworth DJ (2000). Follow-up study eight years after diagnosis of sexual abuse. Archives of Diseases of Childhood 83:132–134

372. Fullilove MT, Fullilove RE, Smith M, Winkler K, Michael C, Panzer PG, Wallace R (1993). Violence, trauma, and post-traumatic stress disorder among women drug users. Journal of Traumatic Stress 6:533–43

374. Fullilove MT (2002). Social and economic causes of depression. J Gend Specif Med 5(2):38–41

G

375. Galenberg AJ (2002). Out of the box. Archives of General Psychiatry 59:281

376. Gara MA, Allen LA, Herzog EP, Woolfolk RL (2000). The abused child as parent: the structure and content of physically abused mothers' perceptions of their babies. Child Abuse & Neglect 24(5)627–39

377. Garfinkle PE, Lin E, Goering P et al. (1995). Bulimia nervosa in a Canadian community sample: prevalence and comparison subgroups. American Journal of Psychiatry 152:1052–8

378. Garfinkle PE, Lin E, Goering P et al. (1996). Purging and nonpurging forms of bulimia nervosa in a community sample. International Journal of Eating Disorders 20:231–8

379. Garland A, Scott J (2002). Using homework in therapy for depression. J Clin Psychol 58(5):489–98

380. Gelijns AC, Their SO (2002). Medical innovation and institutional interdependence: Rethinking university-industry connections. Journal of the American Medical Association 287:72–7

381. George C, Main M (1979). Social interaction of young abused children: approach, avoidance, and aggression. Child Development 50:306–18

382. Giese AA, Thomas MR, Dubovsky SL, Hilty S (1998). The impact of a history of childhood abuse on hospital outcome of affective episodes. Psychiatr Serv. 49(1):77–81

383. Guevara J, Lozano P, Wickizer T, Mell L, Gephart H (2002). Psychotropic medication use in a population of children who have attention-deficit/hyperactivity disorder. Pediatrics 109(5):733–9

384. Gershuny BS, Thayer JF (1999). Relations among psychological trauma, dissociative phenomena, and trauma-related distress: a review and integration. Clin Psychol Rev. 19(5):631–57

385. Gibson LE, Holt JC, Fondacaro KM, Tang TS, Powell TA, Turbitt EL (1999). An examination of antecedent traumas and psychiatric comorbidity among male inmates with PTSD. J Trauma Stress 12(3):473–84

386. Girdano D, Everly G (1979). Controlling stress and tension: A holistic approach. Prentice Hall, NY

387. Gladstone G, Parker G, Wilhelm K, Mitchell P, Austin MP (1999). Characteristics of depressed patients who report childhood sexual abuse. American Journal of Psychiatry 156(3):431–7

388. Glassman AH, Covey LS, Dalack GW, Stetner F (1992). Cigarette smoking, major depression, and schizophrenia. Clin Neuropharmacol. 15 Suppl 1 Pt A:560A–561A

389. Gleuck BC (1963). Chapter 28. Early sexual experiences in schizophrenia. In: Advances in Sex Research

390. Glod CA, Teicher MH (1996). Relationship between early abuse, post-traumatic stress disorder, and activity levels in prepubertal children. Journal of the American Academy of Child and Adolescent Psychiatry 35:1384–1393

391. Glod CA (1993). Long-term consequences of childhood physical and sexual abuse. Arch Psychiatr Nurs. 7(3):163–73

392. Glod CA, Teicher MH, Hartman CR, Harakal T, McGreenery CE (1997). Enduring effects of early abuse on locomotor activity, sleep and circadian rhythms. Annals New York Academy of Science; 821:465–467

393. Goff DC, Brotman AW, Kindlon D, Waites M, Amico E (1991). Self-reports of childhood abuse in chronically psychotic patients. Psychiatry Res. 37(1):73–80

394. Gold ER (1986). Long-term effects of sexual victimization in childhood: An attributional approach. Journal of Consulting and Clinical Psychology 54: 471–475

395. Gold MS, Johnson CR, Stennie K (1997). Chapter 28 Eating disorders. In Lowinson JH et al. (eds.): Substance Abuse: A comprehensive textbook. 3rd ed, Williams & Wilkins, NY

396. Gold SN, Lucenko BA, Elhai JD, Swingle JM, Sellers AH (1999). A comparison of psychological/psychiatric symptomatology of women and men sexually abused as children. Child Abuse & Neglect 23(7):683–92

397. Gold SN, Hill EL, Swingle JM, Elfant AS (1999). Relationship between childhood sexual abuse characteristics and dissociation among women in therapy. Journal of Family Violence, 14:157–171

398. Gold SN (2000). Not Trauma Alone: Therapy for child abuse survivors in family and social context. Brunner-Routledge, Philadelphia

399. Goldberg D (2001). Vulnerability factors for common mental illnesses. British Journal of Psychiatry 178:69–71

400. Goldberg T, Gold J, Greenberg R, Griffin S, Schulz C, Pickar D, Kleinman J, Weinberger D (1993). Contrasts between patients with affective disorders and patients with schizophrenia on a neuropsychological test battery. American Journal of Psychiatry, 150:1355–62

401. Goldberg RT (1994). Childhood abuse, depression, and chronic pain. Clinical Journal of Pain 10:277–281

402. Goldberg R, Goldstein R (2000). A comparison of chronic pain patients and controls on traumatic events in childhood. Disability and Rehab. 22:756–763

403. Golding JM (1996). Sexual assault history and women's reproductive and sexual health. Psychol Women Q. 20:101–21

404. Golding JM (1999). Sexual assault history and headache: five general population studies. J Nerv Ment Dis. 187(10):624–9

405. Goldman SJ, D'Angelo EJ, DeMaso DR, Mezzacappa E (1992). Physical and sexual abuse histories among children with borderline personality disorder. Am J Psychiatry 149(12):1723–6

406. Golier JA, Yehuda R, Bierer LM et al. (2003). The relationship of borderline personality disorder to PTSD and traumatic events. American Journal of Psychiatry 160:2018–24

407. Gomes-Schwartz B, Horowitz J, Sauzier M (1984). The aftermath of sexual abuse: 18 month follow-up. In: Tufts New England Medical Center, Child Psychiatry Division. Sexually Exploited Children: Service and Research Project. Final Report of the Office of Juvenile Justice and Delinquency Prevention. Washington, DC, US Department of Justice

408. Gomes-Schwartz B, Horowitz JM, Sauzier M (1985). Severity of emotional distress among sexually abused preschool, school-age, and adolescent children. Hosp Community Psychiatry 36(5):503–8

409. Gonzales D, Nides MA, Ferry LH, Kustra RP, Jamerson BD, Segall N, Herrero LA, Krishen A, Sweeney A, Buaron K, Metz A (2001). Bupropion SR as an aid to smoking cessation in smokers previously treated with bupropion: a randomized, placebo-controlled study. Clin Pharmacol Ther 69:438–44

410. Goode E (2003). Leading drugs for psychosis come under new scrutiny. NY Times, 20 May

411. Goodman GS, Ghetti S, Quas JA, et al. (2003). A prospective study of memory for child sexual abuse: new findings relevant to the repressed-memory controversy. Psychological Science 14:113–18

412. Goodman L, Rosenberg S, Mueser T, Drake R (1995). Physical and sexual assault prevalence among episodically homeless women with serious mental illness. American Journal of Orthopsychiatry 65:468–78

413. Goodman L, Dutton MA, Harris M (1997). Physical and sexual assault history in women with serious mental illness: Prevalence, correlates, treatment and future research directions. Schizophrenia Bulletin 23:685–96

414. Goodman LA, Thompson KM, Weinfurt K, Corl S, Acker P, Mueser KT, Rosenberg SD (1999). Reliability of reports of violent victimization and post-traumatic stress disorder among men and women with serious mental illness. J Trauma Stress 12(4):587–99

415. Goodman LA, Thompson KM, Weinfurt K, Corl S, Acker P, Mueser KT, Rosenberg SD (1999). Reliability of reports of violent victimization and post-traumatic stress disorder among men and women with serious mental illness. J Trauma Stress 12(4):587–99

416. Goodsitt A (1997). Chapter 11. Eating disorders: a self-psychological perspective. In Garner D, Garfinkle P (eds.) Handbook of Eating Disorders, Guilford Press.

417. Goodwin J, McCarthy T, Divasto P (1981). Prior incest in mothers of abused children. Child Abuse & Neglect 5:87–96

418. Goodwin J, Attias R, McCarty T, Chandler S, Romanik R (1988). Reporting by adult psychiatric patients of childhood sexual abuse. Am J Psychiatry 145(9):1183–4

419. Goodwin JM, Cheeves K, Connell V (1990). Borderline and other severe symptoms in adult survivors of incestuous abuse. Psychiatric Annals 20:22–32

420. Gorcey M, Santiago JM, McCall PF (1986). Psychological consequences for women sexually abused in childhood. Social Psychiatry 21(3): 129–33

421. Gorner P (2002). Top medical journal [NEJM] eases ethics policy. Chicago Tribune, June 13

422. Gottman JM, Katz LF (1989). Effects of marital discord on young children's peer interaction and health. Developmental Psychology 3:373–81

423. Gould DA, Stevens NG, Ward NG, Carlin AS, Sowell HE, Gufstavson B (1994). Self-reported childhood abuse in an adult population in a primary care setting: prevalence, correlates and associated suicide attempts. Archives of Family Medicine 3:252–6

424. Grayston AD, De Luca RV, Boyes DA (1992). Self-esteem, anxiety, and loneliness in preadolescent girls who have experienced sexual abuse. Child Psychiatry Hum Dev 22(4):277–86

425. Grayston AD, De Luca RV (1999). Female perpetrators of child sexual abuse: a review of the clinical and empirical literature. 4:93–106

426. Green B: Problem-based psychiatry. Churchill Livingston, NY 1996

427. Green RJ, Werner PD (1996). Intrusiveness and closeness-caregiving: rethinking the concept of family "Enmeshment." Fam Process 35(2):115–36

428. Greenberg PE, Sisitsky T, Kessler RC, Finkelstein SN, Berndt ER, Davidson JR, Ballenger JC, Fyer AJ (1999). The economic burden of anxiety disorders in the 1990s. J Clin Psychiatry 60(7):427–35

429. Greenfield SF, Strakowski SM, Tohen M, Batson SC, Kolbrener ML (1994). Childhood abuse in first-episode psychosis. Br J Psychiatry 164(6):831–4

430. Greene RW, Biederman J, Zerwas S, Monuteaux MC, Goring JC, Faraone SV (2002). Psychiatric comorbidity, family dysfunction, and social impairment in referred youth with oppositional defiant disorder. Am J Psychiatry 159(7):1214–24

431. Greenwald E, Leitenberg OH, Cado S, Tarran MJ (1990). Childhood sexual abuse: long-term effects on psychological and sexual functioning in a non-clinical and non-student sample of adult women. Child Abuse & Neglect 14 (4): 503–514

432. Grella CE, Joshi V (2003). Treatment processes and outcomes among adolescents with a history of abuse who are in drug treatment. Child Maltreat. Feb; 8(1):7–18

433. Grice DE, Brady KT, Dustan LR, Malcolm R (1995). Sexual and physical assault history and post-traumatic stress disorder in substance-dependent individuals. American Journal of Addictions 4:297–305

434. Grilo CM, Sanislow C, Fehon DC, Martino S, Mc Glashan TH (1999). Psychological and behavioral functioning in adolescent psychiatric inpatients who report histories of childhood abuse. American Journal of Psychiatry 156 (4) 538–543

435. Grilo CM, Masheb RM (2001). Childhood psychological, physical, and sexual maltreatment in outpatients with binge eating disorder: frequency and associations with gender, obesity, and eating-related psychopathology. Obes Res 9(5):320–5

436. Grilo CM, Masheb RM (2002). Childhood maltreatment and personality disorders in adult patients with binge eating disorder. Acta Psychiatr Scand. 106(3):183–8

437. Grossman R, Yehuda R, New A, Schmeidler J, Silverman J, Mitropoulou V, Sta Maria N, Golier J, Siever L (2003). Dexamethasone suppression test findings in subjects with personality disorders: associations with post-traumatic stress disorder and major depression. Am J Psychiatry 160(7):1291–8

438. Guerra NG, Huesmann LR, Spindler A (2003). Community violence exposure, social cognition, and aggression among urban elementary school children. Child Dev. 74(5):1561–76

439. Gurvits TV, Gilbertson MW, Lasko NB, Tarhan AS, Simeon D, Macklin ML, Orr SP, Pitman RK (2000). Neurologic soft signs in chronic post-traumatic stress disorder. Arch Gen Psychiatry. Feb; 57(2):181–6

H

440. Hall RCW, Tice L, Beresford TP, Wooley B, Hall AK (1989). Sexual abuse in patients with anorexia nervosa and bulimia. Psychosomatics 30:73–80

441. Hardman JG, Limbird LE (eds.) (1996). Goodman and Gilman's The Pharmacologic Basis of Therapeutics 9th ed., McGraw Hill, NY

442. Hardt J, Rutter M (2004). Validity of adult retrospective reports of adverse childhood experiences: review of the evidence. Journal of Child Psycology & Psychiatry & Allied Disciplines 45:260–73

443. Harkness KL, Wildes JE (2002). Childhood adversity and anxiety versus dysthymia co-morbidity in major depression. Psychol Med 32(7):1239–49

444. Harrison PA, Lumry AE (1984). Female sexual abuse victims: perspectives on family dysfunction, substance use and psychiatric disorders. Presented at 2nd National Conf for Family Violence Researchers, U New Hampshire, Durham (cited in Jasinski et al. 2000)

445. Hart LE, Mader L, Griffith K, deMendonca M (1989). Effects of sexual and physical abuse: a comparison of adolescent inpatients. Child Psychiatry and Human Development 20:49–57

446. Harter S, Alexander PC, Neimeyer RA (1988). Long-term effects of incestuous child abuse in college women: social adjustment, social cognition and family characteristics. Journal of Consulting and Clinical Psychology 56:5–8

447. Harter SL, Vanecek RJ (2000). Cognitive assumptions and long-term distress of childhood abuse, parental alcoholism, and dysfunctional family environments. Cognitive Therapy and Research 24:445–72

448. Harter SL, Taylor TL (2000). Parental alcoholism, child abuse, and adult adjustment. Journal of Substance Abuse 11(1):31–44

449. Harter SL (2000). Psychosocial adjustment of adult children of alcoholics: a review of the recent empirical literature. Clin Psychol Rev. 20(3):311–37

450. Hartt J, Waller G (2002). Child abuse, dissociation, and core beliefs in bulimic disorders. Child Abuse & Neglect 26:1–16

451. Hasin D, Liu X, Nunes E, McCloud S, Samet S, Endicott J (2002). Effects of major depression on remission and relapse of substance dependence. Arch Gen Psychiatry 59(4):375–80

452. Hastings DP, Kantor GK (2003). Women's victimization history and surgical intervention. AORN J. 77(1):163–8, 170–1, 173–4 passim.

453. Hawke JM, Jainchill N, De Leon G (2003). Posttreatment victimization and violence following residential drug treatment. Child Maltreatment 8:58–71

454. Hasin DS, Grant BF (2002a). Major depression in 6,050 former drinkers: association with past alcohol dependence. Arch Gen Psychiatry 59(9):794–800

455. Hazell P, O'Connell D, Heathcote D, Henry D. Tricyclic drugs for depression in children and adolescents (Cochrane Review). In: The Cochrane Library, Issue 3, 2000

456. Heads T, Taylor P, Leese M (1997). Childhood experiences of patients with schizophrenia and a history of violence: a special hospital sample. Criminal Behavior and Mental Health 7:117–30

457. Heads TC (1997). Risk assessment in schizophrenia. Br J Hosp Med. 57(9):451–3

458. Health Canada in Co-operation with the Schizophrenia Society of Canada (2004). Schizophrenia: A Handbook For Families. http://www.mentalhealth.com/book/p40-sc01.html

459. Healy D (1987). The structure of psychopharmacological revolutions. Psychiatr. Dev. 5, 349–376.

460. Healy D (1991). The marketing of 5-Hydroxytryptamine [serotonin]: depression or anxiety? Br J Psychiatry 158:737–742.

461. Healy D (1998). The Antidepressant Era. Harvard University Press, Cambridge, Mass.

462. Healy D (2000). Good science or good business? Hastings Center Report, 30 No 2, 19–22

463. Healy DR, Tranter R (1991). Pharmacological stress diathesis syndromes, J Psychopharmacol., 1999, 13(3), 287–290. And: In the shadow of the benzodiazepines (Responses to commentaries on the above paper), Ibid, p. 299

464. Healy D (1998). Commentary on J. Moncrieff et al. Meta-analysis of trials comparing antidepressants with active placebos, Brit J Psychiatry, 72, 232–234.

465. Healy D (1993). Images of trauma: from hysteria to PTSD. Chapter 10. Faber & Faber, London

466. Healy D (1999). The three faces of antidepressants. Journal of Mental and Nervous Disease 187:174–180

467. Healy D (2002). The [antidepressant] drugs don't work (also titled "Drug Story"). Documentary on Channel 4, London, UK, May 19

468. Healy D, Savage M, Michael P, Harris M, Cattell D, Carter M, McMonagle T, Sohler N, Susser E (2001). Psychiatric service utilisation: 1896 & 1996 compared. Psychological Medicine 31, 779–790

468a. Healy D (2003). Conspiracy of consensus: How drug companies get round the absence of hard evidence. Mental Health Today November, page 27–30

469. Healy D (2004). Let Them Eat Prozac: The unhealthy relationship between the pharmaceutical industry and depression. NYU Press, NY

470. Healy D (2004b). SSRI risks: new data or renewed scrutiny? Internet report p. 1–5

470a. Healy D (2003). Conspiracy of consensus:

471. Heffernan K, Cloitre M (2000). A comparison of post-traumatic stress disorder with and without borderline personality disorder among women with a history of childhood sexual abuse: etiological and clinical characteristics. J Nerv Ment Dis. Sep; 188(9):589–95

472. Heffernan K, Cloitre M, Tardiff K, Marzuk PM, Portera L, Leon AC (2000). Childhood trauma as a correlate of lifetime opiate use in psychiatric patients. Addict Behav. 25(5):797–803

473. Hegarty JD et al. (1994) One Hundred Years of Schizophrenia: a meta-analysis of the outcome literature. Am. J. Psychiatry 151:1409–1416. (Poorer outcomes in last third of the 20th century and best in the middle third.)

474. Heim C, Newport DJ, Heit S, Graham YP, Wilcox M, Bonsall R, Miller AH, Nemeroff CB (2000). Pituitary-adrenal and autonomic responses to stress in women after sexual and physical abuse in childhood. Journal of the American Medical Association 284:592–7

475. Heins T, Gray A, Tennant M (1990). Persisting hallucinations following childhood sexual abuse. Australian and New Zealand Journal of Psychiatry 24:561–5

476. Henton J, Cate R, Koval J, Lloyd S, Christopher S (1993). Romance and violence in dating relationships. Journal of Family Issues 4:467–82

477. Herman JL (1981). Father-daughter incest. Harvard U. Press, Cambridge, MA

478. Herman JL, Schatzow E (1984). Time-limited group therapy for women with a history of incest. International Journal of Group Psychotherapy 34:605–16

479. Herman JL, Russell DEH, Trocki K (1986). Long-term effects of incestuous abuse in childhood. American Journal of Psychiatry 143:1293–6

480. Herman JL (1986). Histories of violence in an outpatient population. Am J Orthopsychiatry; 56:137–141

481. Herman JL, Russell DEH, Trocki K (1986). Long-term effects of incestuous abuse in childhood. Am J Psychiatry; 143:1293–1296

482. Herman JL, Schatzow E (1987). Recovery and verification of memories of childhood sexual trauma. Psychoanalytic Psychology 4:1–14

483. Herman JL, van der Kolk BA (1987). Traumatic antecedents of borderline personality disorder. In van der Kolk BA (ed.), Psychological trauma. Washington, DC, American Psychiatric Press p 111–26

484. Herman JL (1988). Histories of violence in an outpatient population. In Burgess AW (ed.) Rape and sexual assault, Vol. 2. New York: Garland, p 41–49

485. Herman JL, Perry JC, van der Kolk BA (1989). Childhood trauma in borderline personality disorder. American Journal of Psychiatry 146:490–5

486. Herman JL (1992). Trauma and Recovery. Basic Books, NY, Second Edition 1997

487. Herman JL (1992). Sequelae of prolonged and repeated trauma: Evidence for a complex post-traumatic syndrome. In Davidson JR, Foa EB (eds.), Post-traumatic stress disorder: *DSM-IV* and beyond. Washington, DC: American Psychiatric Press p 213–228

488. Herman JL (1992). Complex PTSD: A syndrome in survivors of prolonged and repeated trauma. J. Traumatic Stress 5:377–391

489. Herman JL (1998). Recovery from psychological trauma. Psychiatry and Clinical Neurosciences 52

490. Hernandez JT (1992). Substance abuse among sexually abused adolescents and their families. J Adolesc Health 13(8):658–62

491. Herrenkohl RC, Russo MJ (2000). Abusive early child rearing and early childhood aggression. Child Maltreatment, February 2001, vol. 6, no. 1, pp. 3–16(14)

492. Herxheimer A (2003). Relationships between the pharmaceutical industry and patients' organizations. BMJ 326:1208–10

493. Hexel M, Sonneck G (2002). Somatoform symptoms, anxiety, and depression in the context of traumatic life experiences by comparing participants with and without psychiatric diagnoses. Psychopathology 35(5):303–12

494. Higgins DJ, McCabe MP (1994). The relationship of child sexual abuse and family violence to adult adjustment: Toward an integrated risk-sequelae model. Journal of Sex Research 31(4):255–66

495. Hill SY, De Bellis MD, Keshavan MS, Lowers L, Shen S, Hall J, Pitts T (2001). Right amygdala volume in adolescent and young adult offspring from families at high risk for developing alcoholism. Biol Psychiatry 1;49(11):894–905

496. Hillis SD, Anda RF, Felitti VJ, Nordenberg D, Marchbanks PA (2000). Adverse childhood experiences and sexually transmitted diseases in men and women: a retrospective study. Pediatrics 106(1):E11

497. Hinshaw SP (2002). Preadolescent girls with attention-deficit/hyperactivity disorder: I. Background characteristics, comorbidity, cognitive and social functioning, and parenting practices. J Consult Clin Psychol. 70(5):1086–98

498. Hoffman-Plotkin D, Twentyman CT (1984). A multimodal assessment of behavioral and cognitive deficits in abused and neglected preschoolers. Child Dev Jun; 55(3):794–802

499. Holowaka DW, King S, Saheb D, Pukall M, Brunet A (2003). Childhood abuse and dissociative symptoms in adult schizophrenia. Schizophrenia Research 60:87–90

500. Honig A, Romme MA, Ensink BJ, Escher SD, Pennings MH, deVries MW (1998). Auditory hallucinations: a comparison between patients and nonpatients. J Nerv Ment Dis 186(10):646–51

501. Hooper PD (1990). Psychological sequelae of sexual abuse in childhood. British Journal of General Practice 40:29–31

502. Hughes JR, Stead LF, Lancaster T (2000). Anxiolytics and antidepressants for smoking cessation (Cochrane Review). In: The Cochrane Library, Issue 3. Oxford: Update Software.

503. Hull AM (2002). Neuroimaging findings in post-traumatic stress disorder: Systematic review. Br J Psychiatry 181(2):102–110

504. Hulme PA (2000). Symptomatology and health care utilization of women primary care patients who experienced childhood sexual abuse. Child Abuse & Neglect 24:1471–84

505. Hunter JA (1991). A comparison of the psychosocial maladjustment of adult males and females sexually molested as children. Journal of Interpersonal Violence 6(2):205–17

506. Hurlbert DF, Apt C, White LC (1992). An empirical examination into the sexuality of women with borderline personality disorder. J Sex Marital Ther 18(3):231–42

507. Hurt H, Malmud E, Brodsky NL, Giannetta J (2001). Exposure to violence, psychological and academic correlates in child witnesses. Archives of Pediatric and Adolescent Medicine; 155:1351–1356.

508. Hussey DL, Singer M (1993). Psychological distress, problem behaviors, and family functioning of sexually abused adolescent inpatients. Journal of the American Academy of Child and Adolescent Psychiatry 32 (5) 954–960

I

509. Irwin HJ (1994). Proneness to dissociation and traumatic childhood events. J Nerv Ment Dis. 182(8):456–60

510. Irwin H, Green M, and Marsh P (1999). Dysfunction in smooth pursuit eye movements and history of childhood trauma. Perceptual and Motor Skills 89:1230–1236.

511. Ito Y, Teicher M, Glod C, and Ackerman E (1998). Preliminary evidence for aberrant cortical development in abused children: A quantitative EEG study. Journal of Neuropsychiatry and Clinical Neurosciences 10:298–307.

512. Ito Y, Teicher MH, Glod CA, Harper D, Magnus E, Gelbard HA (1993). Increased prevalence of electrophysiological abnormalities in children with psychological, physical, and sexual abuse. Journal of Neuropsychiatry and Clinical Neurosciences 5:401–408.

J

513. Jacobson A, Richardson B (1987). Assault experiences of 100 psychiatric inpatients: evidence of the need for routine inquiry. American Journal of Psychiatry 144:908–913.

514. Jacobson A, Kohler JE, Jones-Brown C (1987). The failure of routine assessment to detect histories of assault experienced by psychiatric patients. Hospital and Community Psychiatry 38:386–89

515. Jacobson A (1989). Physical and sexual assault histories among psychiatric outpatients. American Journal of Psychiatry 146(6):755–8

516. Jacobs D, Cohen D (1999). What is really known about psychological alterations produced by psychiatric drugs? The International Journal of Risk and Safety in Medicine Volume 12, Number 1:37–47

517. Jacobson A (1989). Physical and sexual assault histories among psychiatric outpatients. American Journal of Psychiatry 146:751–758

518. Jacobson A, Richardson B (1987). Assault experiences of 100 psychiatric inpatients: evidence of the need for routine inquiry. American Journal of Psychiatry, 144:908–913

519. Jacobson A, Herald C (1990). The relevance of childhood sexual abuse to adult psychiatric inpatient care. Hospital and Community Psychiatry 41:154–8

520. Jacobson NS, Dobson KS, Truax PA, Addis ME, Koerner K, Gollan JK, Gortner E, Prince SE (1996). A component analysis of cognitive behavioral treatment for depression. Journal of Consulting & Clinical Psychology 64:295–304

521. Jaffe P, Wolfe D, Wilson S, Zak L (1986). Similarities in behavioral and social maladjustment among child victims and witnesses to family violence. American Journal of Orthopsychiatry 56:142–6

522. Jasinski JL, Williams LM, Siegel J (2000). Childhood physical and sexual abuse as risk factors for heavy drinking among African-American women: a prospective study. Child Abuse & Neglect 24(8):1061–71

523. James K (1977). Incest: the teenager's perspective. Psychotherapy: Theory, Research & Practice 14(2): 144–6

524. James J, Meyerding J (1977). Early sexual experiences and prostitution. American Journal of Psychiatry 134:1381–5

525. Janus MD, Burgess AW, McCormack A (1987). Histories of sexual abuse in adolescent male runaways. Adolescence 22(86):405–17

526. Jarvis TJ, Copeland J (1997). Child sexual abuse as a predictor of psychiatric co-morbidity and its implications for drug and alcohol treatment. Drug Alcohol Depend. Dec; 49(1):61–9

527. Jellen LK, McCarroll JE, Thayer LE (2001). Child emotional maltreatment: a 2-year study of U.S. Army cases. Child Abuse & Neglect 25(5):623–39

528. Jicks SS, Dean AD, Jicks H (1995). Antidepressants and suicide. British Medical Journal 311:215–8

529. Johnson RL, Shrier DK (1985). Sexual victimization of boys. Journal of Adolescent Health Care 6:372–6

530. Johnson JG, Cohen P, Brown J, Smailes EM, Bernstein DP (1999). Childhood maltreatment increases risk for personality disorders during early adulthood. Archives of General Psychiatry 56:600–606

531. Johnson JG, Smailes EM, Cohen P, Brown J, Bernstein DP (2000). Associations between four types of childhood neglect and personality disorder symptoms during adolescence and early adulthood: findings of a community-based longitudinal study. J Personal Disord 14(2):171–87

532. Johnson JG, Cohen P, Kasen S, Smailes E, Brook JS. (2001). Association of maladaptive parental behavior with psychiatric disorder among parents and their offspring. Arch Gen Psychiatry May 58(5):453–60

533. Johnson DM, Pike JL, Chard KM (2001). Factors predicting PTSD, depression, and dissociative severity in female treatment-seeking childhood sexual abuse survivors. Child Abuse & Neglect 25(1):179–98

534. Johnson J, Weissman MM, Klerman GL (1992). Service utilization and social morbidity associated with depressive symptoms in the community. Journal of the American Medical Association 267 (11): 1478–1483

535. Johnson RM, Kotch JB, Catellier DJ, Winsor JR, Dufort V, Hunter W, Amaya-Jackson L (2002). Adverse behavioral and emotional outcomes from child abuse and witnessed violence. Child Maltreatment 7(3):179–86

536. Jones P, Rodgers B, Murray R, Marmont M (1994). Child developmental risk factors for adult schizophrenia in the British 1946 birth cohort. Lancet 344:1398–1402.

537. Jones L, Hughes M, Unterstaller U (2001). Post-traumatic stress disorder (PTSD) in victims of domestic violence. Trauma, Violence & Abuse 2:99–119

538. Joseph, J (1998). The equal environment assumption of the classical twin method: A critical analysis. Journal of Mind and Behavior, 19, 325–358.

539. Joseph J (1999). A critique of the Finnish Adoptive Family Study of Schizophrenia. Journal of Mind and Behavior, 20, 133–154.

540. Joseph J (1999a). The genetic theory of schizophrenia: A critical overview. Ethical Human Sciences and Services, 1, 119–145.

541. Joseph J (2001). Don Jackson's "A critique of the literature on the genetics of schizophrenia": A reappraisal after 40 years. Genetic, Social, & General Psychology Monographs 127:27–57.

542. Joseph J (2003). The Gene Illusion. PCCS Books, London

543. Jumper S (1995). A meta-analysis of the relationship of child sexual abuse to adult psychological adjustment. Child Abuse & Neglect, 19:715–728.

K

544. Kalb PE, Koehler KG (2002). Legal issues in scientific research. Journal of the American Medical Association 287:85–91

545. Kang SY, Deren S, Goldstein MF (2002). Relationships between childhood abuse and neglect experience and HIV risk behaviors among methadone treatment drop-outs. Child Abuse & Neglect 26(12):1275–89

546. Kaplan SJ, Pelcovitz D, Salzinger S, Weiner M, Mandel FS, Lesser ML, Labruna VE (1998). Adolescent physical abuse: risk for adolescent psychiatric disorders. Am J Psychiatry 155(7):954–9; more at Pediatrics 1999 Jul;104(1 Pt 1):43–9; and J Trauma Stress 2000 Jan;13(1):77–88

547. Kashani JH, Carlson GA (1987). Seriously depressed preschoolers. American Journal of Psychiatry 144:348–50

548. Kashani JH, Beck NC, Burk JP (1987). Predictors of psychopathology in children of patients with major affective disorders. Can J Psychiatry 32(4):287–90

549. Katz LF, Gottman JM (1997). Buffering children from marital conflict and dissolution. J Clin Child Psychol 26(2):157–71

550. Kaufman I, Peck AL, Tagiuri CK (1954). The family constellation and overt incestuous relations between father and daughter. Am J Orthopsychiatry 24(2):266–79

551. Kaufman J (1991). Depressive disorders in maltreated children. Journal of the American Academy of Child and Adolescent Psychiatry 30(2), 257–265.

552. Kaufman J, Birmaher B, Perel J, Dahl RE, Stull S, Brent D, Trubnick L, Al-Shabbout M, Ryan ND (1998). Serotonergic functioning in depressed abused children: clinical and familial correlates. Biological Psychiatry 44:973–8

553. Kaufman J (1991). Depressive disorders in maltreated children. J Am Acad Child Adolesc Psychiatry 30:257–265

554. Kazdin AE, Mosher J, Colbus D, Bell R (1985). Depressive symptoms among physically abused and psychiatrically disturbed children. Journal of Abnormal Psychology 94(3): 298–307

555. Keeler MH. Chapter 47. Alcoholism and affective disorder (p 618) In: Pattison EM & Kaufman R (eds.): Encyclopedic Handbook of Alcoholism, Gardner Press, NY, 1982

556. Kendall-Tackett C, Williams L M, Finkelhor D (1993). Impact of sexual abuse on children: A review and synthesis of recent empirical studies. Psychological Bulletin, 113, 164–180

557. Kendall-Tackett KA, Simon AF (1988). Molestation and the onset of puberty: Data from 365 adults molested as children. Child Abuse & Neglect 12:73–81

558. Kendall-Tackett KA (2000). Physiological correlates of childhood abuse: chronic hyperarousal in PTSD, depression, and irritable bowel syndrome. Child Abuse & Neglect 24(6):799–810

559. Kendler K, Karkowski LM, Prescott CA (1999). Causal relationship between stressful life events and the onset of major depression. American Journal of Psychiatry 156:837–841

560. Kendler K, Bulik C, Silberg J, Hettema J, Myers J, Prescott C (2000). Childhood sexual abuse and adult psychiatric and substance use disorders in women: An epidemiological and co-twin control analysis. Arch Gen Psychiatry 57:953–959

561. Kendler KS, Thornton LM, Prescott CA (2001). Gender differences in the rates of exposure to stressful life events and sensitivity to their depressogenic effects. Am J Psychiatry 158(4):587–93

562. Kendler KS, Gardner CO, Prescott CA (2002). Toward a comprehensive developmental model for major depression in women. Am J Psychiatry 159(7):1133–45

563. Kendler KS, Prescott CA, Myers J, Neale MC (2003). The structure of genetic and environmental risk factors for common psychiatric and substance use disorders in men and women. Arch Gen Psychiatry 60(9):929–37

564. Kennedy BL, Dhaliwal N, Pedley L, Sahner C, Greenberg R, Manshadi MS (2002). Post-traumatic stress disorder in subjects with schizophrenia and bipolar disorder. J Ky Med Assoc 100(9):395–9

565. Kent JT (1976). A follow-up study of abused children. Journal of Pediatric Psychology 1:25–31

566. Kent A, Waller G, Dagnan D (1999). A greater role of emotional than physical or sexual abuse in predicting disordered eating attitudes: the role of mediating variables. International Journal of Eating Disorders 25:159–67

567. Kent A, Waller G (1998). The impact of childhood emotional abuse: and extension of the child abuse and trauma scale. Child Abuse & Neglect 22:393–9

568. Kent A, Waller G (2000). Childhood emotional abuse and eating psychopathology. Clin Psychol Rev. 20(7):887–903

569. Kerig PK, Fedorowicz AE (1999). Assessing maltreatment of children of battered women: methodological and ethical considerations. Child Maltreatment 4(2):103–115

570. Kernic MA, Holt VL, Wolf ME, McKnight B, Huebner CE, Rivara FP (2002). Academic and school health issues among children exposed to maternal intimate partner abuse. Arch Pediatr Adolesc Med. 156(6):549–55

571. Kessler R, Davis C, Kendler R (1997). Childhood adversity and adult psychiatric disorder in the U.S. National Comorbidity Survey. Psychol. Med 27:1101–1119

572. Kiesler CA (1982a). Mental hospitals and alternative care: Noninstitutionalization as potential public policy for mental patients. American Psychologist 37:349–360.

573. Kiesler CA (1982b). Public and professional myths about mental hospitalization: An empirical reassessment of policy-related beliefs. American Psychologist 37:1323–1339

574. Kilpatrick KL, Williams LM (1998). Potential mediators of post-traumatic stress disorder in child witnesses to domestic violence. Child Abuse & Neglect 22:319–30

575. Kilpatrick AC (1986). Some correlates of women's childhood sexual experiences: a retrospective study. Journal of Sex Research 22(2): 221–42

576. Kilpatrick AC (1986). Some correlates of women's childhood sexual experiences. The Journal of Sex Research 22:221–42

577. Kilpatrick DG, Best CL, Veronen LJ, Amick AE, Villeponteaux LA, Ruff GA (1985). Mental health correlates of criminal victimization: a random community survey. J Consult Clin Psychol Dec; 53(6):866–73

578. Kinard EM (1994). Methodological issues and practical problems in conducting research on maltreated children. Child Abuse & Neglect 18(8):645–5

579. Kinard EM (1995). Mother and teacher assessments of behavior problems in abused children. Journal of the American Academy of Child and Adolescent Psychiatry 34 (8):1043–53

580. Kinderman , Cooke, Bentall R (2000). Recent Advances in Understanding Mental Illness and Psychotic Experiences. Leicester, UK: British Psychological Society

581. King CH (1975). The ego and the integration of violence in homicidal youth. American Journal of Orthopsychiatry 45(1):134–45

582. King M, Sibbald B, Ward E, Bower P, Lloyd M, Gabbay M, Byford S (2000). Randomised controlled trial of non-directive counselling, cognitive-behaviour therapy and usual general practitioner care in the management of depression as well as mixed anxiety and depression in primary care. Health Technol Assess. 4(19):1–83

583. King M, Coxell A, Mezey G (2002). Sexual molestation of males: associations with psychological disturbance. Br J Psychiatry 181(2):153–157

583. Kinzl J, Biebl W (1992). Long-term effects of incest: life events triggering mental disorders in female patients with sexual abuse in childhood. Child Abuse & Neglect 16(4):567–73

584. Kinzl JF, Biebl W (1994). Childhood sexual abuse and mental health. Br J Psychiatry 164(5):707

585. Kinzl JF, Traweger C, Guenther V, Biebl W (1994). Family background and sexual abuse associated with eating disorders. Am J Psychiatry 151(8):1127–31

586. Kinzl JF, Mangweth B, Traweger CM, Biebl W (1997). Eating-disordered behavior in males: the impact of adverse childhood experiences. Int J Eat Disord 22(2):131–8

587. Kirkengen AL (2001). Inscribed Bodies: Health Impact of Childhood Sexual Abuse. Kluwer Academic Publishers, Boston

588. Kirsch I, Sapirstein G, Listening to Prozac but Hearing Placebo—A Meta-Analysis of Anti-depressant Medication, June 1998, Prevention and Treatment, vol. One, *http://www.journals.apa.org/prevention*

589. Kirsch I (1998). Reducing noise and hearing placebo more clearly: Rejoinder to comments on Listening to Prozac but Hearing Placebo. Prevention & Treatment, Volume 1, Article 0007r, posted June 26

590. Kirsch I, Moore TJ, Scoboria A, Nicholls SS (2002). The emperor's new drugs: An analysis of anti-depressant medication data submitted to the FDA. Prevention and Treatment, American Psychological Association, *http://www.journals.apa.org/prevention*

591. Kiser LJ, Heston J, Millsap PA, Pruitt DB (1991). Physical and sexual abuse in childhood: relationship with post-traumatic stress disorder. J Am Acad Child Adolesc Psychiatry. 30(5):776–83

592. Kisiel CL, Lyons JS (2001). Dissociation as a mediator of psychopathology among sexually abused children and adolescents. Am J Psychiatry 158(7):1034–9

593. Kluft RP (ed.) (1990). Incest-Related Syndromes of Adult Psychopathology. American Psychiatric Press, NY

594. Kluft ES (1993). Expressive and Functional Therapies in the Treatment of Multiple Personality Disorder. Charles C. Thomas, Springfield, Il

595. Klump KL, Wonderlich S, Lehoux P, Lilenfeld LR, Bulik CM (2002). Does environment matter? A review of nonshared environment and eating disorders. Int J Eat Disord 31(2):118–35

596. Knowles EE, Schroeder DA (1990). Personality characteristics of sons of alcohol abusers. Journal of Studies of Alcohol 142–147

597. Koerner BI (2002). First, you market the disease . . . then you push the pills to treat it . . . the truth about doctors, PR firms and drug companies. The Guardian, 30 July

597a. Koocher G (2004). Three myths about empirically validated therapies. The Independent Practitioner Spring, 2004, vol. 24, #2

598. Kollins SH, MacDonald EK, Rush CR (2001). Assesing the abuse potential of methylphenidate [Ritalin] in nonhuman and human subjects: a review. Pharmacology, Biochemistry & Behavior 68:611–27

599. Krantz G, Ostergren PO (2000). The association between violence victimization and common symptoms in Swedish women. Journal of Epidemiology and Community Health 54:815–821

600. Krause ED, Mendelson T, Lynch TR (2003). Childhood emotional invalidation and adult psychological distress: the mediating role of emotional inhibition. Child Abuse & Neglect 27(2):199–213

601. Kresky-Wolff M, Matthews S, Kalibat F, Mosher LR (1984). Crossing Place: a residential model for crisis intervention. Hosp Community Psychiatry 35(1):72–4

602. Kroll PD, Stock DF, James ME (1985). The behavior of adult alcoholic men abused as children. Journal of Nervous and Mental Disease 173:689–93

603. Kroth JA (1978). Child Sexual Abuse: Analysis of a family therapy approach. Charles C. Thomas, Springfield, Il

604. Krug RS (1989). Adult male report of childhood sexual abuse by mothers: case descriptions, motivations and long-term consequences. Child Abuse & Neglect 13(1):111–9

605. Kuhn TS (1970). The Structure of Scientific Revolutions. Univ Chicago Press

606. Kumar G, Steer RA, Deblinger E (1996). Problems in differentiating sexually from non-sexually abused adolescent psychiatric inpatients by self-reported anxiety, depression, internalization, and externalization. Child Abuse & Neglect 20 (11):1079–1086

607. Kunitz SJ, Levy JE, McCloskey J, Gabriel KR (1998). Alcohol dependence and domestic violence as sequelae of abuse and conduct disorder in childhood. Child Abuse & Neglect 22(11):1079–91

608. Kutchins H, Kirk SA (1997). Making Us Crazy—DSM: The Psychiatric Bible and the creation of mental disorders. The Free Press, NY

609. Kuyken W, Brewin CR (1994). Intrusive memories of childhood abuse during depressive episodes. Behav Res Ther 32(5):525–8

L

610. Lacey JH (1990). Incest, incestuous fantasy & indecency. A clinical catchment area study of normal-weight bulimic women. Br J Psychiatry 157:399–403

611. Ladwig GB, Anderson MD (1989). Substance abuse in women: relationship between chemical dependency in women and past reports of physical and sexual abuse. International Journal of the Addictions, 24: 739–744

612. Lake-White J, Kline CM (1985). Treating the dissociative process in adult victims of childhood incest. Social Case Work 66:394–402

613. Lancet (2001). Editorial 358:854–6

614. Lancet (2002). Just how tainted has medicine become? Editorial 359:1167

615. Langeland W, Hartgers C (1998). Child sexual and physical abuse and alcoholism: a review. Journal of Studies on Alcoholism 59:336–48

617. Langevin R, Wright P, Handy L (1989). Characteristics of sex offenders who were sexually victimized as children. Annals of Sex Research (now Journal of Sexual Abuse) 3:187–204.

618. Langevin R, Paitich D, Orchard B, Handy L, Russon A (1983). Childhood and family background of killers seen for psychiatric assessment: a controlled study. Bull Am Acad Psychiatry Law 11(4):331–41

619. Lansford JE, Dodge KA, Pettit GS, Bates JE, Crozier J, Kaplow J (2002). A 12-year prospective study of the long-term effects of early child physical maltreatment on psychological, behavioral, and academic problems in adolescence. Archives of Pediatric and Adolescent Medicine 156:824–830

620. Lanz JB (1995). Psychological, behavioral, and social characteristics associated with early forced sexual intercourse among pregnant adolescents. Journal of Interpersonal Violence 10 (2):188–200

621. Laporte L, Guttman H (2001). Abusive relationships in families of women with borderline personality disorder, anorexia nervosa and a control group. J Nerv Ment Dis 189(8):522–31

622. Lau JT, Chan KK, Lam PK, Choi PY, Lai KY (2003). Psychological correlates of physical abuse in Hong Kong Chinese adolescents. Child Abuse & Neglect 27(1):63–75

623. The Leadership Council on Child Abuse & Interpersonal Violence (2004). *http://www.leadership-council.org/* (excellent material and advocacy for childhood trauma survivors)

624. Leavitt F (2002). Personal communication. Chicago

625. Lebelle L (2001). Personality disorders. Focus Adolescent Services, MD

626. Lebowitz L, Harvey M, Herman JL (1993). A stage-by-dimension model of recovery from psychological trauma. J. Interpersonal Violence 8:378–391

627. Lechner ME, Vogel ME, Garcia-Shelton LM, Leichter JL, Steibel KR (1993). Self-reported medical problems of adult female survivors of childhood sexual abuse. J Fam Pract 36(6):633–8

628. Lecklitner GL, Malik NM, Aaron SM, Lederman CS (1999). Promoting safety for abused children and battered mothers: Miami-Dade County's modeled dependency court intervention program. Child Maltreatment 4(2):175–182

629. Lecrubier Y, Clerc G, Didi R, et al. Efficacy of St. John's wort extract WS 5570 in major depression: a double-blind, placebo-controlled trial. American Journal of Psychiatry 159:1361–1366

630. Lee JKP, Jackson HJ, Pattison P, Ward T (2002). Developmental risk factors for sexual offending. Child Abuse & Neglect 26:73–92

631. Lehrman NS (2002). Dead Wrong: The drug treatment of depression is one of the great fallacies in the history of medicine. *Redflagsweekly.com*, August 15

632. Lehtinen V et al. (2000). Two-year follow-up of first episode psychosis treated according to an integrated model: Is immediate neuroleptisation always needed? European Psychiatry 15(5): 312–320

633. Leifer M, Shapiro JP, Kassem L (1993). The impact of maternal history and behavior upon foster placement and adjustment in sexually abused girls. Child Abuse & Neglect 17, 755–766

634. Leifer M, Shapiro JP (1995). Longitudinal study of the psychological effects of sexual abuse in African-American girls in foster care and those who remain at home. Journal of Child Sexual Abuse 4:27–44

635. Leserman J, Li Z, Drossman DA, Hu YJ (1998). Selected symptoms associated with sexual and physical abuse history among female patients with gastrointestinal disorders: the impact on subsequent health care visits. Psychol Med 28(2):417–25

636. Leserman J, Li Z, Drossman DA, Li Z (1998). The reliability and validity of a sexual and physical abuse history questionnaire in female patients with gastrointestinal disorders. Behavioral Medicine 21:141–50

637. Levine P, Eckberg M (2000). Victims of Cruelty: Somatic psychotherapy in the treatment of post-traumatic stress disorder. North Atlantic Books, NY

638. Levitan RD, Rector NA, Sheldon T, Goering P (2003). Childhood adversities associated with major depression and/or anxiety disorders in a community sample of Ontario: issues of co-morbidity and specificity. Depress Anxiety 17(1):34–42

639. Leverich GS, McElroy SL, Suppes T, Keck PE Jr, Denicoff KD, Nolen WA, Altshuler LL, Rush AJ, Kupka R, Frye MA, Autio KA, Post RM (2002). Early physical and sexual abuse associated with an adverse course of bipolar illness. Biol Psychiatry 51(4):288–97

640. Lewontin R, Rose S, Kamin L (1984). Not in our genes: biology, ideology, and human nature. Pantheon, NY

641. Lewis DO, Moy E, Jackson LD (1985). Biopsychosocial characteristics of children who later murder: a prospective study. American Journal of Psychiatry 142:1161–7

642. Lewis-Fernandez R, Garrido-Castillo P, Bennasar MC, Parrilla EM, Laria AJ, Ma G, Petkova E (2002). Dissociation, childhood trauma, and *ataque de nervios* among Puerto Rican psychiatric outpatients. Am J Psychiatry 159(9):1603–5

643. Lexclrin J, Bero LA, Djulbergovic B, Clark O (2003). Pharmaceutical industry sponsorship & research outcome & quality: systemic review BMJ 326:1–9

644. Lindberg FH, Distad LJ (1985). Post-traumatic stress disorders in women who experienced childhood incest. Child Abuse & Neglect 9:329

645. Lindberg FH, Distad LJ (1985). Survival responses to incest: adolescents in crisis. Child Abuse & Neglect 9(4):521–6

646. Lindenmayer JP, Bernstein-Hyman R, Grochowski S (1994). Five-factor model of schizophrenia. Initial validation. J Nerv Ment Dis 182(11):631–8

647. Lipman EL, McMillan HL, Boyle MH (2001). Childhood abuse and psychiatric disorders among single and married mothers. Am J Psychiatry 158:73–77

648. Lipschitz D, Kaplan M, Sorkenn J, Faedda G, Chorney P, Asnis G (1996). Prevalence and characteristics of physical and sexual abuse among psychiatric outpatients. Psychiatric Services 47:189–91.

649. Lipschitz D, Winegar R, Nicolaou A, Hartnick, E, Wolfson M, Southwick S (1999). Perceived abuse and neglect as risk factors for suicidal behavior in adolescent inpatients. Journal of Nervous and Mental Disease 187:32–39

650. Lipschitz DS, Rasmusson AM, Anyan W, Cromwell P, Southwick SM (2000). Clinical and functional correlates of post-traumatic stress disorder in urban adolescent girls at a primary care clinic. J Am Acad Child Adolesc Psychiatry Sep; 39(9):1104–11

651. Livingston R (1987). Sexually and physically abused children. Journal of the American Academy of Child and Adolescent Psychiatry 26 (3):413–5

652. Lo B, Wolf LE, Berkeley A (2000). Conflict-of-interest policies for investigators in clinical trials. New England Journal of Medicine 343:1616–20

653. Lobel CM (1992). Relationship between childhood sexual abuse and borderline personality disorder in women psychiatric inpatients. Journal of Child Sexual Abuse 1:63–80

654. Lochner C, du Toit PL, Zungu-Dirwayi N, Marais A, van Kradenburg J, Seedat S, Niehaus DJ, Stein DJ (2002). Childhood trauma in obsessive-compulsive disorder, trichotillomania, and controls. Depress Anxiety 15(2):66–8

655. Loftus EF, Polonsky S, Thompson, T, Fullilove, M. (1994). Memories of childhood sexual abuse. Psychology of Women Quarterly 18:67–84

656. Ludolph PS, Westen D, Misle B, Jackson A, Wixom J, Wiss FC (1990). The borderline diagnosis in adolescents: symptoms and developmental history. Am J Psychiatry 147(4):470–6

657. Lukianowicz N (1972). Incest. British Journal of Psychiatry 120:301–13

658. Lundberg O (1993). The impact of childhood living conditions on illness and mortality in adulthood. Soc Sci Med 36(8):1047–52

659. Lundberg-Love PK, Marmion S, Ford K, Geffner R, Peacock L (1992). The long-term consequences of childhood incestuous victimization upon adult women's psychological symptomatology. Journal of Child Sexual Abuse 1:81–102 107

660. Luntz BK, Widom CS (1994). Antisocial personality disorder in abused and neglected children grown up. American Journal of Psychiatry 151:670–674.

661. Lynskey MT, Fergusson DM (1997). Factors protecting against the development of adjustment difficulties in young adults exposed to childhood sexual abuse. Child Abuse & Neglect 21(12): 1177–90

662. Lyons-Ruth K, Jacobvitz D (1999). Attachment disorganization: Unresolved loss, relational violence, and lapses in behavioral and attentional strategies. In J Cassidy & PR Shaver (eds.) Handbook of attachment: theory, research, and clinical applications (pp. 520–554). Guilford Press, New York

663. Lysaker PH, Meyer PS, Evans JD, Clements CA, Marks KA (2001). Childhood sexual trauma and psychosocial functioning in adults with schizophrenia. Psychiatric Services 52:1485–8

664. Lysaker PH, Wright DE, Clements CA, Plascak-Hallberg CD (2002). Neurocognitive and psychosocial correlates of hostility among persons in a post-acute phase of schizophrenia spectrum disorders. Compr Psychiatry 43(4):319–24

665. Lysaker PH, Wickett AM, Lancaster RS, Davis LW (2004). Neurocognitive deficits and history of childhood abuse in schizophrenia spectrum disorders: Associations with Cluster B personality traits. Schizophrenia Research, in press

M

667. MacEwen KE (1994). Refining the intergenerational transmission hypothesis. Journal of Interpersonal Violence 9:350–365

668. Macfie J, Cicchetti D, Toth SL (2001). Dissociation in maltreated versus nonmaltreated preschool-aged children. Child Abuse & Neglect 25(9):1253–67

669. Macfie J, Cicchetti D, Toth SL (2001). The development of dissociation in maltreated preschool-aged children. Dev Psychopathol. Spring; 13(2):233–54

670. MacMillan HL, Fleming JE, Trocme N, Boyle MH, Wong M, Racine YA, Beardslee WR, Offord DR (1997). Prevalence of child physical and sexual abuse in the community: Results from the Ontario Health Supplement. Journal of the American Medical Association, 278, 131–135

671. MacMillan HL, Fleming JE, Streiner DL, Lin E, Boyle MH, Jamieson E, Duku EK, Walsh CA, Wong MY, Beardslee WR (2001). Childhood abuse and lifetime psychopathology in a community sample. Am J Psychiatry 158(11):1878–83

672. Magdol L, Moffitt TE, Caspi A, Newman DL, Fagan J, Silva PA (1997). Gender differences in partner violence in a birth cohort of 21-year-olds: Bridging the gap between clinical and epidemiological approaches. J Consult Clin Psychol. 65(1):68–7

673. Malinosky-Rummell R, Hansen D (1993). Long-term consequences of childhood physical abuse. Psychological Bulletin 114.68–79

674. Mancini C, Van Ameringen M, MacMillan H (1995). Relationship of childhood sexual and physical abuse to anxiety disorders. Journal of Nervous and Mental Disease 183:309–314

675. Mangweth B, Pope HG Jr, Hudson JI, Olivardia R, Kinzl J, Biebl W (1997). Eating disorders in Austrian men: an intracultural and crosscultural comparison study. Psychother Psychosom 66(4):214–21

676. Manly J, Cichetti D, Barnett D (1994). The impact of subtype, frequency, chronicity, and severity of child maltreatment on social competency and behavior problems. Development and Psychopathology 6:121–4

677. Mann SJ (1999). Healing Hypertension: A Revolutionary New Approach. John Wiley & Sons

678. Margison F (2003). Evidence-based medicine in the treatment of schizophrenia. J Amer Acad Psycho analysis & Dynamic Psychiatry 31(1):177–90

679. Marks IM (1989). The gap between research and policy in mental health care. Journal of the Royal Society of Medicine 82:514–7

680. Marshall RD, Schneier FR, Lin SH, Simpson HB, Vermes D, Liebowitz M (2000). Childhood trauma and dissociative symptoms in panic disorder. Am J Psychiatry 157(3):451–3

681. Martinez A, Israelski D, Walker C, Koopman C (2002). PTSD in women attending human immunodeficiency virus outpatient clinics. AIDS Patient Care & STDs 16:283–91

682. Masterson JF (1988). The Search for the Real Self: Unmasking the personality disorders of our age. Free Press/MacMillan, NY

683. McCann IL, Pearlman LA (1990). Psychological Trauma and the Adult Survivor: Theory, therapy, and transformation. Brunner/Mazel, NY

684. McCauley J, Kern DE, Kolodner K, Dill L., Schroeder AF, DeChant HK, Ryden J, Derogatis L, Bass EB (1997). Clinical characteristics of women with a history of childhood abuse: unhealed wounds. Journal of the American Medical Association 277 (17):1362–1368

685. McClelland L, Mynors-Wallis L, Fahy T, Treasure J (1991). Sexual abuse, disordered personality and eating disorders. Br J Psychiatry Suppl. May (10) 158:63–8

686. McGee D, Wolfe D, Wilson S (1997). Multiple maltreatment experience and adolescent behavior problems: adolescents' perspectives. Development and Psychopathology 9:131–49

687. McGorry PD, Mihalopoulos C, Henry L, Dakis J, Jackson HJ, Flaum M, Harrigan S, McKenzie D, Kulkarni J, Karoly R (1995). Spurious precision: procedural validity of diagnostic assessment in psychotic disorders. Am J Psychiatry 152(2):220–3

688. McKenna C, Ross C (1994). Diagnostic conundrums in substance abusers with psychiatric symptoms: variables suggestive of dual diagnosis (1994). Am J Drug Alcohol Abuse 20(4):397–412

689. McLean LM, Gallop R (2003). Implications of childhood sexual abuse for adult borderline personality disorder and complex PTSD. American Journal of Psychiatry 160:369–371

690. McLeer SV, Deblinger E, Atkins MS, Foa EB, Ralphe DL (1988) Post-traumatic stress disorder in sexually abused children. Journal of the American Academy of Child and Adolescent Psychiatry 27:650–4

691. Mechanic D, Hansell S (1989). Divorce, family conflict, and adolescents' well-being. J Health Soc Behav 30(1):105–16

692. Medawar C (2004). The antidepressant Web—Marketing depression and making medicines work. The current version can be viewed and/or downloaded from this site (*http://www.socialaudit. org.uk*). The original printed version, published in International Journal of Risk & Safety in Medicine (1997) can also be ordered either from Social Audit or from the publishers.

693. Medawar C (1996). Drug education materials for children—are they good enough? In Proc. USP Open Conference, Reston, Va., Sep 29–Oct 1, Children & Medicines: Information isn't just for grown-ups, available from US Pharmacopeia, 12601 Twinbrook Parkway, Rockville, Md 20852, USA

694. Medawar C (1996). Secrecy and medicines. Int J Risk & Safety in Medicine 9:133–141; Medawar C (1993). Drugs, secrecy and society (editorial). BMJ 306:6870, 81–82

695. Medawar C (1994). Defining risk and patients' perceptions of risk, in Proc. USP Open Conference, Communicating risks to patients, Washington DC, available from US Pharmacopeia, 12601 Twinbrook Parkway, Rockville, Md 20852, USA

696. Medawar C (1994). Through the doors of deception? Nature 368:369–370.

697. Medawar C, Hardon A (2004). Medicines out of control? Antidepressants and the conspiracy of goodwill. Transaction Publishers, NY (Askart in Netherlands)

698. Meiselman KC (1980). Personality characteristics of incest history psychotherapy patients: a research note. Arch Sex Behav 9(3):195–7

699. Melander H, Ahlqvist-Rastad J, Meijer G, Beermann B (2003). Evidence b(i)ased medicine—selective reporting from studies sponsored by pharmaceutical industry: review of studies in new drug applications. BMJ 2003 326(7400):1171–3

700. Mennen FE, Meadow D (1995). The relationship of abuse characteristics to symptoms in sexually abused girls. Journal of Interpersonal Violence 10(3):259–74

701. Messman-Moore TL, Long PJ, Siegfried NJ (2000). The revictimization of child sexual abuse survivors: an examination of the adjustment of college women with child sexual abuse, adult sexual assault, and adult physical abuse. Child Maltreatment 5(1):18–27

702. Merrill LL, Thomsen CJ, Gold SR, Milner, JS (2001). Childhood abuse and premilitary sexual assault in male Navy recruits. Journal of Consulting and Clinical Psychology 69:252–261

703. Merrill LL, Thomsen CJ, Sinclair BB, Gold SR, Milner JS (2001). Predicting the impact of child sexual abuse on women: the role of abuse severity, parental support, and coping strategies. J Consult Clin Psychol 69(6):992–1006

704. Merikangas KR, Stolar M, Stevens DE, Goulet J, Presig MA, Fenton B, Zhang H, O'Malley SS, Rounsaville BJ (1998). Familial transmission of substance abuse disorders. Archives of General Psychiatry 55:973–979

705. Mertin P, Mohr PB (2002). Incidence and correlates of post-trauma symptoms in children from backgrounds of domestic violence. Violence Vict. 17(5):555–67

706. Metcalfe M, Oppenheimer R, Dignon A, Palmer RL (1990). Child sexual experiences reported by male psychiatric patients. Psychological Medicine 20:925–9

707. Miller BA, Downs WR, Gondoli DM, Keil A (1987). The role of childhood sexual abuse in the development of alcoholism in women. Violence and Victims 2:157–172

708. Miller BA, Downs WR, Testa M (1993). Interrelationships between victimization experiences and women's alcohol use. Journal of Studies on Alcohol, Supplement no.11, pp. 109–117

709. Miller J, Moeller D, Kaufman A, Divasto P, Fitzsimmons P, Prather D, Christi J (1978). Recidivism among sexual assault victims. American Journal of Psychiatry 135:1003–4

710. Miller J (2002). Personal communication. Philadelphia, PA

711. Miller LJ, Finnerty M (1996). Sexuality, pregnancy, and childrearing among women with schizophrenia-spectrum disorders. Psychiatr Serv 47(5):502–6

712. Mindfreedom (2003). American Psychiatric Association issues a 2nd statement today about hunger strike. Mindfreedom Online, *http://www.mindfreedom.org/mindfreedom/hungerstrikeapa2nd.shtml*

713. Modestin J, Oberson B, Erni T (1997). Possible correlates of *DSM-III-R* personality disorders. Acta Psychiatr Scand 96(6):424–30

713a. Modrow J (1992 & 5). How to Become a Schizophrenic: The case against biological psychiatry. Apollyon Press, Everett, Washington

714. Moeller TP, Bachman GL, Moeller JR (1993). The combined effects of physical, sexual, and emotional abuse during childhood: Long-term health consequences for women. Child Abuse & Neglect 17:623–640.

715. Moisan PA, Sanders-Phillips K, Moisan PM (1997). Ethnic differences in circumstances of abuse and symptoms of depression and anger among sexually abused black and Latino boys. Child Abuse & Neglect 21 (5):473–488

716. Molnar BE, Berkman LF, Buka SL (2001). Psychopathology, childhood sexual abuse and other childhood adversities: relative links to subsequent suicidal behaviour in the U.S. Psychol Med 31(6):965–77

717. Moncrieff J, Drummond D, Candy B, Checinski K, Farmer R, 1996. Sexual abuse in people with alcohol problems. A study of the prevalence of sexual abuse and its relationship to drinking behavior. British Journal of Psychiatry 169:355–360

718. Moncrieff J (1995). Lithium revisited (editorial) British J Psychiatry 167:569–74

719. Moncrieff J, Wessely S, Hardy R (1998). Meta-analysis of trials comparing antidepressants with active placebos. British Journal of Psychiatry 172: 227–231

720. Moncrieff J (1998). Forty years of lithium treatment. Arch Gen Psychiatry 55(1):92–3

721. Morin K, Rakatansky H, Riddick FA, Morse LJ, O'Bannon JM, Goldrich MS, Ray P, Weiss M, Sade RM, Spillman MA (2002). Managing conflicts of interest in the conduct of clinical trials. Journal of The American Medical Association 287:78–84

722. Morris R, Kratochwill T (1983). Treating children's fears and phobia: a behavioral approach. Pergamon Press

723. Morrison J (1989). Childhood sexual histories of women with somatization disorder. American Journal of Psychiatry 146:239–41

724. Morrow KB, Sorell GT (1989). Factors affecting self-esteem, depression, and negative behaviors in sexually abused female adolescents. Journal of Marriage and the Family 51:677–86

725. Morse DS, Suchman AL, Frankel RM (1997). The meaning of symptoms in 10 women with somatization disorder and a history of childhood abuse. Arch Fam Med 6(5):468–76

726. Mosher LR, Menn AZ (1978) Community residential treatment for schizophrenia: Two-year follow-up. Hosp Comm Psych 29:715–723

727. Mosher LR, Bola JR (2000). The Soteria project: Twenty-five years of swimming upriver. Complexity and Change 9:68–74.

728. Mosher LR (1999). Soteria and other alternatives to acute hospitalization: A personal and professional review. Jour Nerv Ment Dis 187:142–149

729. Mosher LR, Burti L (1994) Community mental health: A practical guide. W.W. Norton, NY. Matthews SM, Roper MT, Mosher LR, and Menn AZ (1979). A non-neuroleptic treatment for schizophrenia: Analysis of the two-year post-discharge risk of relapse. Schiz Bull 5:322–333

730. Mosher L, Valone R, Menn A (1995). The treatment of acute psychosis without neuroleptics: Six-week psychopathology outcome data from the Soteria project. International Journal of Social Psychiatry 41:157–73

731. Moss HB, Mezzich A, Yao JK, Gavaler J, Martin CS (1995). Aggressivity among sons of substance-abusing fathers: association with psychiatric disorder in the father and son, paternal personality, pubertal development, and socioeconomic status. Am J Drug Alcohol Abuse 21(2):195–208

732. Moyer D (1997). Childhood sexual abuse and precursors of binge eating in an adolescent female population. International Journal of Eating Disorders 21:23–30

733. Muenzenmaier K, Meyer I, Struening E, Ferber J (1993). Childhood abuse and neglect among women outpatients with chronic mental illness. Hospital and Community Psychiatry 44:666–70

734. Mueser KT, Goodman LB, Trumbetta SL, Rosenberg SD, Osher C, Vidaver R, Auciello P, Foy DW (1998). Trauma and post-traumatic stress disorder in severe mental illness. J Consult Clin Psychol 66(3):493–9

735. Mulder RT, Beautrais AL, Joyce PR, Fergusson DM (1998). Relationship between dissociation, childhood sexual abuse, childhood physical abuse, and mental illness in a general population sample. Am J Psychiatry 155(6):806–11

736. Mullen PE, Romans-Clarkson SE, Walton VA, Herbison GP (1988). Impact of sexual and physical abuse on women's mental health. Lancet 1(8590):841–5

737. Mullen PE, Linsell CR, Parker D (1986). Influence of sleep disruption and calorie restriction on biological markers for depression. Lancet Nov 8; 2(8515):1051–5

738. Mullen PE, Martin JL, Anderson JC, Romans SE, Herbison GP (1993). Childhood sexual abuse and mental health in adult life. British Journal of Psychiatry 163:721–32

739. Mullen PE, Romans-Clarkson SE, Walton VA, Herbison GP (1998). Impact of sexual and physical abuse on women's mental health. Lancet 1:841–845

740. Mullen PE, Martin JL, Anderson JC et al. (1996). The long-term impact of the physical, emotional, and sexual abuse of children: a community study. Child Abuse & Neglect 20:7–21

741. Murphy WD, Coleman E, Hoon E, Scott C (1980). Sexual dysfunction and treatment in alcoholic women. Sexuality and Disability 3:240–55

742. Murphy SM, Kilpatrick DG, Amick-McMullan A, Veronen LJ, Paduhovich J, Best CL, Villeponteaux LA, Saunders BE (1988). Current psychological functioning of child sexual assault survivors. Journal of Interpersonal Violence 3:55–79

743. Murray C, Waller G (2002). Reported sexual abuse and bulimic psychopathology among nonclinical women: the mediating role of shame. Int J Eat Disord 32(2):186–91

N _____

744. Nagata T, Kiriike N, Iketani T, Kawarada Y, Tanaka H (1999). History of childhood sexual or physical abuse in Japanese patients with eating disorders: relationship with dissociation and impulsive behaviours. Psychol Med 29(4):935–42

745. Nagata T, Kaye WH, Kiriike N, Rao R, McConaha C, Plotnicov KH (2001). Physical and sexual abuse histories in patients with eating disorders: a comparison of Japanese and American patients. Psychiatry Clin Neurosci 55(4):333–40

746. Nash M, Hulsey T, Sexton M, Harralson T, Lambert W (1993). Long-term sequelae of childhood sexual abuse: perceived family environment, psychopathology, and dissociation. Journal of Consulting and Clinical Psychology 61:276–283

747. Nelson EC, Heath AC, Madden PA, Cooper ML, Dinwiddie SH, Bucholz KK, Glowinski A, McLaughlin T, Dunne MP, Statham DJ, Martin NG (2002). Association between self-reported childhood sexual abuse and adverse psychosocial outcomes: results from a twin study. Arch Gen Psychiatry 59(2):139–45

748. Neumann DA, Houseamp BM, Poilace VE, Briere J (1996). The long-term sequelae of childhood sexual abuse in women: a meta-analysis review. Child Maltreatment 1:6–16

749. Neumark-Sztainer D, Story M, French SA, Resnick MD (1997). Psychosocial correlates of health compromising behaviors among adolescents. Health Educ Res 12(1):37–52

750. Neurnberger P (1981). Freedom from Stress: A holistic approach. Himalayan International Institute, Honesdale, PA

751. New AS, Yehuda R, Steinberg B, Trestman RL, Mitropoulou V, Coccaro EF, Siever LJ (1996). Self-reported abuse and biological measures in personality disorders. Biological Psychiatry 39:535

752. NIAAA (1974). National Institute on Alcohol and Alcohol Abuse: An assessment of the needs of and resources for children of alcoholic parents. (An extensive interview study of 50 CoAs.) Commissioned study by Booz, Allen and Hamilton, Rockville, MD

753. Nigg JT, Silk KR, Westen D, Lohr NE, Gold LJ, Goodrich S, Ogata S (1991). Object representations in the early memories of sexually abused borderline patients. Am J Psychiatry 148(7):864–9

754. Nijenhuis ER, van Dyck R, Spinhoven P, van der Hart O, Chatrou M, Vanderlinden J, Moene F (1999). Somatoform dissociation discriminates among diagnostic categories over and above general psychopathology. Aust N Z J Psychiatry 33(4):511–20

755. Nijenhuis ER, van Dyck R, ter Kuile MM, Mourits MJ, Spinhoven P, van der Hart O (2003). Evidence for associations among somatoform dissociation, psychological dissociation and reported trauma in patients with chronic pelvic pain. J Psychosom Obstet Gynaecol 24(2):87–98

756. Noblitt R, Perskin PS (2000). Cult and Ritual Abuse: Its history, anthropology, and recent discovery in contemporary America, Revised edition pp. 7–14. Praeger Publishing, Westport, CT

757. Norden KA, Klein DN, Donaldson SK, Pepper CM, Klein LM (1995). Reports of early home environment in *DSM-III-R* personality disorders. Journal of Personality Disorders 9:213–23

758. Norden MJ (1995). Beyond Prozac: Brain-toxic lifestyles, natural antidotes & new generation antidepressants. Regan Books/ HarperCollins, NY

759. Norton J (1982). Expressed emotion, affective style, voice tone and communication deviance as predictors of offspring schizophrenia spectrum disorders. Unpublished doctoral dissertation. Univ. California, Los Angeles

O

760. Ogata SN, Silk KR, Goodrich S, Lohr NE, Western D, Hill EM (1990). Childhood sexual and physical abuse in adult psychiatric patients with borderline personality disorder. American Journal of Psychiatry 147, 100–1013

761. Olivan G (2003). Catch-up growth assessment in long-term physically neglected and emotionally abused preschool aged male children. Child Abuse & Neglect 27:103–8

762. OReilly W (2002). Television and violence effect on children. Fox Channel documentary, April

763. Ouimette PC, Kimerling R, Shaw J, Moos RH (2000). Physical and sexual abuse among women and men with substance use disorders. Alcoholism Treatment Quarterly 18, 7–17

764. Ouimette PC, Wolfe J, Chrestman, KR (1996). Characteristics of PTSD-alcohol abuse comorbidity in women. Journal of Substance Abuse 8, 335–346

P

765. Palmer RL, Oppenheimer R, Dignon A, Chaloner DA, Howells K (1990). Childhood sexual experiences with adults reported by women with eating disorders: an extended series. Br J Psychiatry 156:699–703

766. Palmer RL, Chaloner DA, Oppenheimer R (1992). Childhood sexual experiences with adults reported by female psychiatric patients. British Journal of Psychiatry 160:261–5

767. Palmer RL, Bramble D, Metcalfe M, Oppenheimer R, Smith J (1994). Childhood sexual experiences with adults: adult male psychiatric patients and general practice attenders. British Journal of Psychiatry 165:675–9

768. Pam A (1995). Chapter 1. Biological psychiatry: science or pseudoscience? In Ross CA & Pam A: Pseudoscience in Biological Psychiatry. John Wiley, NY

769. Pam A (1990). A critique of the scientific status of biological psychiatry. Acta Psychiatrica Scandinavica 82:1–35 (Supp l362)

770. Paolucci EO, Genuis ML, Violato C (2001). A meta-analysis of the published research on the effects of child sexual abuse. J Psychol 135(1):17–36

771. Paradise JE, Rose L, Sleeper LA, Nathanson M (1994). Behavior, family function, school performance, and predictors of persistent disturbance in sexually abused children. Pediatrics 93(3):452–9

772. Paris J, Zweig-Frank H, Guzder J (1994). Risk factors for borderline personality in male outpatients. J Nerv Ment Dis 182(7):375–80

773. Paul T, Schroeter K, Dahme B, Nutzinger DO (2002). Self-injurious behavior in women with eating disorders. Am J Psychiatry Mar; 159(3):408–11

774. Pearlman LA (2001). Chapter 9. Treatment of persons with complex PTSD and other trauma-related disruptions of the self. In Wilson JP, Friedman MJ, Lindey JD (eds). Treating Psychological Trauma and PTSD. Guilford, New York

775. Pears KC, Capaldi DM (2001). Intergenerational transmission of abuse: a two-generational prospective study of an at-risk sample. Child Abuse & Neglect 25(11):1439–61

776. Pelcovitz D, Kaplan S, Goldenberg B, Mandel F, Lehane J, Guarrera J (1994). Post-traumatic stress disorder in physically abused adolescents. J Am Acad Child Adolesc Psychiatry 33(3):305–12

777. Pelcovitz D, Kaplan SJ, DeRosa RR, Mandel FS, Salzinger S (2000). Psychiatric disorders in adolescents exposed to domestic violence and physical abuse. Am J Orthopsychiatry 70(3):360–9

778. Pelletier G, Handy L (1999). Chapter 3. Is family dysfunction more harmful than child sexual abuse? A controlled study. In Bagley C, Mallick K (eds.) Child Sexual Abuse in Adult Offenders: New Theory and Research (pp 143–158). Ashgate International, Brookfield, VT

779. Pelletier KR (1977). Mind as Healer. Mind as Slayer: A holistic approach to preventing stress disorders. Delta, NY

780. Pennebaker JW (1999). The effects of traumatic disclosure on physical and mental health: the values of writing and talking about upsetting events. Int J Emerg Ment Health 1(1):9–18

781. Pennebaker JW (2000). Telling stories: the health benefits of narrative. Literature and Medicine 19(1):3–18

782. Perkins DF, Luster (1999). The relationship between sexual abuse and purging: findings from community-wide surveys of female adolescents. Child Abuse & Neglect 23(4):371–82

783. Perry BD (2000). The neurodevelopmental impact of violence in childhood. In D. Schetky & E. Benedek (eds.), Textbook of Child and Adolescent Forensic Psychiatry. American Psychiatric Press, Inc. Washington, DC (available on the Web at:

784. Perry BD (1994). Neurobiological sequelae of childhood trauma: post-traumatic stress disorders in children. In M. Murberg (ed.), Catecholamines in Post-traumatic Stress Disorder: Emerging Concepts. (pp. 253–276). American Psychiatric Press, Washington, DC

785. Perry BD (1999). The memories of states: how the brain stores and retrieves traumatic experience. In J.M. Goodwin & R. Attias (eds.), Splintered Reflections: Images of the Body in Trauma. (pp. 9–38). Basic Books, NY

787. Perry BD, Pollard R (1998). Homeostasis, stress, trauma, and adaptation: A neurodevelopmental view of childhood trauma. Child and Adolescent Psychiatric Clinics of North America, 7, 33–51

788. Perry BD, Azad I (1999). Post-traumatic stress disorders in children and adolescents. Current Opinion in Pediatrics 11:310–16

789. Perry JW (1953/87). The Self in Psychotic Process. Spring Publications, Dallas, TX

790. Perry JC, Herman JL (1992). Trauma and defense in the etiology of borderline personality disorder. In Paris J (ed.), Etiology of borderline personality disorder. American Psychiatric Press Washington, DC 123–140

791. Peters SD (1988). Child sexual abuse and later psychological problems in G Wyatt & G Powell (eds.) The Lasting Effects of Child Sexual Abuse (pp119–123). Sage, Thousand Oaks, CA

792. Petersen M (2003). Court papers suggest scale of drug's use [Neurontin]. NY Times, 30 May

793. Pettigrew J, Burcham J (1997). Effects of childhood sexual abuse in adult female psychiatric patients. Aust N Z J Psychiatry 31(2):208–13

794. Pharris MD, Resnick MD, Blum RW (1997). Protecting against hopelessness and suicidality in sexually abused American Indian adolescents, Journal of Adolescent Health, vol. 21, no. 6, pp. 400–406

795. Pollock VE, Briere J, Schneider L, Knop J, Mednick SA, Goodwin DW (1990). Childhood antecedents of antisocial behavior ; parental alcoholism and physical abusiveness. Am J Psychiatry 147(10):1290–3 / CPA > violence & aggression 131 CT v 70 controls Add

796. Pope HG Jr, Hudson JI (1992). Is childhood sexual abuse a risk factor for bulimia nervosa? Am J Psychiatry 149(4):455–63

797. Pope HG Jr, Hudson JI (1995). Can memories of childhood sexual abuse be repressed? Psychol Med. 25(1):121–6

798. Pope HG Jr, Hudson JI, Bodkin JA, Oliva P (1998). Questionable validity of "dissociative amnesia" in trauma victims. Evidence from prospective studies. Br J Psychiatry 172:210–5; discussion 216–7

800. Pope KS, Brown L (1995). Recovered Memories of Abuse: Assessment, therapy, forensics. American Psychological Association, Wash, DC

801. Portegijs PJM, Jueken FMH, van der Horst FG, Kraan HF, Knotterus JA (1996). A troubled youth: Relations with somatization, depression and anxiety in adulthood. Family Practice 13:1–11

802. Post RM, Leverich GS, Xing G, Weiss RB (2001). Developmental vulnerabilities to the onset and course of bipolar disorder. Dev Psychopathol 13(3):581–98

803. Potter-Efron R, Potter-Efron P (1989). Letting Go of Shame: Understanding how shame affects your life. Hazelden, Center City, MN

804. Potter-Efron R, Potter-Efron P (1995). Letting Go of Anger: The 10 most common anger styles and what to do about them. New Harbinger, NY

805. Power P, Elkins K, Adlard S, Curry C, McGorry P, Harrigan S (1998). Analysis of the initial treatment phase in first-episode psychosis. Br J Psychiatry Suppl 172(33):71–6

806. Preschers UM, Du Mont J, Jundt K, Pfurtner M, Dugan E, Kindermann G (2003). Prevalence of sexual abuse among women seeking gynecological care in Germany. Obstetrics & Gynecology 191:103–8

807. Prevent Child Abuse America (2001). Data available on *http://www.preventchildabuse.org/learn_more/research_docs/cost_analysis.pdf*

808. Pribor EF, Dinwiddie SH (1992). Psychiatric correlates of incest in childhood. American Journal of Psychiatry 149 (1) 52–56

809. Pribor EF, Yutzy SH, Dean JT, Wetzel RD (1993). Briquet's syndrome, dissociation, and abuse. Am J Psychiatry 150(10):1507–11

810. Putnam FW, Guroff JJ, Silberman EK, Barban L, Post RM (1986). The clinical phenomenology of multiple personality disorder: review of 100 recent cases. J Clin Psychiatry Jun; 47(6):285–93

811. Putnam FW (1998). Developmental pathways in sexually abused girls. Presented at Psychological Trauma: Maturational processes and psychotherapeutic interventions. March 20. Harvard Medical School, Boston MA

812. Putnam FW (2003). Ten-year research update review: child sexual abuse. J Am Acad Child Adolesc Psychiatry Mar; 42(3):269–78

Q

813. Quick J (2001). Maintaining the integrity of the clinical evidence base. Bulletin of the World Health Organization 79(12):1093

814. Quitkin FM (1999). Placebos, drug effects, and study design: A clinician's guide. Am J Psychiatry 156:829–836

R

815. Raczek SW (1992). Childhood abuse and personality disorders. Journal of Personality Disorders 6:109–16

816. Randall EJ, Josephson AM, Chowanec G, Thyer BA (1994). The reported prevalence of physical and sexual abuse among a sample of children and adolescents at a public psychiatric hospital. J Trauma Stress 7(4):713–8

817. Rasmussen A (1934). Die bedeutung sexueller attentate auf kinder unter 14. Acta Psychiat et Neurlog 9:351; summarized in Bender & Blau 1937

818. Read JP, Stern AL, Wolfe J, Ouimette PC (1997a). Use of a screening instrument in women's health care: detecting relationships among victimization history, psychological distress, and medical complaints. Women Health 25(3):1–17

819. Read J (1997). Child abuse and psychosis: a literature review and implications for professional practice. Professional Psychology: Research and Practice 28:448–56

820. Read J, Fraser A (1998a). Abuse histories of psychiatric inpatients: To ask or not to ask. Psychiatric Services 49:355–59

821. Read J, Fraser A (1998b). Staff response to abuse histories of psychiatric inpatients. Australian and New Zealand Journal of Psychiatry 32:206–13

822. Read J (1998). Child abuse and severity of disturbance among adult psychiatric inpatients. Child Abuse & Neglect 22:359–68

823. Read J, Perry BD, Moskowitz A, Connolly J (2001). The contribution of early traumatic events to schizophrenia in some patients: a traumagenic neurodevelopmental model. Psychiatry 64(4):319–45

824. Read J (May 2001). The Relationship between Child Abuse and Schizophrenia: Causal, contributory or coincidental? Paper presented at Royal Australian and New Zealand College of Psychiatrists 36th Annual Congress, Canberra

825. Read J, Ross CA (2003). Psychological trauma and psychosis: another reason why people diagnosed schizophrenic must be offered psychological therapies. J Am Acad Psychoanal Dyn Psychiatry 31(1):247–68

826. Regier DA, Farmer ME, Rae DS, Locke BZ, Keith SJ, Judd LL, Goodwin FK (1990). Comorbidity of mental disorders with alcohol and other drug abuse: Results from the epidemiologic catchment area (ECA) study. JAMA 264(19): 2511–2518

827. Regush N (2002). Prescribing untested drugs to children. NY Times April 3

828. Reidy TJ (1977). The aggressive characteristics of abused and neglected children. J Clin Psychol. 33(4):1140–5

829. Relman A (2001). Trust me, I'm a scientist. New Scientist 22 Sept. page 46–7

830. Resnick SG, Bond GR, Mueser KT (2003). Trauma and post-traumatic stress disorder in people with schizophrenia. J Abnorm Psychol. 112(3):415–23

831. Reto CS, Dalenberg CJ, Coe MT (1993). Dissociation and physical abuse as predictors of bulimic symptomatology and impulse dysregulation. Eating Disorders: the Journal of Treatment & Prevention 1(3–4) 226–239

832. Rew L (1989). Childhood sexual exploitation: long-term effects among a group of nursing students. Issues in Mental Health Nursing 10:181–191

833. Reynolds MW, Wallace, Hill, Weist MD, Nabors LA (2001). The relationship between gender, depression, and self-esteem in children who have witnessed domestic violence. Child Abuse & Neglect 25:1201–6

834. Richter J, Eisemann M (2001). Stability of memories of parental rearing among psychiatric inpatients: a replication based on EMBU subscales. Psychopathology 34:318–25

835. Riggs S, Alario AJ, McHorney C (1990). Health risk behaviors and attempted suicide in adolescents who report prior maltreatment. J Pediatr 116(5):815–21

836. Rinne T, de Kloet ER, Wouters L, Goekoop JG, de Rijk RH, van den Brink W (2003). Fluvoxamine reduces responsiveness of HPA axis in adult female BPD patients with a history of sustained childhood abuse. Neuropsychopharmacology 28(1):126–32

837. Roberts GL, Lawrence JM, Williams GM, Raphael B (1998). The impact of domestic violence on women's mental health. Australian and New Zealand of Public Health 22:796–801

838. Robins LN, Schoenberg SP, Holmes SJ, Ratcliff KS, Benham A, Works J (1985). Early home environment and retrospective recall: A test for concordance between siblings with and without psychiatric disorders. American Journal of Orthopsychiatry 55, 27–41.

839. Robin RW, Chester B, Rasmussen JK, Jaranson JM, Goldman D (1997). Prevalence, characteristics and impact of childhood sexual abuse in a southwestern American Indian tribe. Child Abuse & Neglect 21(8):769–87

840. Robins L (1966). Deviant Children Grown Up. Williams and Wilkins, NY

841. Rodnick E, Goldstein M, Lewis J, Doane J (1984). Parental communication style, affect, and role as precursors of offspring schizophrenia-spectrum disorders. In N Watt, E Anthony, L Wynne, J Rolf, eds., Children at Risk for Schizophrenia. Cambridge University Press

842. Rodriguez N, Ryan SW, Rowan AB, Foy DW (1996). Post-traumatic stress disorder in a clinical sample of adult survivors of childhood sexual abuse. Child Abuse & Neglect Oct; 20(10):943–52

843. Roesler TA, McKenzie N (1994). Effects of childhood trauma on psychological functioning in adults sexually abused as children. Journal of Nervous and Mental Disease 182:145–150

844. Roesler T (1994). Reactions to disclosure of childhood sexual abuse: The effect on adult symptoms. Journal of Nervous and Mental Diseases 182, 618–624

845. Rohsenow DJ, Corbett R, Devine D (1988). Molested as children: a hidden contribution to substance abuse? Journal of Substance Abuse Treatment 5:13–18

846. Romans SE, Martin JL, Anderson JC, Herbison GP, Mullen PE (1995). Sexual abuse in childhood and deliberate self-harm. Am J Psychiatry Sep; 152(9):1336–42

847. Romans SE, Martin JL, Anderson JC, O'Shea ML, Mullen PE (1995a). Factors that mediate between child sexual abuse and adult psychological outcome. Psychol Med 25(1):127–42

848. Romans SE, Martin J, Mullen P (1996). Women's self-esteem, a community study of women who report and do not report childhood sexual abuse. British Journal of Psychiatry 169:696–704

849. Romans SE, Gendall KA, Martin JL, Mullen PE (2001). Child sexual abuse and later disordered eating: a New Zealand epidemiological study. Int J Eat Disord 29(4):380–92

850. Romans S, Belaise C, Martin J, Morris E, Raffi A (2002). Childhood abuse and later medical disorders in women. An epidemiological study. Psychother Psychosom 71(3):141–50

851. Roodman AA, Clum GA (2001). Revictimization rates and method variance: a meta-analysis. Clin Psychol Rev Mar; 21(2):183–204

852. Rorty M, Yager J, Rossotto E (1994). Childhood sexual, physical, and psychological abuse in bulimia nervosa. Am J Psychiatry 151(8):1122–6

853. Rorty M, Yager J, Rossotto E (1993). Why and how do women recover from bulimia nervosa? The subjective appraisals of forty women recovered for a year or more. Int J Eat Disord 14(3):249–60

854. Rorty M, Yager J, Rossotto E (1994a). Childhood sexual, physical, and psychological abuse and their relationship to comorbid psychopathology in bulimia nervosa. Int J Eat Disord 16(4):317–34

855. Rose S (2001). Moving on from old dichotomies: Beyond nature-nurture towards a lifetime perspective. British Journal of Psychiatry s3–s7.

856. Rose S, Peabody C, Stratigeas B (1991). Undetected abuse among intensive case management clients. Hospital and Community Psychiatry 42:499–50

857. Rose SM (1991). Acknowledging abuse backgrounds of intensive case management clients. Community Ment Health J 27(4):255–63

858. Rosen C, Ouimette P, Sheik J, Gregg JA, Moos R, (2002). The impact of physical or sexual abuse history on addiction treatment outcomes. Journal of Studies on Alcohol, 63 683–687

859. Rosenberg SD, Mueser KT, Friedman MJ, Gorman PG, Drake RE, Vidaver RM, Torrey WC, Jankowski (2001). Developing effective treatments for post-traumatic disorders among people with severe mental illness. Psychiatric Services 52(11):1453–61

860. Rosenfeld AA (1979). Incidence of a history of incest among 18 female psychiatric patients. American Journal of Psychiatry 136(6):791–5

861. Rosenthal PA, Rosenthal S (1984). Suicidal behavior by preschool children. American Journal of Psychiatry 141:520–5

862. Ross C, Pam A (eds.) (1995). Pseudoscience in Biological Psychiatry: Blaming the body. John Wiley, NY

863. Ross CA, Norton GR, Wozney K (1989). Multiple Personality Disorder: An analysis of 236 cases. Canadian Journal of Psychiatry 34(5):413–418

864. Ross CA, Miller SD, Reagor P, Bjornson L, Fraser GA, Anderson G (1990). Structured Interview Data on 102 Cases of Multiple Personality Disorder from Four Centers. American Journal of Psychiatry 147(5):596–601

865. Ross CA, Kronson J, Koensgen S, Barkman K, Clark P, Rockman G (1992). Dissociative Comorbity in 100 Chemically Dependent Patients. Hospital and Community Psychiatry 43:840–842

866. Ross CA, Anderson G, Clark P (1994). Childhood Abuse and the Positive Symptoms of Schizophrenia, Child and Adolescent Psychiatric Clinics of North America, 45 (5): May

867. Ross CA (2000). The Trauma Model: A solution to the problem of co-morbidity in psychiatry. Manitou Publications, Richardson, TX

868. Ross CA (1995). Chapter 2. Errors of logic in biological psychiatry. In Ross CA & Pam A: Pseudoscience in Biological Psychiatry. John Wiley, NY

869. Ross CA (1995). Chapter 3. Pseudoscience in the American Journal of Psychiatry. In Ross CA & Pam A: Pseudoscience in Biological Psychiatry. John Wiley, NY

870. Ross CA, Joshi S (1992). Schneiderian symptoms and childhood trauma in the general population. Compr Psychiatry 33(4):269–73

871. Roth S, Newman E, Pelcovitz D, van der Kolk B, Mandel FS (1997). Complex PTSD in victims exposed to sexual and physical abuse: Results from the *DSM-IV* field trial for post-traumatic stress disorder. J Trauma Stress 10(4):539–55

872. Rothschild B (2000). The Body Remembers: The psychophysiology of trauma and trauma treatment. Norton, NY

873. Rowan AB, Foy DW (1993). PTSD in child sexual abuse. Journal of Traumatic Stress 6:3–20

874. Rowan AB, Foy DW, Rodriguez N, Ryan S (1994). Post-traumatic stress disorder in a clinical sample of adults sexually abused as children. Child Abuse & Neglect 18:51–61

875. Roy A (1985). Early parental separation and adult depression. Archives of General Psychiatry 42:987–91

876. Roy A (1990). Personality variables in depressed patients and normal controls. Neuropsychobiology 23:119–123

877. Roy A (1996). Aetiology of secondary depression in male alcoholics. Br J Psychiatry 169:753–757

878. Roy A, DeJong J, Lamparski D, Linnoila M (1991). Mental disorders among alcoholics. Arch Gen Psychiatry 48:423–427

879. Roy A (1999). Childhood trauma and depression in alcoholics: Relationship to hostility. Journal of Affective Disorders 56(2–3); 215–8

880. Roy A (2002). Childhood trauma and neuroticism as an adult: possible implication for the development of the common psychiatric disorders and suicidal behaviour. Psychol Med 32(8):1471–4

881. Ruggiero KJ, Mc Leer SV, Dickson JF (2000). Sexual abuse characteristics associated with survivor psychopathology. Child Abuse & Neglect 24(7):951–64

882. Rullo D (2001). Personality disorders. Talk given at Rutgers University Institute on Alcohol and Drug Studies. New Brunswick, NJ

883. Runyon MK, Faust J, Orvaschel H (2002). Differential symptom pattern of post-traumatic stress disorder (PTSD) in maltreated children with and without concurrent depression. Child Abuse & Neglect 26(1):39–53

884. Runyon MK, Kenny MC (2002). Relationship of attributional style, depression, and post-trauma distress among children who suffered physical or sexual abuse. Child Maltreat Aug; 7(3):254–64

885. Russek LG, Schwartz GE (1997). Feelings of parental caring predict health status in midlife: A 35-year follow-up of the Harvard Mastery of Stress Study. J Behav Med 20(1):1–13

S

886. Sacco ML, Farber BA (1999). Reality testing in adult women who report childhood sexual and physical abuse. Child Abuse & Neglect 23(11):1193–203

887. Sadowski CM, Friedrich WN (2000). Psychometric properties of the Trauma Symptom Checklist for Children (TSCC) with psychiatrically hospitalized adolescents. Child Maltreatment 5(4):364–72

888. Safer DJ (2002). Design and reporting modifications in industry-sponsored comparative psychopharmacology trials. J Nerv Ment Dis 190(9):583–92

889. Safren SA, Gershuny BS, Marzol P, Otto MW, Pollack MH (2002). History of childhood abuse in panic disorder, social phobia, and generalized anxiety disorder. J Nerv Ment Dis 190(7):453–6

900. Saigh PA, Mroueh M, Bremner JD (1997). Scholastic impairments among traumatized adolescents. Behav Res Ther 35(5):429–36

901. Saigh PA, Yasik AE, Oberfield RA, Halamandaris PV, McHugh M (2002). An analysis of the internalizing and externalizing behaviors of traumatized urban youth with and without PTSD. J Abnorm Psychol 111(3):462–70

902. Salmon P, Skaife K, Rhodes J (2003). Abuse, dissociation, and somatization in irritable bowel syndrome: towards an explanatory model. J Behavioral Medicine 26(1):1–18

903. Salmon P, Al-Marzooqi SM, Baker G, Reilly J (2003). Childhood family dysfunction and associated abuse in patients with nonepileptic seizures: towards a causal model. Psychosomatic Medicine 65(4):695–700

904. Salter A (1995). Transforming Trauma: A guide to understanding and treating adult survivors of child sexual abuse. Sage, Thousand Oaks, CA

905. Salter D, McMillan D, Richards M, Talbot T, Hodges J, Bentovim A, Hastings R, Stevenson J, Skuse D (2003). Development of sexually abusive behaviour in sexually victimised males: a longitudinal study. Lancet 8;361(9356):471–6

906. Salzinger S, Kaplan S, Pelcovitz D, Samit C, Krieger R (1984). Parent and teacher assessment of children's behavior in child maltreating families. J Am Acad Child Psychiatry 23(4):458–64

907. Sanders B, McRoberts G, Tollefson C (1989). Childhood stress and dissociation in a college population. Dissociation 2:17–23

908. Sanders B, Giolas MH (1991). Dissociation and childhood trauma in psychologically disturbed adolescents. American Journal of Psychiatry 148:50–4

909. Sanders B, Moore DL (1999). Childhood maltreatment and date rape. Journal of Interpersonal Violence 14:115–24

910. Sanford M, Offord D, Boyle M, Pearce A (1992). Ontario child health study: social and school impairment in children age 6–16. Journal of the American Academy of Child and Adolescent Psychiatry 199:60–7

911. Sarno J (1982). Mind Over Back Pain: A Radically New Approach to Diagnosis and Treatment of Back Pain. Berkley Books, NY

912. Sarno J E (1991). Healing Back Pain. Warner Books, NY

913. Sansone RA, Gaither GA, Songer DA (2002). The relationships among childhood abuse, borderline personality, and self-harm behavior in psychiatric inpatients. Violence and Victims 17(1):49–55

914. Sansonnet-Hayden H, Haley G, Marriage K, Fine S (1987). Sexual abuse and psychopathology in hospitalized adolescents. J Am Acad Child Adolesc Psychiatry 26(5):753–7

915. Santa Mina EE, Gallop RM (1998). Childhood sexual and physical abuse and adult self-harm and suicidal behaviour: a literature review. Can J Psychiatry 43(8):793–800

916. Sapolsky RM (2000). Glucocorticoids and hippocampal atrophy in neuropsychiatric disorders. Arch Gen Psychiatry 57(10):925–35

917. Saunders BE, Villeponteaux LA, Lipovsky JA, Kilpatrick DG, Veronen IJ (1992). Child sexual assault as a risk factor for mental disorders among women: a community survey. Journal of Interpersonal Violence 7:189–204

918. Saunders BE, Hanson RF, Kilpatrick DG, Resnick H, Best CL (1991). Prevalence, case characteristics, & long-term psychological correlates of child rape among women: a national survey. Paper presented at the American Orthopsychiatric Association, Toronto, Canada

919. Saunders BE, Kilpatrick DG, Hanson RF, Resnick HS, Walker, ME (1999). Prevalence, case characteristics, and long-term psychological correlates of child rape among women: A national survey. Child Maltreatment 4(3), 187–200

920. Scaer RC (2002). The Body Bears the Burden: Trauma, Dissociation, and Disease. Haworth Press, NY

921. Scaer RC (in press for 2005). Trauma and Meaning: understanding your life (working title) North Atlantic Books, Berkeley, CA

922. Schaff KK, McCanne TR (1998). Relationship of childhood sexual, physical and combined sexual and physical abuse to adult victimization and PTSD. Child Abuse & Neglect 22:1119–33

923. Schaefer MR, Sobieraj K, Hollyfield RL (1988). Prevalence of childhood physical abuse in adult male veteran alcoholics. Child Abuse and Neglect 12:141–9

924. Schetky DH (1988). A review of the literature of the long-term effects of child sexual abuse. In RP Kluft (ed.), Incest Related Syndromes of Adult Psychopathology (pp. 35–54). American Psychiatric Press, Washington, DC

925. Schiffer F, Teicher MH, Papanicolaou AC (1995). Evoked potential evidence for right brain activity during recall of traumatic memories. Journal of Neuropsychiatry and Clinical Neurosciences 7:169–175

926. Schiraldi GR (2000). The PTSD Sourcebook. Lowell House, Los Angeles

927. Schmidt U, Tiller J, Treasure J (1993). Setting the scene for eating disorders: Childhood care, classification and course of illness. Psychological Medicine 23:663–672 203

928. Schore AN (2002). Dysregulation of the right brain: a fundamental mechanism of traumatic attachment and the psychogenesis of pot-traumatic stress disorder. Australian and New Zealand J Psychiatry 36:9–30

929. Schuck AM, Widom CS (2001). Childhood victimization and alcohol symptoms in females: causal inferences and hypothesized mediators. Child Abuse & Neglect 25:1069–92

930. Schuckit M (1983). Alcoholic patients with secondary depression. American Journal of Psychiatry 140 (6): 711–714

931. Schuckit M, Tipp J, Bergman M, Reich W, Hesselbrock V, Smith T (1997). Comparison of induced and independent major depressive disorders in 2,945 alcoholics. Am J Psychiatry 154:948–957

932. Schuckit MA (1999). New findings in the genetics of alcoholism. JAMA 281:1875–1876

933. Scott RL, Stone DA (1986). MMPI profile constellations in incest families. J Consult Clin Psychol Jun; 54(3):364–8

934. Scott RL, Stone DA (1986). MMPI measures of psychological disturbance in adolescent and adult victims of father-daughter incest. J Clin Psychol Mar; 42(2):251–9

935. Scott KD (1992). Childhood sexual abuse: impact on a community's mental health status. Child Abuse & Neglect 16(2):285–95

936. Sedney MA, Brooks B (1984). Factors associated with a history of childhood sexual experience in

a non-clinical female population. Journal of the American Academy of Child Psychiatry 23:215–8

937. Seligman MEP (1995). The effectiveness of psychotherapy: The Consumer Reports study. American Psychologist 50, 965–974. Available *http://www.apa.org/journals/seligman.html*

938. Sendi IB, Blomgren PG (1975). A comparative study of predictive criteria in the predisposition of homicidal adolescents. American Journal of Psychiatry 132:423–7

939. Seng MJ (1989). Child sexual abuse and adolescent prostitution: A comparative analysis. Adolescence xxiv (95) 24:665–75

940. Selye H (1974). Stress without Distress. Lippincott, NY

941. Shaunesey K, Cohen JL, Plummer B, Berman A (1993). Suicidality in hospitalized adolescents: relationship to prior abuse. Am J Orthopsychiatry 63(1):113–9

942. Sharav VH (2002). Conflicts of interest:14th tri-service clinical investigation symposium, US Army medical department and the Henry Jackson foundation for the advancment of military medicine May 5-7

943. Shea MT, Zlotnick C, Weisberg RB (1999). Commonality and specificity of personality disorder profiles in subjects with trauma histories. J Personal Disord 13(3):199–210

944. Shea MT, Zlotnick C, Dolan R, Warshaw MG, Phillips KA, Brown P, Keller MB (2000). Personality disorders, history of trauma, and post-traumatic stress disorder in subjects with anxiety disorders. Compr Psychiatry 41(5):315–25

945. Shearer SL, Peters CP, Quaytman MS, Ogden RL (1990). Frequency and correlates of childhood sexual and physical abuse histories in adult female borderline inpatients. American Journal of Psychiatry, 147: 214–16

946. Sheldrick C (1991). Adult sequelae of child sexual abuse. British Journal of Psychiatry 158 (10): 55–62

947. Shepard M, Raschick M (1999). How child welfare workers assess and intervene around issues of domestic violence. Child Maltreatment 4(2):148–156.

948. Shepherd M (1993). The placebo: from specificity to the non-specific and back. Psychological Medicine 23:569–78

949. Shepherd J, Farrington D, Potts J (2002). Relations between offending, injury and illness. J R Soc Med. 95(11):539–44

950. Sher KJ, Gershuny BS, Peterson L, Raskin G (1997). The role of childhood stressors in intergenerational transmission of alcohol use disorders. Journal of Studies on Alcohol 58:414–27

951. Shetky DH (1990). Chapter 3. A review of the long-term effects of childhood sexual abuse. In Kluft RP (ed.) Incest-Related Syndromes of Adult Psychopathology. American Psychiatric Press, NY

952. Shields A, Cicchetti D (1998). Reactive aggression among maltreated children: the contributions of attention and emotion dysregulation. Journal of Clinical Child Psychology 27:381–95

953. Shields A, Cicchetti D (2001). Parental maltreatment and emotion dysregulation as risk factors for bullying and victimization in middle childhood. Clinical Child Psychology 30(3):349–63

954. Shrier LA, Pierce JD, Emans SJ, DuRant RH (1998). Gender differences in risk behaviors associated with forced or pressured sex. Arch Pediatr Adolesc Med Jan; 152(1):57–63

954a. Schmitz JM, Schneider NG, Jarvik ME (1997). Chapter 25. Nicotine. In Lororinson et al. (eds.) Substance Abuse: A comprehensive textbook. Williams & Wilkins, Baltimore pp. 276–94

955. Shoemaker C, Smit F, Bijl RV, Vollebergh WAM (2002). Bulimia nervosa following psychological and multiple child abuse: support for self-medication hypothesis in a population-based cohort study. International Journal of Eating Disorders 32:381–8

956. Schultz RK, Braun BG, Kluft RP (1989). Multiple personality disorder: Phenomenology of selected variables in comparison to major depression. Dissociation 2, 45–51

957. Sidebotham P, Golding J (2001). Child maltreatment in the "children of the nineties" a longitudinal study of parental risk factors. Child Abuse & Neglect 25(9):1177–200

958. Siebert A (1999). Brain disease hypothesis disconfirmed by all evidence. J. of Ethical Human Sciences and Services 1(2) 179–199.

959. Siegel JM, Burham MA, Stein JA, Golding JM, Sorenson SB (1986). Sexual assault and psychiatric disorder: a preliminary investigation. A Report to the National Institute of Mental Health

960. Silberg JL (2000). Fifteen years of dissociation in maltreated children: where do we go from here? Child Maltreatment 5:119–136(18)

961. Silverman AB, Reinherz HZ, Giaconia, RM (1996). The long-term sequelae of child and adolescent abuse: A longitudinal community study. Child Abuse & Neglect 20:709–723

962. Simmel CA (2002). The effects of early maltreatment and foster care history on adopted foster youths' psychosocial adjustment. Dissertation Abstracts International Vol 63(2-A) Abstract: 2002–95015–160

963. Simos BG (1979). A Time to Grieve: Loss as a universal human experience. Family Services Association of America NY (One of the best books on grieving that I have read.)

964. Simpson TL, Westerberg VS, Little LM, Trujillo M (1994). Screening for childhood physical and sexual abuse among outpatient substance abusers. J. Subst Abuse Treat 11, 347–58

965. Simpson TL (2002). Women's treatment utilization and its relationship to childhood sexual abuse history and lifetime PTSD. Substance Abuse 23(1):17–30.

966. Sloane P, Karpenski E (1942). Effects of incest on the participants. American Journal of Orthopsychiatry 12:666–73

966a. Smith R (2003). Medical journals and pharmaceutical companies: uneasy bedfellows. British Medical Journal May 31; 326(7400):1202-5.

967. Song LY, Singer MI, Anglin TM (1998). Violence exposure and emotional trauma as contributors to adolescents' violent behaviors. Arch Pediatr Adolesc Med 152(6):531–6

968. Spiegel D (1990). Hypnosis, dissociation and trauma: hidden and overt observer. In Singer JL (ed.) Repression and Dissociation, Univ Chicago Press

969. Spiegel D (1993). Dissociation and trauma. In Spiegel D (ed.) Dissociative Disorders: A clinical review. Sidran Press, Lutherville, MD

970. Stahl SM (1998). Selecting an antidepressant by using mechanism of action to enhance efficacy & avoid side effects. Journal of Clinical Psychiatry 59 (suppl 18): 23–9

971. Startup M (1999). Schizotypy, dissociative experiences and childhood abuse: relationships among self-report measures. Br J Clin Psychol 38 (Pt 4):333–44

972. Smith D, Pearce L, Pringle M, Caplan R (1995). Adults with a history of child sexual abuse: Evaluation of a pilot therapy service. British Medical Journal 310:1175–78

973. Smolak L, Levine MP, Sullins E (1990). Are child sexual experiences related to eating disordered attitudes and behaviors in a college sample? Int'l J Eating Disorders 9:167–78

974. Smolak L, Murnen SK (2002). A meta-analytic examination of the relationship between child sexual abuse and eating disorders. Int J Eat Disord 31(2):136–50

975. Springs FE, Friedrich WN (1992). Health risk behaviors and medical sequelae of childhood sexual abuse. Mayo Clin Proc 67(6):527–32

976. Steiger H, Zanko M (1990). Sexual traumata among eating disordered, psychiatric, and normal female groups: Comparison of prevalences and defense styles. Journal of Interpersonal Violence 5:74–86

977. Steiger H, Gauvin L, Israel M, Koerner N, Ng Ying Kin NM, Paris J, Young SN (2001). Association of serotonin and cortisol indices with childhood abuse in bulimia nervosa. Arch Gen Psychiatry 58(9):837–43

978. Steiger H, Koerner N, Engelberg MJ, Israel M, Ng Ying Kin NM, Young SN (2001). Self-destructiveness and serotonin function in bulimia nervosa. Psychiatry Res 103(1):15–26

980. Steiger H, Young SN, Kin NM, Koerner N, Israel M, Lageix P, Paris J (2001). Implications of impulsive and affective symptoms for serotonin function in bulimia nervosa. Psychol Med 31(1):85–95

981. Stein D, Baldwin S (2000). Toward an operational definition of disease in psychiatry and psychology: Implications for diagnosis and treatment. The International Journal of Risk and Safety in Medicine Volume 13 (1):29–46

982. Stein JA, Golding JM, Siegel JM, Burnam MA, Sorenson SB (1988). Long-term psychological sequelae of child sexual abuse: the Los Angeles Epidemiologic Catchment Area Study. In Wyatt GE & Powell GJ (eds): Lasting Effects of Child Sexual Abuse (pp 135–154). Sage. Thousand Oaks, CA

983. Stein MB, Yehuda R, Koverola C, Hanna C (1997). Enhanced dexamethasone suppression of plasma cortisol in adult women traumatized by childhood sexual abuse. Biol Psychiatry Oct 15; 42(8):680–6

984. Stein MB, Koverola C, Hanna C, Torchia MG, McClarty B (1997a). Hippocampal volume in women victimized by childhood sexual abuse. Psychological Medicine 27:1–9

985. Stein MB, Walker JR, Anderson G, Hazen A, Ross CA, Eldridge G, Forde D (1996). Childhood physical and sexual abuse in patients with anxiety disorders and in a community sample. American Journal of Psychiatry 153(2):275–277

986. Steinberg B, Yehuda R, Trestman R, Mitropoulou V, Siever L (1993). Early abuse and biological measures in personality disorder patients. Biological Psychiatry 37:658

987. Steinhausen H (1995). Children of alcoholic parents. A review. European Child and Adolescent Psychiatry 4:1430–152

988. Stermac L, Reist D, Addison M, Miller GM (2002). Childhood risk factors for women's sexual victimization. Journal of Interpersonal Violenc 17(6):647–670

989. Stern AE, Lynch DL, Oates RK, O'Toole BI, Cooney G (1995). Self-esteem, depression, behavior and family functioning in sexually abused girls. Journal of Child Psychology and Psychiatry 36:1077–1089

990. Stets JE, Strauss MA (1989). The marriage license as a hitting license: a comparison of assaults in dating, co-habiting, and married couples. In MA Pirog-Good & JE Stets (eds.) Violence in Dating Relationships pp 33–52. Praeger, NY

991. Stevens SJ, Murphy BS, McKnight K (2003). Traumatic stress and gender differences in relationship to substance abuse, mental health, physical health, and HIV risk behavior in a sample of adolescents enrolled in drug treatment. Child Maltreatment 8(1):46–57

992. Stevenson J (1999). The treatment of the long-term sequelae of child abuse. J Child Psychol Psychiatry Jan; 40(1):89–111

993. Stien P, Kendall J (2002). Stress, Trauma and the Developing Brain: How the new neurobiology is leading to more effective interventions for troubled children. Haworth Press, Binghamton, NY

994. Stone MH (1981). Borderline syndromes: a consideration of subtypes and an overview: directions for research. Psychiatric Clinics of North America 4:3–24

995. Stone MH (1990). Chapter 9. Incest in the borderline patient. In Kluft RP (ed.) Incest-Related Syndromes of Adult Psychopathology. American Psychiatric Press, NY

996. Storosum JG, Elferink AJA, van Zwieten BJ, van der Vrink W, Gersons BPR, van Strik R, Broekmans AW (2001). Short-term efficacy of tricyclic antidepressants revisited: a meta-analytic study. European Neuropsychopharmacology 11:173–80

997. Straw RB (1982). Meta-analysis of deinstitutionalization (doctoral dissertation). University Microfilms, Northwestern University, Ann Arbor, MI

998. Striegel-Moore RH, Dohm FA, Pike KM, Wilfley DE, Fairburn CG (2002). Abuse, bullying, and discrimination as risk factors for binge eating disorder. Am J Psychiatry 159(11):1902–7

999. Stuart GW, Laraia MT, Ballenger JC, Lydiard B (1990). Early family experiences of women with bulimia and depression. Archives of Psychiatric Nursing 4:43–52

1000. Sullivan EV, Fama R, Rosenbloom MJ, Pfefferbaum A (2002). A profile of neuropsychological deficits in alcoholic women. Neuropsychology 16(1):74–83

1001. Summit RC (1983). The child sexual abuse accommodation syndrome. Child Abuse & Neglect 7:177–193

1002. Sundbom E, Henningsson M, Holm U, Soderbergh S, Evengard B (2002). Possible influence of defenses and negative life events on patients with chronic fatigue syndrome: a pilot study. Psychol Rep. 91(3 Pt 1):963–78

1003 . Surtees PG, Ingham JG (1980). Life stress and depressive outcome: Application of a dissipation model to life events. Social Psychiatry 15:21–31

1004 . Swanston HY, Tebbutt JS, O'Toole BI, Oates RK (1997). Sexually abused children 5 years after presentation: a case-control study. Pediatrics 100(4):600–8

1005. Swanston HY, Parkinson PN, Oates RK, O'Toole BI, Plunkett AM, Shrimpton S (2002). Further abuse of sexually abused children. Child Abuse & Neglect 26:115–27

1005. Swett C, Surrey J, Cohen C (1990). Sexual and physical abuse histories and psychiatric symptoms among male psychiatric outpatients. American Journal of Psychiatry 147(5):632–6

1006. Swett C, Cohen C, Surrey J, Compaine A, Chavez R (1991). High rates of alcohol use and history of physical and sexual abuse among women outpatients. American Journal of Drug and Alcohol Abuse 17:49–60

1007. Swett C, Halpert M (1993). Reported history of physical and sexual abuse in relation to dissociation and other symptomatology in women psychiatric inpatients. Journal of Interpersonal Violence 8(4):345–55, 1993

T

1008. Talbot N, Houghtalen R, Duberstein P, Cox C, Giles D, Wynne L (1999). Effects of group treatment for women with a history of childhood sexual abuse. Psychiatric Services 50:686–692.

1009. Taylor RR, Jason LA (2001). Sexual abuse, physical abuse, chronic fatigue, and chronic fatigue syndrome: a community-based study. Journal of Nervous and Mental Disease 189:709–715

1010. Tebbutt J, Swanston H, Oates RK, O'Toole BI (1997). Five years after child sexual abuse: persisting dysfunction and problems of prediction. J Am Acad Child Adolesc Psychiatry 36 (3): 330–9

1011. Teicher MH (2000). Wounds that time wouldn't heal: the neurobiology of childhood abuse. Cerebrum 2, 50–67

1012. Teicher MH, Glod CA, Surrey J, Swett C Jr (1993). Early childhood abuse and limbic system ratings in adult psychiatric outpatients. Journal of Neuropsychiatry and Clinical Neurosciences 5:301–306.

1013. Teicher MH, Ito YN, Glod CA, Schiffer F, Gelbard HA (1994). Early abuse, limbic system dysfunction, and borderline personality disorder. In K. Silk (ed.), Biological and Neurobehavioral Studies of Borderline Personality Disorder, 177–207, American Psychiatric Association Press

1014. Teicher MH, Ito YN, Glod CA, Andersen SL, Dumont N, Ackerman E (1997). Preliminary evidence for abnormal cortical development in physically and sexually abused children using EEG coherence and MRI. Annals New York Academy of Science 821:160–175

1015. Teicher MH, Ito Y, Glod CA, Schiffer F, Ackerman E (1994). Possible effects of early abuse on human brain development, as assessed by EEG coherence. Am J Neuropsychopharmacol 33, 52

1016. Terr LC (1991). Childhood traumas: an outline and overview American Journal of Psychiatry 148:10–20

1017. The Kept University (2000). Atlantic Monthly, March 285 (Part 1–4):3954

1018. Thompson A, Kaplan C (1999). Emotionally abused children presenting to child psychiatry clinics. Child Abuse & Neglect 23:191–196

1019. Thompson KM, Braaten-Antrim R (1998). Youth maltreatment and gang involvement. Journal of Interpersonal Violence 13:328–45

1020. Thompson KM, Wonderlich SA, Crosby RD, Mitchell JE (2001a). Sexual victimization and adolescent weight regulation practices: a test across three community-based samples. Child Abuse & Neglect Feb; 25(2):291–305

1021. Thompson KM, Wonderlich SA, Crosby RD, Mitchell JE (2001b). Sexual violence and weight control techniques among adolescent girls. Int J Eat Disord Mar; 29(2):166–76

1022. Thompson KM, Crosby RD, Wonderlich SA, Mitchell JE, Redland J, Demuth G, Smyth J, Haseltine B (2003). Psychopathology and sexual trauma in childhood and adulthood. Journal of Traumatic Stress 16:78–84

1023. Tienari P (1991). Interaction between genetic vulnerability and family environment. Acta Psychiatrica Scandinavica 84:460–65

1023a. Timimi S et al (2004). A critique of the international consensus statement on ADHD. Clinical Child & Family Psychology Review 7(1), March

1024. Timmermans S, Angell A (2001). Evidence-based medicine, clinical uncertainty, and learning to doctor. J Health Soc Behav 42(4):342–59

1025. Titus JC, Dennis ML, White WL, Scott CK, Funk RR (2003). Gender differences in victimization severity and outcomes among adolescents treated for substance abuse. Child Maltreat 8(1):19–35

1026. Tong L, Oates K, McDowell M (1987). Personality development following sexual abuse. Child Abuse & Neglect 11(3):371–83

1027. Toth SL, Manly JT, Cicchetti D (1992). Child maltreatment and vulnerability to depression. Development and Psychopathology 4:97–112

1028. Toth SL, Cicchetti D (1996). Patterns of relatedness, depressive symptomatology and perceived competence in maltreated children. Journal of Consultant and Clinical Psychology 64 (1):32–41

1029. Toth SL, Cicchetti D, Macfie J, Rogosch FA, Maughan A (2000). Narrative representations of moral-affiliative and conflictual themes and behavioral problems in maltreated preschoolers. J Clin Child Psychol 29(3):307–18

1030. Trickett PK, Susman EJ (1988). Parental perceptions of child-rearing practices in physically abusive and nonabusive families. Developmental Psychology 24, 270–276

1031. Trickett PK, McBride-Chang C, Putnam FW (1994). The classroom performance and behavior of sexually abused females. Development and Psychopathology 6:183–194

1032. Triffleman EG, Marmar CR, Delucci KI, Ronfeldt H (1995). Childhood trauma and post-traumatic stress disorder in substance abuse inpatients. Journal of Nervous and Mental Disease 183:172–6

1033. Trojan O (1994). Sexual experiences of psychotic patients. Int J Adolesc Med Health 7:209–17

1034. Trowell J, Kolvin I, Weeramanthri T, Sadowski H, Berelowitz M, Glasser, D, Leitch I (2002). Psychotherapy for sexually abused girls: psychopathological outcome findings and patterns of change. British Journal of Psychiatry 180:234–47

1035. Tsai M, Feldman-Summers S, Edgar M (1979). Childhood molestation: variables related to differential impacts on psychosexual functioning in adult women. Journal of Abnormal Psychology 88 (4): 407–417

1036. Tufts New England Medical Center, Child Psychiatry Division (1984). Sexually Exploited Children: Service and Research Project. Final Report of the Office of Juvenile Justice and Delinquency Prevention. US Department of Justice, Washington, DC

1037. Tuori T et al (1998). The Finnish National Schizophrenia Project 1981–1987: 10-year evaluation of its results. Acta Psychiatrica Scandinavica 97:10–18

1038. Turkheimer E (1998). Heritability and biological explanation. Psychological Review 105:782–9

U

1039. Ullman SE, Brecklin LR (2002). Sexual assault history and suicidal behavior in a national sample of women. Suicide Life Threat Behav Summer 32(2):117–30

1040. US Dept. of Health and Human Services: A Report of the Surgeon General—executive summary. Rockville, MD, 1999

V

1041. Vaa G, Egner R, Sexton H (2002). Sexually abused women after multimodal group therapy: a long-term follow-up study. Nord J Psychiatry 56:215–21

1042. Valenstein ES (1998). Blaming the Brain: the truth about drugs and mental health. Basic Books, NY

1043. Van Buskirk SS, Cole CF (1983). Characteristics of 8 women seeking therapy for effects of incest. Psychotherapy: Theory, Research, and Practice 20:503–514, 1983

1044. van der Kolk BA (1994). The body keeps the score: memory and the evolving psychobiology of post-traumatic stress. Harv Review of Psychiatry Jan-Feb 1(5):253–65

1045. van der Kolk BA, Fisler RE (1994). Childhood abuse and neglect and loss of self-regulation. Bulletin of the Menninger Clinic 58:145–68

1046. van der Kolk B, Fisler R (1995). Dissociation and the fragmentary nature of traumatic memories: Overview and exploratory study. Journal of Traumatic Stress, 8:505–52

1047. van Egmond M, Garnefski N, Jonker D, Kerkhof A (1993). The relationship between sexual abuse and female suicidal behavior. Crisis 14(3):129–39

1048. Van Etten ME, Taylor S (1998). Comparative efficacy of treatments for post-traumatic stress disorder: A meta-analysis. Clinical Psychology & Psychotherapy 5, 126–144

1049. Van Praag, H (1993). "Make-believes" in psychiatry, or the perils of progress. Clinical and Experimental Psychiatry Monograph No. 7. Brunner/Mazel, New York

1050. Villanueva P, Piero S, Librero J., Pereiro I (2003). Accuracy of pharmaceutical advertisements in medical practice. Lancet 361:27–32

1051. Vize CM, Cooper PJ (1995). Sexual abuse in patients with eating disorders, patients with depression and normal controls: a comparative study. British Journal of Psychiatry 167:80–85

W

1052. Waddington J. Cognitive dysfunction in schizophrenia: organic vulnerability factor or state marker for tardive dyskinesia? Brain and Cognition 23, 56–70

1053. Waldinger RJ, Swett C Jr, Frank A, Miller K (1994). Levels of dissociation and histories of reported abuse among women outpatients. J Nerv Ment Dis 182(11):625–30

1054. Walker E, Cudeck R, Mednick S, Schulsinger F (1981). Effects of parental absence and institutionalization on the development of clinical symptoms in high-risk children. Acta Psychiatrica Scandinvica 63:95–109

1055. Walker EA, Katon WJ, Hansom J, Harrop-Griffiths J, Holm L, Jones ML, Hickok L, Jemelka RP (1992). Medical and psychiatric symptoms in women with childhood sexual abuse. Psychosom Med 54(6):658–64

1056. Walker E, Diforio D, Baum, K (1998). Developmental neuropathology and the precursors of schizophrenia. Acta Psychiatric Scandinavica, 97:1–9

1057. Walker EA, Katon WJ, Nerass K, Jemelka RP, Massoth D (1992). Dissociation in women with chronic pelvic pain. American Journal of Psychiatry 149:534–7

1058. Walker EA, Gelfand AN, Gellfand MD, Koss MP, Katon WJ (1995). Medical and psychiatric symptoms in female gastroenterology clinic-patients with histories of sexual victimization. General Hospital Psychiatry 17:85–92

1059. Walker EA, Unutzer J, Rutter C, Gelfand A, Saunders K, Von Korff M, Koss MP, Katon W (1999). Costs of healthcare use by women HMO members with a history of childhood abuse and neglect. Archives of General Psychiatry 56:609–13.

1060. Walker EA, Gelfand A, Katon WJ, Koss MP, Von Korff M, Bernstein D, Russo J (1999). Adult health status of women with histories of childhood abuse and neglect. Am J Med 107(4):332–9

1061. Walker E, DiFornio D (1997). Schizophrenia: A neural diathesis-stress model. Psychological Review 104:667–85

1062. Wallen J, Berman K (1992). Possible indicators of childhood sexual abuse for individuals in substance abuse treatment. Journal of Child Sexual Abuse 1 (3): 63–74 217

1063. Waller G, Halek C, Crisp AH (1993). When is sexual abuse relevant to bulimic disorders? European Eating Disorders Review 1:143–51

1064. Waller G, Roddock A, Pitts C (1993). Sexual abuse as a factor in anorexia nervosa: evidence from two separate case series. J Psychosom Res 37(8):873–9

1065. Waller G (1994). Childhood sexual abuse and borderline personality disorder in the eating disorders. Child Abuse & Neglect 18(1):97–101

1066. Waller G, Meyer C, Ohanian V, Elliott P, Dickson C, Sellings J (2001). The psychopathology of bulimic women who report childhood sexual abuse: the mediating role of core beliefs. J Nerv Ment Dis 189(10):700–8

1067. Walling MK, Reiter RC, O'Hara MW et al. (1994). Abuse history & chronic pain in women: 1. prevalences of sexual abuse and physical abuse. Obstetrics & Gynecology 84:193–9

1068. Walling MK, O'Hara MW, Reiter RC et al. (1994). Abuse history & chronic pain in women: II A multi vanafe analysis of abuse and psychological morbidity. Obstetrics & Gynecology 84:200–6

1069. Walrath C, Ybarra M, Holden EW, Liao Q, Santiago R, Leaf (2003). Children with reported histories of sexual abuse: utilizing multiple perspectives to understand clinical and psychosocial profiles. Child Abuse & Neglect 27(5):509–24

1070. Warner R (ed.) (1995). Alternatives to the mental hospital for acute psychiatric treatment. American Psychiatric Press, Wash DC

1071. Weaver TL, Clum GA (1993). Early family environments and traumatic experiences with borderline personality disorder. Journal of Consulting and Clinical Psychology 61:1068–75

1072. Weinstein D, Staffelbach D, Biaggio M (2000). Attention-deficit hyperactivity disorder and posttraumatic stress disorder: differential diagnosis in childhood sexual abuse. Clin Psychol Rev 20(3):359–78

1073. Weiss MJ, Wagner SH (1998). What explains the negative consequences of adverse childhood experiences on adult health? Insights from cognitive and neuroscience research. Am J Prev Med 14(4):356–60

1074. Welch SL, Fairburn GC (1994). Sexual abuse and bulimia nervosa. American Journal of Psychiatry 151:402–7

1075. Welch SL, Fairburn CG (1996). Childhood sexual and physical abuse as risk factors for the development of bulimia nervosa: a community-based case control study. Child Abuse & Neglect 20(7):633–42

1076. Westen D, Ludolph P, Misle B, Ruffins S, Block J (1990). Physical and sexual abuse in adolescent girls with borderline personality disorder. Am J Orthopsychiatry 60(1):55–66

1077. Wexler B, Lyons L, Lyons H, Mazure C (1997). Physical and sexual abuse during childhood and development of psychiatric illness during adulthood. J Nerv Ment Dis 185:522–4

1078. Whealin JM, Jackson JL (2002). Childhood unwanted sexual attention and young women's present self-concept. Journal of Interpersonal Violence 17(8): 854–871

1079. Whiffen VE, Clark SE (1997). Does victimization account for sex differences in depressive symptoms? Br J Clin Psychol 36 (Pt 2):185–93

1080. Whitfield, BH (1995). Spiritual Awakenings: Insights of the near-death experience and other doorways to our soul. Health Communications, Deerfield Beach, FL

1081. Whitfield BH (1998). Final Passage: Sharing the journey as this life ends. Health Communications, Deerfield Beach, FL

1082. Whitfield CL (1988). Editorial: Update on alcoholism & chemical dependence. American Journal of Medicine, Oct

1083. Whitfield CL (1988). Chapter 11. Alcoholism, other drug misuse, and violence: an overview. In Field JR, Hertzberg LJ, S & Ostrum G (eds): Violent Behavior: Assessment & Intervention Vol 1. Spectrum Publications, Jamaica, NY

1084. Whitfield CL (1997). Chapter 72. Co-dependence, addictions and related disorders. in Lowinson J, Millman R, et al. (eds.) Comprehensive Textbook of Substance Abuse. Williams & Wilkins, Baltimore, 1991; Updated in 1997 edition

1085. Whitfield CL, Anda RF, Dube SR, Felitti VJ (2003). Violent childhood experiences and the risk of intimate partner violence in adults: assessment in a large health maintenance organization. Journal of Interpersonal Violence 18(2):166–85

1086. Whitfield CL, Silberg J, Fink P (eds.) (2001). Exposing misinformation concerning child sexual abuse and adult survivors. Journal of Child Sexual Abuse 9(3–4):1–8, special volume also published separately by Haworth Press, Binghamton, NY, 2002

1087. Whitfield CL, Stock WE (1996). Traumatic amnesia in 100 survivors of childhood sexual abuse. Presented at the national conference on trauma & memory (peer-reviewed), Univ. of New Hampshire, July

1088. Whitfield CL (1998). Adverse childhood experience and trauma (editorial). American Journal of Preventive Medicine, 14(4):361–364, May

1089. Whitfield CL (1995). Memory and Abuse: Remembering and healing the wounds of trauma. (p. 238–242) Health Communications, Deerfield Beach FL

1090. Whitfield CL (2003). The Truth about Depression: Choices for Healing. Health Communications, Deerfield Beach FL

1091. Whitfield CL (1998). Internal evidence and corroboration of traumatic memories of child sexual abuse with addictive disorders. Sexual Addiction & Compulsivity 5:269–292

1092. Whitfield CL (1997). Internal verification and corroboration of traumatic memories. Journal of Child Sexual Abuse 6(3):99–122

1093. Whitfield CL (2001). The false memory defense: using disinformation in and out of court. Journal of Child Sexual Abuse 9(3–4):53–78

1094. Whitfield CL (1993). Boundaries and Relationships: Knowing, protecting and enjoying the self. Health Communications, Deerfield Beach, FL

1095. Whitfield, CL (1991). A Gift to Myself. Health Communications, Deerfield Beach, FL

1096. Whitfield CL (2003). My Recovery: A personal plan for healing. Health Communications, Deerfield Beach, FL

1097. Whitfield CL, Anda RA, Felitti VF, Dube S (2004). Adverse childhood experiences and subsequent hallucinations. (in submission)

1098. Widom CS, Shepard RL (1996). Accuracy of adult recollections of childhood victimization: Part 1. Childhood physical abuse. Psychological Assessment 8:412–421

1099. Widom CS, Morris S (1997). Accuracy of adult recollections of childhood victimization: Part 2. Childhood sexual abuse. Psychological Assessment 9:34–46

1100. Widom CS (1999). Post-traumatic stress disorder in abused and neglected children grown up. American Journal of Psychiatry 156:1223–1229

1101. Widom CS, Ireland TO, Glynn PG (1995). Alcohol abuse in abused and neglected children followed-up: are they at increased risk? Journal of the Study of Alcohol, 56: 207–217

1102. Williams HJ, Wagner HL, Calam RM (1992). Eating attitudes in survivors of unwanted sexual experiences. Br J Clin Psychol 31 (Pt 2):203–6

1103. Willis DJ (2003). The drugging of young children: why is psychology mute? The Clinical Psychologist 56:1–3

1104. Wilsnack RW, Wilsnack SC, Krisjainson P, Harris TR (1998). Ten-year prediction of women's drinking behavior in a national representative sample. Women's Health: Research on Gender, Behavior and Policy 4(3):199–230

1105. Wilsnack SC, Vogeltanz ND, Klassen AD, Harris TR (1997). Childhood sexual abuse and women's substance abuse: national survey findings. Journal of Studies on Alcohol 58:264–71

1106. Wilsnack SC, Wonderlich SA, Kristjanson AF, Vogeltanz-Holm ND, Wilsnack RW (2002). Self-reports of forgetting and remembering childhood sexual abuse in a nationally representative sample of US women. Child Abuse & Neglect 26(2):139–47

1107. Wilson JP, Friedman MJ, Lindey JD (2001). Treating Psychological Trauma and PTSD. Guilford, New York

1108. Wind TW, Silvern L (1992). Type and extent of child abuse as predictors of adult functioning. Journal of Family Violence 7, 261–281

1109. Winfield I, George LK, Swartz M, Blazer DG (1990). Sexual assault and psychiatric disorders among a community sample of women. Am J Psychiatry 147(3):335–41

1110. Windle M, Windle RC, Scheidt DM, Miller GB (1995). Physical and sexual abuse and associated mental disorders among alcoholic inpatients. American Journal of Psychiatry 152:1322–8

1111. Windle M, Windle RC (2001). Depressive symptoms and cigarette smoking among middle adolescence: prospective associations and intrapersonal and interpersonal influences. J Consult Clin Psychol 69(2):215–26

1112. Wolfe DA, Mosk MD (1983). Behavioral comparisons of children from abusive and distressed families. J Consult Clin Psychol 51(5):702–8

1113. Wolfsdorf BA, Zlotnick C (2001). Affect management in group therapy for women with post-traumatic stress disorder and histories of childhood sexual abuse. J Clin Psychol Feb; 57(2):169–81

1114. Wonderlich S, Wusnack R, Wisnack S, Harris TR (1996). Childhood sexual abuse and bulimic behavior in a nationally representative sample. American Journal of Public Health 86, 1082–1086

1115. Wonderlich SA, Brewerton TD, Jocic Z, Dansky BS, Abbott DW (1997). Relationship of childhood sexual abuse and eating disorders. J Am Acad Child Adolesc Psychiatry 36(8):1107–15

1116. Wonderlich S, Crosby R, Mitchell J, Thompson K, Redlin J, Demuth G, Smyth J (2001). Pathways mediating sexual abuse and eating disturbance in children. Int J Eat Disord 29(3):270–9

1117. Wood BL (1987). Children of Alcoholism: The struggle for self and intimacy in adult life. University Press, NY

1118. World Health Organization (1979) Schizophrenia: An international follow-up study. John Wiley & Sons, NY

1119. Wozniak J, Crawford MH, Biederman J, Faraone SV, Spencer TJ, Taylor A, Blier HK (1999). Antecedents and complications of trauma in boys with ADHD: findings from a longitudinal study. J Am Acad Child Adolesc Psychiatry 38(1):48–55

1120. Wright DC, Woo WL, Muller RT, Fernandes CB, Kraftcheck ER (2003). An investigation of trauma-centered inpatient treatment for adult survivors of abuse. Child Abuse & Neglect 27(4):393–406

1121. Wurr JC, Partridge IM (1996). The prevalence of a history of childhood sexual abuse in an acute adult in patient population. Child Abuse & Neglect 20:867–72

1122. Wurtele SK, Kaplan GM, Keairnes M (1990). Childhood sexual abuse among chronic pain patients. Clin J Pain 6(2):110–3

1123. Wyatt GE (1985). The sexual abuse of Afro-American and White American women in childhood. Child Abuse & Neglect 9:507–519

Y

1124. Yama MF, Tovey SL, Forgas BS, Teegarden LA (1992). Joint consequences of parental alcoholism and childhood sexual abuse, and their partial mediation by family environment. Violenc & Victimology 7(4):313–25

1125. Yama MF, Tovey SL, Fogas BS (1993). Childhood family environment and sexual abuse as predictors of anxiety and depression in adult women. American Journal of Orthopsychiatry 63:136–141

1126. Yaryura-Tobias JA, Neziroglu FA, Kaplan S (1995). Self-mutilation, anorexia, and dysmenorrhea in obsessive-compulsive disorder. International Journal of Eating Disorders 17(1):33–38

1127. Yen S, Shea MT, Battle CL et al. (2002). Traumatic exposure and PTSD in borderline, schizotypal, avoidant, and obsessive-compulsive personality disorders. Journal of Nervous & Mental Disease 190:510–8

1128. Young EA, Abelson JL, Curtis GC, Nesse RM (1997). Childhood adversity and vulnerability to mood and anxiety disorders. Depress Anxiety 5(2):66–72

1129. Young EB (1990). The role of incest in relapse. Journal of Psychoactive Drugs 22:249–258

1130. Yucel B, Ozyalcin S, Sertel HO, Camlica H, Ketenci A, Talu GK (2002). Childhood traumatic events and dissociative experiences in patients with chronic headache and low back pain. Clin J Pain 18(6):394–401

Z

1132. Zanarini MC, Gunderson JG, Marino MF, Schwartz EO, Frankenburg FR (1989). Childhood experiences of borderline patients. Comprehensive Psychiatry 30:18–25

1133. Zlotnick C, Ryan CE, Miller IW, Keitner GI (1995). Childhood abuse and recovery from major depression. Child Abuse & Neglect 19:1513–1516

1134. Zlotnick C, Shea MT, Pearlstein T, Simpson E, Costello E, Begin A (1996). The relationship between dissociative symptoms, alexithymia, impulsivity, sexual abuse, and self-mutilation. Compr Psychiatry 37(1):12–6

1135. Zlotnick C, Hohlstein LA, Shea MT, Pearlstein T, Recupero P, Bidadi K (1996). The relationship between sexual abuse and eating pathology. Int J Eat Disord 20(2):129–34

1136. Zlotnick C (1999). Antisocial personality disorder, affect dysregulation and childhood abuse among incarcerated women. J Personal Disord 13(1):90–5

1137. Zlotnick C, Mattia JI, Zimmerman M (2001). The relationship between post-traumatic stress disorder, childhood trauma and alexithymia in an outpatient sample. Journal of Traumatic Stress 14:177–188

1138. Zlotnick C, Mattia J, Zimmerman M (2001). Clinical features of survivors of sexual abuse with major depression. Child Abuse & Neglect 25(3):357–67

1139. Zlotnick C, Franklin CL, Zimmerman M (2002). Is comorbidity of post-traumatic stress disorder and borderline personality disorder related to greater pathology and impairment? Am J Psychiatry 159(11):1940–3

Index

More from the Author